MW01233835

HOME FRONT

UNIVERSITY PRESS OF FLORIDA

Florida A&M University, Tallahassee
Florida Atlantic University, Boca Raton
Florida Gulf Coast University, Ft. Myers
Florida International University, Miami
Florida State University, Tallahassee
New College of Florida, Sarasota
University of Central Florida, Orlando
University of Florida, Gainesville
University of North Florida, Jacksonville
University of South Florida, Tampa
University of West Florida, Pensacola

NORTH CAROLINA DURING WORLD WAR II

JULIAN M. PLEASANTS

University Press of Florida

Gainesville · Tallahassee · Tampa · Boca Raton

Pensacola · Orlando · Miami · Jacksonville · Ft. Myers · Sarasota

This book may be available in an electronic edition.

22 21 20 19 18 17   6 5 4 3 2 1

Library of Congress Cataloging-in-Publication Data
Names: Pleasants, Julian M., author.
Title: Home front : North Carolina during World War II / Julian M. Pleasants.
Description: Gainesville : University Press of Florida, 2017. | Includes
bibliographical references and index.
Identifiers: LCCN 2016049598 | ISBN 9780813054254 (cloth)
Subjects: LCSH: World War, 1939–1945—North Carolina. | North
Carolina—History—20th century. | North Carolina—History, Military—20th
century.
Classification: LCC D769.85.N8 P55 2017 | DDC 940.53/756—dc23
LC record available at https://lccn.loc.gov/2016049598

The University Press of Florida is the scholarly publishing agency for the State
University System of Florida, comprising Florida A&M University, Florida Atlantic
University, Florida Gulf Coast University, Florida International University, Florida
State University, New College of Florida, University of Central Florida, University
of Florida, University of North Florida, University of South Florida, and University of
West Florida.

University Press of Florida
15 Northwest 15th Street
Gainesville, FL 32611-2079
http://upress.ufl.edu

CONTENTS

FIGURES

ACKNOWLEDGMENTS

The state of North Carolina played a vital role in the conduct of World War II, and the story of the state's contribution to the war effort deserves more elaborate and expanded coverage than has been provided by previous historians. Sarah Lemmon and Nancy Midgette did an excellent job with their book *North Carolina and the Two World Wars*, but the history of the state during World War II had so many interesting individuals and important activities that it seemed appropriate to provide coverage in greater detail.

This book is designed to be both descriptive and analytical. The main purpose is to focus on the events and people that helped shape the state during a crucial period in its history. The emphasis is on the home front, not military combat, and how customs, tradition, and attitudes were modified by this extraordinary event. There are numerous books on the military aspects of the war, but not as much research has been devoted to what was happening at home while the troops were off at war. It is especially important to understand how the war altered the lives of individuals and how it impacted various communities, from large cities like Charlotte to small hamlets like Hoffman. The far-reaching changes to the economy, to the social fabric, to education, and to cultural mores were similar to those experienced by other southern states, but specific circumstances made North Carolina's reaction to events unique.

In chronicling and explaining the changes that reshaped the state, the emphasis will be, as much as possible, on how selected individuals remembered the war. In an attempt to humanize events and circumstances, it is imperative to allow people to communicate their own recollections of the war. Extensive use of oral histories always runs the risk of inaccuracy and the limitations of human memory. However, first-person accounts of why a young man decided to join the army or why a young black woman chose the Women's Army Corps (WACs) or why a nurse volunteered for combat duty help the reader to understand the circumstances and thinking behind such monumental and life-altering personal decisions. Intimate stories of a mother desperate for some ingredients to make a cake for her family's Christmas dinner, the heartbreaking response to the loss of a loved one, the difficulties faced by women in the military, the working conditions in a textile mill, and the trauma of a military physical allow us into the minds and emotions of those telling their stories.

In some areas (in particular women at war, submarine warfare, prisoners of war, and racial issues) I have relied heavily on several excellent general histories. Otherwise I have tried to tell the story from as many primary sources as possible and to make the book accessible for the general reader. In compiling this book, I have consulted many very good local histories, especially Stephen H. Dew's *The Queen City at War*; two informative histories of Camp Mackall; Mary Best's edited work *North Carolina's Shining Hour*; Melton McLaurin's *The Marines of Montford Point*; and many other fine works. I have relied on state newspapers for interesting incidents and anecdotes that might not otherwise have been discovered. As my basic newspaper source I used the *Raleigh News and Observer*, which at the time had the most complete coverage of state government and state-wide events.

As with any undertaking of this nature, many people assisted me in my work and offered sage advice and pertinent comments about how to improve the manuscript. Bob Anthony and the staff at the North Carolina Collection at Chapel Hill are to be commended for their courtesy, knowledge of the archives, and infinite patience in assisting a technologically deficient researcher. Similar kudos go to the staff at the Southern Historical Collection at the University of North Carolina (UNC) and the State Archives in Raleigh. Jason Tomberlin at the North Carolina Collection is as knowledgeable, talented, and understanding as any archivist with whom I have interacted. Kim Anderson at the State Archives was invaluable in helping me find appropriate photographs. Elise Anderson did an outstanding job of patiently assisting me in sorting through the excellent photographic archives at the Greensboro Historical Museum. Sheila Bumgarner at the Charlotte Mecklenburg Library provided me access to valuable letters and other archival material. The two readers for the University Press of Florida contributed many constructive comments that strengthened the book.

D. G. Martin, a wonderful friend, read some of the early work and had many beneficial suggestions. John Saunders read the entire manuscript and saved me from many errors due to his extraordinary knowledge of North Carolina. Gary Mormino, a superb historian and good friend, offered many wise and insightful suggestions that improved the book significantly. An outstanding and thorough researcher, he provided me with some wonderful and relevant quotations.

The editorial and personal support from Sian Hunter and Meredith Babb and from other staff members of the University Press of Florida made the entire experience enjoyable and worthwhile. Ali Sundook and Michele Fiyak-Burkley did outstanding work in formatting and bringing the project to fruition. Kathy Lewis, the copy editor, improved the manuscript significantly with her accurate and much appreciated corrections.

The terms "Negro" and "colored" were standard usage by newspapers and individuals during World War II and in the early postwar era. Those names are used in this book only in quotations, as "black" and "African American" are now the more accepted terms.

INTRODUCTION

Studs Terkel, in his illuminating history of World War II, *The Good War*, interviewed a graying veteran, who, like most of his compatriots, recalled the powerful influence that the war had on his life. "World War II has affected me in many ways ever since. In a short period of time, I had the most tremendous experiences of all of life: of fear, of jubilance, of misery, of hope, of comradeship, and of endless excitement. I honestly feel grateful for having been a witness to an event as monumental as anything in history and, in a very small way, a participant."[1]

World War II had an extraordinary impact on every aspect of American life. Many historians see World War II as a turning point, a watershed in American history. The United States and its allies spent billions of dollars and lost millions of lives fighting and defeating the Axis powers. In almost every way—militarily, socially, politically, economically, culturally, racially, educationally, and demographically—postwar America was significantly different from prewar America. World War II was the transforming event that forged modern America and the crucible that reshaped the lives of those who lived through it.

John Egerton eloquently described the importance of World War II:

It was World War II, more than the Great Depression or the New Deal, that ushered in the modern age. The war turned hard times into hopeful times, it moved people up and out, it changed our ways of thinking and working and living. It ended in a cataclysmic flash of blinding light and searing heat, a paradoxical mushroom symbol of death and birth; it heralded the realignment of nations, the coming of new technology, the beginning of the Cold War. Practically everything about this war, from the way we got into it to the way we got out of it, suggested transformation. After this, the times and the experience seemed to tell us nothing will ever be the same again; this is an end and a beginning.[2]

The attack on Pearl Harbor on December 7, 1941, produced fear, anger, and anxiety about the future of America and the survival of democracy, but Americans believed to the core that they were involved in a righteous war and would eventually prevail. The Americans who had survived the Great Depression and were now called upon to sacrifice lives, livelihoods, and family in a united effort to win the war later became known as the Greatest Generation. After the war ended, these veterans did not brag about their exploits and sacrifices; they eagerly returned to their families and jobs to help make America prosper.

World War II was a unique experience for everyone. Studs Terkel called it *The Good War*, and in many ways the sense of community and the need to pull together to win the war found wider expression during 1941–1945 than at any other time in American history. Because democracy and America's future were in peril, the country was united by a common bond, a shared purpose, and a can-do spirit that solidified relationships and led to increased concern for one another.

While this sense of community and cooperation in pursuit of one goal was essential to the survival of freedom and democracy, America was not a place of unalloyed happiness or success. There continued to be crime, disloyalty, divorces, racial conflict, and social upheavals, but the American public by and large supported the war effort and expressed their patriotism over and over. People proudly sang "The Star-Spangled Banner" at baseball games and other events and encouraged friends to do whatever they could to help the war effort. In the front windows of their homes families displayed a Blue Star for each family member serving in the armed forces. One North Carolina family had six stars in their window. Sadly, other families displayed a Gold Star for each family member killed in the war. The Gold Star spoke more poignantly than any memorial or eulogy about the great sacrifice that the family had made.

Despite some hardship and the loss of loved ones, those who lived through the war years admitted that it was the most exciting period of their lives and that more happened to them then than at any other time. Many citizens had a chance to work at interesting and important jobs and to travel to new cities and meet new people—all in a noble and righteous cause that gave them a sense of purpose that they had not known before. The hard-earned victory over fascism gave Americans a renewed confidence in their country and a newfound security. By the end of 1945 the United States, the country that suffered the least and profited the most from the war, was the wealthiest and most powerful nation in the world.

While praising World War II as a heroic effort to save the world from tyranny, observers also commented on the brutality and callousness of combat: the Nazis' extermination of Jews and other enemies of the German state; the sadistic torture of prisoners by the Japanese; and the unbelievable loss of life, estimated at 60 million, suffered by all participants. It took two generations for Western Europe to recover from the physical, emotional, and economic destruction of the war.

In *Wartime* Paul Fussell reminded his readers of the horrors of war: "For the past fifty years the Allied war effort has been sanitized and romanticized almost beyond recognition." Americans, according to Fussell, referred to the conflict as being justified and necessary and in so doing made it appear that the war was not such a bad thing after all. Fussell recalled the barbarous and terrifying savagery of war. He quoted Marguerite Higgins, the first female war correspondent, about the "mosaic of misery" that she found while reporting on the war in Europe: ruined cities, dead bodies everywhere, some mangled and torn apart, some blinded, others horribly disfigured. Fussell recalled that George Gordon, Lord Byron, defined war as "the feast of vultures; the waste of life." Once started, war had to run its course and had to be won at all costs—and the costs were always high.[3]

For the most part, the United States suffered less from the vicissitudes of war than many other countries. America lost 405,000 service members but did not have as many troops die in battle as other Allied nations did; nor had America been scarred by bombs and battle. At home America did not always live up to the nation's commitment to freedom and equality. While the war increased job opportunities and living standards, Jim Crow remained the law in most states and the military continued to be segregated. Women, while having new chances at jobs, were still victims of discrimination. Some 112,000 American citizens of Japanese ancestry were unconstitutionally incarcerated for a large part of the war. So World War II was not always a good war for everyone, but it was for most a just war and a successful war—a great triumph of American will, unity, and virtue. After all, America did not seek territorial gains or a vengeful peace but used its resources to help rebuild Western Europe after the war through the Marshall Plan.

The war changed the United States in fundamental ways. World War II produced national prosperity and increased living standards, especially among minorities and the poor, leading to a rapidly developing middle class. Increased industrial production strengthened and diversified the economies of the South. A great population growth occurred in the Sunbelt states and in urban areas as rural residents moved to cities for defense jobs and other economic opportunities. In spite of discrimination, in general the war improved the status and prospects of African Americans and some women. By challenging the conventional wisdom about the place of women and African Americans in society, the war helped pave the way for civil rights and the postwar women's movement.[4]

The impact of the war was perhaps greater in the South and in North Carolina than elsewhere in the nation. The conflict began the transformation and restructuring of the South from a rural, provincial, poor, racist society to a modern, industrialized, urbanized region. From 1940 to 1945 approximately 1.6 million citizens, including many African Americans, left the region for other parts of the country. The South's rural population declined by 20 percent. At the same time, an ethnically diverse group of Americans moved into the South for jobs and for training at the many military bases. The influx of "outsiders" also challenged the long-held views of southerners about regional stereotypes and race.[5]

At the outset of the war, North Carolina was one of the poorest states in the union, with its per capita income ranked forty-fifth out of forty-eight states. Only one-third of the 67,000 miles of roads in the state were paved, and 66 percent of the state was rural. Over one-third of the farms had no electricity; only one in eight farms had a telephone. North Carolina had the highest rate of draft rejections by the United States Selective Service in World War II of any state. Illiteracy and a lack of education, especially in the rural areas of the state, were primary reasons for the exclusion of many draftees. White citizens over twenty-five had completed only an average of 7.9 years in school and African Americans an average of 5.9 years.

Another reason for a large number of rejections was poor health—especially a lack of dental care. There were no regional hospitals in the state. Many rural residents suffered from rickets, pellagra, and malnutrition.[6]

If any set of statistics indicated the desperate plight of many people of the Tar Heel State, the high rejection rate from the Selective Service was proof of the great need for better health care and education. North Carolina had been known as the Rip Van Winkle state for years, but the war would now set in motion changes that would awaken the state to its fullest potential.

A major change came as a result of the construction of a series of major military bases in the state and the organization of an additional fifty military establishments. The rapid construction and expansion of camps like Fort Bragg, by the end of the war the largest army base in the nation, led to many new jobs and was a great boost to the economy, with increased need for lumber and other supplies. In addition to Fort Bragg, the army established an infantry training center at Camp Butner; an antiaircraft training facility at Camp Davis; a combat engineer installation at Camp Sutton in Monroe; and a large airborne training center for parachute and glider troops in Camp Mackall, near Hoffman. The U.S. Marines built the Cherry Point Marine Corps Air Base for preparing fighter and bomber pilots for combat and expanded Camp Lejeune in Jacksonville, a major training base for infantry, armor, artillery, and amphibious warfare. Lejeune welcomed the first women marines, and near Lejeune on Montford Point the Marine Corps set up the first training center for African American marines. Lejeune was also the home of the "devil dogs," trained for use in canine warfare.

The United States Army Air Force (also known as the U.S. Army Air Corps: it later became a separate branch of service, the U.S. Air Force) was just as active. It set up an Overseas Replacement Depot in Greensboro and a troop carrier and glider training base at Laurinburg-Maxton Army Air Base. The most prominent base was Pope Air Force Base, adjacent to Fort Bragg, where troop carriers, gliders, and fighters were located.

The United States Navy was less of a presence in the state, as most of its installations were already located elsewhere. The navy did open Naval Air Stations in Elizabeth City, Southport, Manteo, and Ocracoke. Southport was used for ship repairs and antisubmarine defense, and Manteo was a carrier fighter aircraft training base. There was a navy blimp station in Weeksville.

These new bases brought in a large influx of service members and workers, who often overwhelmed the local facilities, especially in housing and transportation. The diverse group of soldiers relocating into the state hailed from all over the country. These new residents challenged the status quo in North Carolina and brought in new ideas and cultural change.

In addition to military bases, other government and industrial facilities were also set up in the state. Carrboro had a munitions factory. Fairchild Aviation established a plant in Mebane to build the AT-21, a training plane for aircraft gunners. Many small and large local businesses converted to wartime production. The J. A. Jones Construction Company, the largest construction company in the state, won many lucrative government contracts building army bases, barracks, and other buildings.

The United States government spent $2 billion ($32 billion in 2014 dollars) directly in the state for goods, services, construction costs, and salaries. The economic impact of military bases and government contracts was huge. Workers who had never done more than pick cotton and slop pigs were making blankets and milling lumber, while others installed complicated electrical panels on airplanes. As defense spending accelerated the shift of the population from rural to urban, the subsequent social and economic changes enhanced the economic opportunities of many Tar Heels.

The state made economic contributions to the war effort in many ways. The North Carolina Shipbuilding Company in Wilmington produced some 243 vessels during the years 1941 to 1946, including 126 cargo and troop transport ships, known as Liberty ships. The company employed a large contingent of women, and 20 to 30 percent of the workers were African American. The shipbuilding industry and military installations changed Wilmington in many important areas. Within a year after the war began, the population had increased by almost 20,000, to a total of 43,000. By the end of 1943 the number had increased to near 100,000. This huge influx of people created increased demands for housing, transportation, medical care, police services, and restaurants.

The cotton and textile industries, including giants like Hanes Knitting Company, Burlington Mills, and Cannon Mills, played an important part in the war effort by supplying socks, underwear, bandages, camouflage cloth, blankets, towels, tent fabric, work clothes, and uniforms. During the war 70 percent of the state's textile products were designated for military use. The mills had to hire and train thousands of new employees, and plants found it necessary to run three production shifts in order to meet the demand.

North Carolina became one of the nation's largest suppliers of agricultural products. The remarkable production was achieved despite a shortage of farm labor due to drafts, enlistments, and the move by many from the farms to the textile mills and defense plants. The main crops for the state were cotton, sweet and Irish potatoes, hay and wheat, peanuts, beef, and pork. A major source of income was the sale of tobacco. In the 1940s almost everyone smoked and few were willing to forego that pleasure/ habit. North Carolina supplied the Allied fighting forces with tons of to-bacco products. The war reinvigorated the timber and mineral industries, gave textiles and tobacco their greatest market ever, and enabled farmers and other manufacturing firms to achieve economic success heretofore unimagined.

As the industrial and agricultural entities in the state geared up for the war effort, citizens of the Outer Banks experienced the war firsthand. When German U-boats initiated submarine warfare off the North Caro-lina coast shortly after Pearl Harbor, they found the unescorted merchant vessels plying their trade on the East Coast easy pickings. Cruising one of the most congested sea lanes in the world, the U-boats sank some eighty vessels off the coast of North Carolina, with the loss of hundreds of lives and millions of dollars of cargo essential for the war effort. The U.S. Navy, woefully unprepared for the unexpected attacks, lacked an effective anti-submarine warfare program. The U-boats rampaged virtually unimpeded in the area around Ocracoke and the Barrier Islands in what became known as "Torpedo Junction." By August 1942 the U.S. Navy had turned the tide by instituting a full-fledged convoy system with a sufficient num-ber of destroyers and corvettes to interdict the submarine attacks.

Wars have social consequences. World War II altered the daily lives of North Carolinians in ways not experienced before. Many husbands and fathers went off to war, leaving wives and families to care for themselves. Some women went into textile factories and munitions plants, but most stayed home raising children and volunteering for scrap drives and war bond sales. Families almost immediately felt economic distress with the loss of breadwinners and the unavailability of items that they had been used to having in large quantities. The shortage of rubber, gasoline, meat, sugar, shoes, coal, cotton, autos, aluminum, and other basic and essential items made life more difficult, but most Americans did not suffer greatly. In many cases, families had to resort to substitutes. Tires were recapped, and later came the use of synthetic rubber. Margarine was a substitute for butter, and dried eggs were used in powdered form instead of fresh farm eggs. A popular wartime refrain was "Use it up, wear it out, make it do, or do without."

In order to ensure sufficient supplies for the military, the federal gov-ernment, under the auspices of the Office of Price Administration (OPA), set up price controls and a nationwide rationing program for essential items such as gasoline and rubber. Gasoline was critical to the war effort. Some individuals were restricted to five gallons a week, there was a ban on pleasure driving, and the national speed limit was reduced to thirty-five miles an hour. Although inconvenient, rationing and coupon books would be a way of life until the end of the war. There were numerous examples of hoarding and black market sales, of course, but overall the system worked.

In countless other ways, the public supported the war effort. Thousands of rural and urban dwellers planted Victory Gardens, producing a large percentage of home-grown vegetables needed by the military. Citizens, especially schoolchildren, participated in scrap drives (rubber, tin, discarded steel and iron) and deposited these items in a central location. Scrap drives gave citizens, particularly the youth of the state, a sense of participation and doing their part.

Raising money to pay for the huge cost of war was essential if the Allied powers were to prevail. Money generated from income taxes was not sufficient to provide the necessary funds, so the government ended up borrowing money from citizens and banks by selling war bonds or victory bonds. The federal government conducted seven war bond drives and one victory bond drive, selling a total of $156.9 billion in bonds to an estimated 85 million investors. Citizens of North Carolina were enthusiastic supporters of the war bond sales, exceeding all quotas during the war.

North Carolina contributed some 370,000 men and women to the armed forces during World War II, a number that included 75,000 African Americans. More military were trained in North Carolina than in any other state. Over 7,000 made the ultimate sacrifice. Seven Tar Heels earned the nation's highest award, the Congressional Medal of Honor. Colonel Robert Morgan from Asheville piloted the famous B-17 bomber *Memphis Belle*. Thomas W. Ferebee of Mocksville was the bombardier of the *Enola Gay*, the plane that dropped the world's first atomic bomb on Hiroshima. Major General William C. Lee pioneered the concept of airborne units.

North Carolina universities and colleges also assisted the war effort. Many institutions of higher learning were deprived of their student body as thousands of young men aged eighteen to twenty-one either were drafted or volunteered for service. Without students, it was difficult for colleges to keep their doors open, so many institutions agreed to set up military training programs on their campuses. The U.S. Navy designated the University of North Carolina (UNC) at Chapel Hill as one of only four navy Pre-flight School training centers in the country. By the summer of

1942 the campus had 1,875 cadets, including two future presidents of the United States, Gerald R. Ford and George Herbert Walker Bush. Some 18,700 young men eventually completed their indoctrination at UNC.

While in training, the Pre-Flight School programs fielded athletic teams that played local universities and other military bases. In baseball the Cloudbusters, as they were called, featured many former Major Leaguers, including Ted Williams. The Cloudbusters football team was just as impressive, with Otto Graham, a future all-pro at quarterback and excellent coaches such as Paul "Bear" Bryant. The navy's first all-black band, the B-1 Band, was recruited from North Carolina natives and stationed at the Pre-Flight School. The acceptance of black B-1 Band members as naval personnel was a meaningful step toward integrating the military.

World War II could not have been won without the help and support of women, especially in war production. Women were not drafted in World War II, but the federal and state governments encouraged them to join the female military branches of the army, air force, navy, coast guard, and marines. They served as WACs (Women's Army Corps), WASPs (Women Air Force Service Pilots), WAVEs (Women Accepted for Emergency Volunteer Services), SPARs (from the coast guard motto *Semper Paratus*), and women marines. A total of 7,000 Tar Heel women joined the military, with 4,000 serving in the WACs. Other women trained as nurses and joined hospital units all over the world, often serving in combat zones.

The war mobilization and the important expansion of manufacturing gave women opportunities that they never had before. Some women began to work outside the home for the first time, filling jobs vacated by men in service—"freeing a man to fight." They worked in agriculture, textile mills, tobacco factories, and shipbuilding and took on highly skilled jobs in defense industries, becoming welders and riveters and occupying positions previously reserved only for men. Other women worked as secretaries in Washington or for military units. These jobs gave women a newfound sense of self-confidence and self-knowledge. Many women emerged from the experience stronger and more independent than they had been before.

A majority of women did not work in an industrial or military capacity but continued to raise their families and serve as nurses and schoolteachers. Women spent countless hours volunteering to plant Victory Gardens, roll bandages for the Red Cross, sponsor USOs (United Services Organizations), and support war bond drives—all significant contributions to the war effort.

The Allies shipped approximately 50,000 Italian prisoners of war (POWs) and 378,000 German POWs to the United States. North Carolina received a large number of this group, housing 3,000 Italians at Camp Butner, where they were used primarily in cutting lumber and harvesting peanuts. The military sent 10,000 Germans to six base camps and twelve branch camps across the state. Each of the major POW sites had branch camps where the prisoners were assigned specific tasks. The Germans proved to be such good workers that the army hired out some of them to local businesses and farmers. The POWs were treated humanely overall, and local citizens who worked with the POWs generally got along well with them.

The American military, with a few minor exceptions, remained racially segregated during the war. African Americans who fought for their country sought what they called the "Double V": victory over tyranny and fascism abroad and victory over discrimination and hatred at home. African American leaders argued that black soldiers who were willing to fight and die for their country deserved equal rights in all areas. Although President Franklin Roosevelt had issued Executive Order 8802, which forbade discrimination in defense industries and established the Fair Employment Practices Committee to ensure equality in hiring and in job placement, the tradition of segregation and discrimination in the South and North Carolina prevailed. African Americans decried the hypocrisy of white citizens who denounced Hitler's racism and apartheid policies but accepted the same discrimination at home.

World War II provided realistic chances for black Americans to challenge white domination. Acknowledging that the war had increased racial tensions, black middle-class spokespeople hoped that the war would present an opportunity to discuss the essential question of racial segregation and discrimination. Some serious racial clashes occurred around the state, but most African Americans wholeheartedly backed the war effort despite the conflicts and animosity. The overwhelming majority of black troops served honorably and were glad to have the opportunity to fight for their country.

World War II did create cracks in the system of white supremacy in North Carolina and the nation and marked a genuine watershed in racial politics in the state. African Americans began moving away from a traditional acceptance of Jim Crow and moving toward decades of civil rights activism.

The conclusion of World War II on August 14, 1945, found the state of North Carolina drastically different than it was on December 7, 1941. The state had lost 7,000 of its native sons and daughters, and many more had suffered serious injuries. Over 350,000 Tar Heels served directly in the armed forces as the state did its part in winning the war.

North Carolina was much better off than it had been prior to 1941. Its manufacturing plants and farms had hired a large number of new employees and, working at full capacity, had provided essential supplies necessary for winning the war. The war ended the Great Depression, and wartime spending provided an economic stimulus the state had never experienced. By 1945 the state had a large budget surplus and was able to purchase land, hospitals, and military buildings that were no longer needed by the federal government at reasonable prices. Many of the military airfields, such as Raleigh-Durham, were bought cheaply from the federal government and turned into commercial airports, helping the state build its infrastructure for future development.

In 1945 rural residents in the state who had moved to cities for defense jobs as North Carolina rapidly transformed itself into a more urbanized society had new challenges and opportunities. Higher education survived the war and received a wonderful boost with the GI Bill, which would lead to a large number of veterans entering college. All in all, despite all the sacrifices, World War II was beneficial to the Rip Van Winkle state and helped move North Carolina toward becoming a more productive, energetic, and enterprising state.

PRELUDE TO WAR

THE YEARS 1931–1941

The two principal antagonists of World War II came to power at almost the same time. Adolf Hitler, leader of the National Socialist Party, the largest party in the Reichstag, became chancellor of Germany on January 30, 1933. Franklin D. Roosevelt, elected by a large majority of his fellow Americans, took office on March 4, 1933, at the height of the Great Depression. They were two totally different leaders: one seeking war and world domination, the other hoping to preserve peace in the world.

The origins of World War II, in large part, resided in Adolf Hitler's twisted and apocalyptic vision of world supremacy. Hitler, mortified by Germany's defeat in World War I, wanted to reverse what he saw as the crippling legacy of the Treaty of Versailles, which had saddled the Weimar Republic with an insurmountable debt and had virtually eliminated Germany's military power. In order to exact revenge for the unfair terms of the Versailles Treaty, Hitler founded the National Socialist or Nazi Party. An articulate and fiery orator, Hitler aroused German nationalistic fervor and blamed Germany's economic ills on the Versailles Treaty and a worldwide Jewish conspiracy. He pledged to revive German economic and military power, to eliminate the Bolshevik threat from Russia, and to purify the "Aryan race" from the contamination of Jewish influence.

Hitler's powerful diatribes began to attract thousands of adherents. As the Nazi Party grew in influence in 1932, Herr Hitler became the most powerful political leader in Germany. In what John Keegan described as "the most remarkable and complete economic, political and military revolutions ever carried through by one man in a comparable space of time," Hitler became chancellor of Germany and quickly consolidated his power.[1] The new Führer (leader) became the undisputed dictator of Germany. Every aspect of German life was brought under Nazi rule. Hitler enforced his authority through the military, the Gestapo, and local party officials.

Once securely in power, Hitler set out to undermine the Treaty of Versailles by withdrawing from the League of Nations, rearming the German military, and secretly planning for the conquest of Europe. His first step in controlling Germany's borders was the reoccupation of the Rhineland in March 1936. France and the other European countries issued warnings but accepted the German action, which emboldened Hitler to continue his plan to subjugate the rest of Europe. Most leaders in the United States and other Western countries did not understand Hitler's fanaticism and did not take his ambitions seriously.

Fascism was on the move in Europe and had triumphed in Italy with the emergence of the boisterous dictator Benito Mussolini, who came to power in 1922. In 1937 Germany and Italy signed an agreement known as the Rome-Berlin Axis. Now Hitler had a partner in arms—a decision that he would later regret. These two fascist nations were joined by Japan, a rapidly growing Asian power. Japan, with expansionist plans of its own, had invaded Manchuria in 1931 and would later ruthlessly attack China in July 1937. The League of Nations formally proclaimed that Japan was an aggressor for its actions in Manchuria and China but did nothing more. The Americans were upset and angry at the Japanese depredations but were generally powerless to act because of strong isolationist sentiment in the country and because Congress passed a series of strict neutrality bills that restricted President Roosevelt's actions.

American public opinion in the 1930s overwhelmingly opposed any action that might lead to an entanglement with foreign powers. Many believed that America had been unwillingly and unwittingly drawn into World War I and thought that the United States, separated from Europe by a vast ocean, could and should remain aloof from any European conflicts. The isolationists favored security through a fortress America and espoused their views in such organizations as America First. Supported by luminaries such as Charles Lindbergh, America First had a powerful influence on Congress and public opinion.[2]

The Neutrality Act of 1935 occurred against a backdrop of war between

Italy and Ethiopia, Germany's military resurgence, an expansionist Japan, and a deepening pacifism at home. The act outlined a firm position of neutrality, warned Americans not to travel on vessels from either Italy or Ethiopia, and declared an arms, munitions, and trade embargo against both countries. Roosevelt signed the legislation, although he thought that aggressors should be barred from buying munitions and lamented that the act did not give him enough discretionary power to decide which belligerents would fall into that category.

One of the most vociferous proponents of isolationism was the first-term senator from North Carolina, Robert "Our Bob" Reynolds. Reynolds opposed any involvement with any other nation under any circumstances. He recognized that "the world has gone crazy, . . . but it shall not get the wealth and flesh of this country in a war." Until December 7, 1941, Reynolds would rail against any proposal, including membership in the World Court, that might lead America into an unwanted war.[3]

President Franklin Roosevelt understood that America could not long remain out of international conflicts and wanted to prepare for possible hostilities, but Congress was adamant in support of neutrality. By 1936 the fight was essentially over who would control U.S. policy in wartime— the president or the Congress. Because public opinion was strongly in favor of neutrality, Congress held the upper hand. Although Roosevelt felt stymied, he continued to demand the repeal of the mandatory embargo policy so that he would have the authority to use embargoes against those he considered America's enemies while not punishing America's allies.

Meanwhile, in Germany Hitler recognized that the impotent League of Nations would not enforce the provisions of the Versailles Treaty. He noted that the other world powers had also ignored invasions and depredations by Germany, Japan, and Italy. Because of this inaction by the world's military powers, Hitler became more aggressive in his expansionist strategy. On March 12, 1938, German troops marched into Vienna and Hitler declared an *Anschluss* (union) with the German-speaking people of Austria. As he had anticipated, Britain and France protested but did little else. The European nations decided that the best strategy was to appease Hitler by allowing him to take control of some German-speaking countries in hopes that this would satisfy his territorial demands. This appeasement strategy played into Hitler's hands and merely heightened his lust for more territory.

Hitler next demanded the German-speaking part of Czechoslovakia, the Sudetenland. When Czechoslovakia refused to cede the territory, Hitler threatened to invade. British prime minister Neville Chamberlain and French premier Edouard Daladier met with the Czech president, Eduard Benes, at the Munich Conference in 1938 and persuaded Benes to give up the Sudetenland in exchange for Hitler's promise that "this is the last territorial claim I have to make in Europe." The Munich Agreement was the high point and greatest failure of appeasement diplomacy. No country wanted to go to war over the Sudetenland and in 1939 no European country, especially Czechoslovakia, had the military might to stop Hitler. Had the European powers intervened after Germany took the Rhineland, they might have halted Hitler's expansion. By 1939 it was too late. The appeasement strategy could only delay war, not prevent it. Chamberlain hailed the Munich agreement, claiming that it meant "Peace for our time." Winston Churchill knew better: "England and France had to choose between war and dishonor. They chose dishonor; they will have war."[4]

Six months later Hitler marched into Prague and took the rest of Czechoslovakia, while Mussolini seized Albania. Now Hitler was poised to move against Poland. Britain and France, at last fully aware of Hitler's goals, concluded security treaties with Poland, guaranteeing its independence and territorial integrity in case of an invasion. The rape of Czechoslovakia had persuaded the French and British that Hitler's next move had to be stopped. Roosevelt did his best to accept the neutrality acts, although he thought that the legislation would end up hurting America's allies rather than keeping America out of a war that it could not ultimately avoid. As the neutrality acts currently stood, the embargoes would apply not only to Germany and Italy but also to America's friends, Britain and France. FDR wanted the neutrality acts revised so that Britain and France could purchase arms from the United States.

Undeterred by Britain's and France's guarantee of Poland's borders, on August 22, 1939, Hitler cleverly prevented the possibility of a two-front war by agreeing to a nonaggression pact with Russia. The United States and the Allied nations were caught off guard by Germany's bold maneuver. At this juncture Poland was doomed. At 4:45 a.m. on September 1, 1939, German guns fired on Polish troops as German tanks crossed the border into Poland. The first shots of World War II had been fired. Germany's blitzkrieg (lightning warfare) quickly wiped out all Polish resistance by October 6. Poland had been conquered in five weeks. Contrary to their promises, France and England had done very little to protect the integrity of Poland. Hitler now sent his forces to enforce the Siegfried line and to prepare for an attack on France and Britain.[5]

The residents of North Carolina were not unduly alarmed about the beginning of World War II. They knew that the fighting would impact travel and trade, but most considered themselves safe because they were thousands of miles away from what was essentially a European quarrel. Citizens in Charlotte could see no direct threat to the United States and thought that the war was irrelevant to their vital interests.[6]

Two days after the invasion of Poland, President Roosevelt made an appeal for national unity in a "Fireside Chat" and declared: "This nation will remain a neutral nation, but I cannot ask that every American remain neutral in thought as well. Even a neutral cannot be asked to close his mind or his conscience." The president said that he hoped America would be able to stay out of this war, although he knew that was unlikely, and most Americans agreed with that sentiment.[7]

For a period during 1939–1940, in what became known as the "phony war," Tar Heels began to believe that there would be no more fighting and that Hitler would be satisfied with his current territorial gains. Hitler, however, was merely gathering strength for his next objective. In April 1940 Denmark and Norway fell to the German juggernaut. The Allies did little other than to denounce the incursions. On May 10, 1940, the hammer fell. The Germans invaded Holland and the German blitzkrieg overwhelmed the valiant Dutch army. When the Nazis crushed Belgium, Britain and France finally responded militarily. But German air superiority was complete, and the German panzers pummeled the French and British resisters, forcing them back to the channel port of Dunkirk. Fortunately for the Allies, Hitler called a two-day halt to the attack, so some 337,000 French and British soldiers were able to escape capture. This miracle evacuation at Dunkirk happened because hundreds of naval ships and small civilian craft, facing withering fire from the Luftwaffe, managed to ferry the soldiers to safety. If these 337,000 troops had been captured, the war would have been much more difficult for the Allies.

Hitler forced France, weakened by inadequate defense and heavy losses, into an ignominious surrender on June 25, 1940. He now turned his attention to the island of Great Britain and put in place his plan to conquer it, code-named Operation Sea Lion. Desirous of air superiority, the German Luftwaffe launched a long-term, devastating bombing attack on British cities and air bases. Only the heroic action of the Royal Air Force (RAF), radar, and the leadership of the new prime minister, Winston Churchill, enabled the British to survive the Battle of Britain to fight another day.

The RAF suffered massive losses during the Battle of Britain, especially during the critical months of August and September 1940. If Hitler and Hermann Goering had realized how effective their attacks had been, they might have accelerated them and could have defeated England. Hitler, in a strategic error, decided to shift the attack from the radar stations and fighter bases and committed the Luftwaffe to a terror bombing on British cities. Hitler expected British morale to collapse, but the British people refused to break. Hitler, who was losing many planes, admitted defeat and gave up the fight. The survival of an independent Britain was a huge turning point in the war.[8]

The defeat of France finally ended American illusions and awakened the country to the real threat of a German Empire. If Britain collapsed, then Germany would control the powerful British fleet and the Atlantic Ocean would no longer be a barrier to German expansion. Now Roosevelt shifted foreign policy from neutrality to the status of a nonbelligerent and committed the United States to give all aid to the Allies short of war. By 1939 FDR had recognized that his nation was woefully unprepared to fight a global war. Despite protests from a large number of isolationists, Roosevelt moved boldly, calling for a military buildup and the production of 50,000 planes per year. Congress voted the unheard-of sum of $17 billion for defense. Soon American factories were humming for the first time since the 1920s, turning out 17,000 planes and 9,000 tanks before the end of 1940.

When Churchill wrote FDR asking for some destroyers to protect British convoys in the Atlantic, Roosevelt responded by giving the British fifty older destroyers in exchange for leases to eight British military bases. By giving military aid to one of the belligerents America had now moved from neutrality into a state of limited war.[9] At the president's request, Congress enacted the first peacetime military draft in the nation's history. The Burke-Wadsworth bill, passed in September 1940, required the registration of all males between the ages of twenty-one and thirty-six. The isolationists fought the bill because they believed that a peacetime draft was a major step toward involving America in the European war. Senator Bob Reynolds, at this time the ranking member of the powerful Military Affairs Committee, surprised his critics by voting for the bill, since a strong defense was the best way to keep the country out of war.[10]

In the midst of the ongoing debate over America's willingness to come to the aid of Great Britain, Roosevelt decided to run for a third term as president. Although there was no constitutional limitation on the number of terms served by a president, the tradition had been to restrict presidents to two terms. FDR's decision was unprecedented in American history. But the nation was in a severe crisis, and FDR believed that America needed a steady and experienced hand at the helm. With the Republican nominee, Wendell Willkie, gaining momentum by attacking FDR as a warmonger whose policies would force America into the war, Roosevelt made unqualified assurances of peace. "I have said this before, but I shall say it again and again, your boys are not going to be sent into any foreign war." FDR, however, knew that America would eventually enter the war and hoped that sooner or later an attack by the totalitarian powers would force such a decision. In 1940 reelection was the most important goal. In order to win, FDR felt he had to mislead the American people.[11]

By late in 1940 North Carolinians began to realize that they were in a serious world crisis and that the state had to prepare for a war that was rapidly closing in on them. Charlotteans responded with a dramatic increase in patriotic fervor and reverence for the American flag. The Veterans of Foreign Wars (VFW) and the American Legion sponsored rallies promoting patriotism. The city put American flags in every classroom and all over the city and encouraged teachers to emphasize patriotic themes in class. Charlotte bragged about being ultrapatriotic. The *Charlotte Observer* attacked those who failed to display the proper zeal for their country. "Anybody who fails to contribute is in a fair way to be thought of as a Nazi-sympathizer, Hitler-lover or just a plain tight-wad and cheapskate."[12] FDR won a huge electoral victory in 1944 by a margin of 449 to 82 for Willkie. Bolstered by a public mandate and a third term, FDR recognized that it was essential for England to stay in the war and knew that he had to act quickly because the British had run out of funds to pay for U.S. military goods that it needed to stay in the war. Roosevelt devised a clever approach to overcome the restrictions of the various Neutrality Acts. Rather than sell goods to the Allies, he would lend or lease the supplies to Britain, which would repay the United States after the war ended. Urging America to be "the great arsenal of democracy," FDR asked Congress to revise America's neutrality policy.[13]

Under Roosevelt's prodding, Congress passed a bill "To Promote the Defense of the United States," emphasizing the defense aspect of the aid and downplaying any American military intervention. While the isolationists vigorously opposed the measure, public opinion favored aid to America's allies. After two months of contentious debate, the "Cash and Carry" bill allowed Britain and France to purchase American goods if they paid cash and transported them in their own vessels. Roosevelt had the sole authority to permit the sale, lease, or lending of war material and other supplies to any country that the president deemed vital to the defense of the United States. Totally committed to the survival of Great Britain, Roosevelt could now supply them with guns, tanks, and planes. In effect, America had declared economic warfare on Germany.

Most Americans favored the bill and believed that lend-lease was the best option to keep America out of the war. Governor Clyde R. Hoey of North Carolina said that it was "safer to sell supplies than to send men and if England and France can win this war that is our best security for peace." Most newspapers in the state agreed with Hoey. Senator Josiah Bailey voted for the bill, but Senator Reynolds, continuing his anti-British and unilateralist sentiment, vigorously rejected the bill. Why should America pay to save Britain? Demonstrating his ignorance of international affairs, Reynolds explained that the threat to the United States from Hitler was no greater than the threat to America from Napoleon Bonaparte in 1808. As expected, many Tar Heels denounced Reynolds's views. One writer was astonished at the senator's isolationist views in a time of crisis and upset that he opposed a bill favored by 90 percent of the state.[14]

In 1941, from the point of view of many observers, Hitler seemed invincible. He had already moved into the Balkans, conquering Greece, Romania, Yugoslavia, and Crete while penetrating into North Africa. On June 22, 1941, in what Max Hastings called the defining moment of the war, Hitler astonished the world by invading Russia. Hitler had long planned to invade the Soviet Union, partly to fulfill his objective of lebensraum (more living space for the German people). He had long exhibited a strong disdain for Slavic people, whom he considered Untermenschen (inferior people), and wanted to impose the superior German system on the supposedly lower races. He wanted to push back the borders of Russia, create a new empire in the east, and destroy Bolshevism. Hitler insisted that he could conquer Russia in a short period. All that one had to do, he declared, was kick in the door and the entire rotten structure would come crashing down. He knew that the Soviet military had been badly hurt by Joseph Stalin's purges in the 1930s and did not expect the Russians to put up much of a fight.

With hubris of the highest order, Hitler assumed that his highly trained and powerful military and a superior Aryan race would easily overrun the Russians. Fortunately for the Allies, Hitler made the same critical mistake as Napoleon did when he invaded Russia in 1812. Hitler misjudged the vast territory that he had to conquer, underestimated the devastating impact of the severe Russian winters, and did not recognize the industrial and military capacity of the Russian people, who would fight to the end to protect Mother Russia. Germany now had to fight a two-front war. Hitler's decision to invade Russia proved to be his most fateful judgment of the war. Germany would be bogged down fighting the Russians for the remainder of the war and Hitler would lose large numbers of men and supplies. Without Russia on their side, the Allies might well have lost World War II.

Operation Barbarossa, as the invasion was called, began on June 22, 1941. On that date some 3.6 million Axis troops poured into Russian territory and began to advance on a 900-mile front from the Black Sea to the Baltic. Stalin had been surprised by the audacious move, and in the first days of the invasion Germany achieved monumental victories. Hitler expected that the war would be won by August and that Germany would soon hold a victory parade in Moscow.[15]

Since Allied unity was essential to stopping the German war machine, FDR arranged to meet with Winston Churchill at a conference off the coast of Newfoundland in August 1941. Roosevelt would not agree to enter the war at that time, but he and Churchill discussed the best ways to defeat Germany and contain Japan. The meeting resulted in the Atlantic Charter, a joint declaration of war aims and Allied commitment to the Four Freedoms—freedom from want, freedom from fear, freedom of speech, and freedom of religion. The charter reaffirmed the universal principle of freedom of the seas and free trade as well as self-determination for all people. The final part of the charter proposed a postwar international organization to keep the peace. Roosevelt hoped that the Atlantic Charter would explain the Allied war aims to the rest of the world and would educate the American people about what was at stake.[16]

America and England faced a difficult task protecting the lend-lease supplies being sent to Great Britain. The German U-boats had inflicted severe material and psychological damage to the Allied war effort by repeated sinking of ships in the Atlantic. Operating in groups of "wolf packs," the German submarines were effective in disrupting merchant marine traffic in the Atlantic. The British responded with convoys, merchant ships protected by destroyers and corvettes, but this strategy offered only partial protection for Britain's lifeline. Churchill knew that what he called the Battle of the Atlantic had to be won if Britain were to survive.

Roosevelt offered significant help to England by allowing American destroyers to accompany British ships as far as Iceland and by granting permission for U.S. naval vessels to sink any enemy ships that violated the American zone of neutrality. When a German U-boat attacked the USS *Greer* in September 1941, FDR used that hostile act as a pretext for announcing an undeclared naval war against Germany in the North Atlantic. Furthermore, FDR persuaded Congress to allow the arming of American merchant ships and to permit them to sail into war zones. With all the naval activity in the Atlantic, clashes between American warships and German U-boats were inevitable. On October 17, 1941, a German U-boat sank a U.S. destroyer, the USS *Kearny*, with the loss of 17 lives. Two weeks later another U.S. destroyer, the *Reuben James*, went to the bottom, killing 115 sailors. These losses outraged Americans and strengthened public opinion in favor of war. FDR knew that he could not get a declaration of war at this point but privately hoped that a significant military act of war by the Axis powers would unite all Americans in support of the war.[17]

Pearl Harbor

Now that the United States was unofficially at war with Germany, Roosevelt expected that sooner or later another U-boat incident would be serious enough to enable him to ask for a declaration of war. The president, however, was looking in the wrong direction: the immediate threat came from Asia. The militaristic Japanese government, firmly fixed on creating a Japanese Empire in Asia, had invaded Manchuria in 1931 and attacked China in 1937. The Japanese lacked certain key raw materials for expansion, primarily oil, and had their eyes on much of Southeast Asia, especially the oil and rubber resources in Dutch East India.

The war in China had been a critical mistake for Japan's military future, but the Japanese refused to withdraw from China despite their losses and continued to defy insistent American demands that they withdraw. Japan was dependent on the United States for shipments of scrap iron, steel, and oil, so Roosevelt used economic pressure to dislodge the Japanese. But the strategy failed. Motivated by its traditional warrior mentality, Japan believed in the virtue of making war for its own sake, and its citizens were honored to sacrifice their lives for their country. General Hideki Tojo and other militant leaders promoted the country's expansionist agenda. In September 1940 Japan joined with Germany and Italy in the Tripartite Agreement, creating the Rome-Tokyo-Berlin Axis. This agreement bound the three nations to help each other if one of the signees was attacked by a power not currently involved in the fighting, a pact clearly aimed at the United States.

America responded to Japan's refusal to get out of conquered territories by embargoing all shipments of steel and scrap iron to Japan. But Roosevelt did not want war with Japan in 1941, as Germany was the main focus and the greatest danger. FDR wanted to delay Japan's ambitions with a combination of economic pressure and diplomacy, hoping to stall Japanese military designs until America could speed up its preparation for war.

The Japanese government initially hoped to avoid war with the United States in 1941 and thought that diplomatic endeavors would allow continued trade with the United States without giving up Japanese gains in China and Indo-China. The military, convinced that only success on the battlefield would enable Japan to achieve its goals, chafed at the unending and unsuccessful diplomatic maneuvers. When the United States joined with Britain and Holland to impose embargoes that cut off nine-tenths of Japan's oil supply and reduced its foreign trade by three-quarters, Japan had no oil resources of its own and could not maintain a viable economy without oil. The nation was now at a crossroads. The Japanese could acquiesce in American restrictions and depart from conquered territories or could continue negotiations and prepare for immediate war. Encouraged by Emperor Hirohito, the Japanese government chose to continue discussions while gearing up for war.

General Hideki Tojo, formerly the war minister, became prime minister in October 1941, and placed a deadline on successful negotiations. If no agreement had been reached with the United States by November 1941, Japan would go to war. Tojo knew that Japan would have to conquer Southeast Asia to gain the raw materials needed for economic success and thought that the time was right for Japan to achieve its rightful dominance over Asia—an Asia freed from Western influence. Hitler's invasion of Russia had eliminated the possibility of a two-front war with Russia. America was engaged in thwarting Hitler and Germany, and Hitler had promised to declare war on the United States if Japanese actions provoked a war.

The Japanese army and navy were eager to launch what was at best a grandiose scheme. Japan, a nation of small islands, did not have the economic wherewithal to conquer the United States. Japan took a huge risk in its decision to go to war, because the nation would end up with either a complete victory or a complete defeat. The Japanese saw Americans as soft and cowardly and were convinced that they would easily defeat the U.S. forces.

FDR condemned the Japanese for sending troops into Indo-China and accused Japan of combining peaceful comments with warlike actions. He warned the Japanese that America and Britain were prepared to fight if the Japanese forces attacked anywhere in the area. The Japanese denied any aggressive intent but had already decided on war. The United States had made a huge intelligence breakthrough by cracking the Japanese diplomatic code. The decoded messages were named "Magic" and enabled American intelligence to learn about key decisions made by the Japanese government. The United States learned on November 7, 1941, that an aggressive move by Japan was expected by the end of the month if bargaining had ended.[18] Through Magic intercepts U.S. officials knew that the Japanese planned an attack in the Pacific but were not certain where or when. The commanders at Pearl Harbor, Admiral Husband E. Kimmel and General Walter C. Short, had been warned on November 27 of a possible attack by the Japanese and were told to execute appropriate defense deployment. Unfortunately the two commanders did little other than plan for sabotage. The American commanders and the leaders in Washington assumed that the attacks would come in the Philippines, never expecting a raid on American soil.

Most historians do not think that FDR deliberately goaded Japan into an attack on Pearl Harbor, but the attack certainly served his purposes, as it united the American people and galvanized them into action. The Japanese made a critical error by attacking American soil. If Japan had confined the invasion to Guam, the Philippines, and East Asia, FDR would have had a much harder time persuading the American people to go to war.[19]

The Japanese attack fleet had been at sea from November 26 to December 7 and had covered some 3,000 miles. By keeping out of the sea lanes, reducing smoke, keeping radio silence, preventing any waste being thrown overboard, and observing total blackout conditions, the Japanese convoy escaped detection. On December 7, 1941, Japan launched one of the most daring and damaging surprise attacks in military history. Shortly after 6 a.m. local time, four aircraft carriers launched two waves of 360 Japanese torpedo and dive bombers escorted by Zero fighters. At 7:55 a.m. the first wave of the dive bombers blasted American battleships and airfields. The attack lasted two hours and did considerable damage.

The Japanese had achieved total and complete surprise. First of all, the attack came early in the morning on a Sunday, generally accepted as a holiday. Many residents of Pearl Harbor were still asleep, some were in church, and a sizable number of navy personnel were hung over from excessive partying on Saturday night. Local observers were so shocked when the planes flew overhead, emblazoned with the bright red rising sun on the wings, that they initially thought that they were witnessing practice maneuvers. Their mistaken judgment ended when the bombs exploded. The U.S. Army, which had responsibility for defending the base, had chosen the least rigorous of three possible alerts. The antisabotage alert ordered that the planes be parked together to make it easier to guard them against sabotage. The planes lined up wing tip to wing tip at Hickam Field were an enticing target for the Japanese. The antiaircraft guns were not readily available and the ammunition was locked away in warehouses. Some of the ammunition had been issued in 1918. The navy also chose the lowest alert level, meaning that there were no barrage balloons, no torpedo nets, and no reconnaissance planes and only manned 25 percent of its antiaircraft guns.

Despite ever-growing signs that an attack was imminent, the security forces simply would not believe that an attack was happening. One destroyer radioed twice that he had attacked, fired on, and sunk what he thought was an enemy sub, but his warnings were ignored. Around 7 a.m. one of the spotter stations noticed a large blip on the radar screen. It was dismissed as an anomaly, but the blip got bigger and bigger. One officer said that it was probably a flock of birds. If so, fifty of them were coming at 180 miles per hour. The spotter again approached the commanding officer with a warning, but the officer told him not to worry about it. If there were planes coming to Pearl Harbor, surely they were friendly planes.

The Japanese achieved a huge success at Pearl Harbor. The raiders sank or crippled 18 warships, including the battleships *California*, *Oklahoma*, and *West Virginia*; destroyed or damaged 188 planes on the ground; and extensively damaged 5 airfields and killed 2,403 Americans—1,000 forever entombed in the battleship *Arizona*, which exploded in a huge orange ball and sank. The Japanese losses were minimal: 29 planes, 45 pilots, and crewmen, 1 regular submarine, and 4 midget subs.

The attack had exceeded Japan's most optimistic predictions and had surprised Admiral Chuichi Nagumo, who led the mission. The commanders talked briefly about embarking on a second mission against the repair facilities and oil storage tanks, because the defenses were so weak and Pearl Harbor was virtually defenseless, but the commander decided that he had achieved enough success for the day. Had they chosen to attack one more time, the damage would have been so devastating that it would have crippled the Pacific fleet for many months.

On December 7 Japanese forces also destroyed American airfields in the Philippines and attacked Guam, Wake Island, Hong Kong, Malaya, Burma, the Dutch East Indies, and Singapore. Japanese forces soon reigned supreme in all of these areas and began to assert military control of their newly conquered territory.

Fortunately the U.S aircraft carriers were not at Pearl Harbor. This was a significant factor, because the carriers would form the crux of America's retaliatory force. What appeared to be a momentous Japanese victory was in reality a grossly misconceived operation. It awakened the fury of the Americans, who from this point on were committed to total war and victory. By attacking American soil and shedding American blood, although they did not know it at the time, the Japanese had condemned themselves to defeat. Tojo had aroused a sleeping giant and in the process had angered and united all Americans, even the isolationists, in support of war.

Pearl Harbor gave President Roosevelt exactly what he needed to issue a clarion call for war. The next day, December 8, 1941, speaking before a cheering joint session of Congress and with 60 million Americans listening over the radio, FDR condemned the dastardly sneak attack on Pearl Harbor as a "date which will live in infamy." Admitting severe damage from the attack, Roosevelt rallied the confused and frightened American people with soaring rhetoric. "No matter how long it may take us to overcome this premeditated invasion, the American people, in their righteous might, will win through to absolute victory. . . . With confidence in our armed forces, with the unbounding determination of our people, we will gain the inevitable triumph, so help us God." That same day Congress voted for a declaration of war against Japan with only one dissenting vote, by Jeannette Rankin, a pacifist from Montana. Isolation had ended. Three days later, as part of the Tripartite Pact, Germany and Italy declared war on the United States. America responded in kind on the same day.[20] Now the United States was engaged in the greatest war in human history.

North Carolina's reaction to Pearl Harbor was immediate, forceful, and unified. On December 8, 1941, the *Raleigh News and Observer*'s headline was "Japan Declares War on the United States."[21] Charlotte newspaper carriers selling an extra edition of the *Charlotte News* hit the streets, shouting: "War, War!" Other state newspapers announced the attack and urged all citizens, even the pacifists, to unite to defeat the totalitarian powers.

All of the isolationists in the Senate, save one, now called for unity and endorsed the goal of winning the war. Senator Bob Reynolds initially declared that even after the Japanese attack he remained fully against war and wanted to know more details before he could say anything about declaring war. He somehow managed to blame the British not the Japanese for the attack. Reynolds, realizing that he had blundered badly, tried to repair his error by issuing a formal statement denouncing the Japanese for two-timing and double-crossing the United States while pretending to work for peace. "In view of this unwarranted, deceitful, murderous and uncalled for attack on us, there is nothing left to do but to go to it 100 percent." Although late rallying to the cause, Reynolds enthusiastically voted for a declaration of war against Japan on December 8.[22]

The morning of December 8 in North Carolina was sunny but cold. Most residents went about their Sunday activities without a clue about what was happening in Hawaii. Churchgoers were coming home for their Sunday dinners, while others attended a movie or a football game. At 2:22 p.m. the music from "Sammy Kaye's Sunday Serenade" was abruptly interrupted with the news that the Japanese had attacked Pearl Harbor. When the same news was announced at a semipro football game between the Charlotte Clippers and the Norfolk Shamrocks in Legion Memorial Stadium, the crowd sat shocked and silent then arose with a loud cheer. The announcer instructed all military personnel to return at once to their bases.[23] Worshipers at the Peace of Prince in Raleigh heard the news coming out of church. In Memorial Auditorium the audience was listening to G. F. Handel's *Messiah* when the announcement came.

Very few had ever heard of Pearl Harbor, but everyone knew the significance of the newscast. America was now at war. Some simply did not believe the news, calling it a hoax. Most listeners were angry and vowed to defeat the Japanese at all costs and expressed belief in the ultimate triumph of American arms. Patriotic rallies were held in various towns and cities to promote unity and rally the people for the long fight ahead.[24]

All Americans remembered exactly where they were and what they were doing when they heard the news about Pearl Harbor. James Waynick had just returned from his grandfather's funeral and was hanging around the local soda shop when he heard the radio announcement. Like other young men of his day, Waynick had some vague knowledge of the conflict in Europe against Germany but did not know anything about Japan and admitted that he had no idea what impact the war would have on his world.[25] Twenty-year-old Robert Thomas knew immediately that he had to join the army and fight for his country. The American flag "meant a lot to me." Combining his patriotism with his love of God and family, he felt he had no choice but to defend what he believed.[26] William Riggs and two of his buddies were riding around Fayetteville, N.C., in a 1938 model Ford V8 listening to a program on the radio by Andre Kostelanetz, a well-known orchestra director, when the program was interrupted by the announcement of Pearl Harbor. Riggs was not completely shocked because he had been keeping up with the negotiations in the newspapers. Unlike some of his buddies, he knew that the fighting would be difficult and that defeating the "Japs" would not be a picnic.[27]

J. D. Lancaster had a unique and vivid memory of the attack because he was standing on the deck of the USS *Arizona*. Lancaster, a seaman second class, had just finished breakfast and had ventured to the deck when the attack began. He saw a flying fragment slice his commanding officer in two and seconds later was blown off the deck into the oily and burning water. He swam over to the battleship *West Virginia* and manned an antiaircraft gun. Lancaster was one of only ninety members of the crew who survived and the only North Carolinian. Some 1,103 of his shipmates died in the assault.[28] Claude E. Pike, who was attending the V-7 Officer Training Program in Chicago, was having a nice dinner with a family there when the news came over the radio. His unit was put on full alert, and he "remembered vividly the folly of standing a four hour watch that freezing night on top of the building, searching for Japanese planes that might come over and bomb us."[29]

The overall response from North Carolinians in support of the war was enthusiastic and instantaneous. Upon hearing the news, Ed Newton, son of the police chief in Southern Pines, N.C., immediately made his way to Raleigh to be first in line at the U.S Naval Recruiting Station. He was said to be the first North Carolinian to sign up for military service.[30]

Army, navy, and marine recruiting stations opened early on December 8 and geared up for the rush of enlistees. And they came in droves. In Raleigh alone 768 men had volunteered for service by December 16. Six University of North Carolina students immediately enlisted as aviation cadets. In Greenville, N.C., ten prisoners volunteered to serve in the army as a suicide squad and offered to return, if alive, to finish out the rest of their sentences. Colonel John D. Langston commented on the unusual request by the prisoners. "The story was an inspiring one. If the peril of the nation can so revive the ideals of those who have sinned against our laws, what may we expect from those who are not so handicapped."[31]

A sixty-year-old auditor from the state Department of Revenue offered his services. "While I'm not as young as I once was, I am still in good physical condition, not in a notably bad mental condition" and "can render worthwhile service to our Uncle." He was turned away with thanks for his offer.[32] Congressman Harold D. Cooley had promised in a campaign for Congress in 1934 to put on a uniform if war was declared. He said that the minute he cast a vote to send North Carolinians to war he would surrender his seat in Congress and "shoulder my musket and march . . . upon the field of battle and into the jaws of death." Cooley tried to enlist in the army, which turned him down and told him to stay in Congress.[33]

Mildred McIver recalled being with a soldier from Camp Davis when she heard the terrible news. "I remember being frightened to death. There was such a state of fear. It was a terrible, terrible fear." Katherine Cameron expressed the views of many North Carolinians when she reported that the news paralyzed her. She thought: "We're Americans. We've been attacked. This just can't happen." Charles M. Paty of Charlotte heard the reports and immediately announced that he was going to join up. He was an only child, so his parents resisted the idea, but as Paty recalled: "I was in no mood to listen to logic." He argued that he did not want to fight the Japanese on the banks of the Catawba River. Initially turned down by the navy because he did not have his parents' permission and because he was too skinny, Paty returned home, got the required permission, ate a lot of bananas, and was accepted by the navy.[34]

Eleanor Peck, in a December 12 letter to her father, caught the mood of many Tar Heels: "Well, it looks as though you were wrong when you said the U.S. wouldn't get into the war. I can think of no greater miscalculation on the part of the Japs than just what they have done as far as crystallizing public opinion in America. I suppose people are madder than hell at what happened."[35] They were.

The *Raleigh News and Observer*, in a December 8 editorial, remarked that the sneak attack had given America "the unquestioned power of absolute unity." North Carolinians had no will for war, but now they were determined and confident that America would destroy the Japanese military machine. The paper knew that the war would not be easy. Japan would not have attacked if it thought that the totalitarian powers would not prevail. The newspaper sought to bolster its readers' hopes and encourage a full commitment to the war effort. "Dead Americans in Honolulu created not only sad hearts but steel ones. We are ready. We are not afraid. Beyond every sacrifice America recognizes no possibility but victory and is ready to pay every price to insure it."[36]

Governor J. Melville Broughton, knowing that he had to prepare the state for a long conflict, sprang into action the day after the Pearl Harbor attack to prevent sabotage and subversive activities. The governor ordered the Home Guard and civilian defense organizations to organize and explained that he would allocate responsibility to each unit to protect all vital industries, bridges and power plants, and other structures that might be in danger of sabotage. He used his police power to assign the state Highway Patrol to assist in these efforts and to place all fire departments and police departments on a wartime footing. The governor's ambitious desire to shore up civilian defenses resonated throughout the state. In Roxboro extra guards were put on industrial plants. In Halifax County the Defense Council announced a group of "V-Men" to go around the county and discuss defense measures.[37]

North Carolina was now poised to make a great leap ahead from being the backward, rural, poorly educated, southern backwater state of 1940 into becoming a more modern, industrialized entity. In 1940 the state's population was 3,571,623, evenly divided between males and females. There were 1,003,988 nonwhites in the state. North Carolina had very few foreign-born citizens—9,046 in urban areas and 2,055 in the rural parts of the state. Approximately 70 percent of the state was rural. North Carolina ranked very low in most economic indices, even among other southern states. As late as 1950 the median income for families was $2,121; in rural sections the average was $1,304. State payrolls were low because the key industries—tobacco, textiles, farming, and furniture manufacturing—paid notoriously low wages. The state had been very slow to build up its infrastructure and develop an industrial base.

Raleigh, the capital city, with a population of 46,490 in 1941, demonstrated the slow and uneven economic development in the state. State government was small, employing 3,300 individuals. The forty-four industries in Raleigh had hired 1,191 workers. The city (hardly an industrial giant) had only three commercial banks and two building and loan associations. It was served by a small municipal airport, two main line railroads, and three passenger bus lines—and this was the state capital. These statistics demonstrate the difficult economic circumstances in the state, even in the larger cities.

About 53 percent of the state's population had incomes of less than

$2,000. In terms of employment 42 percent of the workforce was engaged in farming-related industries and only 28 percent worked in manufacturing jobs. Nonwhite residents were about one-third of the population and by every standard—employment, education, health care, and voting rights—they languished behind whites and their opportunities were limited.

Illiteracy and health issues were major problems. Only 54.8 percent of whites, both rural and urban, attended school. Only 16 percent completed high school. Rickets, pellagra, bad teeth, and malnourishment were common in the poorer communities. The lack of community colleges, underfunded schools, and a limited number of paved roads provided few opportunities for advancement for those in rural areas—many of whom had to live without telephones and electricity.[38]

Despite the negative economic circumstances, North Carolina had excellent higher education, progressive state leaders, and the resources to fuel an economic revolution. The state would undergo totally unexpected and dramatic changes in the next four years, which would remake the state and would reorder the lives of its citizens.

A Call to Duty

The Selective Service Act of 1940

Now that America was committed to the defeat of the Axis powers, the nation had to organize its people and materiel for the long haul. Most pressing was the need for a large body of trained soldiers to carry the burden of fighting. Unfortunately for the nation's armed services, prior to 1940 the public and the isolationists were vehemently opposed to any act that might draw the United States into a military conflict. Therefore there had not been a military buildup or any call-up and training of new troops.

In September 1939 the U.S. Army was in woeful shape and would not be able to resist an invasion by even the weakest nation. It was nineteenth in the world in size with a meager total of 174,000 men, ahead of Bulgaria but behind Portugal. Its so-called divisions, which were dispersed in bases all over the country, were at half strength. Because of the scattered camps, the military had virtually no opportunity to train the soldiers in cohesive units. The army's equipment was obsolete and inadequate. The army had very little ammunition, no combat planes, and only one fully armored unit to combat Hitler's blitzkrieg. Some troops were without any modern weapons and were forced to use broomsticks to simulate machine guns.[1]

By 1940 George C. Marshall, the army chief of staff, knew that America would almost certainly be drawn into the European conflict. He wanted to conscript an army of at least 2 million soldiers as soon as possible. If war did come, which appeared more likely each day, Marshall's job was to prepare an army capable of fighting a lengthy ground war. Marshall understood that recruitment alone would not raise the necessary number of soldiers in a short period and favored setting up a peacetime draft. As late as the summer of 1940, however, the U.S. Congress, many newspaper critics, and the isolationists vigorously opposed any draft or buildup of the U.S. Army. Incredible as it might seem today, the opposition to Marshall's attempt to institute a draft and raise an army continued unabated until just before Pearl Harbor. Some congressional representatives and isolationists went so far as to urge Marshall to reduce the size of the army. Even Great Britain opposed an American draft, fearing that a decision to spend large sums of money on the army buildup would endanger the American military aid given to Great Britain.

The Training and Selective Service Act of 1940

General Marshall knew that it would be difficult to get a draft bill passed if the impetus came from the military, so he worked assiduously to get public opinion behind the concept of universal military training. He persuaded a distinguished group of prominent business leaders, conservatives, veterans of World War I, graduates of Ivy League colleges, and the *New York Times* to back the effort. This group of adherents appealed for public support and tirelessly lobbied Congress. President Roosevelt, running for a third term and fearful of being characterized as a warmonger, was initially reluctant to come out publicly in favor of the draft but finally lent his approval, recognizing the importance of a draft bill. The secretary of war, Henry Stimson, constantly lobbied Congress, as did General Marshall, who testified several times before congressional committees.

Despite frantic efforts to derail the Burke-Wadsworth bill, the first peacetime conscription bill in the nation's history, it passed the Senate by a vote of 58–31 on August 28, 1940. On September 7 the House approved the bill by a vote of 263–149. Because of Germany's stunning defeat of France and due to the effective lobbying by Marshall, Roosevelt, and key civilian proponents, public opinion had changed to the point that 71 percent of the people favored some sort of draft legislation. The possibility of war seemed imminent, so it became imperative to select and train the personnel of the armed forces through a compulsory draft system. In the meantime President Roosevelt, as commander-in-chief, ordered all National Guard and Reserve units mobilized for active duty.

The Selective Training and Service Act of 1940, as it was known, was signed into law by President Roosevelt on September 16, 1940. The president had to compromise to get the bill passed by promising that no drafted troops would be sent to take part in any European wars. The bill recognized the obligation of all citizens to serve their country in a time of national crisis and promised a "fair and just" system of conscription. Every male citizen between the ages of twenty-one and thirty-six was required to register for the draft. The term of service was fixed at twelve months, but the act cautioned that the term could be extended by the president if necessary for the national defense. The bill assigned a quota to each state based on its population and the number of men available for training and service.

Several paragraphs of the bill were devoted to exceptions, exemptions, and deferments from service and training. These included men already in the armed forces; federal, state, and local officials of the legislative, executive, and judicial branches; anyone deemed by the president to be necessary to the maintenance of the national health, safety, or interest; and ministers of religion. Students would be deferred until July 1, 1941, allowing them to complete their school year, and a provision included noncombatant service for those who opposed the war. No bounties were to be given, no substitutes were allowed, and no payment to escape service would be accepted. The act gave the president the authority to create a Selective Service system and spelled out the penalties for failing to register—a fine of $10,000 or five years in prison or both.[2] The acceptance of the Selective Service Act by American citizens and its effective implementation would be the key to the mobilization of America's defenses.

One year later, when the extension of the Selective Service Act came up, congressional resistance was greater than before. Isolationists feared that because the United States had acquired an army, it would be used to enter the war. George Marshall took the lead on getting the draft extended by pointing out that America's newly acquired strength would vanish if the extension was not approved. Despite worsening relations with the Japanese, increasingly effective Nazi U-boat attacks in the Battle of the Atlantic, and German military successes, the isolationist sentiment remained strong. The country simply did not want to accept the reality of an impending conflict. One congressman saw the extension of the Selective Service Act as "part and parcel of a vast conspiracy" to force the country into war.[3]

In August 1941, after a bitter battle in Congress, the Selective Service Extension Act of 1941 passed the Senate by a two-to-one margin but passed the House by a single vote. The defeat of this bill would have been a major setback for Roosevelt's attempt to prepare the nation for war and would have been a disaster for the army. Without the extension, the first draft of conscripts would have been released from active duty, leaving the army in a shambles. The bill squeaked through primarily on the force of General Marshall's persuasive arguments. The army and to some degree the nation were saved by one vote.[4] One can only imagine what would have happened to the United States if there had been a drastically reduced army when the Japanese attacked Pearl Harbor.

The Selective Service in 1940 had been designed to provide a workable system for the induction of millions of trained men into the military. The emphasis was on the word "selective." The Selective Service not only had to choose men to fight but also had to keep others at home, working in the fields and factories to furnish the material necessary for winning the war.

The response in North Carolina to the Selective Service Act of 1940 was overwhelmingly positive.[5] Tar Heel men were so eager to get into service that many volunteered and signed up before the draft. These impatient young men cited many different reasons for their willingness to serve. Many saw this as their patriotic duty. Others wanted to get a job after the years of a depressed economy, and twenty-one dollars a month and three meals a day seemed a pretty good option. Some just wanted to embark on an adventure—they did not want to spend their lives in small-town North Carolina working at a textile mill. It should be noted that the great majority of men did not go to war or even into the armed forces during the war. Just one out of every three men aged seventeen to thirty-five, a total of 16 million men, served in the military during World War II. One-fourth of them never left the United States, and only a minority served in actual combat zones.[6]

As was the case with many enlistees, Manfred T. Blanchard joined the army prior to the draft partly because he was enticed by the spiffy uniforms and thought that it would be the kind of life he would enjoy.[7] Wendell Haire remarked that the navy uniforms were the prettiest he ever saw and thought that joining the navy would result in "a lot of adventure."[8] Bill Lashley volunteered for the draft and intended to join the army, but on the way to the recruiting station he ran into a marine recruiter who persuaded him to join the U.S. Marines. Lashley had always admired the Marine Corps, so he bypassed the army and signed with the Leathernecks.[9]

The Selective Service Act segregated the draft, with white and black men having to register separately. Women were not included in the draft. Each person who registered for the draft was assigned a draft number, and a national lottery would determine when the individual would be drafted. On October 30, 1940, Secretary Stimson drew the numbers at random from a fishbowl and so determined the fate of each registrant.

Those men whose numbers were not initially called could go about their daily activities until they were summoned to duty. Some registrants were not drafted until 1942 or 1943, and some were never called. Of the 52,542 men who registered in Mecklenburg County, 76 percent were never drafted. Most of those who were not called up either had a defense job or had physical, mental, or health problems.

In the first year of the war only single men were drafted; married men were deferred. By the end of 1942, with most single men in service, draft boards began calling married men without children and finally, after October 1943, even men with children. As the need for fighting men increased, the list of exemptions was drastically reduced. In December 1943 a North Carolina father of nine, age thirty-seven, was ushered into service.[10]

The Selective Service Organization in North Carolina

Setting up the infrastructure of the Selective Service system was a complicated and difficult task. The act had intentionally decentralized the operation of the system so that the actual work would be done by each state headquarters and in turn by the local draft boards. At the national level, headquarters set the overall standards and determined the order in which men were to be drafted. In addition, Washington employed trained military personnel to decide overall policy. At the local level, to preserve a democratic system, civilian personnel operated the machinery: the power to determine an individual's status lay with the local draft board.

The state and local boards had no control over the impersonal number selected by the lottery and could not (without a good reason) relieve from service a man whom chance had selected. Otherwise, each local board, while being held to uniform policies by state headquarters, retained the right of determining the classification of the individuals drafted in the area under its supervision. For the most part each state interpreted national regulations in light of its needs.

The local Selective Service Boards, known as draft boards, were manned by volunteers who worked many hours without any compensation, trying as best they could to make sense of confusing and constantly changing directives from state and national headquarters. The red tape was almost beyond comprehension, as the local boards had to interpret two volumes of Selective Service regulations. These boards tried to be fair in all cases that appeared before them, but they were often under tremendous pressure from parents and local leaders. The boards were inevitably inundated with criticism, both just and unjust, for their decisions. If they allowed the mayor's son to be classified 4-F for weak eyesight, they were accused of favoring the powerful at the expense of the poor.

Brigadier General Lewis B. Hershey directed the overall system on a federal level. North Carolina, led by Governor Clyde R. Hoey, organized the state system. After December 8, 1940, personnel at state headquarters began to wear uniforms, but the statewide system remained strictly civilian. North Carolina had 155 local draft boards, 7 appeal boards, and 6 medical advisory boards. All clerical and staff employees working for the Selective Service administration were part of the federal civil service and thus were federal employees.[11]

The number of local boards for each county was determined by population. The ideal area serviced by a draft board contained a population of about 30,000 people, but each county had to have at least one board. Thirty of the larger North Carolina counties had two draft boards, while sixty-one counties had only one. The nine largest counties had from three to five boards. Most of the tribunals were composed of three members, but seven boards had four members. The state determined the territorial jurisdiction of each governing board.

The most difficult task in planning for the inception of the draft was the selection of the members of the draft board. Governor Hoey requested that prominent local officials make recommendations to him since they would know the right persons to be entrusted with such a delicate task. The local officials (such as mayors, judges, and city council members) should recommend individuals highly respected in the community and choose only those who would be free from political bias. Because there was no compensation for this difficult task, not even money for travel, the governor hoped that the men (only men served on the boards) selected would be eager to serve their country without remuneration. Surprisingly, despite the long hours and difficult decision making, the local boards had very few resignations. Some of those who left the board entered military service, and a few had health problems that prevented them from serving. Otherwise the members served without complaint.

The draft system generally worked because those appointed to the local boards were thought to be relatively free from racial discrimination and bias. The board members were usually business and community leaders and knew the economic situation and the family background of many of the men with whom they were dealing. The system relied on a democratic concept whereby the local members had a better gauge of individual situations than those at the state or federal level. In a state where approximately one-third of the population was black, however, only four blacks were chosen for local draft boards. As one would expect in a segregated society, the boards' members were overwhelmingly from the middle and upper classes of the white community.

North Carolina had seven district appeal boards to hear the entreaties of men who believed that they had been improperly classified. The membership of the appeal boards ideally represented a myriad of interests: labor, law, industry, and medicine. The appeal board members heard the oral presentations by those who were appealing their classification, read briefs for each case, and made a final decision. The Selective Service also required advisory groups to help registrants fill out the forms that would be the basis for classification. A prison appeal board dealt with prisoners who sought parole in exchange for entering the armed forces.

The state was divided into six medical districts, staffed by physicians and nurses, who determined the physical and mental fitness of registrants. Each local board had at least one examining physician and one dentist to perform physicals.

When official registration began on October 16, 1940, not all of the local boards had been formally established. Originally the act required the registration of all males between the ages of twenty-one and thirty-six. This requirement was amended on December 11, 1942, to include those men between eighteen and forty-five. Eventually the administration set up six different registration periods for draftees, with different ages and requirements on each occasion. The fourth registration period was perhaps the most controversial, because it enrolled men from forty-five to sixty-five who would never be called into the military. The government did this deliberately for the psychological effect that it would have on the nation—every man, regardless of age, was required to enroll in the fight for freedom. Those who failed to report for examination or induction were declared delinquent. Delinquency was not a matter for the local draft boards; enforcement was the responsibility of the Department of Justice and the federal district attorneys.

Figure 2.1. Men report for draft registration in Greensboro, N.C., in 1942. By permission of Carol W. Martin/Greensboro Historical Museum.

For the initial registration, rules and instructions as well as Registration Cards were passed out to the volunteer registrars. Many of the volunteers were schoolteachers and public employees taking a day away from their regular jobs. The one-day registration event on October 16 proved to be successful, as radio, state officials, and newspapers had alerted the public about exactly what was happening and when. On opening day, with American and state flags flying in public places, the nation enrolled 16 million men. The call to arms was carried out in a systematic manner, with a sense of unity and with very few individual objections or complaints.

Before the end of November 1940 the first group of draftees selected from Charlotte, N.C., had taken their physical and mental examinations and had been ordered to report to Fort Bragg. The Charlotte city fathers provided a ceremonial send-off for the group, with bands playing patriotic music and officials giving each inductee an American flag. The new draftees, after a hearty meal, had to suffer through several patriotic speeches before being finally loaded on buses, ready to serve their country.[12]

Bill Stansfield, a recent draftee, humorously recalled that he had received a letter in the mail that said "your friends and neighbors [local draft board] have selected you to serve your country." Stansfield described the circumstances when he and a bunch of his buddies from Rockingham County took their physicals. He remembered "119 good old boys . . . , standing in line with absolutely no clothes on, one behind the other and not too close." Stansfield recalled that all of his group passed the physical but described how close he came to being rejected. The doctor asked him how he got along with girls. "At that particular time," he said, "I wasn't getting along with my girlfriend too well and I thought for a while before I gave him an answer. Finally, I said, 'all right I reckon.' The doctor grinned and said, soldier you just passed your physical, you're in the Army now. Later on, I realized that the doctor was a psychiatrist and I'm lucky I gave him the right answer. Had I given him the wrong answer I would have been 4F until the days of Bill Clinton."[13]

The order to report for induction, from "the President of the United States to . . . ," read as follows: "Having submitted yourself to a local board composed of your neighbors for the purpose of training and service in the land or naval forces of the United States, you are hereby notified that you have been selected for training and service therein." The draftee was advised to put his affairs in order and notify employees in case he was accepted. (He could still be rejected during the induction process.) The draftee was to go to the local board, which would provide transportation to the induction site. Failure to report was a violation of the Selective Training and Service Act of 1940 and subject to fine and imprisonment.[14]

Classifying the Registrants

The local draft board's initial problem was how to classify each registrant. No classification was permanent, as a change in the needs of the military or a change in a person's status could lead to a reclassification. The local board based its classification determination on a questionnaire, filled out by the registrants and returned to the board. The board also provided special forms for conscientious objectors and forms to be used on appeals for deferments.

There were four main classes of draftees. Class 1 was composed of men immediately available for military service. Class 2 was made up of men deferred by reason of occupations in fields that supported the national health and safety or in war production or in an essential agricultural profession. Class 3 was made up of men with dependents and extreme dependency problems that would cause a severe hardship to wife, parents, or child. Class 4 was composed of men deferred for various reasons, such as age and unfitness.

What seemed like a simple process was vastly more complicated than the basic four classes, because each class had a number of subcategories. Class 1 included 1-A (available for service) and 1-A-O (available only for noncombatant service due to conscientious objection). 1-B meant limited service for physical reasons. 1-C meant that the man was already a member of the armed forces or had completed military service. 1-D was a student fit for military service. 1-E was a student fit for limited military service. 1-H was a man temporarily deferred because of age.

Class 4 posed a particularly vexing problem for the local boards, because it dealt with deferments and who qualified for them. The rules made a clear distinction between a deferment and an exemption. Any deferment was temporary: the individual could be reclassified if conditions changed. An exemption meant that the individual was completely exempt from any military service, although as noted that classification could also change. Class 4 contained several categories. 4-A was someone deferred by reason of age or completed military service. 4-B was an official deferred by law. 4-D was a minister of religion. 4-E was a conscientious objector, available only for civilian duty. 4-F was a man found unfit for military service for mental or physical reasons.

As all citizens recognized, the regulations had many gray areas. Was a self-proclaimed minister of the gospel eligible for deferment? Exactly what was necessary for a 4-F designation? Should a draftee be exempted for flat feet? What about a man who was nearsighted? Could just anyone claim to be a conscientious objector? How did the draft board evaluate such claims?

The rules were unclear at the outset of the process, and each draft board had to develop its own set of criteria. Unfortunately, the rules and regulations changed constantly, so the local boards had a difficult time keeping up with all the revisions. The rules changed partly because the nation needed more troops as the war progressed and had to expand the eligible numbers and reduce the number of deferments and exemptions. There was always a conflict between the needs of the military and workforce issues for industry and farming. The draft boards needed to keep a proper balance between workers needed for production goals and soldiers necessary for military success. If the United States did not have enough skilled workers making ammunition, airplanes, and uniforms, the country could not win the war. Farm products were also essential to the survival and fitness of the troops.

Many employers asked for occupational deferments based on the vital importance of skilled workers to their company—the "necessary man." When the government judged an industry or business to be critical to the war effort, its employees could be eligible for deferment. For example, North Carolina was an essential source of mica and produced more of it than any other state. Mica was necessary for the production of important munitions, so its mining was considered a critical industry. Some local boards, however, thought that young men were working in mica production just to avoid military service—"digging for deferment."[15] The local boards had to determine if the industry was important enough and the worker skilled enough for a deferment.

One case typified many of the difficult assessments that the draft boards had to make. The board had to decide if a bank clerk at a very important and powerful financial company was irreplaceable. After due diligence, the board determined that he was not irreplaceable (that other workers could do his job) and classified him 1-A. In the later years of the war it became more difficult to secure occupational deferments and harder to gain deferment because of age but easier to be excused for agricultural pursuits.

Special groups such as teachers, bus drivers, highway patrol officers, members of the Civil Air Patrol, and government employees thought that they were entitled to deferment and constantly besieged the local boards to obtain that status. As a general rule, the draft boards did not allow group deferments.

A draftee could appeal his classification by filing a written notice to the district Appeals Board but could not challenge the determination of his mental or physical condition by his attending physician. The Appeals Board had the responsibility of reviewing all appeals in regard to occupational deferments. By March 1947 the North Carolina Appeals Boards had heard 62,505 cases. Even after the Appeals Board's final judgment, applicants had the right of final appeal to the president of the United States. The president reviewed 431 of the most controversial cases and upheld the boards in 134 cases. He changed the boards' decisions in 297 cases.[16]

For the most part men in the state accepted the draft system without much grumbling or complaining. A sampling of public opinion around the state revealed that, while people in Chowan County were disturbed about the war, there were remarkably few complaints about the draft system. In Rocky Mount the draft board performed its duties "in a manner that meets with general approval." In Chatham County, according to the lieutenant governor, W. P. Horton, "there have been far less complaints about the draft than there were during World War I."[17]

After being drafted, the men arriving at the induction center spent a day full of activity and anxiety. The draftees, usually fifty in a group, were unloaded from the bus and escorted to the latrine—a military term unfamiliar to most, but one that they all learned quickly. The draftees then officially registered and listened to an orientation talk. The examiners warned them not to eat too much before the medical exam and reassured them about the nature of the exam to eliminate any nervousness.

At this point high school graduates were separated from the rest and like the other draftees were given a psychological test for possible neuroses or psychoses. If they passed, they took the physical exam. Men without a high school diploma were given a sixteen-item qualifying literacy test. A sample question: "How many inches in one and one-half feet?" If they failed that test the inductees were given a test to see if they could follow simple instructions. If an individual did not pass this second test, and if the officer was convinced that the selectee was not a malingerer, he was rejected for service for being below the intelligence standard at that time. A surprisingly large number of potential inductees in North Carolina fell into this category. Once the men had passed their physical exam, blood test, and psychological evaluation they were sworn into service, issued uniforms, and marched to the reception center.[18]

The Selective Service system tried to ensure that morale remained high during wartime and kept churches involved in the important role of maintaining spiritual strength and moral courage by granting deferments to ministers of religion. The Selective Service Act allowed some students to complete their schoolwork before going into service, especially if they were studying in certain specialized fields such as physics, engineering, medicine, dentistry, pharmacy, and other occupations needed for the war effort. The government kept schools running by deferring school administrators and some teachers, many of whom were in vocational education. The act also protected local, state, and national governmental agencies involved in war work with deferments.

The issue of family dependency was especially important to the Selective Service. The act established a Class 3 category for those families who would suffer "undue hardship" by the designation of a husband or son as eligible for the military, as the agency wanted to limit the disruption of families as much as possible. The applicant for a hardship exemption had to prove that the family would be seriously harmed by the absence of the breadwinner. In the early stage married men were excused but the local boards had to be careful, because an increasing number of registrants got married just to avoid military service. Men with a large number of children were usually excused. In January 1942 North Carolina draft boards approved 68 percent of dependency applications, but this number went down as the war continued due to a heightened need for troops and a tightening of the deferment policy. The status of a dependent could also be applied to parents or grandparents. A good example was the case of James Waynick. Waynick, a North Carolina native, received deferred status because his father was old and disabled, his mother was ill, and James was the only wage earner in the family.[19]

As the draft expanded, the federal government came to realize that many of the draftees came from very poor economic circumstances. The government concluded that enlisted men, who received a rather modest salary, needed help looking after their families while in service and set up a program to supply a monthly allowance for each military family. The Servicemen's Dependents Allowance Act of 1942 was designed to provide family allowances for the dependents of enlisted soldiers. The monthly allowance for a wife with no child was $50. Of this sum, the soldier contributed $22 from his monthly pay and the government contributed $28. For a wife and one child, the amount was $62; for two children, $72; and so on.[20]

Conscientious Objectors

One category that aroused heated passions on both sides was the status of conscientious objectors (COs). The law granted the deferment of registrants conscientiously opposed to military duty of any kind. Those opposed only to combat duty were classified as 1-A-O and put in noncombatant service. Those who refused noncombatant duty because they believed that any work for the military supported the war machine were classified 4-E and placed into government Civilian Public Service Camps to perform "work of national importance."[21]

The refusal to bear arms based on moral and religious principles had existed in North Carolina since its foundation as a colony. Initially only those of certain pacifist sects (Quakers, Moravians, and Mennonites) were recognized as conscientious objectors. Later that category was expanded to anyone with a demonstrable aversion to killing.[22] The Society of Friends or Quakers and the Jehovah's Witnesses furnished most of the COs in North Carolina, but there were very few individuals in the state who actually registered for CO status. By March 1, 1943, at the height of requests for CO status, only 171 men (0.02 percent of all registrants in the state) were so classified. Of that number, 7 were black and 164 were white. The cumulative total of COs on all grounds during World War II in North Carolina was 422. Of the men, 10 were reclassified as 1-A and made available for military service, while 23 were reclassified as 1-A-O and placed into noncombatant service. Most of the other conscientious objectors served time in the Civilian Public Service Camps, usually from twelve to eighteen months, although 7 were held for over four years. And 20 claimants who refused to work in noncombatant service or spend time in the public service camps were sentenced to prison.[23]

In North Carolina many of those seeking CO status were members of the Jehovah's Witnesses religious sect and were put in a special category by the state board. The sect members were given job-related deferments as "ministers of religion," rather than being deferred due to religious beliefs. Later on the state board changed the rules, and the Jehovah's Witnesses lost their "minister of religion" deferment.

Although the Mecklenburg County board never approved a single person for CO status, many citizens and the local newspapers in Charlotte and other cities still considered men applying for a CO classification to be cowards and an embarrassment to the community.[24] Some draft board members held a negative view of COs. One commented that they should be branded with an "O" on their forehead, while another thought they should be placed in army camps and relegated to KP (kitchen patrol) or similar duty. Lawyers on some of the draft boards believed that most of the requests for CO status were for the purpose of evasion and requested that the classification be abolished.[25] Despite the complaints, the designation remained.

The several highly publicized cases of conscientious objectors in the state included the saga of Joseph Felmet, a native of Asheville. While a student at the University of North Carolina (UNC), Felmet became very active in the pacifist movement on campus. According to his Federal Bureau of Investigation (FBI) file, on January 17, 1941, he participated in a walkout on campus to protest militarism and conscription. In October 1941 he sent out postcards announcing a meeting of all pacifists to discuss means of avoiding the draft as a conscientious objector. He later told the FBI that he was not a Communist but a socialist and a pacifist. Felmet, a contentious and disputatious individual, was on the FBI's radar for any number of reasons from the time he arrived at UNC.

Felmet had registered with his local draft board as required on February 16, 1942. When he registered, he signified that he was conscientiously opposed to participation in the act of killing a human being, even in self-defense. He filled out the special form for COs and explained that he was also opposed to noncombatant military service because any such service aided the war effort. As a result of his request, on November 25, 1942, Felmet was classified as 4-E, a conscientious objector available only for civilian duty, and assigned to Civilian Public Service Camp 52 in Powellsville, Maryland. Here he was to do "work of national importance" under civilian not military control.

After working in the camp for several weeks, he complained that he was spending time in meaningless work and that his civilian assignment did not properly recognize his position as a conscientious objector. He petitioned General Lewis Hershey at the National Selective Service Headquarters for a reclassification to 1-A-O, a conscientious objector eligible for noncombatant military duty. His request was granted on April 14, 1943.

As expected, Felmet received a notice from the local Draft Board in Salisbury, Maryland, to report for induction into the Armed Forces for noncombatant military duty on June 25, 1943. He decided not to report for induction, however, and decamped to New York. Felmet then asked that he be allowed to go into the Medical Corps as a protest against the destructiveness of war. In the Medical Corps he would be serving as an "angel of mercy" and would also be receiving compensation for his work. Felmet believed that his work for the Medical Corps would be a stronger statement of his pacifism than working in a Civilian Public Service Camp. He continued to insist that his failure to report for duty was not a criminal act but was a result of conscientious objection.

Aware of Felmet's several attempts to evade duty, the local draft board concluded that moral or ethical opposition to the war did not qualify for a CO classification, which could be obtained only for religious reasons. Felmet then quickly became a member of the Jehovah's Witnesses, but the draft board dismissed this ploy as yet another attempt to avoid service. The local board reported him overdue for enlistment. On November 8,

1943, the Federal Grand Jury in Asheville indicted him for draft evasion. On November 10, 1943, the U.S. District Court sentenced him to one year and one day in a federal penitentiary. The court suspended his original sentence on the condition that he work in a hospital to be determined by the attorney general.

Despite his earlier request to serve in the Medical Corps, however, Felmet now refused to serve in a hospital. The FBI declared him a fugitive. He was arrested, prosecuted, and served six months and twenty days in the federal penitentiary in Ashland, Kentucky. A perusal of the FBI investigation of Felmet indicates that they perceived him as a radical and did not take seriously his late claim of being a Jehovah's Witness. Felmet was certainly a socialist and an agitator, but it is difficult to ascertain whether he was a genuine pacifist. His failure to report for duty and his unwillingness to serve in a hospital after protesting the horrors of war undercut his avowed pacifism. Felmet's case demonstrated the difficulty the draft boards had dealing with COs.[26]

Jehovah's Witnesses in North Carolina figured in several important CO cases. In March 1943 Carl Byers was sentenced to four years at a Federal Reformatory in West Virginia for failing to report for duty as ordered by his draft board. Byers claimed that he was a minister of the gospel (although he had joined the Jehovah's Witnesses after his induction notice) and tried to take the stand in court with a Bible in his hand to give religious reasons why he should not have to serve. The court did not allow him to testify, because the draft board had already made its decision and neither the draftee nor the court could change the decision of a fact-finding agency.[27]

Two other Jehovah's Witnesses, Robert Farris of Wilson and Nathaniel Miller Jr. of Warren County, were also convicted of failing to report for duty. Both were sentenced to eighteen months in a federal reformatory and chose prison sentences rather than reporting for noncombatant military service or for work at a Public Civilian Service Camp because they were opposed to performing any kind of duties, direct or indirect, that supported the war effort.[28] The Society of Friends (Quakers) had beliefs similar to those of the Jehovah's Witnesses. Clarence Ray Thomas, a Quaker since the age of fifteen, explained the Quaker view toward war. The Quakers tried consistently to practice the Christian principles of love and goodwill toward all. They worked actively against military training and service and for peace and for the removal of the causes of war.[29]

The Jehovah's Witnesses, like other religious groups, certainly seemed sincere in their beliefs, because they were willing to go to prison rather than work in any job that would support the war effort. This hard-core belief in pacifism was typical for many of the inhabitants of the only Civilian Public Service Camp in North Carolina, at Buck Creek Camp near Marion. The Friends Service Committee of the Quaker Church operated the facility, which opened in late August 1941. All of the public service camps were operated by religious organizations under the direction of the National Selective Service Board at no cost to the government. The expenses of the men in camp, usually $35 per month, were paid by the individual, his family, or the church.

At the Buck Creek encampment the 118 residents worked eight hours a day on landscaping projects on the Blue Ridge Parkway, but several volunteered to go into a war zone, where they felt they were more urgently needed. Many COs perceived that it was not their job to preach pacifism but to show by their actions that they were living up to their philosophy of helping others and relieving human suffering. Some stayed in the United States and worked in public health, in insane asylums or hospitals, or with underprivileged children. Others volunteered for war zones in Burma and the Philippines to help war victims.

The initial group of conscientious objectors who arrived at the Buck Creek camp made clear their reasons for opposing war. "We take the attitude that we can't make a better world by destroying the things we have already achieved. Progress is constructive, not destructive." They believed that everyone had a right to live and that no one had the right to take another's life, for any reason.[30] Inhabitants of the Buck Creek Camp exhibited the true values of pacifism by their willingness to work for the good of humanity even at the risk of their lives in combat zones.

Clarence Ray Thomas, a Quaker, reflected the views of most COs. He had been declared 4-E and sent to the Buck Creek Camp in March 1943 to do work of national importance for "no pay, no free food, no travel expenses. We provided our own clothes and those who could were asked to pay $35 a month for board. We signed papers that the US Government was not responsible for anything that happened to us." Thomas and the others made rail fences, cut dead wood, developed campgrounds, and worked on the roads of the Blue Ridge Parkway.[31]

Greensboro's Charles Hendrick, also a Quaker, knew that as a pacifist he would be unable to bear arms against an enemy. He believed that he could not aid the military in any way, so he spent the war at the Buck Creek Camp. He explained his decision: "I was sympathetic to issues raised by the war and to the need for solving problems, but not by killing people. The government set up these C.O. camps where I felt I could serve my country but not kill people." Hendrick said that for the most part people understood why he made the decision that he did and tolerated his position. The mood of a country at war, however, made being a CO an unpopular choice. "But I knew for me it was the right thing to do. One time I went into Marion to buy a bathing suit. When the salesperson asked me where I was stationed, I told him I was at Buck Creek. He said: 'I don't have anything to sell you.'"[32]

Clarence Thomas also encountered hostility when people learned that he was a conscientious objector. A military officer told Thomas that he "hated his guts," and a member of the draft board made negative and hateful remarks to him. On another occasion a man giving out gas rationing stamps "was pretty rough on me, but I learned to just let it roll off and keep a'going."[33]

The public was disdainful of those who tried to avoid service, and some critics branded them as cowards and un-American. Festus Woodall, writing in the *Raleigh News and Observer*, expressed those views rather forcefully. "This is no time to lag. Throughout our land there are young men—upstarts—having recently married, hiding under their wives [sic] petticoats, seeking to avoid the draft. They seem to take the attitude: 'Let Bill or Tom go do the job, it is no business of mine.' I say with all the emphasis at my command, I have no patience with these softies. These parasites have won contempt from the masses."[34]

Delinquency

As the military expected, a few men were willing to take significant risks, even prison, to avoid going into service. Those attempting to evade the military participated in numerous schemes. Some claimed CO status, while others got married and hurried to have a child. One man left the induction line and convinced his brother, who was suffering from a severe hernia, to take his place in line. The brother was rejected, and neither one served. Another way to avoid being classified as 1-A was to get a job in defense work, even if the man planned to stay in that employment only long enough to get a deferment—a ploy known as "job skipping." Another option was to get a boss to request that an employee's job, regardless of its significance, be classified as necessary for the health and safety of the nation.

Draftees tried every trick possible to stay out, including deliberately failing the literacy exam. Some persuaded or bribed physicians to declare that they were mentally unstable or physically unfit. Others intentionally failed the eye test. Draftees feigned every kind of illness imaginable, complaining about bad knees, bad backs, flat feet, cancer, tuberculosis, diabetes, and rare diseases that they hoped the physicians had never heard of. One young man even put the thermometer next to the radiator to increase his body temperature. The doctors had witnessed every scam imaginable and were not fooled by a body temperature of 110 degrees from a perfectly healthy inductee. One individual put a grain of corn in each ear, sealed his ears with wax, and pleaded hearing loss. Another draftee went down to the river and deposited his clothes on the bank, leaving a suicide note indicating that he had drowned himself. The authorities dragged the river but did not find his body and abandoned the search, presuming that he was dead. The young deserter might have gotten away with this particular scam except that he was arrested a few days later for being drunk and disorderly in a neighboring town.[35]

One inductee was released after insisting that he was homosexual (which was not true). Alone among the belligerent nations in World War II, the United States screened for homosexuality during the induction procedure. Psychiatrists held that homosexuality constituted a personality type unfit for military service. Thousands of homosexuals were disqualified from entry into the armed forces. Those in service were treated as deviant and psychiatric cases and given the same dishonorable discharge as drug addicts and other undesirables. Even after the war discrimination against gays was routine and the military frequently investigated homosexuals as security risks.[36]

Golden Moore went AWOL (Absent without Leave) from Camp Davis because he did not like army life and did not intend to go back. But he changed his mind after attending church at the Church of Christ Jesus in Wilson. The preacher told his flock that "[you] must be loyal to your country and not desert it in its time of need." Moore, moved by the sermon, went to the police station in Wilson after church and declared that he was ready to go back to Camp Davis. "The preacher was right, I got to be loyal and can't desert my country when I am needed."[37]

Some citizens, out of fear of death or bodily harm in the military, were willing to resort to self-mutilation or take their own lives rather than go to war. Grover Smith, age thirty-four, killed himself with a shotgun less than twelve hours before being inducted into the army.[38] Darow Ray Creel of Kinston committed suicide when army officers arrived at his home to take him into custody after he was twenty-three days overdue at Camp Blanding, Florida.[39] Calf Carpenter, who had been ordered to report to Fort Bragg for duty, shot off the top of his head with a double-barreled shotgun rather than serve.[40] There were also examples of draftees blowing off a big toe with a gun or cutting off a right index finger to avoid service. The thinking was that someone needed an index finger to pull a trigger, so without said appendage the military would surely turn him away.[41] To their chagrin, some of those with minor self-inflicted wounds were taken into service anyway.

The Rejection Rate

After the war ended many Tar Heels were surprised to learn that North Carolina had a higher rate of draft rejections than any other state. In some induction stations over 50 percent of those sent for examination were rejected for physical, mental, or moral reasons. The official rejection rate for the state of North Carolina during World War II was 44.6 percent. These men were classified as 4-F and did not have to serve unless their classification was changed at some later date. Draftees were unfit for service if they had a severe case of polio, bad teeth, a serious disease, a clubfoot, tuberculosis, venereal disease, or cardiovascular defects or were blind in one eye. The military did not accept epileptics, and in general anyone with a hernia was excused except for limited military service. As the war progressed the Selective Service began to relax the standards for flat feet, being overweight, and being underweight. Those with remediable defects such as weight problems or physical weakness were often put on a program of physical rehabilitation.

By 1944 the army needed more manpower and lowered the standards for literacy, accepting functionally illiterate men. If those with learning issues could learn to read at a fourth grade level after sixteen weeks of tutoring, they would be accepted for service. Cedric Jones from Wake County was one of the reading instructors. He realized that many of the rural boys had gone to work at an early age and never really had a chance to learn to read. Jones was pleased that most of them made the most of their opportunity and were ultimately able to develop talents that they did not know they had. "Not only did they pass the Army test, but this was the opportunity they needed to start . . . a life more meaningful because they could read and explain themselves." They could get better jobs and feel more comfortable in social surroundings.[42]

Most of the Tar Heels who were denied entrance into the military were excused for reasons of health. Physical rejections accounted for 72.2 percent of those eliminated and moral and mental problems for 27.2 percent. The categories under mental defects included emotional instability, chronic drunkenness, drug addiction, and what was called mental deficiency, defined as both an educational and intelligence deficiency ("morons," "idiots," and "imbeciles"). In the moral category, all felons were initially classified as 4-F.

Many observers in 1941 realized that the state's health system was totally inadequate to handle even the basic health care for the poorer element of society and those in isolated areas. One-third of the counties did not have a single hospital bed, and the infant mortality rate was among the highest in the nation. Men were rejected due to numerous examples of venereal diseases, hernias, bad teeth, cardiovascular problems, tuberculosis, malnutrition, hearing loss, ringworm, and other diseases and conditions often found in rural areas. A large number of inductees were excluded because of illiteracy. All that was required for the military was to have the ability to read the English language as prescribed for the fourth grade grammar school. Failing to meet this standard accounted for 12.5 percent of those excluded in North Carolina, meaning that the state had a large number of functional illiterates. The black population in the state had a very high rate of exclusion for reasons of illiteracy.[43]

The rejection numbers were embarrassing to state officials. The figures demonstrated that the state was in a desperate situation as far as the health and education of its citizens were concerned. The *Raleigh News and Observer* recognized the reality of the circumstances and reminded the state legislature that "removal of this stigma in the vitally important matter of health is the first concern of the State." The newspaper pointed out that provision of adequate medical care was an urgent and immediate need but that no single remedy would remove "the deplorable and shocking conditions revealed by the draft rejection figure." The *News and Observer* argued that the school system had to be strengthened and the compulsory school attendance law strictly enforced. The editors noted that many of those excluded from service came from areas with low per capita income. The state had to find a way to improve its ranking of forty-third in the nation in per capita income in order to raise the standard of living and health care for all.[44]

Despite many changes in regulations, overworked draft boards, and sometimes confusing instructions, the Selective Service System in North Carolina did a very good job in funneling inexperienced draftees into the military services. There were very few complaints about the fairness of the system overall and the effectiveness of the appeal boards. The state supplied some 540,000 troops for all services during World War II, and Tar Heels served with honor. The dramatic number of rejections by the Selective Service caused North Carolina to take stock of its political, economic, health, and educational system and provided the impetus to press forward and make the changes necessary to improve conditions in the state.

A CALL TO ARMS

MILITARY PREPAREDNESS

North Carolina had already experienced an economic impact as the country prepared for military expansion before Pearl Harbor. Although few would have predicted it at the time, North Carolina was to have an important role in the nation's military, industrial, and economic development from 1940 to 1945. More than 2 million fighting men and women were trained for combat in more than one hundred bases, installations, facilities, and camps in the state. A large number of major military establishments and many other facilities were used in supporting the military buildup and the training of troops.

When America began the enormous task of rearming in 1940, Governor J. Melville Broughton, in his January 9, 1941, inaugural address to the citizens of the state, issued a call to arms. "Democracies throughout the earth are not only being challenged; they are being flaunted and over thrown. Not since the beginning of our national history has our own democracy been so gravely threatened." Broughton pledged that North Carolina would do its part and would continue its long tradition of aiding the nation in time of crisis. From Kings Mountain to the trenches of World War I, intoned Broughton, the "heroism of North Carolina has been attested by the blood of her sons who died in the front lines of victory."[1]

Broughton announced that the United States was about to embark on a major building program in North Carolina. Not only did the country lack

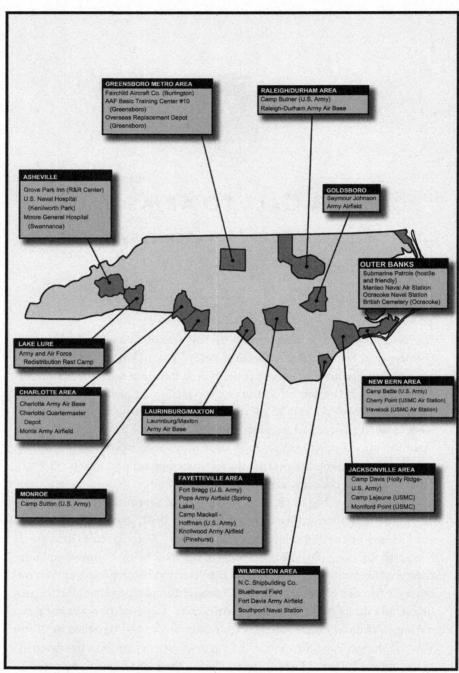

GREENSBORO METRO AREA
Fairchild Aircraft Co. (Burlington)
AAF Basic Training Center #10
  (Greensboro)
Overseas Replacement Depot
  (Greensboro)

RALEIGH/DURHAM AREA
Camp Butner (U.S. Army)
Raleigh-Durham Army Air Base

ASHEVILLE
Grove Park Inn (R&R Center)
U.S. Naval Hospital
  (Kenilworth Park)
Moore General Hospital
  (Swannanoa)

GOLDSBORO
Seymour Johnson
Army Airfield

OUTER BANKS
Submarine Patrols (hostile
  and friendly)
Manteo Naval Air Station
Ocracoke Naval Station
British Cemetery (Ocracoke)

LAKE LURE
Army and Air Force
  Redistribution Rest Camp

CHARLOTTE AREA
Charlotte Army Air Base
Charlotte Quartermaster
  Depot
Morris Army Airfield

LAURINBURG/MAXTON
Laurinburg/Maxton
Army Air Base

NEW BERN AREA
Camp Battle (U.S. Army)
Cherry Point (USMC Air Station)
Havelock (USMC Air Station)

MONROE
Camp Sutton (U.S. Army)

FAYETTEVILLE AREA
Fort Bragg (U.S. Army)
Pope Army Airfield (Spring
  Lake)
Camp Mackall -
  Hoffman (U.S. Army)
Knollwood Army Airfield
  (Pinehurst)

JACKSONVILLE AREA
Camp Davis (Holly Ridge-
  U.S. Army)
Camp Lejeune (USMC)
Montford Point (USMC)

WILMINGTON AREA
N.C. Shipbuilding Co.
Bluethenal Field
Fort Davis Army Airfield
Southport Naval Station

Figure 3.1. North Carolina's military and defense facilities in World War II, 1940–1945.
By permission of Eric Knisley.

arms, ammunition, uniforms, and training officers, but it had so few existing army, navy, and marine posts that new bases would have to be constructed immediately. Because of the warmer climate, cheaper land and labor, and the low density of population, the federal government decided to build most of these new bases in North Carolina and the South, known as "Fortress Dixie." The federal government eventually spent over $4 billion in the construction of military bases and training centers. George Tindall described the South "as more campground than arsenal."[2]

By 1940 military base construction had become a major industry in the state. The state had suffered from high unemployment and sluggish growth during the Great Depression, but by the summer of 1940 construction workers were pouring into building sites at Fort Bragg, Camp Davis, and numerous other places where remarkable feats of building and engineering were under way. After the United States entered the war and the need for troops expanded, the construction contracts flowed out of Washington. Every time a new contract was let, thousands of workers gained a decent paycheck, signaling the beginning of the end of the economic depression in North Carolina.

Operating under a federal directive to complete their work as quickly and efficiently as possible, and with the fate of the free world in the balance, the construction companies and their workers in North Carolina achieved spectacular successes. Military boomtowns sprang up all over the state. Most of the camps were built in rural areas where construction machinery and materials had to be brought in. The camps had few if any amenities, so the workers had to build theaters, chapels, gyms, recreation centers, hospitals, and post exchanges (PXs) in addition to the barracks, training centers, and command offices. As the bases were erected all over the state, the effect on the communities was considerable. Workers now had wages to spend at local stores, construction projects used local goods and services, and new roads were being built: as a result these rural, isolated local towns began to see a huge economic revival.[3]

The army had by far the largest number of bases and trainees in the state. All of the large training facilities in the state were served by the Charlotte Quartermaster Depot, the U.S. Army logistics center and one of nine quartermaster distribution centers established at strategic points around the nation. The Charlotte Depot, while utilizing 1.2 million square feet in six warehouses on forty-two acres of land, supplied bases in the Carolinas with huge amounts of food, clothing, and traditional military equipment but also tremendous amounts of everyday items—tents, pillows, sheets, cots, toothpicks, uniforms, flags, bars of soap, and a thousand other items. The depot employed 2,500 civilians in addition to a staff of 80 army officers. Working three shifts, seven days a week, the personnel were capable of unloading, sorting, storing, and distributing up to forty carloads of freight daily.[4]

The U.S. Army Air Force (AAF) built and maintained eight airfields in the state. It also pioneered a new method for rehabilitating battle-fatigued veterans. The Lake Lure Rest and Redistribution Center, occupying the former Lake Lure Inn, was used as a rest camp for the approximately 5,000 returning combat crews processed during the center's two-year existence. The AAF discovered that ten to twenty days of rest for fliers and their wives helped to deter combat fatigue and prepared aviators for future assignments. It was the first center of its kind in the nation.[5]

The U.S. Navy had a much smaller presence in the state. It built an aviation training and maintenance base at Weeksville Naval Air Station outside of Elizabeth City. This base used blimps (lighter-than-air craft) for long-range antisubmarine patrols. The blimps had a cruising speed of sixty miles per hour, could stay aloft for thirty-eight hours, could hover over a single spot, and had a range of 220 miles. The airships were 252 feet long and carried a crew of eighteen. They were armed with fifty-caliber machine guns and depth charges for antisubmarine work. After 1943 radar made a formidable weapon out of blimps, which could spot a periscope ten miles away. The Marine Corps had a very powerful and long-lasting influence on the state, with large bases at Camp Lejeune and at Cherry Point.[6]

Army Bases

Fort Bragg

Army bases had a dramatic influence on the outcome of the war and on the economic development of the state, but the first and most influential of these was Fort Bragg, named for Braxton Bragg, a Confederate general and a native North Carolinian.

In the summer of 1940, when the United States began its mobilization against the threat of war, Fayetteville was a languid southern town with some 17,428 residents, while the military population at Fort Bragg and Pope Air Field numbered around 5,000. The army decided to make Fort Bragg a centerpiece in its military preparations, giving it a major role in the army's expansion. In August 1940 the post was designated as the training center for the Ninth Infantry Division and the home for all artillery units.

Thousands of troops (including a young Captain William Westmoreland, later commander of U.S. forces in Vietnam) and workers flowed into Fayetteville, but the camp did not have the necessary facilities to accommodate such a large influx of newcomers. A temporary tent city for the workers went up, but this encampment was inadequate. Many of the workers had to find housing in neighboring communities, some as far as a hundred miles away.

The army's focus was on a one-year, rapid expansion of the base. The federal government spent the unheard of sum of $44 million for infrastructure—new roads, sewers, power lines, training fields, and recreation buildings. In nine months a building miracle took place. As of September 1940 Bragg had 376 assorted buildings and 5,406 troops. In June 1941, nine months later, Fort Bragg had 3,135 buildings and 67,000 troops. In December 1941 the number of troops exceeded 90,000, an increase of 85,000 in fourteen months. At the peak of production, the 28,500 workers at Bragg were putting up a new building at the rate of one every thirty-two minutes. Sixty-five carloads of building materials arrived each day on the Cape Fear Railroad and the Atlantic Coast Line railway. By the end of the expansion project, Fort Bragg was the largest military base in the state and Fayetteville became the state's third largest city.

One example of the extraordinary efficiency in construction at Fort Bragg came on September 17, 1940, when the T. A. Loving Construction Company began work on the Ninth Division Cantonment. After only 109 days, the company had erected 586 modern, comfortable buildings with central heating. The buildings in the cantonment included 253 barracks (63 men in each barrack), 80 mess halls, 80 day rooms, and 80 company administration buildings. The fort had 11 infirmaries, 10 post exchanges, 2 fire stations, 5 recreation buildings, a post office, and 3 theaters. In the middle of the construction, the post had to call in more than 4,900 new workers, primarily black, from the surrounding area to complete the work on time.[7]

Fort Bragg would be the home of not only the Ninth Infantry Division but also the 82nd and 101st Airborne Divisions. The 82nd and the 101st parachuted behind enemy lines on D-Day and fought in the Battle of the Bulge. More than fifty artillery battalions that were formed at Bragg participated in every theater of the war.[8] The fort also included the all-black 41st Engineers and the 76th Coast Artillery.[9]

As was true of most small towns in the state, Fayetteville had neither the funds nor the expertise to cope with the increased population and the myriad demands for goods and services. The roads were crowded and inadequate, housing for families and workers was insufficient, and the food supply could not keep up with the growing number of hungry visitors. Nonetheless, the townspeople made a major effort to welcome their new neighbors. For Christmas 1940 the people of Fayetteville opened their homes to soldiers who were stationed far from home. The army added to the festivities by supplying 12 tons of turkey and 300 pounds of candy.[10]

Governor J. Melville Broughton praised the spirit and attitude of Tar Heels who responded positively to the national crisis. He lauded the North Carolina workers, architects, and contractors who had done a superior job in completing military projects efficiently and on time. He pointed out that county, city, civic, and religious organizations throughout the state "cooperated magnificently in giving this great army of men the most courteous and hospitable treatment." The governor expected that the state would continue to provide great service and strong cooperation.[11]

The primary function of Fort Bragg was the intensive and rigorous training of troops for combat. Brigadier General William C. Lee, a native of Dunn, N.C., pioneered the concept of parachute operations. Lee concentrated on the development of tactical and training doctrines and standardization of material and equipment. Paratrooper training was still in its infancy, so the training programs at Bragg and later at Camp Mackall would be essential to Allied success in the later stages of the war.

Because of the long, stressful, and difficult training programs, the troops needed opportunities for relaxation—a place to "blow off steam." As the fort was being built, they had very few opportunities for entertainment or social activities. Roy Parker Jr. described the situation in his book on Cumberland County: "On Saturday night the nearby country town of Fayetteville heaved and rocked and every bar was packed. The main bar, the Pump, was often the scene of fights between parachute soldiers and glider troops; between men of the 82nd and 101st; between the Airborne and the rest of the Army—and between everybody and the Military Police."[12] On one fairly typical occasion in March 1943 a free-for-all erupted between eight Fort Bragg paratroopers and the local police in the neighboring town of Clinton, N.C. The police chief claimed that the incident had been started by the soldiers in a local café when a soldier hit the chief over the head with a bottle. The police retaliated and shot one soldier in the stomach. Two policemen and one soldier ended up in the hospital, and four paratroopers were invited to spend the night in the city jail.[13]

This imbroglio was by no means unusual around military bases. The troops at Fort Bragg sought women, liquor, and entertainment all over the region and frequently crossed swords with the local constabulary. The excessive amount of public drunkenness created significant problems for military authorities. The few USO clubs could be supervised by the army, but it became increasingly difficult to regulate a proliferating array of beer joints springing up close to the base. The Military Police tried to control the situation by jailing soldiers, discharging them from the army, or using fines and company punishment, but soldiers were going to drink and party when off duty. There was no way the military or the local authorities could completely curtail these activities.

In Fayetteville the city fathers, churches, and other civic groups constantly preached temperance and called for harsher penalties for drinking. The Woman's Christian Temperance Union (WCTU) asked the governor to close all legal liquor stores and bars for the duration of the war. It argued that intoxicating liquor was an unnecessary luxury and a dangerous commodity that wasted millions of dollars of basic food (grains) needed for defense. "The mothers of our land are glad to give their sons in service to the country but they do not want them returned as drunkards."[14] The problem had no viable solution, but the local authorities did the best they could to control the situation without denying soldiers the opportunity to drink.

Perhaps even more worrisome to the military was the problem of prostitution and venereal disease. On October 27, 1941, Governor Broughton called upon military authorities and local police to exercise greater vigor in the apprehension and prosecution of cases of prostitution and other forms of vice. The governor observed that the incidence of venereal disease had increased exponentially and urged all police officers, prosecutors, and judges to cooperate in curtailing this serious condition.[15]

The federal and state governments, along with numerous social agencies, attempted to restrain venereal disease (particularly in the armed forces) through the distribution of condoms and the repression of female prostitution. Their concern was not just morality: military leaders saw venereal disease as a dangerous health issue that would incapacitate thousands of soldiers and undermine the war effort. Government agencies, including the U.S. Health Service, recommended an aggressive program of education about the danger of the disease and the prevention of infection. The key would be early diagnosis and treatment, so all contacts between military personnel and infected civilians were to be reported to medical officers and state health authorities.[16]

Congress joined the fight by passing the May Act, which made prostitution within specified areas around military bases a federal crime. The penalty was a misdemeanor, punished by a fine of not more than $1,000 or by imprisonment for not more than one year. The bill was very specific, forbidding anyone "to engage in prostitution or to aid and abet prostitution or to procure or solicit for the purposes of prostitution, or to keep or set up a house of ill fame, brothel or bawdy house or to receive any person for purposes of lewdness, assignation or prostitution into any vehicle, conveyance, place, structure or building."[17] The act did not precisely define lewdness or prostitution; nor did it clarify what a bawdy house was. The theory was that the enforcers would know it when they saw it.

The act focused on eliminating "amateur prostitutes" variously known as victory girls, khaki-wackies, chippies, and pick-ups. In typical hyperbole, the USO warned that these promiscuous women looked nice but often harbored VD. A federal committee noted that prostitutes were more dangerous to the community than a mad dog. "Rabies can be recognized. Gonorrhea and syphilis cannot."[18]

Immediately after the passage of the May Act, many social groups, especially the churches, stepped up their denunciation of the evils of prostitution and the cruel exploitation of women. One problem facing the regulators was the difficulty of differentiating between professional ladies of the evening and innocent women who flirted with military men or attended dances or participated in social activities with soldiers. It became difficult to separate acceptable morale-maintaining sexuality from dangerous promiscuous sexuality, as practiced by working prostitutes. Of course, there was always a double standard. The spread of disease was blamed on the prostitutes and call girls who preyed upon the soldiers, not vice versa. Males were often seen as victims, and their behavior was viewed as natural for men.

At the time, resolving the threat was crucial because venereal disease was difficult to treat or to cure and medical care was painful, costly, and lengthy. Penicillin did not become available until 1944 and then only in limited quantities. Prostitutes infected men with venereal diseases that were not easily cured, so the resultant loss of manpower could cripple the war effort.[19]

In mid-June 1942 Governor Broughton concluded that local law enforcement had failed to control the spread of venereal disease and called on the federal government vigorously to enforce the May Act. The *Raleigh News and Observer* approved the decision. "The presence of these disease infected prostitutes openly plying their trade . . . constitutes a national peril to the health and morals of the country's youth which is now being mobilized for the serous business of war."[20] On July 1, 1942, the Federal Bureau of Investigation (FBI), after sending 158 agents to the area, invoked the May Act in twelve counties surrounding Fort Bragg. In one county 161 persons were arrested; in another county 140 "prostitutes" were detained and tested for venereal disease, with 53 testing positive. There were some serious legal concerns about federal encroachment on states' rights, arrests without warrants, and arrests on mere suspicion or lack of evidence. Local police arrested women without recourse to habeas corpus or other individual rights. But these constitutional issues did not deter the repression effort.[21]

Throughout the war the FBI and local authorities continued to pursue a vigorous enforcement of the May Act. In September 1942 the FBI arrested twenty-seven women in the Fort Bragg area. They were tried and convicted in Federal District Court. A week later the FBI seized a taxi driver for aiding and abetting prostitution by importing women in his taxi. In November 1942 the FBI captured nine white women and four black women for violating the May Act.[22]

Desperately trying to avoid problems with drinking, illicit sexual encounters, fighting, and gambling at Fort Bragg, the army constructed many recreation centers on base and sponsored individual and team sports—putting in baseball fields, tennis courts, golf courses, basketball goals, and swimming pools, in the hope that the GIs would burn off some of the energy that might otherwise go to excessive partying. The army also decided that base movie theaters would keep the troops entertained and off the streets. By 1943 Fort Bragg had eleven motion picture theaters, with one theater reserved for black troops. The movie houses operated every night of the week and could accommodate 30,000 troops a night. The theaters received first-run films before the public did, and the soldiers had to pay only a small fee to enter. Civilians were not allowed to attend except with special permission. The larger theaters were also used for USO shows and visiting entertainers such as the comedian Bob Hope and Gene Autry and Roy Rogers, the singing cowboys.[23]

Some of the important visitors who came to Fort Bragg during the war included President Franklin Roosevelt and British prime minister Winston Churchill. World leaders notwithstanding, perhaps the most exciting event for the troops was when Mickey Rooney, the number one box office movie star in America, visited the base accompanied by his new bride, the glamorous Ava Gardner, a native North Carolinian. In keeping with America's longtime fascination and obsession with celebrities, over 15,000 fans came to see Mickey and Ava. Surrounded by public relations officers, military spokesmen, managers, military police, and photographers, Mickey and Ava had to fight their way through a boisterous crowd of well-wishers. Although designed as a public service event, their visit became a media circus.[24]

Local service clubs in the geographical vicinity of Fort Bragg sponsored weekly dances for the troops. The local clubs would vet and approve a list of young women to participate in Friday night dances at the post. They had to be over eighteen, unmarried, and socially acceptable. The event was very strictly regulated, and any violation of the rules led to the woman's suspension from the list. Two chaperones accompanied the women to the dance in autos or buses and escorted each one back to her front door. At the dance couples were not allowed to leave the floor and the women could leave only en masse at the end of the dance. If a soldier left the dance floor, he could not return. Many of the young women returned Friday after Friday. Each week there was a new set of partners, as army units were limited in the number of times they could participate. Only four hundred tickets were allotted to each battalion for the dance, which occasionally led to fights or substantial bribes in order to get a ticket.[25]

A lanky, boyish-looking GI at Fort Bragg, Private Marion Hargrove, took advantage of his leisure time to write a series of vignettes about life in the barracks. He sent these humorous stories about the trials and tribulations of army boot camp to the *Charlotte News*, where he had been a features editor before being drafted. The articles were later edited into a book, *See Here, Private Hargrove*. It became an instant best seller—"the most popular humor book of World War II"—and sold over 2.2 million copies.[26]

Self-described as "the epitome of the happy but confused civilian in uniform," Hargrove penned many interesting anecdotes about his life as a private and the challenges that a raw recruit faced in the soulless military. He warned newcomers about the adversity they would face: "Two weeks from now, you will be thoroughly disgusted with your new job. You will have been herded from place to place, you will have wandered in nakedness and bewilderment through miles of physical examinations, you will look upon privacy and individuality as things you left behind you in a golden civilian society. . . . You will writhe and fume under what you consider brutality and you will wonder how an enlightened nation can permit such atrocity in its army." Despite his experience in the newspaper business, the army, as it was wont to do, made Hargrove a cook. He protested that he had no culinary skills, noting that the only egg that he had ever tried to fry was used as a tire patch. The other cooks in his unit included former postal clerks, railroad engineers, bricklayers, and one blacksmith. Not one had experience in a kitchen. Hargrove was not only woefully unprepared for being a cook or for military life in general but possessed a contrary streak that landed him in trouble on a daily basis. The essence of Hargrove's military experience was summed up by his drill sergeant: "See, here, Private Hargrove. Can't you try just once to do something right? Don't you want to be a credit to the platoon?"[27]

When reveille sounded, Hargrove slept. When his fellow trainees turned left, Hargrove veered right. When his buddies left with weekend passes, Private Hargrove peeled potatoes. According to his sergeant: "On the drill field Saturday morning, you pulled forty-eight boners out of fifty marching commands. Everything you did was backwards. Friday morning you fell out for reveille without your leggings. Saturday you had your leggings, but no field hat. Monday morning neither of your shoes was tied and none of your shirt buttons were buttoned." Hargrove protested that reveille was way too early in the morning and that he could not be faulted for his mistakes since he was never fully awake. He described a typical day:

I am very enthusiastic about Army life. We lie around in bed every morning until at least six o'clock. This, of course, gives us plenty of time to get washed and dressed and make the bunks, etc. by 6:10. At 6:15 we stand outside and some asshole blows a bugle. After we are reasonably chilled, we grope our way through the darkness to the mess hall. There we have a hearty breakfast consisting of an unidentified liquid and a choice of white or rye crusts. After gorging ourselves with this delicious repast, we waddle our way back to the barracks. We have nothing to do until 7:30 so we just sit around and scrub toilets, mop the floors, wash the windows, and pick up all the matchsticks and cigarette butts within a radius of 2,000 feet of the barracks.

Hargrove later wrote about the great fun of going out and "basking in the warm Carolina sunshine" on long walks with a light pack "weighing 217 pounds."[28]

Complaining about army chow has been an essential and universal part of the military experience since Valley Forge. The hero of Neil Simon's *Biloxi Blues*, Eugene Jerome, is served creamed chipped beef on toast for breakfast for the first time in his life, an offering known throughout the military world as SOS: "shit on a shingle." This breakfast delicacy was thoroughly despised by all who tried it. After tasting the glop, one of Eugene's friends comments: "They ought to drop this stuff over Germany. The whole country would come out with their hands up." Eugene, a Brooklyn boy, notes: "I saw this in the Bronx Zoo. The gorillas were throwing it

Figure 3.2. Soldiers going through chow line inside the Mess Hall at the Basic Training Center in Greensboro, N.C., 1943. By permission of Carol W. Martin/Greensboro Historical Museum.

at each other."[29] No matter how plentiful the grub, soldiers always had inventive and derogatory comments about the cooks and their cooking expertise. If all the cooks were like Private Hargrove, the diners had legitimate complaints.

After the war Hargrove wrote a second book about his wartime experiences, but it was not a big success. He later wrote screenplays for Hollywood movies, including the screenplay for *The Music Man*, and several episodes for the television shows *Maverick*, *I Spy*, and *The Waltons*. Hargrove died in 2003 in Long Beach, California.[30]

Private Hargrove was not the only military man to complain about the military's unerring ability to assign totally unqualified soldiers to the wrong job. Alex R. Josephs was a Charlotte lawyer waiting for assignment. "When they found out I was a lawyer, they sent me to the medical corps." A friend also waiting for an assignment was asked if he knew anything about bridges. He did not but facetiously said, "I painted a sign on a bridge once." That clever riposte got him assigned to the engineers. Billy C. Coleman and some of his buddies went down to the university to sign up for military service. Arbitrarily one was placed in the U.S. Army Air Force, three in the army, and Coleman was assigned to the navy after they discovered that he could not swim.[31]

Fort Bragg continued to flourish and operate as a military base for airborne troops after the end of the war and by 2014 was the largest military base in the country, with the third largest military population. Fort Bragg had more generals than anywhere other than the Pentagon and accounted for 10 percent of the state's economy.[32]

Camp Mackall

Grover Cleveland Caddell, a typical teenager, grew up in the tiny town of Hoffman, a farming community not far from Fort Bragg. In the summer of 1942 the war had had very little impact on Caddell or his community other than rationing. Early one morning in July 1942 everything changed. Grover Caddell stepped out of his house and witnessed an awesome and unexpected sight. He spied seven Waco CG-4A gliders and dozens of parachutists landing in the field across from his house.[33] The paratroopers had arrived. Caddell, his family, and Hoffman were about to experience profound changes in their lives.

The War Department decided the military needed a base to train paratroopers, so in 1942 it built Camp Mackall, which would become the largest airborne training camp in the country. Three of the army's five air-borne divisions (the 11th, 13th, and 17th) were formed at the camp and troops from the 82nd and 101st airborne divisions trained there. At its wartime peak the camp had over 30,000 soldiers and support staff.

The government chose tiny Hoffman, in the Sandhills area of North Carolina, as the site for Camp Mackall for a variety of reasons. The government owned 65,000 acres in the area and would not have to spend time and money buying up individual properties. Many large and reasonably level areas were suitable for parachute drop zones and glider landings. The region boasted of a good climate, the sandy soil assured quick drainage, there was plenty of water, and the rural area was remarkably clear of air traffic—essential for parachute training. Finally, U.S. Highway 1 and the Seaboard Coast Line Railroad ran through the center of the town, giving the site significant transportation advantages. Hoffman was also close to Fort Bragg and the Laurinburg-Maxton Air Base.[34]

On November 9, 1942, the citizens of Hoffman were awakened by the rumblings of heavy moving equipment, trucks, buses, and autos as construction officially started. The J. A. Jones Construction Company of Charlotte won the army contract but faced the daunting task of building in an isolated rural area. The camp was a marvel of wartime construction. On November 7, 1942, it consisted of 65,000 acres of wilderness. By the completion of the contract four months later, the company had paved 68 miles of new roads and constructed 15 miles of railroad track, 3 all-weather runways (each 5,000 feet long), a 1,200-bed hospital, 5 movie theaters, boxing rings and baseball diamonds, 12 chapels, and over 1,700 buildings.

In order to complete the work on time, the Jones Company needed thousands of workers. They offered jobs to both white and black laborers at the same weekly wage of $23.80 for 53 hours of work. Equal pay for minority workers was unusual at the time and created some resentment among white workers, but the company retained its policy. Although the vast majority of the 6,000 workers were white, a significant number of black people who already lived in the Sandhills responded eagerly to newspaper ads seeking their services. As was the custom, the work crews were usually racially segregated. Little interracial conflict occurred during the building of the base.

Significant difficulties arose in providing food, transportation, and lodging in such an out-of-the-way place, but local families took in boarders, eateries popped up everywhere, and workers commuted from nearby communities such as Aberdeen and Raeford. By May 3, 1943, approximately six months after building began, Camp Mackall was completed. The J. A. Jones Construction Company won an "E" award (for efficiency with rapid completion at low cost) presented by the army.[35]

In order to help preserve order and discipline, the camp organized a six-man mounted police detachment. Gasoline, tires, and motor vehicles were in short supply, so the Military Police used horses to cover the large area and rough terrain. The MPs spent much of their time directing traffic, searching the forests for lost parachutists, recapturing prisoners who escaped from the camp stockade, and setting up a night guard on a nearby watermelon farm, from which the melons had been mysteriously disappearing.[36]

The camp was named in the memory of John Thomas Mackall, the first American airborne trooper to die in combat. Private Mackall had been killed after landing behind enemy lines in northern Algeria, as part of Operation Torch.[37] Alda Newton, Mackall's mother, became a Gold Star Mother on her son's death. The military issued a Gold Star to all mothers whose children made the supreme sacrifice in offering their lives for their country. The Gold Star was usually posted in the front windows of the homes of the grieving families. Unfortunately, before the war was over, Mrs. Newton had two Gold Stars in her window.

During World War II Camp Mackall served as a testing ground for the army's new airborne concept, a laboratory for equipment, tactics, and logistics. The new strategy of engaging the enemy by dropping paratroopers into the battle zone, known as vertical envelopment, had been developed by General William C. Lee. The German military had already successfully used gliders and paratroopers while landing in Crete, so the U.S. Army decided that it needed gliders to carry the troops. The army arranged for the 193rd Glider Infantry Regiment and glider pilots to receive instruction at Camp Mackall in conjunction with five different airborne divisions. The development of the airborne divisions was such a high priority that the training camp was constantly monitored by high-ranking visitors. British prime minister Winston Churchill, American secretary of war Henry Stimson, General George Marshall, and British vice admiral Louis Mountbatten visited the camp.[38]

The glider pilots, paratroopers, and air-landed infantry trained together. The training regimen, especially physical conditioning, was long and arduous. In the first six weeks the airborne soldier learned to operate all the weapons in a platoon and became proficient in hand-to-hand combat, grenade work, knife fighting, scouting, patrolling, and, an essential skill, parachute packing. The next six weeks were devoted to squad and platoon training and small unit jumps. The final four weeks emphasized company and battalion maneuvers. By the end of sixteen weeks each battalion had been trained to function effectively in combat.[39]

Easy Company, 506th Parachute Infantry Regiment, 101st Airborne Division, the "Band of Brothers" immortalized by Stephen Ambrose in his book of the same name, trained at Mackall. Ambrose described the jump training. Each of the paratroopers carried rifles, small arms, food, ammunition, hand grenades, maps, high explosives, and additional items. Many of the maneuvers focused on quick troop movements and the ability to operate behind enemy lines. E Company and its battalion were superbly trained, as they would need to be, and scored a 97 on the standard physical fitness test, the highest score ever recorded for a battalion in the army. Eventually E Company would land at Utah Beach on D-Day. It fought in Holland, the Battle of the Bulge, and the Rhineland campaign and captured Hitler's Eagle's Nest at Berchtesgaden. By the end of the war E Company, according to Ambrose, "was as good a rifle company as there was in the world." These brave men took terrible casualties during the war.[40]

Social activities for the troops at Mackall were essential because there was little entertainment close to Hoffman. The military installed forty-two pay stations for private telephone calls and erected seven service clubs on base for dances, bingo, group singing, and shuffleboard. The military set up twenty-one post exchanges, which featured sixty barbers, five soda fountains, two cafeterias, a bakery, a tailor, and dry cleaning shops. The PX sold soap, hot dogs, sandwiches, cigarettes, and candy bars. In one year the 375 civilian employees of the twenty-one PXs sold over $5 million in goods and services. The base also had three libraries, a bank, and six open-air beer gardens, noted primarily for the fierceness of the many fights among patrons. Camp Mackall sponsored a weekly newspaper, *Geronimo*, that constantly gave fulsome praise to the regimental mascot, "a cadaverous, bleary-eyed, beer-swilling, tobacco chewing goat," also named Geronimo.[41]

John Lowden, a glider pilot who trained at Mackall, complained about the lack of a decent watering hole. About the only place to get a real drink was a roadside restaurant/beer joint near the base. The only option for alcohol other than the local beer joint was to buy one pint a week with a coupon book or "drink rot-gut provided by a local bootlegger." The problem was that the beer joint was controlled by paratroopers, who did not welcome glider pilots. Lowden and his friends decided to challenge the paratroopers. As expected, a serious fight broke out between the troopers and the pilots. Eventually both sides realized "the futility and foolishness of the encounter," and the brawl ended. After a few beers the now friendly paratroopers and pilots agreed that they would make an unbeatable combination in combat.[42]

Like Fort Bragg, Camp Mackall faced problems with prostitution. A physician at the camp notified authorities that ladies of the evening frequented a café in Hamlet and a hotel in Rockingham and reported that three women in one house "dated" thirty-one soldiers in one night at $5 a date. The doctor claimed that 90 percent of the "victory belles" had venereal disease (an obvious exaggeration) and asked the FBI to clean up the vice.[43]

After four years of hectic activity, Camp Mackall officially became inactive on January 31, 1946. The base, like all other bases, gave rise to a series of meaningful changes in the community. In Hoffman, however, the impact of the base was different than in Fayetteville, Greensboro, and other large towns. Primarily a farming community, Hoffman had been hard hit by the Great Depression, so the community generally welcomed the influx of 30,000 workers and troops. The *Richmond County Journal* commented on the ways in which the camp affected the locals. "For some Richmond County citizens, this project will work a hardship; to others it will be an inconvenience, but to the majority it will be welcomed as a means of livelihood." There was a significant cash flow into the community. Many citizens got jobs on the post, local stores had a huge surge in business, and others made money by renting out rooms in their homes. The inhabitants tried not to overcharge for goods and services or take advantage of the paratroopers. One woman said: "We were all so aware of where they were going and what price they were paying . . . we wanted . . . to do what we could for them." Hoffman experienced dramatic economic growth during the war but returned to its former status once the camp folded. The town simply did not have the population or infrastructure to prosper.[44] Cities like Fayetteville boomed, but the smaller towns of Hoffman and Butner did not reap as many long term rewards from its wartime experience.

Camp Butner

As the fighting intensified overseas, the War Department recognized the urgent need of establishing additional military bases for the training of soldiers. Business and civic leaders in Oxford and Durham, learning of the possible expansion of bases, encouraged the army to build in their area as a shot in the arm for the local economy. Eventually, the federal government purchased 40,300 acres of agricultural land in southern Granville County, for what was then known as the Camp Butner Reservation. Camp Butner was named after General Henry Wolfe Butner, a native of Surry County, who died in 1937 following a very distinguished military career.

As was the case in many other military bases, when the government purchased the land in February 1942, several tobacco farmers resisted the loss of their land but eventually accepted the inevitable. As at Fort Bragg and Mackall, the cantonment was cleared and built by 25,000 workers, including 8,000 carpenters, in a remarkably short period.[45] One potentially volatile situation in the construction of the base occurred when workers discovered that one of the contractors, Wikstrom, paid black workers the same wage as white employees. The other companies ganged up on Wikstrom and forced it to reduce the pay of black workers.[46]

Some 35,000 troops had arrived on base by August 1, 1942. Governor Broughton welcomed Camp Butner's personnel to North Carolina and outlined the state's strategic role in supporting the war effort. The *Raleigh News and Observer* also extended a cordial welcome to the soldiers at Butner, located less than thirty miles from Raleigh.[47]

Camp Butner's primary mission was to process and train infantry combat divisions and various artillery and engineering units in the shortest possible time for deployment and redeployment to the European and Pacific theaters. The army set up drill fields, obstacle and bayonet courses, modern firing ranges, and other training aids over a large area. One exhausted trainee expressed his sentiments about the rigorous training regimen in a poem:

"Ode to Sarge"—The Soldier's Psalm

The Sarge is my Shepard [*sic*], I shall not want.
He maketh me pick up burnt matches.
He leadeth me through mud puddles.
He guideth me over the course of obstacles for my health's sake.
Yea though I walk through the valleys, I must climb up the hills.
He anointeth my head with abuses, my cup runneth over.
Surely cadence and KP will follow me all the days of my life.
And I will dwell in the hair of my sergeant forever.[48]

The camp was the home of the 78th Infantry "Lightning" Division, re-activated in August 1942. From October 1942 through March 1943 the 78th trained other units for combat then went into action in Germany, fighting its way through the Siegfried Line and distinguishing itself in combat by capturing 16 German towns and 2,248 prisoners.[49]

Camp Butner was home to a large military hospital staffed by well-trained physicians and Women's Army Corps (WAC) nurses and designed to handle casualties from the European front. Camp Butner also housed German and Italian prisoners of war.

Camp Butner was used for the demobilization and deactivation of army units at the end of the war.[50] With the invaluable assistance of Butner natives, the camp provided health care, entertainment, and exercise for these returning combat veterans. Butner focused on the well-being of the soldiers who suffered from both mental and physical scars from long months of fierce fighting and difficult conditions. The troops had been away from home for a long time. The readjustment period was problem-atic for many—they needed sympathy and support. The troops received kindness and encouragement in full measure from the local residents. The camp commandant expressed his gratitude to local families who took the veterans into their homes. "You can't begin to experience the thrill that comes to these boys when they sit down to a big meal and again know that there is such a thing as a home."[51]

After the end of the war the army turned the camp over to the state, which made excellent use of the remaining buildings. It set up an Alcohol and Drug Abuse Treatment Center, the C. A. Dillon School for Juvenile Delinquents, the John Umstead mental hospital, a federal correctional institution, and a training center for the North Carolina National Guard.[52]

Camp Davis

To military observers, Hoffman seemed like a metropolis compared to Holly Ridge, N.C., the site of Camp Davis. The little town, just thirty miles north of Wilmington on Highway 17, consisted of a store or two, two fill-ing stations, a half-dozen homes, and a population of twenty-eight. The camp was thrown up in five months, while the population zoomed from 28 to over 100,000 at its peak in 1943. Camp Davis was the most extraor-dinary thing ever to hit the region and became a thriving camp overnight, with buildings sprouting up like mushrooms. To the local inhabitants, used to a slow-moving tempo, it seemed as if a gold rush had engulfed the town. The mad scramble for jobs, construction activity, and incoming troops simply overwhelmed the residents.

The base was named for Major General Richmond P. Davis, a native of Statesville, a World War I hero. The camp was home to the Coast Artillery Anti-Aircraft Regiments, with some 46,000 acres designated as target ranges. The Camp Davis cadre trained six artillery units, four white and two black. With the establishment of a center for testing and developing new antiaircraft weapons, Davis became the most complete antiaircraft post anywhere in the United States. The first troops arrived in April 1941 and immediately began intensive training.

The army experimented with the use of large barrage balloons at Camp Davis as a defense weapon against airplanes. The balloons, which could rise as high as 15,000 feet while attached to heavy cables, forced attacking planes to a higher altitude, where it was more difficult to score direct hits. The main antiaircraft defense weapon, however, was the 90-mm gun, the largest weapon used by the Coast Artillery. The "90," manned by a crew of fifteen men, could fire eighteen rounds per minute from a sixteen-foot barrel. The projectiles weighed twenty-three pounds each and could do heavy damage when on target. Quite mobile for a large gun, the crew could assemble the "90" for action in thirteen minutes.

In order to achieve accuracy with their weapons, the gunners needed targets on which to practice. The military came to the conclusion that it would be practical to use female pilots to perform such noncombat duties as transporting of planes from base to base and towing targets for the gunners, thus freeing up male pilots for combat flying. Commanders viewed the job of towing targets for green air gunners and ground artillery as a dangerous but extremely important task.

By 1943 the Women's Air Service Pilots (WASPs) had become a vital part of the antiaircraft training at Camp Davis. The "Darlings of Flight" or "Flying Flappers" initially had a difficult time proving their worth to skeptical commanders and gunners, but they quickly demonstrated their skill and courage. From 1942 to 1944 the U.S. Army Air Force trained 1,074 WASPs, who ended up flying 60 million miles in every type of aircraft in the air force, including the B-29 Super Fortress.[53] By the end of 1944 Camp Davis had over 2,000 women on base—mainly WACs, army nurses, librarians, secretaries, recreation workers, and Women Ordnance Workers (WOWs).

As at the other military bases, outside entertainment was an important event for the troops. Betty Grable, the troops' favorite movie pin-up, came for a visit, as did Kay Kyser's band, playing such favorites as "White Cliffs of Dover" and "Praise the Lord and Pass the Ammunition." The highlight of the war years for the troops was the all-star boxing show brought to the camp by the world heavyweight champion, Sergeant Joe Louis. Over 5,000 spectators crammed into every bleacher and ringside seat to see the spectacle.

The deafening roar of the 90-mm guns was stilled when the camp officially ceased operations on September 30, 1944. During the last few months of its existence the camp served as a redistribution and convalescent center, but by 1944 those facilities were closed. Personnel shifted to other air force bases.[54]

Camp Sutton

Built in 1942 near Monroe, N.C., the camp was named after Frank Howie Sutton, who joined the Royal Canadian Air Force before America's entrance into the war. He was the first Union County man to die fighting the Axis powers.[55] Established as an expanded and overflow training facility for about 18,000 troops, Camp Sutton trained the U.S. Army Corps of Engineers in the specialized skills used in building fixed bridges and pontoon bridges. Base depot companies, base equipment companies, dump truck companies, utilities detachments, bakery units, salvage and repair companies, and construction battalions also underwent indoctrination at Camp Sutton. Several Graves Registration Units received instruction at the camp. During its later years the camp housed prisoners of war.

Citizens of Monroe recalled that the camp was a very significant development in the community's history because soldiers from all over the country introduced the insular Monrovians to the outside world. The old-timers remembered how important the base was in economic terms, as Monroe flourished during the war. The army deactivated Camp Sutton in January 1945, sooner than planned because of racial tension between the black and white soldiers. In August 1944 a race riot developed when white Monroe residents stoned a busload of black soldiers. The racial animosity never receded and gave the military another reason to terminate a facility that had outlived its usefulness.[56]

The kind of training that the army developed at Camp Sutton might not have been as glamorous as airborne maneuvers and Marine Corps invasion tactics, but the work done at this base was crucial to the success of the war. Someone had to bake the bread, string the wire, drive the trucks, build the bridges, repair the equipment, and construct the buildings; otherwise the military could not function. For every fighting man there were numerous personnel behind the lines who provided the necessities of war that enabled the front lines troops to succeed.

Marine Bases

Camp Lejeune

Camp Lejeune was the major training base for the First Marine division and marine amphibious exercises and was the largest all-purpose Marine base in the world as the site of the first African-American Marines at Montford Point, the Women Marines, the Seabees, the Devil Dogs, the Marine Field Medical Service, and the Marine Corps Engineering School.

On February 8, 1941, Congress approved $15 million to establish a Marine Corps Base in eastern North Carolina. At the same time the War Department planned a large marine air base (later Cherry Point) to operate in conjunction with the main base. The Marine Corps chose a 10,000-acre site in Onslow County because the geography, climate, oceanfront location, and isolation of the area made the site on the New River an ideal spot for a training center. The eleven miles of beachfront was not dissimilar to the beaches of some of the Pacific islands and would be a perfect place to practice amphibious landings. The base would be close to deep-water ports at Morehead City and Wilmington and a few miles from the town of Jacksonville, the county seat of Onslow County. Jacksonville had a population of only 873 people in 1940. The county was isolated, rural, and poor and a bastion of segregation.[57]

The base was later named for John Archer Lejeune, who won distinction as commander of the Second Division in World War I and had been the commandant of the Marine Corps in the 1920s. When the First Marine Division arrived in late September 1941, only tents and a few buildings were available. In 1942 the builders focused on permanent construction. When completed, the camp was self-sufficient, providing its own electric power, and had its own hospital, school, library, and newspaper. The base had 3,150 buildings, 130 miles of paved highways, 150 miles of electric lines, and 165 miles of telephone lines. In sixty days the Marine Corps built an eight-mile railroad track to connect the new base with the Atlantic Coast Line in Jacksonville. The rail line provided access to the port at Morehead City and the air base at Cherry Point.[58]

One of the more difficult problems faced by the Marine Corps was the displacement of Onslow County residents. The establishment of the base was successful in many ways, but it brought havoc and distress to some 720 families who were forced to yield their property to the government. Some, including 100 black families, were left homeless and in a few cases destitute. The federal government resettlement program could take up to five years, and an average of two years elapsed between the time the families were evicted and the receipt of compensation for their property. Even after two years many had not yet received adequate recompense.[59]

Marlene Blake recalled the bitterness her family felt over their eviction from their home. Her father had been so proud of purchasing 55 acres of land and a house with money he earned as a sharecropper. The family was devastated when they learned that they had one year to vacate the property that they had worked so hard and so long to obtain. Two days after they left the house was demolished. Since they had not been reimbursed by the government and did not have the money to buy another house, they were forced to live in a dairy barn with another displaced family. Without land her father had no job. Marlene really did not know what the future would hold. "It was hard when they took your home away from you. . . . The home you had worked hard for and planned was gone. The government loaded up the families who no longer had any land, moved them over the boundary and put their things out in the road."[60] The government's activities certainly seemed cruel and heartless, but it had a military base to build, which took first priority.

Marines were posted to Lejeune after completing boot training at Parris Island, S.C., and at Quantico, Va. The Marine Corps emphasized intensive specialist training in order to prepare individuals for every kind of combat duty. The focus was on guerrilla warfare, hand-to-hand combat, ship-to-shore assault, jungle operations, and beach defense. The specialty units, like communications personnel and the engineers, learned to establish lines of communication and supply lines under combat conditions. The Seabees, navy combat engineers, were taught to utilize ingenuity in restoring airfields and bases seized from the enemy. The navy manned the landing barges, lighters, and Higgins boats used in amphibious warfare and trained closely with the marines in perfecting the process of getting large numbers of troops ashore under enemy gunfire.[61]

Billy Arthur, the diminutive publisher of the *News and Views* (Jacksonville, N.C.), "The Only Newspaper in the World That Gives a Whoop about Onslow County," spent many days on base observing the lifestyle of the marines. The weather was hot and muggy, the training arduous, and the mosquitos ferocious. Arthur discovered that most of the new residents wished they were elsewhere. There was absolutely nothing to do for entertainment except for a trip into Jacksonville, which still offered nothing to do. Jacksonville had one movie theater, a few beer parlors, and several cafes. One of the eateries was the Snappy Lunch. On the outside wall of the establishment the owner had painted: "Seating 22,000—22 at a time." Even if the marines wanted to visit Jacksonville, only six buses were available and the bus station was a ticket counter in the back of a gas station. Traveling farther away than Jacksonville was even more problematic.[62]

Soldiers from Camp Davis had taken over Wilmington, the largest nearby city, so the marines gravitated to the village of Kinston, N.C., their favorite liberty town. The marines liked Kinston, but the affection was not returned by the locals, who resented the boisterous, hard-charging Leathernecks who came into their peaceful village yelling, drinking, and fighting. On a typical weekend some 4,000 to 6,000 marines would crowd the streets of Kinston. Their drunken behavior, an influx of prostitutes, and the subsequent rise in venereal disease was out of control and the Marine Corps put Kinston out of bounds for all naval and military personnel. The local constabulary and town council of the city went to Camp Lejeune and asked that the ban be lifted, because the town merchants were losing a bonanza in dollars. The city council told the commandant that the Kinston police department had begun an energetic roundup of prostitutes and vagrants and would quickly clean up the "vice, immorality and disease" in the town. Kinston's urgent appeal failed. The ban was not lifted.[63]

Mrs. Wilson Hall expressed the relief that many Kinston townspeople felt when the ban was declared. She noted that the city of Kinston would have been better off if it had never heard of Camp Lejeune. She realized that the merchants had made good money off of the marines, but the town had to consider the future welfare of the young women of Kinston, who had gone "completely crazy over the servicemen." Kinston, continued Mrs. Hall, had been a clean and decent town. "I hate to say it about my home town, but it's a wicked place. I hope it will soon be cleaned up."[64] Marine private Dan Weingrad responded to her letter. "So Mrs. Hall wishes that she had never heard of Camp Lejeune. I imagine Tojo feels quite the same." Weingrad pointed out that there was a military base near his hometown and that the citizens of his town "had accepted the soldiers for what they are—American boys far from home. The servicemen are your sons, not the dregs of the nation's slums—the service has not changed them." Now that Kinston was out of bounds, continued Weingrad, Mrs. Hall and her friends can "save their grease, collect scrap, buy war bonds and call themselves patriots—and there won't be any filthy, low saviors of a nation to bother them."[65]

The incidents in Kinston were repeated all over the state. Townspeople in many of the communities near military bases, regardless of size, faced the problem of dealing with excessive drinking, prostitution, and general mayhem when military personnel were released for a weekend of fun and frolic. The merchants loved the military visits and some were getting rich off GIs on liberty, but other citizens resented the disruption of their lives and the increasing immorality. As always, there had to be a balance. The marines were training hard and were about to put their lives on the line for their country. They believed they deserved the chance to party when off duty and on many occasions viewed the locals as puritanical and un-welcoming. In the end, the great majority of North Carolinians supported the troops. Civilians understood that these soldiers were young men far from home, living under very difficult circumstances, and that they would be, as Private Weingrad put it, saviors of the country.

Because of the extreme isolation of Camp Lejeune, the Marine Corps set up a big circus tent for USO shows and camp events. Perhaps due to the dangerous nature of the marines' job, or to sustain their spiritual beliefs, the Marine Corps assigned fifteen permanent chaplains to the base. The base had four chapels and Protestant and Catholic services every Sunday. The marines arranged for a Jewish chaplain and special chaplains for the women marines and the Montford Point Marines.[66] One Catholic chap-lain, Father Joseph Patrick Mannion, known to the men as "Padre," de-cided that if he were to be a proper chaplain to the paramarines, he needed to jump with them. "I thought the paramarines ought to have their own chaplain, one who would go right with them in battle just as chaplains accompany men . . . in the front lines of battle." The marine commander approved of Mannion's jumping because it was good psychology: when the young kids saw the 34-year-old Mannion jump, they thought, "Well, if that old boy can do it, then I can do it."[67]

One of the highlights of 1944 was the visit of President Franklin Roo-sevelt, on his way home from Warm Springs, his Georgia vacation home. The president visited for two hours and stopped at least a dozen times to view various units or to speak with commanders and individuals. He spent quite some time in conversation with the women marines.[68] It was a significant morale boost to the Marine Corps. Bill Lashley, a native North Carolinian, recalled that FDR interviewed his unit. "It was quite thrilling to have him come by."[69]

Montford Point Marines

On June 1, 1942, the Marine Corps, breaking a 167-year-old tradition, started enlisting African Americans. It had little choice: the commander-in-chief had ordered the only branch of the military that still excluded blacks to integrate forthwith. The Marine Corps opposed the move, stating that it would rather have 5,000 whites than 25,000 blacks, but reluctantly began the recruitment of black marines. The corps insisted on a strict policy of segregation of the unit and opened its first training facility in Montford Point, a remote area of Camp Lejeune.

The first black recruits arrived at Montford Point on August 26, 1942. All of the officers, staff, and instructors were white. The white officers greeted all 1,200 new recruits with undisguised disdain and open hostility. By late 1943 the Marine Corps had replaced the original white drill instructors with black noncommissioned officers who had demonstrated leadership qualities. There were no black commissioned officers: the officer corps remained all white. A basic rule at Montford Point was that a black man could not give an order to a white marine at any time.

In opening a training base for black marines in North Carolina, the corps apparently never considered the difficulties that black soldiers would encounter in the segregated South. In addition to the blatant racism that they faced in camp, the Montford Point Marines came up against even greater problems when off base. While in uniform serving their country, they endured every form of racial discrimination imaginable. On buses they were forced to the rear; on trains they were restricted to segregated cars; in theaters they were segregated; and restaurants refused to serve them. Whites insulted them on the streets and hurled racial epithets at them almost every time they appeared in public. The black marines managed to endure this constant abuse and served their country with distinction.[70]

Melton McLaurin, in his fine book on the Montford Point Marines, explained that their story was one of "honor, duty and patriotism. . . . It is also the story of achievement and ultimate triumph in the face of unrelenting racial prejudice, of an unyielding determination to prove their mettle as fighting men to a nation that endorsed a policy of segregation based upon the doctrine of white supremacy. Even the Marine Corps they joined did not welcome them."[71]

As many as 19,000 African Americans served in the U.S. Marine Corps during World War II; two-thirds of that number had duty stations overseas. Most of the young men who expected to see combat were disappointed, as the majority were assigned to duty stations outside of any combat zone. On the battlefields they were used as stewards, drew guard duty, or were posted to ammunition and depot companies. Frustrated by their experiences, the Montford Point Marines blamed their lack of combat duty on racial discrimination.

A few members of the ammunition and depot companies did see action in some of the bloodiest battles in the war—at Iwo Jima, Okinawa, and Peleliu. Originally assigned as stretcher bearers to evacuate the wounded from the field of battle, of necessity they became riflemen engaged in hand-to-hand combat and earned respect from their comrades for their bravery and performance under fire. On Saipan a dozen black Leathernecks were ordered into battle and advanced bravely against the enemy despite intense rifle and mortar fire, killing about fifteen Japanese soldiers.[72]

Many of the men who signed up for Montford Point joined for reasons similar to those of their white counterparts—the desire for a decent job, travel, and escape from the racist South as well as admiration for the marines. Herman Darden Jr. had seen John Wayne in the film *Fighting Devil Dogs* and decided then and there that he wanted to be a marine. When Darden told his parents that he had joined the Marine Corps, his father told his mother: "I told you he was crazy."[73]

Boot camp proved to be an endurance test for all of the new recruits, especially in the summer when temperatures hovered above 90 degrees. The black marines got the same training as the white marines. The drill instructors (DIs) were tough on them, but they did what they were told. Glenn White remembered how it was. "It was yes sir, and no sir, and no, not too many no sirs. I did exactly what they said and that was all. We didn't give them no back lip." Joseph Carpenter thought that they would have it easier when the black drill instructors took over but found that it was worse because the black DIs were determined to make them real marines and prepare them to be better than anyone else.[74] The Marine Corps shut down the Montford Point base in September 1949. After President

Harry Truman's Executive Order 9981, which ended segregation in the armed forces, the Marine Corps slowly integrated its ranks.[75]

Belatedly, the American government recognized the contribution of the Montford Point Marines to the war effort: on June 27, 2012, they were awarded the Congressional Gold Medal.[76] In 2013 the Marine Corps honored Hubert Poole of Raleigh for his contributions to his country in World War II. The citation read: "The diversity of today's Marine Corps was paved in large part by the selfless dedication to duty of the Montford Point Marines." Poole told the *News and Observer* in 2003 that he did not like some of the experiences, "but I think it made me a better person. It taught me that you were not going to have things the way you want them all the time. You have to improvise. Do hard thinking and pray."[77] The Montford Point Marines did their duty and achieved an inspiring and compelling record of service to their country.

Marine Devil Dogs

The War Dog Training Company was set up at Camp Lejeune on January 7, 1943. Over 450 dogs, mostly doberman pinschers, were prepared in Boot Camp for combat action. Over 1,000 dogs served in the Marine Corps in World War II. The dogs were selected because of their intelligence, loyalty, sense of smell, stamina, and dependability. Each of the dogs had two trainers who taught them complete obedience to any commands and instructed them to attack strangers upon orders. The dogs went through attack classes and extensive physical endurance tests and were subjected to explosions and loud noises to see how they would respond in combat conditions. The Devil Dog cadre trained the dogs with patience and firmness, praise and scolding, rather than with force or punishment.

The dogs were specially trained to search out the enemy in hiding, to detect booby traps and mines, and to alert the marines of an approaching enemy. The dogs had such a keen sense of smell and hearing that they could alert their handlers far in advance of an enemy ambush or attack. The dogs would warn their handlers without barking and could tell when humans were present as far away as several hundred yards. The dogs did not bark, so enemies were unaware that they had been spotted. Other dogs were used to carry messages, ammunition, and medical supplies in saddlebags to units that could not be reached otherwise due to enemy fire. Each dog had its own method of alerting its handler: some lifted their heads, others sniffed or pointed their nose in the direction of the enemy, and some raised the hackles on their backs when they suspected something ahead. Mine dogs were invaluable—they were taught to recognize trip wires, mines, booby traps, and other explosive devices hidden from view. Many Japanese mines were made of clay, so the metal detectors could not locate them. The dogs could smell out almost anything. The dogs would indicate the exact location of the mine by stopping about three paces in front of the mine or booby trap, sitting down, and refusing to move forward.

The Marine Corps sent the first platoon of dogs into combat against the Japanese in the Bougainville landings in November 1943. The Japanese had been sneaking up on American ranks at night and killing sleeping marines. The dogs did a remarkable job in warning of the enemy and also were used to scout ahead of the advancing line. Six of the dogs were cited for outstanding performance of duty. Caesar, a German shepherd, was the only means of communication between M Company and headquarters. Although wounded, he continued to carry messages back and forth. Otto flushed out a Japanese machine-gun nest, saving many American lives.

Captain William W. Putney commanded a Marine Corps dog platoon in the heavy fighting on Guam. In his memoir, *Always Faithful*, he described the remarkable success of the Devil Dogs. Again and again timely warning by the dogs saved countless lives. There was, of course, a strong bond between dog and handler. Whenever a dog sacrificed his life, the unit mourned. When Carl Bliss's dog Hobo died in action, he put his hand on the dog's head and murmured, "Nobody ever got by you." He then began to sob and turned away. The sacrifices of the lost dogs were recognized by all the marines. Captain Putney put it best. "They died; we lived." Many of the dead dogs on Guam were buried in the Marine War Dog Cemetery. As one marine officer declared, "The dog was a Marine, by God, and he deserved to be buried in the cemetery with the rest of the Marines."[78]

U.S. Marine Corps Air Station, Cherry Point

As part of the extraordinary training center for the U.S. Marines on the east coast, the corps established an elaborate and extensive air station at Cherry Point, N.C., in close proximity to Camp Lejeune. It was fitting that the government chose this site because North Carolina gave birth to aviation when Orville and Wilbur Wright flew, for the first time, in a heavier than air machine at nearby Kitty Hawk, N.C.

Construction began on the 11,155-acre site on the Neuse River, halfway between New Bern and Morehead City, on July 9, 1941. The building of Cherry Point, designed to be the "largest, most modern and most important Marine Air Station in the world," cost $85 million, one of the largest construction projects of World War II. The workers mixed and laid some 500,000 cubic yards of concrete for the runways—equivalent to 27 miles of a 20-foot-wide highway—making the base one of the largest airfields in the world. A twelve-mile railroad connected the base to the Atlantic and North Carolina Railway.[79]

The first marines arrived at Cherry Point on December 10, 1941, just three days after Pearl Harbor. The marines used the base for advanced training, as all of the pilots had already undergone basic flight training and had received their gold wings. The chief function of marine aviators was to support ground forces in landing operations and to provide aerial defense for advanced bases. The marines focused on mobility and concentrated striking power, so marine pilots were essential to success in ground battle. Fighting squadrons, dive-bombers, and observation squadrons flew practice missions at Cherry Point. Pilots had to fly both seaplanes and landplanes and had to operate with equal familiarity from the flight deck of carriers or in offshore landings.

Cherry Point and the Marine Corps land base at Lejeune often cooperated in staging exercises, resolving problems, and simulating actual combat conditions. North Carolina could claim one of the most powerful military establishments on the globe, where the toughest soldiers were trained in every type of fighting—on land, on sea, and in the air.

The Cherry Point commanders did as much as possible to provide entertainment for the troops—movie theaters, service clubs, dances, sports, and post exchanges. The Leathernecks, however, liked to party on a more extensive scale than allowed on base and maintained a fierce rivalry with army troops stationed only a few miles away at Camp Davis. The army and marines often clashed while on rest and relaxation (R and R) in Jacksonville or Wilmington. The spats were mostly verbal encounters, but occasionally significant brawls broke out. The marines clearly considered themselves vastly superior to any other branch of service, as demonstrated by the third, seldom heard, verse of the Marine Hymn. Most people are familiar with the first verse. "From the Halls of Montezuma, to the shores of Tripoli," but not the third verse:

Here's health to you and to the Corps
Which we are proud to serve;

In many a strife we've fought for life
And never lost our nerve;
If the Army and the Navy
Ever gaze on Heaven's scenes;
They will find the streets are guarded
BY THE UNITED STATES MARINES.[80]

Air Force Bases

Basic Training Unit #10—Greensboro

In late 1942 the mayor and administrators of the city of Greensboro, a blue-collar town of 60,000 people, saw the dramatic development of military bases in other parts of the state and wanted their share of government largesse to help alleviate the persistent suffering from the Great Depression. Greensboro was a likely spot for a base because it was a major city with plenty of shops and seven movie theaters and the only large town in the state that allowed "Sunday beer." The city had eliminated the restrictive Sunday Blue Laws and allowed movie theaters, bowling alleys,

Figure 3.3. Newly arrived recruits just off the train at the Basic Training Center line up with their luggage ready for transport to the base. By permission of Carol W. Martin/Greensboro Historical Museum.

and all sports venues, except pool halls, to be open to the public. Greensboro was a young town, with half of its citizens under thirty years of age and only 6 percent over sixty.

As the war progressed, the U.S. Army Air Force needed more trained soldiers for overseas service and began looking for a suitable site. Greensboro had a good central location, excellent transportation connections, numerous recreational and cultural facilities, uncrowded schools, and some vacant housing. When the city offered to help develop 652 acres of land in the downtown area, the air force had its new base.

The base in Greensboro functioned as the Army Air Force Basic Training Center (BTC) #10 from March 1, 1943, until May 1, 1944. The new recruits, fresh from civilian life, had to master the fundamentals of military life in a four-week or an eight-week course. They learned judo, how to drill, how to handle weapons, and how to protect themselves against chemical warfare. BTC #10, however, was an army air force training center, not a marine boot camp. The purpose was to familiarize the troops with military life and get them into decent physical shape. After this preliminary training the men went to other bases for advanced training as pilots, crewmen, mechanics, weather observers, and clerks. The BTC graduated some 87,500 men during its fourteen months of operation.

By 1944 the post had trained most of the skilled personnel that the army air force needed for the war. At this point in the war the air force needed a center to process airmen for overseas duty and then redistribute the troops rotating back from overseas service to new assignments. Thus on May 1, 1944, BTC #10 ceased operations and became the army air force's principal eastern Overseas Replacement Depot (ORD). Here individual soldiers were processed, reassigned to new duty, and shipped out, mainly to Europe. The Greensboro base was closed in September 1946.

Life in Greensboro was good. Unlike the isolated bases in Hoffman, Holly Ridge, and Cherry Point, the base was in downtown Greensboro, where soldiers could use one of the three bus lines connecting the camp with the city. The entertainment options were more than even the most avid sybarite could ask for. The citizens of Greensboro went out of their way to welcome the troops and frequently invited them into their homes, volunteered to staff USO clubs, and organized social outings for anyone interested. The camp added to the options by providing four more movie theaters, ten post exchanges, officers' and enlisted men's clubs, three large gymnasiums, and five chapels. The base PX was a popular destination. In August 1943 the PX sold millions of cigarettes, 30,000 cases of Coke,

200 gallons of ice cream, 100,000 boxes of stationery, and 90,000 giant Hershey bars. Sports, mainly boxing, basketball, and baseball, were available around the clock.[81]

The Greensboro USO Club offered "wholesome" services with hostesses in constant attendance. The club was in great demand and entertained thousands of visitors from May 15, 1943, until 1946. Open from 11 a.m. until 11 p.m. on weekdays and from 9 a.m. until 11 p.m. on weekends, the USO club offered reading and game rooms, a library, a snack bar, and frequent dances. The African American troops, some 6,674 living in separate quarters, did not get their USO club until August 1944.[82]

The base had an excellent camp newspaper, initially called *Ten-Shun*, that kept the troops posted on events in the city and operations on the post. The first issue explained bus routes and taxi fares and informed the troops about service clubs at the Presbyterian Church and Temple Emanuel.[83] The paper provided information about the USO Traveler's Aid and details about the hours of the Young Men's Christian Association (YMCA) and the public library and explained that the local Red Cross would help with family illness and money matters. If a soldier became ill, the Red Cross would pay for housing for the spouse. Each weekly paper had a listing of the available movies and entertainment and featured many ads from city restaurants and stores.

The professional members of the city pitched in with support to help alleviate any serious problems the GIs might have. The American Bar Association offered free legal advice about divorce, debt, and mortgages. Volunteers manned the public telephone exchange, working seven hours a day, so that soldiers could call their spouses, sweethearts, or parents. The exchange was always jammed with soldiers, who often had to wait two hours to make a call.[84]

Much of the camp newspaper was taken up with gossip on the ins and outs of the troops, their former jobs, celebrities in camp, new fathers, amusing anecdotes, and the results of sports contests. Among the celebrities were Sergeant Charlton "Chuck" Heston (later Moses and Ben Hur), who was married in the Greensboro Methodist Church on March 17, 1944. Michael Ponce de Leon, a direct descendant of the Spanish explorer, drew cartoons for the paper. Private Thomas A. Sousa, son of the great bandmaster and march king John Philip Sousa, constantly had to explain why he could not sing, play, or read a note. "I'm just not musical."[85] On May 15, 1943, the paper observed "the educated fingers of Private Elmer Bernstein, New York concert pianist," manicuring the lawn in front of

Barracks 12.[86] The men loved the personal references to events and colorful pranks: "Private Sklar: what's this about a snake in your bed?" There was a reference to Private Quinn, who had complained about sore feet on the drill field but was seen in town the very same evening, tripping the light fantastic until dawn. "Oh, the healing powers of a beautiful redhead."[87]

When the Greensboro base closed in 1946, the commanding officer gave an address to the troops. When soldiers returned to civilian life, he hoped they would hold onto the friendships made at the camp and in Greensboro. "Most of us will have different interests, settle in different parts of the country and return to different income brackets. But these army associations should rise above these differences. They should be a constant reminder of what we fought for and how we worked in true democratic fashion, without regard to race, religion, or social status, to achieve our final victory."[88] One could quibble over the reference to race, but the other sentiments rang true for those who served their country.

Morris Field—Charlotte Army Air Base

The mayor of Charlotte, Ben Douglas, an enthusiastic booster of the city, wanted to make the city a key link in the air transportation industry. In June 1940, when the War Department proposed creating eighteen new army airfields, Mayor Douglas saw a great opportunity to expand the city airport. After he sponsored a campaign touting Charlotte's advantages, the War Department selected Charlotte as the site for one of the new bases.

The city gave the army a twenty-five-year lease, free of charge, for 476 acres. The army agreed to allow the city to continue to operate the municipal terminal and consented to spending an initial amount of $1,235,000 to pay for widening and lengthening the three runways and for the construction of 100 buildings to administer and house the troops. The airport was dedicated on April 21, 1941 by Governor Broughton and Fiorello La Guardia, the mayor of New York City. After reviewing a mile-long parade featuring the Central High School band marching down West Trade Street, LaGuardia told the 10,000 visitors that the airbase was essential because America was "challenged by Adolf Hitler now."[89]

The primary purpose of the base was to train pilots and maintenance crews for fighter planes and light bombers and to serve as a link in the

Eastern Air Defense Zone. Morris Field occupied a strategic position for handling local and cross-country traffic. As the major source of information for the troops, Morris Field put out a camp newspaper, cleverly titled the *Morris Code*. Most of the news had to do with base activities and the interactions between the "flyboys" and the local women. A Corporal Robider, a notorious playboy, apparently was persuaded by his buddies to place a formal announcement in the paper. "I am no longer available to the bachelor girls of Charlotte. It is with regret and chagrin that I am forced to announce my impending marriage."[90]

The War Department announced the deactivation of Morris Field on May 31, 1945. The air field was officially deeded back to the city at no cost in May 1946. Charlotte had benefited from the economic stimulus of two thousand soldiers, continued to use the municipal airport during the war, and inherited a $6 million airport after its total investment of $150,000.[91]

One problem faced by the army air corps in Charlotte was the restrictive, puritanical "Sunday Laws" or "blue laws." Thirty-five cities in the state, including Greensboro, allowed Sunday movies. But Charlotte, the largest city in the state, did not. In 1940 every type of commerce other than hotels, restaurants, drug stores, transportation, and emergency services was strictly prohibited. Especially irksome for soldiers was the prohibition of any kind of commercial amusement, including movies and sports. The military and the active, energetic young men on base constantly complained about the outmoded and narrow laws and hypocritical views of the city council. Despite the protests, the city council and the churches in the city fought vigorously against any liberalization of the laws.[92]

But the city did what it could to entertain the troops. The Charlotte Defense Recreation Committee claimed that 1,191 homes in Charlotte had provided hospitality, 6,781 soldiers had been weekend guests, and some 8,431 troops had enjoyed Sunday dinner in those homes by the end of 1942. The churches were very active in catering to the soldiers. Some 31 churches had put on 124 parties and 48 suppers for 20,000 troops.[93]

By the end of 1941 the city council had decided to grant one of the army's key demands and allowed motion pictures and sports on Sunday between 1:30 p.m. and 6:30 p.m. and after 9 p.m. The public response to this change in policy was overwhelmingly favorable. More soldiers now were seen around the city on weekends, an economic windfall for the merchants. As Stephen Dew noted in his fine book *The Queen City at War*,

Charlotteans were the first Americans liberated by the military forces. The citizens had fought the city council for years to amend the Blue Laws, but changes were not made until the military led the way.[94]

Seymour Johnson Air Force Base

In August 1940 the War Department, in search of delicious eastern North Carolina barbecue, designated the municipal airport near Goldsboro, N.C., as essential to national defense. By October 30, 1942, the AAF had opened the headquarters for an Army Air Force Technical School. The field was named for the navy's Lt. Seymour A. Johnson, a native of Goldsboro and a graduate of Annapolis, who died in an air crash in Maryland in March 1941. It is the only air force base named for a naval officer. At the peak of its strength the field hosted 27,000 troops and trained over 250,000 troops during the course of the war. The base later welcomed cadets preparing to become officers in the army air corps and served as a site for the preparation of officers and enlisted men for overseas duty. The 326th bomber group arrived in October 1943, and the base began training replacement pilots for the P-47 Thunderbolt aircraft. The base was deactivated in May 1946.[95]

When the massive influx of troops, workers, and wives arrived in Goldsboro, they created serious overcrowding and housing problems. Blanche Egerton Baker, a Goldsboro housewife, wrote a book about her experiences during the war, called *Mrs. G.I. Joe*. She complained that her quiet little town of twenty thousand suddenly had to cope with all the new residents, but she and her husband decided to open up their home to help alleviate the housing problem. At first they housed the workers on the base, but later they welcomed wives and visitors on a one-night or two-night basis. Mrs. Baker recalled that the need for rooms was so acute that the city had to set up housing desks at the railroad and bus station and in the lobby of the city's largest hotel.

Mrs. Baker discovered that people were sitting up all night in the lobby of the hotel and in the railroad station and some even had to take a night's lodging in the city jail. Determined to help, she opened up all the rooms in her house. In addition to the guest rooms, "it wasn't long before not only the living room, but the attic and occasionally the hall and kitchen were used as sleeping quarters." Whenever the housing staff called, she tried to accommodate anyone in need of a room. Mrs. Baker and her husband had been living alone and welcomed the company. They made quite a bit of money by renting rooms but did not charge when the person could not afford the fee. She and her husband had a wonderful experience meeting kind and interesting folks from all over the country. There were, as expected, a few drunks and discourteous guests, but she praised everyone for making do under difficult circumstances. She fondly remembered "those days when the house teemed with boys and girls, the brave boys who were willing to give their all for their country, and the brave girls who left their all to come to be with their husbands."[96]

Laurinburg-Maxton Army Air Base

Wartime exigencies often lead to technological innovation. When Major General William C. Lee decided to combine the use of paratroopers and gliders for airborne assaults; the army air force constructed the Laurinburg-Maxton Army Air Base (L-MAAB), the largest glider base in the world. The base had a prime location, only fifteen miles from Camp Mackall and close to Fort Bragg.

Activated on August 28, 1942, and essentially completed by October 31, 1942, the 4,644-acre base contained three 6,500-foot-long runways that formed a triangle. At the center of the triangle was a 510-acre area of Bermuda grass that served as the landing site for the gliders. The principal function of L-MAAB was to furnish equipment facilities, supplies, and protection for the training of the Troop Carrier Transport Command and Glider Troops for their coordinated maneuvers with paratroopers, infantry, artillery, and engineering units.

The majority of the aircraft at Maxton featured the CG-4A "Waco" gliders. Designed by the Waco Aircraft Company and manufactured by Ford Motor Company, the CG-4A gliders were huge. With a wingspan of eighty feet and weighing over 4,000 pounds when empty, the glider could carry thirteen fully equipped soldiers, a jeep with a four-man crew, and a 75-mm howitzer plus supplies and ammunition. The gliders were made primarily out of wood with metal tubing and canvas. The gliders were towed by C-47s Dakotas, which connected to the glider by a tow rope.

The base schooled C-47 pilots in the intricate art of towing a glider. The glider pilots found it difficult to land an unpowered aircraft once it was released from the C-47, as the glider pilot had limited control over exactly where and when he landed. Gliders frequently smashed into trees, buildings, or rocks. There was almost always some damage to the glider when landing, making the profession of glider pilot a difficult one. An experienced glider pilot remarked: "It took guts to fly a glider beyond enemy lines on a one-way mission."[97]

Laurinburg-Maxton trained glider pilots in advanced techniques and ground fighting. Once the glider landed, the pilots were as vulnerable to combat as were the airborne infantry that they carried. Units and personnel that trained at the base participated in the Operation Torch landings in North Africa in November 1942 and in airborne assaults in New Guinea, Operation Market Garden, and most important the D-Day invasion of Normandy. The base was closed at the end of the war. With the advent of helicopters, there was no longer any need for gliders.[98]

The building of such a large number of military bases in North Carolina had a huge impact on the state and its citizens. From 1940 until the end of the war the constant sound of bulldozers, hammers, saws, and concrete mixers could be heard in numerous towns and villages. With the arrival of large numbers of workers, soldiers, wives, and clerical personnel some communities, like Goldsboro, seemingly doubled in population overnight. The economic benefit was extraordinary, a welcome respite from the dark days of the Great Depression. Many new well-paying jobs were available. The local merchants, especially bar and restaurant owners, profited mightily from the appearance of new townspeople eager for entertainment and a wholesome meal.

The federal government spent some $2 billion in the state. Much of the investment in infrastructure (roads, sewer lines, buildings) reverted to the use of the state at the end of the war. Airfields in Raleigh, Laurinburg-Maxton, Wilmington, Charlotte (now Charlotte Douglas International Airport), and other sites were deeded to the cities or the state. Permanent buildings in Greensboro, Camp Butner (Umstead Center for Mental Health), and Laurinburg-Maxton (Scotland Memorial Hospital) were used for public needs. The largest bases (Fort Bragg, Lejeune, and Cherry Point) have grown and prospered, making North Carolina a continuously important site for military bases in the nation. A few smaller communities like Butner, Hoffman, and Holy Ridge were barely touched by all the activity except for a four-year boon to local business. Some residents in the smaller towns suffered hardship when the government bought up their land and moved them off of what was now government property. Overall, however, the defense buildup was a great benefit to the state.

The contributions by the state of North Carolina and its citizens were prodigious. Airborne troops learned how to fight at Fort Bragg and Camp Mackall; Cherry Point taught Thunderbolt pilots how to attack the enemy;

and the Quartermaster Center in Charlotte supplied the necessities for carrying on the war. More than 2 million troops were trained in the state in more than one hundred bases, camps, and installations. Civilians at every level welcomed the troops and tried to make their stay in their communities as pleasant as possible. They supplied housing and entertainment, volunteered for numerous activities, and for the most part let the troops know how important they were for the war effort. In many ways, as we shall see, farmers, carpenters, textile workers, clerks, scientists, lumber mill operators, welders, machinists, and other civilian workers played a big part in winning the war.

Arsenal of Democracy

The Economic Impact of the War

Supporting America's war effort from 1940 until 1945 required North Carolina to strive for a total mobilization of its workforce and its resources. Governor Broughton called on all the state's citizens to work hard to produce the tools and necessities to win the war. Fortunately, North Carolina was well positioned to respond favorably to production demands. The state boasted a good climate, lots of cheap land and lumber, important raw materials, a strong textile industry, a farming industry that ranked third or fourth nationally in the volume and value of agricultural products, a large supply of labor for construction, good shipbuilding facilities, a decent transportation system, and an excellent state university system.[1]

On the negative side, North Carolina did not possess a strong manufacturing base; lacked electricity, telephones, and roads in rural areas; did not have a large supply of well-educated and skilled workers; and had been devastated by the Great Depression. The war changed all that. The federal government's expenditure of $2 billion from 1940 to 1945 directly in the state for the purchase of manufactured goods and in defense contracts ushered in an economic boom unimaginable in 1939.

In 1940 the South, including North Carolina, was still essentially a peasant and rural society, shackled by the two-crop system of cotton and tobacco. John Egerton explained that compared to other Americans "Southerners in 1940 were still the poorest, the sickest, the worst housed and clothed and fed, the most violent, the least educated, the least skilled and the most lacking in latitude and power." While Egerton exaggerated the circumstances in some instances, his overall evaluation held up to close scrutiny. His description generally applied to North Carolina as well as the lower South. Egerton recognized that the economic revival during World War II:

> finally blew away eighty years of stagnation dating all the way back to the Civil War. For the first time in its history, the South experienced a genuine bloom of economic opportunity, a broad-based and sustained flowering that brightened virtually every corner of the society. Industry, agriculture and government fed this surge with new facilities, new crops, new services. The war effort opened up millions of new jobs nationally for both uniformed and civilian personnel; more than that, it transported hundreds of thousands of them out of the narrow confines of their native environment and into a wide world of exotic people, places and ideas. At last, Southerners were no longer hopelessly stranded, isolated, idle and broke; they were on the move and the general direction was up.[2]

Historian George Tindall concluded that income in the state multiplied about two and one-half times during the war and full employment raised the per capita income. As a result, retail sales increased and the demand for farm products, textiles, tobacco, and other items skyrocketed. This new prosperity drew new industries to the state, led to the creation of local capital for investment, and developed a pool of skilled workers and experienced managers. Farmworkers who did not know what a rivet was learned how to build airplanes or be a welder in a shipyard or install a sophisticated electrical panel in an airplane. More important than the physical changes, argued Tindall, were the intangibles: "The demonstration of industrial potential, new habits of mind, a recognition that industrialization required community services."[3]

The war raised the effective industrial capacity of the South some 40 percent during the war, but much of the expansion proved ephemeral, especially in ordnance works, aircraft, and shipbuilding. The industrial output, particularly in smaller industries, continued after the war, just not at the same level as wartime production. Tindall noted that World War II created another dramatic change in the South as it put people on the move: to big cities, to training bases, to war plants, and overseas in combat roles.[4]

On the national level the War Production Board supervised essential industrial planning. Mobilizing the economy for war not only changed economic parameters in the nation but also had a transformative impact on the federal government in Washington. The number of federal civilian employees quadrupled as expenditures soared elevenfold. The federal government spent more than $300 billion during the war, twice as much money expended from 1940 to 1945 as it had disbursed from 1789 to 1940. The power of the executive branch increased enormously as the federal government controlled materials, production, and labor while rationing goods, setting prices, and taxing more heavily than it ever had.

From the outset the many mobilization agencies used rewards rather than punishment to persuade large manufacturers to convert to defense production. The major automobile producers and other corporations initially resisted the government's entreaties, fearful of a New Deal socialist takeover of big business. The federal agencies, however, provided subsidies, low-cost loans, and tax write-offs plus an appeal to patriotism to entice corporations to make or build military items. President Roosevelt and his advisors realized that in a capitalist society businesses had to make money; they would not work without a reasonable profit. Government contracts were written with what was called a "cost-plus" arrangement. This meant that the government guaranteed that the manufacturer would be paid the cost of the production plus a fixed profit—a win-win scenario. The government got its defense products, businesses earned guaranteed profits, and jobs were created for everyone.

Many of FDR's key advisors on defense policy were lawyers, financiers, and business executives from industrial giants such as General Motors and U.S. Steel who knew how the system worked. Most of the prime early contracts went to large established firms, like Ford Motor Company. The nation simply could not wait to build new factories and develop expertise but had to use the system already in place. To speed up the process, many of the early contracts were awarded without competitive bidding. Final authority over procurement and contracts remained under government and military control.

The essential purpose of all defense contracts was to ensure the speedy, high-quality, efficient production of war goods. Despite overlapping authority, too many alphabet agencies, and often inefficient management, the mobilization of industry eventually succeeded—partly due to luck but primarily due to the industriousness and ingenuity of American workers and managers.[5]

First of all, America had to provide enough food and agricultural products for both the military and civilian population. In order to meet the critical needs of a nation at war, the U.S. government constantly urged each state to increase its production and industrial capacity to the maximum and in particular called on farming states to grow more and better farm goods for the military, because a war could not be won without adequate food.

Farming

North Carolina's greatest gift to the war effort probably was its agricultural production. One of the state's major assets was its farming community, which already ranked high in the volume and value of its products. After 1940 the state's farmers experienced a greatly expanded demand for their products and in turn, despite shortages of labor, achieved a significant increase in the volume of goods.[6] The state, however, was still agriculturally backward compared to other states. Many farms did not have running water, electricity, or telephones, and most relied on mules rather than tractors. The agricultural boom touched off by World War II would alleviate many of those problems and would rescue the state's farms from the economic woes of the Great Depression.[7]

A major problem for farming in North Carolina and elsewhere was scarce agricultural labor. The farm population in the South decreased by a remarkable 3.5 million between 1940 and 1945. Many rural folk went into the armed services; others left the farm for the city, seeking high-paying jobs in industry or textiles. Larger cities such as Greensboro and Charlotte, as well as military bases, saw a massive increase in population as farm workers moved from rural dead-end jobs and poverty and flocked to larger towns. Orion Blizzard left his farm in search of better pay. He went into construction work at Camp Davis and prospered.[8] Lauch Faircloth remarked that the average farm wage in 1939 was about 50 cents a day. By 1940 those working on military bases were getting $7.20 a day. "Who is going to plow a mule for fifty cents a day when you can drive to Camp Lejeune or Fort Bragg and you would make $7.20 a day?"[9] Thomas Fuller left the farm to work for the railroad and expressed the views of many who followed in his footsteps. "You can make a living on a farm, but there's no money in a farm."[10]

During the war America was a nation on the move, and many native Tar Heels left the state altogether. About 15 million Americans moved across county lines and 8 million across state lines. One in five citizens made an important geographical move.[11] So many rural residents left the farms that farmers were desperate to attract enough labor to bring in the crops.

Governor Broughton early on recognized the need to expand agricultural production in the state. The governor advocated for more diversified farming by increases in the production of poultry, beef cattle, hogs, and sheep.[12] Broughton understood that the true function of government was to aid farmers with marketing facilities, credit at reasonable rates, fair freight rates, better transportation from farm to the market, research assistance from North Carolina State College, and expanded extension services. The governor wanted to help the farmers without overwhelming them with regulations and too many public agencies. He believed farmers would perform better if they could work unfettered by government interference but benefit from government advice and funding.[13] Victor Crosby, an innovative, progressive farmer in Iredell County, took advantage of government assistance by enrolling in a night course on agricultural production. The course helped him maximize his production of food and fiber. He also borrowed money from the Farm Credit Administration (FCA) to purchase new machinery such as a cultivator and a corn picker, which further enhanced his efficiency and yield.[14]

The state and federal governments took other active steps to help the farmer. The Selective Service classified farming as an essential war industry and deferred farm labor in the draft, furloughing some who had already been drafted. This move, plus an appeal for schoolchildren, women, retirees, and other volunteers to assist in the harvesting of essential crops, proved to be invaluable in solving the labor problem. Each county set out to coordinate farm labor and farm machinery, as not enough machinery was available for the harvesting of crops. The State Department of Agriculture and the N.C. State College of Agriculture also coordinated in finding solutions for shortages of feed and fertilizer, without which the 278,000 farms in the state could not function effectively.

There was a statewide emphasis on conservation of food and an increase in the size and diversity of Victory Gardens. State officials urged an increase in electricity, telephones, and power plants to help farmers increase their yield. North Carolina power companies scheduled over $12,000,000 in expansion. The Tidewater Power Company reported that it had built fifty-one miles of new transmission lines. Bell Telephone and Carolina Telephone and Telegraph announced that business had increased 30 percent after they extended lines in rural areas.[15] A statewide Civilian

Service Corps, a mobile army of 28,000 volunteers, assisted farmers with their Victory Gardens, emphasizing fresh fruits and vegetables that could be eaten or canned.[16]

Aided by schoolchildren and business owners, farmers responded to the vital need for agricultural products by increasing the size of their yields and their Victory Gardens. Thomas Snipes worked hard to expand his harvest by crop rotation and enhanced fertilizer but was also self-sufficient by growing his own vegetables and supplying his own eggs, milk, butter, and meat. Like many of his rural compatriots, Snipes was a down-home, wise, uncomplicated individual. "We're just what I call average country people. I always worked and made a living somehow. I never accumulated a whole heap and never particularly wanted a whole heap. Just to make a decent, honest living—that's about all there is in the world anyhow. It's not a person's needs that hurts [sic], it's their wants."[17]

Farmers realized that their future success depended on greater diversification and heeded agricultural commissioner Kerr Scott's admonition to work on "food, feed and fibre." They increased the production of soybeans and peanuts, bought more dairy and beef cattle, and expanded the production of pork and poultry. By the end of 1942 the dairy industry had improved so much that North Carolina was shipping milk to military camps in railway tank cars and for the first time the state had developed a substantial export business.[18]

By the middle of the war, farm prices had risen dramatically and farmers enjoyed rare prosperity. Their success in better use of farm machinery, improved crop rotation, and soil improvement helped the state achieve new standards of production. A spirit of cooperation abounded, as farmers overcame the difficulties of a shortage of labor, machinery, and fertilizer by cooperation and ingenuity. Automobile mechanics volunteered to fix tractors and other farm machinery, so no crops rotted in the field for lack of help in harvesting. The slogan was "No idle labor, no idle land, no idle machines."

North Carolina produced 374 million pounds of peanuts in one year (1944), as compared with the previous average of 250 pounds per year. Farmers grew 9,000,000 bushels of Irish potatoes in 1942, an increase of 30 percent over the previous year. In 1942 farmers doubled the output of wheat from 4 million to 8 million bushels. Perishable crops such as strawberries, cucumbers, and squash also increased.[19] In 1944 the state canned approximately 28 million quarts of fruits and vegetables—twice the amount canned in the years prior to 1941.[20]

The production of cotton and tobacco, the two primary crops before 1940, continued to make great gains. North Carolina tobacco manufacturing companies dominated the industry in 1940 and were the most productive in the country. Tobacco had been classified by the government as an essential industry largely due to the morale factor—supplying cigarettes to both civilian and military personnel. The American Tobacco Company sold millions of Lucky Strike cigarettes to the military. Other tobacco giants, including Brown and Williamson and Liggett-Myers, did the same. Camel cigarettes, produced by the R. J. Reynolds Company, became the most popular cigarette in the country. The product was so named because the tobacco was similar to the blend used by the then fashionable Egyptian cigarettes. The company used "Old Joe," a circus camel, as a marketing device with the slogan "I'll Walk a Mile for a Camel."[21]

Overall developments during World War II brought major changes to southern agriculture. Lauch Faircloth, a farmer, entrepreneur, and later United States senator, explained that before World War II farming was a way of life. Before the war the first goal of agriculture was for the landowner and the worker to subsist. With so many unemployed, a farm was successful if it could turn a small profit with hogs, vegetables, and tobacco. The mechanical revolution and diversification in crops and livestock led to a new age in farming. The transition was from one man and a mule to one man and a tractor, if available, that could do six times as much work as the mule. From 1940 to 1944 farm income went from $2 billion to $4.7 billion in the South and per capita farm income soared from $150 to $454. With more electrification and use of tractors the influence of the small farmer would be reduced, resulting in a movement toward organized agribusiness. With greater demand for produce and fewer workers, farms had to become more efficient to thrive.[22]

The war years affected rural crop growers in ways other than in terms of economics. The migration of rural citizens and their new experiences changed their outlook on life and opened them up to new ideas. When they returned home to the farm they had experienced life in the cities with new jobs and more money. The standard of living had improved after the war, so many rural inhabitants left the farm for nonfarm jobs, entered college, or moved to the city. By 1946 North Carolina farmers had not escaped poverty and isolation and were still the forgotten people in the state, but they took pride in the extraordinary contribution that they had made to the war effort. They knew the war was not won just on the battlefield and that food was essential to the Allied success. A poem by

Thomas Lomax Hunter, favored by some of the farmers, expressed their views succinctly:

> In laying adversaries low
> War's greatest weapon is the plow.
> Success'n war, depends, my son
> On making corn and wheat to grow;
> And victory will by him be won
> Who hoes the most successful row.
> On those who till and plant and grow
> And feed the swine and milk the cow,
> We should our medals now bestow—
> War's greatest weapon is the plow.[23]

Construction

As discussed in the chapter on military bases, North Carolina's construction companies enjoyed a booming business from 1940 to 1944, as the government paid huge sums to private companies to build military facilities in the state. The companies had the rare opportunity to choose from a wide variety of no-bid, cost-plus contracts. Blythe Brothers and Goode Construction Company had a very successful run in Charlotte, but the dominant force in the industry was J. A. Jones Construction Company, led by the president and principal stockholder, J. A. Jones. The company invested its energies in building military cantonments and Liberty ships.

In January 1940 J. A. Jones was one of fourteen companies called to Washington, D.C., by the Defense Department to learn about the plans to build new military bases. The J. A. Jones Company ended up with government contracts to construct thirteen military bases, mainly in the South: Fort Jackson in Columbia, S.C.; Camp Gordon in Augusta, Ga.; the AAF Replacement Center in Greensboro; and Camp Mackall in Hoffman. Jones had to hire and train a large number of new workers, gain access to lumber and raw materials, and organize each of his many work groups. He developed construction proficiency that revolutionized the industry by using assembly-line techniques with prefabricated materials. The company won several "E" awards for excellence in building. The award for building Camp Mackall read as follows: "We have come to depend upon you not only for meeting and more often exceeding, contract schedules, but also for the high type of your finished jobs."[24]

In March 1942 J. A. Jones was contacted by an admiral in Washington to see if the company would be interested in making ships. Jones replied: "You mean boats?" The admiral: "You may call them boats, I am referring to ocean going vessels." Jones replied that he was not interested either way, because they were a building construction company. When Edwin L. Jones Sr., the secretary and treasurer of the organization, found out about the rejection of the admiral's offer, he immediately put together a feasibility study on how to build oceangoing vessels with specific information about hiring skilled workers and obtaining the steel and other necessary equipment. By virtue of his audacity and vision, Edwin Jones acquired an initial government contract to build thirty-three Liberty ships. J. A. Jones Construction Company was now in the shipbuilding business and constructed 212 Liberty ships. Using some of the same assembly-line concepts used in building bases, J. A. Jones Company turned out its first ship in seventy-nine days. Always innovative, the company hired and trained several female welders despite negative comments about "women folks" in coveralls "puttering" around the navy yard.[25]

The company was not finished with new surprises for its workforce. In May 1943 General Leslie R. Groves, head of the top secret Manhattan Project in Oak Ridge, Tennessee, asked Edwin Jones if he had ever built a power plant. Jones said yes. Groves asked: "When can you start?" Jones replied: "Tomorrow." The J. A. Jones company's work with the Manhattan Project in the development and production of the atomic bomb was probably its most significant contribution to the war. The company constructed a 238,000-kilowatt electric plant in ten months; built the half-mile long K-25 gaseous diffusion plant; and completed a city for 12,000 workers—with shopping and recreation facilities, cafeterias, roads, utilities, and housing.[26] Many other state construction companies, both large and small, profited from the numerous government contracts in the state, of course, but J. A. Jones was a national leader in the field and built a remarkable reputation as an efficient and inventive company.

Textiles

Long a stable and prosperous business in the state, the textile industry produced an amazing array of products for the military. More North Carolinians were employed in textiles than in all the other industries combined. With the wartime demand for a greatly increased number of goods, textile companies developed more sophisticated machinery, produced better and more durable yarns and fabrics, and improved the process of dyeing and finishing the products. The mills were able to produce cloth that was fire retardant and crease resistant, and the workers could tailor the material to the desired softness, crispness, or luster. Rayon replaced silk in the making of stockings. The resultant product was stronger, more elastic, and resistant to abrasion and wear. The state succeeded as a major textile producer because it had a large population of cheap available labor with wages below the national average, sufficient power resources, good transportation facilities, and no unions.

Gordon Berkstressor, an executive with J. P. Stevens and Fieldcrest, pointed out that during World War II textile mills were asked to produce more goods for both the war effort and the civilian population when it was hard to get good raw material and difficult to get replacement parts for machines. Berkstressor complained that young white males, long considered to be the best labor force, were away serving in the army. Thus a certain portion of the labor force had to be replaced by black workers, who had toiled in the mills but had been relegated to menial jobs like yard work and sweeping. Berkstressor admitted that putting blacks into more skilled positions created all sorts of antagonism and opposition from white workers, but the owners had little choice. Eventually the owners were pleasantly surprised at the quality of skilled work turned out by these former menial workers. "They all got educated during World War II."[27]

Many of the factories were in rural areas where workers lived in mill villages in houses owned by the company and rented to the workers. The mill villages and the workforce were controlled by the companies. Although some owners provided good amenities for the workers, the basic concept was paternalism.[28]

While opportunities for work had increased, the working and living conditions in the textile mills remained difficult. Paul Cline, who worked for J. P. Stevens, described life in the mills for his parents in the 1930s. If the worker didn't make enough and had a big family, it "was a struggle. You had to knuckle under. It was almost like slavery. They tell you what to do, you couldn't do this and you couldn't do that. They tried to run your life—tell you what to do outside the mill." Cline, working in the 1940s, said the job was not as bad as during his parents' time "but it's almost as bad." About the only difference in working conditions was that it was no longer like a penitentiary—you could go home at night. Cline worried that the excessive heat in the summer was dangerous to his health. "I know it to be 110 [degrees] on the second shift where I worked. You get so hot in

Figure 4.1. Two women workers at a cotton mill in Gastonia, N.C. Courtesy of the State Archives of North Carolina.

there, you nearly stifle to death." He noted that there was only one water hose and one water fountain and that he did not expect things to change. The company did very little for the worker's benefit, recalled Cline. Whatever was done, "it was for the company's benefit."[29]

Ethel Faucette was fairly typical of the women textile workers during the 1930s and 1940s. Like many in her community, she finished school only through the eighth grade: "I got married and I did not go back to school anymore." Ethel, her parents, and her siblings all went to work for

Glencoe Mills. She complained that the mill was hot in the summer and freezing in the winter and that the noise from the machines was so loud that "you couldn't hear nothing." You had to yell at the person standing next to you just to be heard.[30] Most people preferred to work in the hosiery mills or the furniture mills rather than in the cotton mills because the pay was better, the work easier, and the factory less dusty.[31]

Burlington Mills, led by an astute entrepreneur, J. Spencer Love, built a modern, integrated corporate structure. Love, one of the first to recognize the potential of artificial fibers, became a pioneer in the production of rayon, making Burlington a leader in the field. He also experimented with the development of nylon, to be used in making parachutes. During the war the company produced more than fifty products for the military. Due to innovation, a commitment to research, and sound management, by 1962 Love had created the largest textile manufacturing company in the world, with 130 plants in sixteen states and seven foreign countries.[32]

Cannon Mills, presided over by its authoritarian owner, Charles Cannon, made towels, percale sheets, pillow cases, and women's hosiery for the government. Strongly patriotic, Cannon made a "To Hell with Hitler" towel. Due to labor shortages, Cannon, a hard-charging innovator, wanted to retain workers and boost morale, so he increased wages to one of the highest rates in the industry and built a YMCA, permanent housing, and movie theaters. He hired women and put them in jobs traditionally available to men only. At one time Kannapolis was the largest unincorporated town in America. Cannon ruled the town and his company like a feudal lord.[33]

Textile mills all over the state operated at full blast during the war, usually running three shifts. As the demand for goods increased, the textile factories achieved their goals by employing some 200,000 workers. State textile production in 1941 was the greatest in history and would be even greater in 1942. Particularly important were cotton textiles, needed to replace silk, nylon, and wool fabrics being diverted to the armed forces.[34] In September 1944 Governor Broughton reported that the increase in cotton production had exceeded normal production by 100 percent, with a 66 percent rise in personnel. So great and so wide was the variety of production that the governor claimed that every soldier and sailor in service either wore or carried some article manufactured in North Carolina.[35]

A brief survey of the textile manufacturers gives some idea of the extraordinary kinds of items made in the state. O. L. Shackleford in Kinston made camouflage netting; Raven Cotton Mill produced pup tents, tarpaulins, medical litters, and barracks bags. Elizabeth City boasted of products made by the American Enca company, primarily rayon for parachutes and high-strength rayon cord used in bomber tires. Erwin Cotton Mills in Dunn turned out tons of blue denim, and Chatham Manufacturing Company crafted army, navy, and marine blankets. Fred Norman, a homesick young soldier from North Carolina, facing the bitter cold and the ferocious Nazi attack in the Battle of the Bulge, was comforted when he noticed that one of the warm blankets supplied by the army had been made by Chatham Blankets. He said it felt good to touch the familiar softness of a blanket made in his home state while isolated in such a cold, dark, and dangerous place.[36]

Hanes Hosiery in Winston-Salem was a major supplier of wool shirts, olive drab shorts, underwear, and hosiery of all kinds. The Tip Top Hosiery Mill in Asheboro added to the state's reputation for fine socks and hosiery. Holt Manufacturing Company in Fayetteville mass-produced leather and canvas gloves for the military. The Wellco Shoe Company in Waynesville crafted hospital slippers. Cramerton Mills in Cramerton, with a workforce of 2,000, produced trousers and twill uniforms and turned out 1 million yards of cloth during the war.[37]

Stedman Manufacturing Company in Randolph County produced T-shirts for the navy, while McCrary Industries made nylon yarn used for parachutes, ponchos, and men's and women's stockings.[38] Alda Womack of Mooresville was part of a growing female workforce that flocked to the textile mills. Proud of her new job and better pay, she made towels for the navy in the Hanes Plant in Cliffside. Like most other women workers who put in a full day at the mill, Alda also canned, grew vegetables, and bought war bonds.[39]

Munitions and Arms

The state focused on textiles, farm products, and furniture but also manufactured other important items for the military. When the Defense Department encouraged small manufacturers to sign up to produce hundreds of types of equipment ranging from flame throwers to ammunition, several small firms in the state answered the call. The Vultee Aircraft Corporation in Elizabeth City modified all types of aircraft for the navy. The Southern Steel Stamping Company produced parts for grenade launchers and fuses for fragmentation bombs, while the Peden Steel Company in Raleigh made barges for the navy.

Impressed with Charlotte's central location and its labor supply, the munitions division of U.S. Rubber Company, which had many contracts for rubber products, especially tires, set up a shell-loading facility (known locally as the Shell Plant). Here the employees assembled sixty different parts and nine different explosives in order to produce 40-mm and 75-mm antiaircraft shells.

U.S. Rubber Company needed lots of employees, primarily women, who were more adept at handling dangerous ammunition, and needed them immediately. The company advertised for workers in local newspapers. One ad carried the banner headline. "WANTED: WOMEN FOR WAR WORK. AT ONCE." The company encouraged women to

> enlist as soldiers in a production line. . . . A call to women like YOU, who have maybe never worked before . . . to women who don't need the money . . . but patriotic women who want the terrible war over as soon as possible. YOU can hasten that day by making the munitions of war to blast the AXIS on land, sea and air.
> THIS IS YOUR WAR, TOO. WILL YOU HELP?

U.S. Rubber promised good working conditions, cafeterias, a group insurance plan, adequate bus facilities, lockers, showers, and future pay increases.[40]

Construction of the 2,000-acre facility was completed in January 1943 at a cost of $20 million. The plant operated 272 buildings connected by thirty-two miles of gravel roads along Highway 49, nine miles south of Charlotte. The plant employed approximately 7,500 workers—three-fourths women, one-third of those black. Most of the supervisors were men. To accommodate the workforce, assigned to three eight-hour shifts, the company provided a laundry that handled 8,312 coveralls and towels daily, a main cafeteria plus six smaller ones (meals were served around the clock), a hospital, and for obvious reasons, a fire department, with four trucks and one ambulance.

The Shell Plant was an extremely dangerous place to work, and the employees took their jobs seriously. As a safety precaution recreational activities were not allowed on the premises. No rings could be worn. All workers had to have a photo ID and wear steel-toed shoes and blue overalls. Remarkably, there were very few accidents. The facility achieved impressive speed and safety records. On its peak day of production, the plant manufactured 213,143 rounds in twenty-four hours.

One of the largest employers in the county, the Shell Plant was a boon for women, many of whom had never worked outside of the home. The money was good, and they were proud of their record and their contribution to the war effort.[41] Frances P. Falls remarked that the workers got along very well and did not have "any fusses or fights." She recalled making 65 cents per hour and earning $22.80 for a week with overtime. She was happy to set aside $6.25 to buy war bonds, "just one more way I could do my part."[42]

Annie Poole worked on the shell assembly line because "they needed people to work for defense and you wanted to defend your country the best you could. It was the onliest thing I could do, I couldn't go where the action was." Dot Cornwell had a four-hour bus ride to work at the Shell Plant. After a dangerous and demanding eight-hour workday, she had little free time. "Come home and eat and sleep and that's just about it." After the plant closed, Dot took a big cut in pay when she returned home to Lincolnton, to the five and dime store where she had previously worked. Luciel McNeel, a black worker, was excited about having such a good paying job. She talked about how well white women and black women got along working side by side. After the war, when there were no more shells to make, "we all had to go back into segregated society making $3 a week . . . we couldn't get a job working with white people. You couldn't even sit on the bus with them."[43]

Another rubber company, Firestone in Winston-Salem, made pontoons for constructing bridges. The National Carbon Company, maker of Eveready batteries, operated in a former textile mill in Thrift, N.C., and made almost 3 million different-sized batteries used to power the army's two-way radios. Edwards Company, a small business in Sanford, made hydraulic aircraft equipment used on the Curtis Hell Diver and the B-29 bomber.[44] The National Munitions Corporation of Carrboro produced bazooka shells and 20-mm high explosive antiaircraft shells for the navy. Men packed shells with a high-grade explosive while women applied the detonators. The plant eventually employed as many as 16,000 workers and operated for three shifts a day for almost three years. The workers could fill 400–500 cases of ammunition per shift. Except for one incident, the factory had an enviable safety record and earned three army-navy "E" citations for war production excellence.[45]

Although the Carrboro plant was safe, the transportation of explosives turned out to be a dangerous proposition. On March 7, 1942, near Selma, N.C., a truck carrying thirty thousand pounds of black gunpowder, hand grenades, and other explosives, blew up with a thunderous roar after a collision with a passenger car. The blast, which could be seen and heard fifty miles away, wrecked nearby buildings, dug a large crater into the highway, and killed four people. The death toll would not have been so high except that several spectators ignored the warning to stand back from the still burning truck. They stood around gawking at the wreck, while eating and drinking and commenting on the fire. Unaware of the potential power of the blast, the onlookers were standing much too close to the burning vehicle when it exploded. In addition to the four deaths, several of the spectators were seriously injured and had to be transported to nearby hospitals.[46]

While the state ranked high in Defense Department efficiency ratings, there were some abject failures. The Fairchild Engine and Airplane Corporation had been awarded contracts worth $63,000,000 to build 475 gunnery training planes, the AT-21 Gunner, for the army air force. Fairchild employed 2,350 workers in Burlington to achieve that goal. When Fairchild failed to meet its goals, a government investigation in December 1943 revealed "general wastage, inefficiency and extravagance" in the plant. Plant guards were being paid $325 a month, a huge salary at that time, and so-called skilled workers, who were anything but, made $48 a day. "Excessive" sums were spent for travel, telephone, and office supplies and the company designated $106,407 for miscellaneous items. The investigator reported his results to Congress, which then held hearings on the issues and demanded greater efficiency from the corporation. The president of Fairchild blamed the delay on research problems and assured Congress that the planes would be forthcoming. In the end Fairchild spent more than $13 million of defense contract money and made only one plane. In May 1944 the government ordered the company to curtail production. The company then announced the gradual layoff of all workers and closed the plant.[47]

Minerals and Chemicals

While North Carolina was not known for its mineral resources, private firms operated over 400 mines during the war. The state did have some important minerals and, recognizing the potential for mining, set up a Bureau of Mines to coordinate mining activities. The Bureau of Mines established a research facility at North Carolina State College to discover new uses for the minerals.

Mica was mined in large quantities in the Blue Ridge Mountains. The

Asheville Mica Company made twenty-six electrical instruments using mica, an aluminum silicate. It was made into thin flexible strips often used in window glass and also used as an insulator and a metallic lubricant for high-speed machine guns. By the end of the war North Carolina was producing half of all the mica mined in the United States. The state was also one of the leading producers of feldspar, utilized in optical glasses, spark plugs, and porcelain. Chromite, although in limited supply, was perfect for armor plating and steel alloys.

There was some gold mining in various parts of the state, although the output was slim. Coal mining was more widespread, but again had limited output. Mining of any type was hard, dusty, and dangerous, as Dock Hall testified. Hall worked as a chucker in a coal mine, which meant that he poured water on steam drills to cool them down and changed drill bits when necessary. He thought it was "a pretty tough job" with limited pay, but he never had any problems with black lung disease. Hall reckoned that the eight-hour shifts were hard on the workers, but it was a living. He complained that there was little entertainment in the area except to drink liquor and listen to fiddling.[48]

The state produced significant quantities of bauxite, tin, fertilizer, and bromide. The Carolina Aluminum Plant in Badin made enough aluminum to construct more than 6,000 B-29 bombers. Vick Chemical Company made several chemicals available to the armed forces. The Smith Douglas Fertilizer Company helped meet the farmers' increasing demand for fertilizer. Millions of gallons of water came out of the sea to flow through the Ethyl-Dow processing plant, leaving behind bromide to be used in high-test gasoline.[49] North Carolina was one of only three areas in the United States suitable for the mining of tin. The supply of tin from South America, Malaya, and China had been cut off by the Japanese, so manufacturers opened two mines in the state. The production level was low but important: tin was necessary as plating for bearings in engines, as a corrosion-preventing coating for cans of food and for tinfoil, and as a pliable wrapping for soap, candy, and tobacco.[50] Governor Broughton praised the miners' work in producing materials as vital to the defeat of the enemy as soldiers on the battle front.[51]

In order to mine and develop all of the state's natural resources, the state had to increase its hydroelectric power by an enormous amount. One of the keys to expanding aluminum production was the building of Fontana Dam in western Graham County. The Aluminum Company of America (ALCOA) hoped to find a power source for the massive amounts of electricity needed at its aluminum production plant. ALCOA cooperated with the Tennessee Valley Authority (TVA) to build the massive Fontana Dam. The Fontana Agreement gave the TVA possession and control of the dam, while guaranteeing that ALCOA would be the primary beneficiary of the dam's electrical output for at least twenty years.

The excavation for Fontana Dam started shortly after Pearl Harbor in January 1942, and the company poured the first bucket of concrete in February 1943. Highways, bridges, and rail lines had to be built to bring in construction equipment, supplies, and workers to the remote site on the Little Tennessee River. The TVA built a community for 5,000 workers and families with 19 dormitories, a cafeteria for 1,000 people, a recreation facility, and a softball field. The permanent village, a mile downstream from the construction site, included 400 permanent houses, 400 trailers, a movie theater, a 550-bed hospital, libraries, and 2 racially segregated schools.

After 2.8 million cubic yards of concrete and 34.5 million man hours of work, ALCOA completed the dam in November 1944, at a final cost of $74.7 million. Because the workers were on three shifts for seven days a week, the dam was constructed in half the time that it would have taken in peacetime. To inspire the workers, military marches and big band music were piped in over the public address system. Signs everywhere reminded the workers of their patriotic mission for the war effort. The new power-generating units were put into operation in January 1945, in time to provide crucial energy for aluminum production at the end of the war. Some of this energy made possible the accelerated production of nuclear material at Oak Ridge, Tennessee, necessary for the completion of the atomic bomb.

After the war Fontana developed into a multipurpose dam providing electric power, flood control, recreation, and navigation. The reservoir was more than 11,000 acres and had a 240-mile shoreline. At 480 feet, it was the highest dam east of the Rockies and essential for the industrial development of the state.

Since the building of the dam required the purchase of over 68,000 acres of land, some 1,311 families and 60 miles of roads had to be relocated. The TVA offered the families $37 per acre for their land. Although losing their homes was a significant sacrifice, the local families viewed the dam as an essential war project and had no choice but to do what was required of them. The towns of Proctor, Judson, Bushnell, and Sugar Fork were completely inundated by the lake. Using their strength of character and skills, the displaced mountain folk had to make new lives for themselves. One family bought an old general store, while another man built cabins and small boats to rent. With electricity now available throughout the region, the local lads returning from overseas service understood that great changes had occurred while they were at war, not only in themselves but to some degree in their mountain way of life.[52]

Furniture and the Lumber Industry

With the huge increase in construction and shipbuilding at the start of the war, timber production in the state more than doubled from 1939 to 1941. The state became a national leader, with over 3,000 sawmills in operation. Much of the lumber was used for pulpwood, veneer, and paper. Native wood, especially pine and hardwoods, was eagerly grabbed up by the furniture industry. Rankin Lumber Company in Fayetteville cut 20,000 feet per day of yellow long leaf pine for the navy.[53]

Furniture had been an important product in North Carolina since the colonial era. By 1939 the state was the national leader in the total production of wood household furniture. The furniture business boomed during the war, as factories made a number of wood products. The woodworking plants in the state manufactured chairs, boxes, upholstered furniture, desks, shelves, venetian blinds, coffins, crates, beds, and other items for the military and civilian population.

The Broyhill Furniture Company expanded significantly in the 1940s and moved from making inexpensive furniture to more upscale, medium-priced bedroom and upholstered furniture. The company succeeded because it increased its national advertising, modernized its factories, and hired a larger paid sales staff. The 109 plants in North Carolina manufacturing furniture employed 19,600 workers in 1942 and paid out wages of $31 million. The total production of furniture in 1942 totaled over $53 million in sales.[54]

From 1940 to 1945 more goods were manufactured, more people were employed, and more plants and factories were engaged in around-the-clock operations than ever before in the state's history. Nearly three-quarters of a million people were employed in industrial pursuits in North Carolina. A huge benefit from all this labor was a steady increase in income. In 1939 the state's per capita income was 57.2 percent of the national average, but by 1945 it had risen to 63.6 percent. When J. S. Dorton assessed the state's economic development during the war, he discovered that the largest industry was textiles, followed by tobacco, then logging and lumber, the furniture industry, and dairy products.[55]

Retail Sales and Transportation

The state's transportation system underwent a dramatic reorganization due to war demands. Commercial airlines expanded with the need to transport people and goods. Eastern Air Lines was the key provider of commercial air service in the state. In August 1943 the Civil Aeronautics Board (CAB) approved Delta Airlines for new routes to the Midwest, while authorizing two commuter airlines, Southern Airways and Southeast Airlines, for local service. The state's airports were quickly expanded and served both the military and the slowly increasing civilian traffic. North Carolina was a key center for the trucking industry, which had to add a large number of trucks and vans to carry freight around the state. The truckers faced the same problem as did the bus lines—the lack of tires, gasoline, and drivers—but managed to succeed in spite of these difficulties. Most intercity bus passengers were carried by five lines: Atlantic Greyhound, Carolina Coach, Queen City Coach, Smoky Mountain Trailways, and Pan-American Bus Lines.

Most passengers went by either rail or bus, with trains usually jam-packed with military personnel, military wives, families, and business people. Some citizens went to visit family and occasionally on vacation, but personal travel was limited due to the exigencies of the war. The major rail lines were the Seaboard Airline Railroad, the Atlantic Coast Line, and the Southern Railway. The Seaboard Airline Railway operated 3,857 miles of track and opened an important freight yard in Hamlet, where the lines to Florida met those to Atlanta and Richmond.[56] The Atlantic Coast Line Railroad, with lucrative traffic between the northeastern cities and Florida, also had an excellent transportation service that attracted industry to the state. Their main north–south rail lines that ran through Rocky Mount, Wilmington, and Fayetteville offered dependable service, with dining and sleeping cars on most trains.[57]

The railroads flourished as never before, because automobile use was restricted and railroad travel was the best option for long trips. The railroads earned large sums transporting military personnel. But some, like the Atlantic Coast Line, made their money by hauling freight. In order to service regional businesses, some rail and bus lines limited their services to the local area. The Cape Fear Railroad handled all the troops and baggage between Fayetteville and Fort Bragg. The Queen City Coach Company did the same for Morris Field and other sites in Charlotte.

The state's banks played a pivotal role in providing start-up capital for new businesses, promoting commercial transactions, and assisting the transfer of money from Washington, D.C., to state enterprises. The largest banks in Charlotte during the war were Wachovia, Union National, Commercial National, and American Trust. Wachovia, with Robert Hanes as the chief executive officer, mobilized its resources at the outbreak of war and loaned more than $75 million to area industries. The bank lent some money to defense industries, but most of the funds were earmarked for local industries so that they could expand to keep up with increasing wartime demand. Hanes believed it essential that adequate credit be available for small businesses. He surmised that without banking support many small businesses would have failed. The only branch of the Federal Reserve Bank in the Carolinas was in Charlotte, so it was a banking center from the outset of the war. This heightened commercial and banking activity was the precursor to the beginning of the twenty-first century, when Charlotte would become the banking capital of the South.[58]

As the wartime boom revived old industries and brought new companies and customers to the state, retail merchants witnessed a large increase in sales and profits. The huge demand for consumer goods was fueled to some degree by the larger pay packets for working families. The retailer was described as "a soldier on the home front" because of the contribution to the war effort in providing goods, adhering to rationing restrictions, and promoting war bonds.[59]

Two of the state's largest and best-known department stores, Belk and J. B. Ivey, were located in Charlotte. Both companies had developed a chain of stores around the state, with Belk opening thirty new stores between Pearl Harbor and the end of the war. Belk generated a profit growth of two and a half times as great as before the war. The essential difficulty was always in finding enough merchandise to sell and hiring experienced managers. In 1941, anticipating an allotment and rationing system once America entered the war, Belk placed the largest possible orders for goods. When rationing came about, Belk was in better shape with its large supply of merchandise than those stores that had not anticipated the changes.[60] Some local companies were hurt by the shift to defense production. No longer having cars to sell, Spence Motors in Burlington began selling phonograph records. Hughes Motors shifted over to the sale of horses, saddles, and farm equipment. Kelly Springfield Tires had to close because rubber was no longer available. Because of the gas rationing, Melville Dairy had to start delivering milk by horse and cart.[61]

Shipbuilding

At a time when the British Empire was in grave danger due to the successful German U-boat campaign, President Franklin D. Roosevelt recognized that Great Britain might not survive without a huge influx of needed supplies. More ships were needed to carry the goods, so Roosevelt declared merchant vessels to be a defense priority and ordered the U.S. Maritime Commission to build ships on an emergency basis. On January 31, 1941, the Maritime Commission called for two hundred new ships to be built. Unfortunately there were not enough shipyards to construct the new vessels and the industry suffered from a lack of skilled managers and workers. The Maritime Commission set out to remedy that problem with a crash program of constructing new shipyards.

Roosevelt decided to build many of the shipyards in the South partly because he wanted to aid the economic development there. He realized that the region lacked skilled managers, skilled workers, and machine shops, but the South had a warm climate for year-round construction, adequate supplies of lumber, and large numbers of unskilled workers whose hiring would reduce unemployment in the area.

Initially Governor Broughton and others wanted a yard at Morehead City, but they were overruled by the Maritime Commission when the Newport News Shipbuilding and Dry Dock Company proposed a subsidiary yard to build Liberty ships in Wilmington.[62] The North Carolina Shipbuilding Company was located on a 57-acre site on the east bank of the Cape Fear River, about three miles south of the center of Wilmington. Construction on the $5,140,000 plant began on February 3, 1941. Within three months construction had proceeded to the point where it was feasible to lay the keels for the first two vessels. Awarded a $37,500,000 contract by the Maritime Commission to build thirty-seven ships, the company expanded its facilities by building three more shipways and a pier as well as providing additional electric power in order to meet its commitment. Later on it added an administration building, a cafeteria, a warehouse, and a machine shop. Nineteen miles of standard railway tracks connected all of the buildings.

Along with the increased military population in the area, the shipbuilding industry helped change Wilmington from a small, post-Depression coastal town into a significant industrial center. The population rose from 33,000 to 50,000 in the first year, as farmers and unemployed workers moved to the city looking for work. Manufacturing employment in Wilmington numbered around 2,606 in 1939, but by 1943 employment peaked at about 24,000, with most of the increase due to shipbuilding. In 1943 there were 20,000 workers at the shipyard, working a seven-day week with three shifts each day. *State* magazine described the industrial plant at work: "Day and night it represents a scene of bustling activity. There is the consistent rat-a-tat-tat of the riveters, chippers and caulkers, the whine of many motors, the pounding of steel hammers, the clash of steel against steel."[63]

Upon arrival, the new shipbuilding employees easily found jobs but faced some serious problems. In addition to the increased traffic and lack of transportation, workers had to deal with a housing shortage and an inadequate food supply. In October 1942 the city reported a shortage of 3,000 housing units. The federal government did its best to rectify the problem by putting up 1,700 permanent structures, mainly dormitories, apartment units, and one-bedroom and two-bedroom dwellings. The construction of 4,000 mobile and prefabricated homes helped, but thousands were forced to rely on garage apartments, rented rooms, and rooming houses for shelter.[64]

Arthur Miller, the famous American playwright and author of *The Death of a Salesman*, while working for the Library of Congress, was sent to Wilmington to determine how the local population had adjusted to the huge increase in population and the sudden, unprecedented prosperity. In Wilmington from October 15 until November 5, 1941, Miller interviewed a group of women living in the shipyard's trailer camp about how they viewed their new existence. Most complained about the lack of housing but seemed happy to be somewhere with good employment opportunities.

Miller asked a bus driver about the housing shortage. "Everything is full up," he said. Many families shared rooms. Some workers lived in tents, old railroad cars, and tobacco barns, while others literally rented cots in hallways and pantries. The city manager and the police chief lamented the new problems that the city faced—crowded streets, traffic jams, and an increase in crime and prostitution. The police chief planned to hire ten additional officers and purchase more patrol cars. The city leaders also discussed a skyrocketing demand for public services such as street cleaning and road repair and an expansion of the local hospital. Some of the elderly long-time residents complained about the loss of a small town feeling and intimacy. The old rhythms of the city had changed, and the newcomers threatened to tear the old social fabric apart at the seams. Nonetheless, Miller concluded that Wilmington approached the future with optimism and energy.[65]

Agnes Meyer, a sociologist, traveled around the country to urban and rural areas, studying and describing the social impact of the war on American citizens. As a self-described "correspondent on the home front," Meyer observed what she viewed as intolerable social conditions and decried the government's decision to go into war mode without sufficient concern for the welfare of the individual worker. Unlike Miller, Meyer painted a desolate picture of the working conditions in New Hanover County. She denounced the inadequate food supply, blaming the problem on the incompetence and inefficiency with which the government managed the war effort. Meyer said that she "would not be a worker in Wilmington if you gave me the whole city." In contrast to the chaos created by governmental agencies, Meyer found efficiency in private enterprise, in particular the North Carolina Shipbuilding Company, which was the most efficient producer of Liberty ships in the nation. Meyer believed that the company cafeteria demonstrated how private business achieved success where a government enterprise failed.[66]

Meyer, a social gadfly and proponent of free enterprise, overstated the conditions in Wilmington. Most of the local restaurants that she trashed were run by private enterprise. The restaurants simply could not get enough food because the government had allocated the scarce resources to the workers at the shipyard, a critical industry, and to nearby Camp Davis. Conditions were surely difficult, with food and housing shortages for the general population in Wilmington. But the citizens made do with what they had, as elsewhere in America.

Another issue of grave concern for the shipbuilding company and the town authorities was a shortage of transportation. If employees could not get to work, the plant could not function. Since housing in the city was limited, many workers were forced to live in the surrounding communities and commute to the yard. Twenty-six employees traveled round trip from Fairmont, N.C., a journey of eighty-five miles each day. The company used 140 trucks and buses to carry 1,639 workers to the yard. The Maritime Commission purchased 11 large trailer buses. Some workers came by bicycle or local buses or walked to work. The transportation system devised by the company, despite difficulty with gas and tire rationing, ultimately proved successful in getting employees to their jobs.

With 20,000 workers in 1943, the North Carolina Shipbuilding Company injected $52 million into the town's economy. The labor shortage in Wilmington was less serious than in most regions. But when shortages did occur, the company turned to black workers and women.[67] At the peak of production in 1943, the Wilmington shipyard employed 1,628 female workers—about one out of a hundred. But by 1944 women were 10 percent of the workforce. Women first were used as tool checkers. When several passed the difficult master welder's test, however, it quickly became apparent that they could perform skilled jobs as well as the men. Women worked as welders, woodworking machine operators, messengers, chauffeurs, and drill press operators.

Women were hired "with the understanding that they are to do a man's job and are to be treated the same as the men are treated. Each woman must carry on her work without favor and must do any work requested." The company thoroughly and carefully prepared for the integration of women into the workforce. It provided them with a special counselor, assigned them to "suitable" jobs and generally gave them the same training, pay raises, food, and safety and medical facilities as the men. In addition, women workers were provided with forty-four restrooms (with a ten-minute limit for visits) as well as day-care facilities for women with children. Women performed at a superior level while working at the Wilmington shipyard. They were loyal and highly motivated and had higher attendance rates than the men. Although pressed into duty with little formal training, women workers did superior work in what had been exclusively a male domain. Their performance went a long way toward changing men's attitudes toward women as war workers.[68] *The North Carolina Shipbuilder*, the company magazine, constantly praised women for their skills and hard work, especially lauding the performance of Edith Phillips and Nell Rector, the first two women welders.[69]

More problematic for the company was the use of black workers. Over six thousand workers, 30 percent of the workforce, were black, an unprecedented number for a skilled industry in the South, especially when the majority of other shipyards were racially segregated. The new hires were successfully trained as riveters, riggers, drillers, shipwrights, and other skilled jobs. Integrated crews and work assignments were common. Although the cafeteria and lockers were segregated and many tasks were performed by all-black crews, some blacks worked side by side with whites.

While Roosevelt's Executive Order 8802 had outlawed racial discrimination in the workplace, the immediate need for a large number of skilled workers, not the governmental decree, led to the integration of the Wilmington shipyard. Despite Jim Crow laws and general white antipathy toward black workers, blacks and whites consistently worked well together. Some racial animosity occurred when white workers saw the black workers as trespassing on a white domain and taking away "white" jobs. The security forces generally kept a lid on racial antagonism, and there were few racial incidents. In many ways the working conditions in Wilmington were a remarkable achievement. Blacks clearly played an important role in the success of the company.[70]

The owners of the company went out of their way to make the lives of the black workers more comfortable and frequently expressed gratitude for their work. In July 1943 the company launched the Liberty ship S.S. *John Merrick*, named for the black founder of the North Carolina Mutual Life Insurance Company, one of the largest black businesses in the world. Born in slavery and raised in poverty, Merrick was the first black person to have a ship named in his honor. Black workers were proud to have played a part in building the ship. The company owners ran an ad in the *Colored Shipbuilder*: "With every good wish for our colored employees." The Todd Furniture Company also purchased an ad. "We salute the Colored Workers of the N.C. Shipbuilding Company."[71]

The black workers had an annual yearbook, *The Colored Shipbuilder*, published for the employees of the North Carolina Shipbuilding Company. In the July 1944 issue, the editor expressed great pride in the work done by the black workers in Wilmington. The editor, Thomas Jervay, praised the management of the company for giving the black workers a fair chance at a decent job. As the result of the company's enlightened attitude, hundreds of black men who three years ago had been farmers, bellhops, schoolteachers, and common laborers were now trained mechanics enjoying the wages of a skilled worker. Jervay observed that the black workers had shown the world that they could produce in the right circumstances. But he reminded his readers that they had to consolidate their gains and improve on the past and that thrift, sobriety, and common sense should be the watchwords of the future.[72]

Between 1941 and 1946 the Carolina Shipbuilding Company produced 243 vessels; 126 were Liberty ships that ended up carrying two-thirds of the U.S. cargo during the war. The Liberty ships were 440 feet long, 66 feet wide, and, with 2,500 horsepower, were capable of cruising at eleven knots. Each vessel could carry the equivalent of three hundred railroad cars. The shipyard excelled in innovative production techniques. Its Lib-

Figure 4.2. Launching of the USS *Zebulon B. Vance* on December 6, 1941. This was the first of 243 vessels built by the North Carolina Shipbuilding Company. Courtesy of the State Archives of North Carolina.

erty ships were the first group that used welding instead of riveting in building the hull.

The first Liberty ship launched was the *Zebulon B. Vance*, named after the state's Civil War governor. Christened on December 6, 1941, just one day prior to Pearl Harbor, the ship had been completed in five months and was the first in the "bridge of ships" across the Atlantic promised by President Roosevelt. Captain Edward McCauley, a member of the Maritime Commission and principal speaker, addressed the crowd at the christening: "Let this ship be a warning to those who would trample the rights of man beneath their blood-soiled boots. This great ship is a product of American labor, a labor that is free and unfettered; a labor that knows the only course of a free people lies in democracy."[73]

The North Carolina Shipbuilding Company won numerous awards for efficiency and a high-quality product. At the end of 1943 it was producing one ship a month, and it built ships at the lowest average cost per ship of any of the yards building Liberty ships. The last ship was launched on April

16, 1946.[74] The shipbuilding business would fall off substantially after the war, but the state retained important seaports in Wilmington and Morehead City.

Labor

Laboring men and women during World War II were delighted with the many opportunities for higher pay and skilled work in important industries. After living through the Great Depression and high unemployment, the citizens of the state welcomed the chance to save their homes and farms and work toward a better life. The key to the economic revival was higher pay across the board and the consequent increase in purchasing power. For example, pay for textile workers increased by 50 percent during the war, which gave formerly low-paid workers the chance to purchase more household goods, hook up to electricity, and perhaps get telephone service. In some ways the full employment during the war and increased wages enabled workers to begin the long path to membership in the middle class.

For the most part, North Carolina labor unions were quiescent during the war and did not call many strikes. When workers walked off the job, most of those strikes were of the wildcat variety, not approved by the labor unions. Shortly after Pearl Harbor, President Roosevelt had negotiated an agreement whereby there would be no strikes by labor and no lockouts by management. The federal government established the National War Labor Board (NWLB) to head off any labor strife that might in any way imperil the war effort. The NWLB was very successful in resolving numerous labor disputes. Only when a significant challenge to war production occurred did the government assume control of plants shut down by work stoppages.

Because wages were controlled by the federal government, workers demanded fringe benefits to help them meet the rising cost of living. The NWLB allowed companies to provide job upgrades, increased overtime pay, pensions, and health insurance to make up for the lack of a pay increase. Workers also pleaded for better working conditions, shorter hours, and better housing, but the labor unions did not push their agenda by going on strike. In fact on several occasions the labor unions did all they could to prevent walkouts. Despite the union's efforts, there were still wildcat strikes nationwide during the war. But most of these walkouts were short-lived and had no substantial impact on overall war production.

Despite good jobs and improved pay, many workers still had important grievances, as wages tended to lag behind prices and profits. Manufacturers, with their government-guaranteed cost-plus contracts, enjoyed soaring profits during the war. Although the no-strike pledge hampered workers because they could not use their most potent weapon, labor unions adhered to the pledge because they did not want to lose clout with government agencies and lose contracts for their members. The unions did not want to seem unpatriotic and inflame antilabor attitudes in Congress and among the public.

Nonetheless, the wildcat strikes and national walkouts by the coal miners and other workers eroded the strength and status of organized labor. The workers had real grievances, as many laborers, such as the coal miners, worked long hours under difficult conditions without medical care or long-term contracts. Despite this, the public viewed any walkout as irresponsible, unpatriotic, and self-serving. These views and the increasing number of wildcat walkouts led to a growing antiunion sentiment in the state.[75] T. W. Massengale's letter to the *Raleigh News and Observer* was typical. He expressed his disdain for the strikers for shirking their duty. He noted that the boys on the front line never thought of striking. Massengale considered it wrong that boys could be drafted to fight but strikers could not be drafted to work. He proposed putting all the strikers in the army and sending them to the front lines, where they could be put to work burying the soldiers who gave their lives while the workers were on strike.[76]

Governor Broughton, like the governors of the other southern states, got into the act with his "Work or Fight" proclamation. Because North Carolina was confronted with its most critical labor shortage in history, the governor declared that all classes and groups had a public and moral duty to engage in productive work. The governor insisted that every able-bodied person should be either fighting or working. Broughton urged law enforcement officers and public officials to go to places where idlers gathered and find out why they were not at work. He encouraged the Selective Service to check on those deferred on physical grounds to ascertain if they were physically unable to work.[77] The governor had no authority to mandate employment, even in wartime, but he hoped that if he called out the slackers perhaps public opinion would shame them into either working or joining the armed forces.

Several fairly important wildcat strikes occurred in North Carolina during the war. In 1942 eight hundred hosiery workers in twelve High

Point textile mills went on strike for a 10 percent wage increase. Governor Broughton intervened, because the walkout would hold up war production. A week later, persuaded by appeals from government officials, the laborers called off the job action. The end of the walkout cleared the way for the textile mills to make 17 million pairs of army socks.[78] The making of socks might not seem important, but it would be if you happened to be in the Battle of the Bulge fighting frostbite or in an Asian jungle trying to prevent trench foot. Both of these ailments sidelined a number of men badly needed at the front, so warm and clean socks were essential to an effective military.

The industrial action at America Enka Corporation in Asheville where three thousand workers went on strike was critical, because the company made rayon cord that was necessary for the manufacture of tires. The workers had petty grievances over lunch periods and shift differentials. When the two sides could not resolve the dispute, President Roosevelt ordered the War Department to take over control of the plant.[79] The strike could have been very harmful, as the army had a constant and desperate need for tires. Without the tires, supplies and ammunition could not get to the front and American military success in Europe would have been hindered. Lieutenant Colonel Paul Hines, chief of the labor branch of the U.S. Army Command, appealed to the workers to return to the plant: "Every hour of the production of the rayon cord used in tires that is lost at Enka means a loss of about 150–200 tires that are badly needed just now. . . . On one highway in France we are chewing up 5,000 tires a day."[80] Under significant pressure, the strikers returned to work but labor had once again raised the ire of the public, who viewed the walkout as un-American.

Perhaps the most controversial strike was at the Cocker Machine and Foundry Company in Gastonia. The company made high-tenacity rayon also used for tires and the equipment and parts needed for the manufacture of the rayon. The army had called for a 60 percent increase in the manufacture of rayon, but with the walkout in this plant the entire production line was threatened. After workers refused the War Labor Board's demand to return to work, the military took over the plant. Despite protests from labor unions and a fear of government control of private industries, the government justified its action. The product was critical to the war effort, so a continued strike would imperil the success of soldiers overseas. The dispute was peaceful, with no troops present, but military personnel ran the plant. The *Raleigh News and Observer* called the strike inexcusable during wartime and a blot on the otherwise splendid labor relations in the state.[81] The Truman administration did not intend to stand idly by as America and its Allies were closing in on Germany with a good chance to end the war. It might have been a bit high-handed to take over the mill, but this was wartime, the tires were essential, and Truman intended that there would be no interruption of production.

Despite some wildcat strikes and work stoppages, labor unions in America emerged from the war in good shape by exceeding production quotas and limiting large strikes. The war years were a time of great advances for labor on a national level, less so in the South. Union membership increased from 9 million to 15 million members. One-third of the nation's nonfarm labor force had been unionized. Union members earned better wages, perks, and working conditions, and the Congress of Industrial Organizations (CIO) grew substantially. After the war the CIO organized mass production industries such as steel, rubber, and automobiles. Labor now had more clout with government and an enhanced role in labor-management relations.[82]

The situation for labor unions would be vastly different in North Carolina, which remained a right-to-work state. Very few plants unionized in the state, as R. J. Reynolds, Cannon Mills, J. P. Stevens, and other large industries fought off the union movement with money, legal challenges, and increased benefits to the workers. Despite some strikes and constant attempts at unionization, unions never achieved significant success in the state after the war. When Roy Auton, a worker in hosiery mills, was asked about joining a union, he replied: "I don't think I would if I lived to be two hundred."[83] Murphy Sigmon, also a hosiery mill worker, agreed: "We never did have no big hassles over unions down there. Once or twice while I was working there they tried to unionize it, but they [the workers] voted it down."[84] The workers, isolated and poorly educated, were easily persuaded by mill owners that unions were dangerous: outsiders would come in and change their traditional way of life. The mill workers were innately suspicious of outsiders, particularly those from New York and the northern states, who clearly did not understand the southern way of life. It was better to stay with a master that they knew than take a chance with a rogue agency that might end up integrating the plant. Several workers, when asked why they opposed the union, could not come up with a clear response. They would admit they did not know much about unions, but had always been "agin 'em."

The wartime economic expansion provided great benefits for the state. Its industrial output increased significantly, as did production in farm goods, textiles, lumber, mining, and shipbuilding. The state mobilized underutilized resources (such as mining) and converted labor, machinery, and material to war production. With innovation, new technology, and an increase in electric power; the state became more efficient and more diversified in its economy. North Carolina still relied heavily on tobacco, textiles, and furniture. But other industries were beginning to take root. The state's workers enjoyed higher wages, full employment, greater purchasing power, and rising living standards along with rising expectations and a sense of optimism for the future.[85]

With the end of the war, many defense plants shut down and unemployment once again became a concern. In Wilmington the shipyard closed in 1946 due to lack of demand. Camp Mackall closed and left the town of Hoffman as it had been in the past. With no need to produce munitions in Carrboro or shells in Charlotte, the state reverted to its more agrarian state. But nothing would ever be the same. The Depression had been vanquished and the economic changes during the war set North Carolina on a path to industrial and economic success.

TORPEDO JUNCTION

SUBMARINE WARFARE OFF
THE NORTH CAROLINA COAST

From the sixteenth century to the present some 5,000 shipwrecks have been reported in the Outer Banks of North Carolina, a series of barrier islands with constantly changing sandbars. A history of rough weather has always made the North Carolina coast, known as the "Graveyard of the Atlantic," dangerous for shipping. The area around Cape Fear, Cape Hatteras, and Cape Lookout is particularly treacherous due to numerous sandbars. There the warmer northbound Gulf Stream collides with the colder Arctic currents, creating a wild vortex of winds and waves that only skilled mariners can negotiate.[1]

While coastal residents were aware of the hazardous conditions off the Barrier Islands, they could not have foreseen that the most perilous time for ships traversing the North Carolina coast would be from January to July 1942, after America's entrance into World War II. Americans and North Carolinians could never have imagined that German U-boats (*Unterseeboote* or submarines) would dare to venture into American waters and wantonly and callously decimate Allied shipping. The residents of the North Carolina coast, believing that they were thousands of miles from a faraway war, were shocked to see the burning hulks of transport ships sinking just miles off the coast. Wreckage and bodies from the stricken ships washed ashore, alarming the residents and raising the specter of a

German invasion. Governor J. Melville Broughton noted that not since the War of 1812 had any foreign enemy approached so close to the North Carolina coast.

The period between January and July 1942, the most active phase of German U-boat attacks, accounted for some 90 percent of the nearly eighty vessels sunk off of the North Carolina coast. Twenty-seven cargo ships, with an aggregate tonnage of 109,795 tons, were dispatched to the bottom within sight of the Cape Hatteras lighthouse. The winds and the ocean currents around Cape Hatteras forced some vessels using the shipping lanes to stay close to shore. This improved the U-boats' advantage, because the merchant ships had less room to maneuver. Southbound ships, not wanting to sail against the powerful Gulf Stream, were forced closer to the jutting North Carolina coast—a natural choke point and an area constantly monitored by the German U-boats. Other ships, trying to avoid the treacherous shoals, chose to move farther out to sea into the open waters, making them easy prey for the dangerous U-boats. Any option chosen by merchant vessels could be exploited by the U-boats. For merchant ships, the turn around the extended portion of Cape Hatteras was difficult in the best of times, let alone when trying to avoid a submarine attack.

Because North Carolina was located midway along the eastern seaboard, German subs could wait in ambush and easily attack international merchant ships and trading vessels moving north and south along one of the most congested sea lanes in the world. The cumbersome, slow-moving cargo ships carrying great loads of machinery, oil, sugar, steel, and iron, silhouetted against the lights of the industrial cities of the eastern seaboard, were sitting ducks for the German subs that lay in wait. Historians and observers later referred to the easy poaching of merchant vessels as the "Great Atlantic Turkey Shoot." The hotspot just off Hatteras Point, where so many vessels were attacked, was known as "Torpedo Junction."

The German U-boats did not target naval vessels. They attacked tankers and freighters and their cargoes (the "sinew" of war), thus waging economic warfare against the United States and England. By preventing tons of supplies, especially oil, food, and raw materials, from reaching the Allied war effort, the Nazis hoped to destroy much of the merchant lifeblood that was keeping England in the war.[2]

One of the most crucial, underestimated, and frequently ignored keys to military victory is the science of logistics. No matter how brilliant the strategic and tactical planning of a military commander is, the war cannot be won without the necessary supplies—oil, weapons, ammunition, food, clothes, water, heavy equipment, and other vital needs. Since 1940 the United States had been an "Arsenal of Democracy," supplying England with much of the necessary materiel to resist a German invasion.

In February 1941 the United States Congress passed the Committee to Defend America by Aiding the Allies bill or Lend Lease as it was commonly known. The isolationists in America, including North Carolina's senator Robert R. Reynolds, vigorously opposed any effort that might lead America into an armed conflict. President Franklin Roosevelt helped to sell the concept by explaining that if his neighbor's house caught on fire he would gladly lend him his water hose to prevent the conflagration from spreading. When the fire was out, he would welcome the return of his hose. In effect, Lend Lease allowed England to borrow war supplies with the promise to repay the Americans at the end of the war. The supplies, especially oil, ammunition, wheat, butter, rubber, beef, copper, explosives, and military equipment, were urgently needed. Germany had begun devastating air raids against England, and Great Britain was finding it difficult to maintain the viability of its population and to sustain its war machine.

Winning the Battle of the Atlantic against the dreaded U-boat attacks was essential to the survival of Great Britain. Germany had built a large fleet of submarines and had initiated unlimited warfare on merchant vessels cruising the Atlantic with supplies for Britain. The German U-boats achieved great success against enemy merchant vessels in the Atlantic in 1941, sinking 328 merchant ships with a tonnage of over 1,500,000 tons. Admiral Karl Doenitz, commander of the German U-boat fleet, had adapted an effective attack strategy. Torpedo boats were outgunned by enemy destroyers. He demonstrated that "packs" of submarines, on the surface of the ocean, would be most effective at night (radar was too primitive at this time to give accurate range or early warnings). The U-boats, using their superior speed, could inflict vast damage by concerted raids in numbers that would overwhelm the escorts. When a convoy was sighted, the U-boats were directed to the area by radio signal. The submarines would then attack. This powerful "wolf pack" technique threatened to turn the war in Germany's favor.

At this juncture Roosevelt was unwilling to arm U.S. naval ships to combat German depredations on the sea, but he did emphasize greater industrial production in America to make up for the losses. America also began to make up for the depletion of merchant vessels by building bigger and faster tankers. By October 1942 American shipyards were launching three new Liberty ships each day. By that time a more effective convoy system with more destroyers and corvettes and an improved ASDIC (sonar, the echo-sounder used to detect submerged submarines) had reduced the number of sinkings in the Atlantic. More important, the British code breakers at Bletchley Park, England, managed to crack the German Naval Enigma code. Since Britain often knew the size and location of the German wolf packs, this newly gleaned information frequently enabled the convoys to avoid the U-boat attacks.[3]

Torpedo Junction: U-Boat Warfare off the North Carolina Coast

Admiral Doenitz, realizing that the tide was changing in the Battle for the Atlantic, decided to turn his attention to the east coast of the United States. He determined that his U-boats could make the trip to the United States and have enough fuel left over for seven to fifteen days of attacks before returning to Germany. Doenitz reasoned that the war would be won or lost in the battle against Allied commerce. He knew that America's east coast defenses were virtually nonexistent and that all shipping would be vulnerable to an organized attack.

Doenitz called his attack plan operation Paukenschlag (Operation Drumbeat), surmising that the surprise attacks would be as sudden and as jarring as beating on a kettle drum. The admiral further believed that attacks off the U.S. coast would have an even greater impact than the Japanese attack on Pearl Harbor did because they would reveal American vulnerability. The sinkings would terrify the civilian population. Americans would be stunned to realize that the enemy was destroying ships just miles off the U.S. coast. He knew that American naval and air forces were at this time weak and inexperienced. Doenitz reveled at the thought of his highly trained and experienced submariners going after unescorted ships in American waters.[4]

Doenitz realized that the merchant ships would have a difficult time running the gauntlet of German U-boats, especially because the element of surprise favored the Germans. Doenitz, who had some ninety-one submarines in his fleet, initially dispatched five of the long-range subs to the American east coast, including U-123, U-130, U-66, U-109, and U-125. The German U-boat attacks began in earnest thirty-eight days after Pearl Harbor.

The most aggressive and militant of the five German commanders, Captain Reinhard Hardegen, was a superb naval officer. On five war patrols he managed to sink twenty-five ships with a total of 136,661 tons. To understand his achievements, historian Michael Gannon pointed out that of the 863 U-boats that put to sea in World War II, 754 did not return to their bases; of the 39,000 men who served in U-boats, 27,491 died and 5,000 others were taken prisoner. All submarine warfare was dangerous and involved enormous risks. Just to launch a U-boat was an act of bravery.[5]

After venturing into American waters off Newfoundland, Captain Hardegen made his way southward to Cape Hatteras. On his voyage he was amazed at the bright lights and numerous car headlights visible on American shores—a far cry from blacked-out Europe. After the captain sank his first ship, he informed his crew: "Listen to me, everyone. We're here just like a wolf in the middle of a flock of sheep. We've just sunk a tanker and the Americans still haven't realized that there's a submarine in the area. So much the better for us. Let's take advantage of the situation."[6]

The U-123, a Type VIIB submarine, was a typical medium-sized U-boat only 218 feet long, 20 ¼ feet wide in the middle, and 15 ½ feet high from the keel to the top of the conning tower. The 770-ton VIIB housed a crew of forty-five crewmen, two 1,400-horsepower diesel engines, two 275-horsepower electric motors, five torpedo tubes (four in the bow, one aft), and the steering and control systems. The Type VII carried fourteen torpedoes, had a range of 6,500 miles on the surface, and was a killing machine designed for only one purpose—to sink enemy ships.

All the crew and the necessary equipment and supplies were jammed into a narrow steel cylinder. The inner dimensions of the U-boat were 150 feet long and 20 feet at its widest point. Some observers described this as an iron coffin, but the German submariners were a hardy lot and managed to cope with their suffocating environment even though it had only one toilet for the entire crew. They were under water much of the time, jammed together with little room for maneuver and no privacy. Very little water was available, and none for bathing. The sickening odor of diesel fuel was everywhere, but these German officers and men were the personification of order and discipline. Although they were waging unconditional warfare on behalf of an evil Nazi regime, the submariners should get some credit for overcoming their fears and the difficult conditions.

Hardegen and the other U-boat captains made the most of their opportunities and began to wreak havoc all along the eastern seaboard, as the American authorities were woefully unprepared to stop the onslaught. The U-boats would lie on the sandy bottom during the day and surface at night. The Germans preferred to attack on the surface at night because visibility was low. The large tankers, even with lookouts, had a difficult time spotting a low-lying submarine, while the tankers were easily visible in contrast to the lights on the shore. The subs could make better speed on the surface, 17–19 knots compared to 7 knots underwater, and the shallow coastal waters were more dangerous for the U-boats if they were submerged. On the surface, the U-boats could use their 3.5-inch guns to finish off sinking ships, thus preserving precious torpedoes.

Admiral Doenitz had instructed his U-boat commanders to show no mercy to the enemy. "Rescue no one and take no one with you. Have no care for the ship's boats. Weather conditions and the proximity of land are of no account. Care only for your own boat and strive to achieve the next success as soon as possible. We must be hard in this war. The enemy started this war in order to destroy us; therefore nothing else matters." Brutally efficient in the early months of the conflict, German submariners usually fired only one torpedo (seldom more than two), waited for the crew of the stricken ship to disembark, and then finished the job with the 3.5-inch deck gun. There was only one known incident of a German U-boat commander deliberately killing survivors in the water. The early attacks, while lethal, did not lead to a mass annihilation of the ships' crews. Due to the warmer Gulf Stream waters and the closer proximity to shore, many rescue efforts were successful.[7]

On January 18, 1942, the U-66, skippered by Captain Richard Zapp, was lying in wait off Cape Hatteras. The U-66 spotted the *Allan Jackson,* a Standard Oil of New Jersey tanker carrying 72,280 barrels of oil, bound for New York. Although no German U-boats had been sighted in the area, Captain Felix Kretchmer decided to black out the ship as a precaution. He also made certain that the lifeboats had been supplied with sufficient food, water, and distress signals but was not overly concerned with a possible sub attack. He was lying in his bunk, fully clothed, when the first torpedo from the U-66 struck. Second mate Melvin A. Rand had shouted an alarm, but a violent explosion rocked the bridge before anyone could react. A second torpedo, close behind, hit in the middle of two oil tanks and the ship began to break apart, engulfed in flames.

Rand, realizing the ship was rapidly sinking, jumped overboard and swam for his life. Captain Kretchmer had been knocked from his bunk by the explosions and found himself trapped in his cabin. He managed to squeeze out through a tiny porthole and swam valiantly to avoid the suction of the sinking vessel. There had been no time to sound Abandon Ship or to warn the thirty-five crew members.

A boatswain, Rolf Clausen, managed to lower one lifeboat. The surviving crew members had to row vigorously to gain passage through the fiery wall of burning oil. As the ship was sinking, one member of the crew ran below decks to rescue eighty dollars stashed in his locker. This proved to be a bad decision. Rescuers later found his burned body floating on the surface, with his eighty dollars intact. Clausen and his fellow survivors rowed away from the wreck and were rescued the next morning by the American destroyer *Roe*. The *Roe* also picked up Captain Kretchmer and Melvin Rand, but twenty-two of the crew had perished.

David Best, a British merchant seaman, had signed on as a mate on the *Alan Jackson*. Best remembered that as they passed up the North Carolina coast he could see all the lights on the coast. "There was no blackout. Americans were not, I wouldn't say unconcerned, but . . . their lights were on" and formed a backdrop for the merchant vessels. Because of the silhouette, Best recalled that "they picked us off." He recalled the fear that a seaman felt when struck by a torpedo: "When you get hit by a torpedo, you hear a thud. Then there's about a three second silence. Then the explosion." Best, in the aft of the ship when the first torpedo hit amidships, was able to get into the one lifeboat and managed to row through the oil fire on the surface to be rescued the following morning.[8]

Hardegen and the other U-boat captains were having a field day and kept wondering where the coastal defenses were. Where was the American navy? They saw no evidence that the Americans were switching over to wartime conditions. Nor did the United States appear to have any concrete plan to thwart the U-boat attacks. While the submarine attacks took the Americans by surprise, the U.S. Naval and Coast Guard defense system initially did little to minimize the impact of the U-boat attacks. Every day tons of irreplaceable cargo was lost.

Even after two months of war the merchant ships were still sailing independently and did not bother to zigzag or vary speed to make the U-boats' job more difficult. The ships' skippers often ignored security and talked to each other on their radios, providing valuable information for the lurking U-boats. The coastal defense stations sent out information over the air about where and when aircraft would be patrolling and gave information about rescue work in progress. The U-boat skippers could not believe their good fortune and made the most of the important information carelessly revealed by the Americans. Captain Johann Mohr composed a poem for Admiral Doenitz, celebrating his U-boat's success:

The new-moon night is black as ink
Off Hatteras the tankers sink
While sadly Roosevelt counts the score
Some fifty thousand tons, by Mohr.[9]

The *City of Atlanta* was the next ship off the North Carolina coast to visit Davy Jones's Locker. The 1904 vintage American vessel was moving south at around 12 knots when Captain Hardegen of the U-123 unleashed one torpedo. The torpedo hit aft, destroying the radio shack and killing many men outright. The ship immediately listed to port and sank quickly. Hardegen, surprised that the vessel had gone down so fast, checked for survivors but did not see any.

The lifeboats on the *City of Atlanta* were inoperative, so the crew grabbed on to whatever debris they could find. George Tavelle held onto a bench from the ship's dining room and narrowly avoided being pulled under when the ship went down. Unfortunately for the survivors from the *City of Atlanta*, the water was cold and choppy. They could clearly see the lights on Cape Hatteras, but no one onshore had spotted the sinking ship. As the cold numbed the men, one by one they lost their grip on the debris and surrendered to the sea. At daybreak, six hours later, only three of the forty-six crew members were alive to be rescued.[10]

Robert Fennell, a crewman on the *City of Atlanta*, thought that he was having a horrible nightmare when the torpedo hit. Fennell "awoke with a jolt and couldn't understand why an entire wall of his cabin was missing. There had been a deafening blast, what he thought sounded like a pistol going off beside his ear. Oddly, the pounding of the engine crankshafts had stopped, but other terrifying sounds had replaced it—the unmistakable hissing of escaping steam, the screech of steel plates being violently twisted and torn asunder, and a torrent of surging seawater pouring into the sides of the ship." Realizing they had been torpedoed, Fennell grabbed his lifebelt and made his way to the outer deck as the ship began to list significantly to port. At that point he remembered he had left the photo of his wife, Mary, and risked life and limb to return to his cabin and retrieve the picture. He was never quite certain why he had done so except that he had to have that picture. Luckily, Fennell found floating debris to hang on to and was eventually rescued.[11]

During the last ten days of January 1942 eight more ships went down between New England and the Carolinas. One of the most devastating attacks occurred on January 27, 1942, when Captain Richard Zapp of U-66 had two kills within just a few minutes. The first ship hit was the British tanker *Empire Gem*, bound for Britain with a load of 10,600 tons of gasoline. The ship had its running lights on under a moonlit sky and was just passing another vessel, the *Venore*, when it took two torpedoes in the aft tanks. The ship burst into flames as the gasoline ignited. The flames quickly enveloped the ship, which burned down to the water line. All but three crew members, who were rescued by the U.S. Coast Guard, perished.

Mac Womac, from the Cape Hatteras Coast Guard station, set out in the treacherous seas with his comrades in a 36-foot motor lifeboat to rescue any survivors. "We could see the orange glow in the sky a long time before we got to it." When Womac arrived at the *Empire Gem*, the stricken ship was ablaze and about to sink. They passed through raging fires, clouds of thick black smoke, and physical and human debris from the ship. Due to the heat of the fires, the rescuers could do little to help. "All we could do," said Womack, "was go around and around hoping to pick up somebody that was alive." Eventually Womac and his mates did save the captain and his radioman.[12]

The dramatic fire from the *Empire Gem* exposed the *Venore*, an American tanker carrying 22,300 tons of iron ore. The U-66 hit the tanker with one torpedo and the *Venore* tried to run for it. A second torpedo fired by U-66 hit home and the captain ordered the crew to abandon ship. Some twenty-one crewmen managed to get away safely in a lifeboat. They rowed toward land, subsisting on rations of sea biscuits and water. Thirty-nine hours later they were rescued by the tanker *Tennessee*. The remaining twenty-two crewmen, including the captain, were never found.[13]

Burning oil was the seaman's worst nightmare. Ed Chaney, a ship's quartermaster, described the moment the torpedo hit his tanker: "There was a sickening thud and the boat seemed to slide sideways, then came the explosion. . . . It was just a few moments until . . . the entire ship was encircled by fire." Chaney tried to man a lifeboat, but the rope fouled and he was dumped into the sea. As he began swimming away from the burning ship, he saw one man get sucked into the still-rotating propellers. His clothes soaked with oil, Chaney suddenly was surrounded by fire. "I ducked and swam under the water. Every time I would come up for a breath, I sucked in fire and smoke until it was almost impossible to dive again." After ten or fifteen minutes he swam clear of the fire. Only eleven members of the crew, rescued by the coast guard from Oak Island, escaped the burning wreck. The attack had taken place so close to the shore that several hundred residents of Wrightsville and Carolina beaches heard the blast and witnessed the flames.[14]

Incidents like this were repeated over and over from January until May 1942. The last sixteen days of March were the most devastating time for vessels off the eastern seaboard. During that period the Germans sank thirty-one ships, with the loss of 683 people. The staggering loss of cargo hurt the Allied chances of providing Britain with much needed supplies. As an example, in the brief two-day period from March 14 until March 16, German U-boats sank the *British Resource*, a medium-sized tanker; the *Olean*, an American-owned tanker; the *Australia*, an American tanker wiped out by a single torpedo; the 8,073-ton tanker *San Demetrio*; the Chilean freighter *Tolten*, with only one survivor; and the *Ceiba*, a United Fruit Company ship carrying a load of bananas. When thousands of bananas from the *Ceiba* floated to the surface, Captain Mohr of U-124 cursed his luck because he had wasted a torpedo on a fruit ship.[15]

The U.S. Navy had yet to work out an effective defensive system to thwart the U-boat attacks. The destroyers did their best, but they had been trained to attack and defeat enemy destroyers. They were shorthanded and not effectively equipped to search for enemy subs. The ship's crew viewed their task as virtually impossible—looking for a tiny submarine in hundreds of square miles of ocean. Despite the boring, endless days of unsuccessfully looking for U-boats, the crew recognized that the rescue of survivors from the damaged ships was their most important task.

The *Jesse Roper* had a chance to justify its mission by rescuing shipwreck survivors. One of the more extraordinary rescues occurred after the scuttling of the *City of New York*, a passenger ship from Cape Town, South Africa, bound for New York. After learning that the vessel had been mortally wounded by a torpedo, the destroyer *Roper* raced to the rescue and managed to save four lifeboats full of survivors who had almost perished in stormy seas.

The most dramatic part of the rescue effort concerned Desanka Mohorovic, traveling with her two-year-old daughter to meet her husband in New York. Nearly nine months pregnant, she hoped to make it to New York before the baby was born. As the *City of New York* began to sink, Mrs. Mohorovic found herself in a lifeboat giving birth. Fortunately, Dr. L. H. Conly, the ship's doctor, had followed her into the lifeboat. Unfortunately a huge wave knocked him off balance and he suffered two broken ribs. Under the most difficult of circumstances, in a leaky, open lifeboat on a dark, cold March night with ten- to fifteen-foot waves, Dr. Conly managed to save the baby and keep him warm until rescued. The twenty-one survivors were at sea for thirty-seven hours before being delivered to safety. When the *Roper* found the lifeboat, it was rising and falling on ten-foot seas. It became very difficult to lift the survivors from the lifeboat onto the destroyer. Amazingly, a member of the crew managed to grab the slippery eight-pound baby as it was hoisted aboard.

The new baby was named Jesse Roper Mohorovic, in honor of the rescue ship. The crew was thrilled about the rescue of the survivors and excited that the baby had been named after the ship. Hamilton W. Howe, captain of the *Roper*, remarked: "That was a real shot in the arm. The fact that we were able . . . to save these people and the fact that one of them was this baby, it really made a difference." The crew and passengers raised money in honor of the newborn and made him a boatswain's mate. When the mother was asked by immigration officials where her son had been born, she replied "somewhere in the Atlantic" and noted that he was as healthy as if he had been born in the "most magnificent hospital." Jesse Roper Mohorovic had been born in a lifeboat belonging to a ship in the United State Navy and landed first on American soil, so he was an American citizen. The press continually referred to him as the miracle "lifeboat baby."[16]

Blackouts and Saboteurs

The numerous sinkings had a dramatic impact on those who lived along the North Carolina shore, especially people on the Barrier Islands. Many old-timers recalled the difficult times in early 1942, when the Turkey Shoot was at its height. Residents often heard the loud explosions and witnessed the night sky lit up with flames from a burning ship. One citizen recalled hearing those "explosions almost any time of day or night, and it would shake the houses . . . and damaged the plaster in some of the houses."[17]

Another citizen of Okracoke said that the people got used to the explosions. "It would mostly be in the distance, the explosions were. We wasn't [*sic*] too scared. It just became a regular, routine thing of hearing all this going on, all these explosions." Faced with savage weather and an uncertain economic future, Outer Bankers had been living precariously all their lives. They were sympathetic to those seamen who had been drowned and burned in oil but were stoical and unafraid of the unfolding war just miles from their homes.[18] Nonetheless, night after night the locals would see explosions. It sometimes appeared that the whole ocean was on fire.

Great oil slicks blackened the pristine beaches, along with debris from the shattered ships and water-ruined crates of cargo. Occasionally a drowned seaman floated in with the tide. The carnage and devastation was hard to ignore.

On one occasion the school principal on Harkers' Island noticed that the boys in the school, who usually went barefoot, wore Florsheim shoes. The shoes, part of a cargo washed up on shore, had been quickly confiscated by the local fishermen, whose children wore them proudly. Gibb Gray, a young schoolboy from Avon, remembered when the *Dixie Arrow* was torpedoed south of the Cape Hatteras Lighthouse: "I was on my way to school, and just before we got to the school house the whole ground shook, a violent explosion." Gray and his mates, intrigued by the smoke and explosion, skipped school and went right over to the beach to watch for lifeboats and survivors.[19]

Other unusual happenings live on in local lore. Jim Gaskill, an Okracoker, was lost at sea when his ship, *Caribsea*, fell victim to a U-boat attack off of Okracoke. Third mate Gaskill, along with twenty-one of his shipmates, was killed instantly when two torpedoes hit his ship. The ship went down in less than three minutes, and his body was never found. According to island historians, three days later a man walking on the beach at Ocracoke Island found Jim Gaskill's third mate license and a wooden oar marked *Caribsea*. The oar had floated through Ocracoke Inlet and washed ashore very close to where the Gaskills lived. On another occasion, after the British ship *San Delfino* went down, some of the crew, including Otis Bryant, were adrift in a lifeboat on a dark night and had no idea where they were. They heard waves crashing on the shore and rowed in that direction. The survivors landed on a deserted beach and waited until dawn to assess their status. When morning came, Otis exclaimed: "I know where I am. I was born and raised here. That's Ocracoke lighthouse over yonder." Some survivors were luckier than others.[20]

Some of the injured merchantmen from shipwrecks were picked up and taken into Southport, to the Dosher Memorial Hospital, a small facility that had been overwhelmed by the influx of badly injured and burned patients. After the sinking of the oil tanker *John D. Gill*, several of the rescued crew members were brought to the hospital. Josephine Hickman, a Red Cross volunteer, described the scene: "We didn't even think half of them could hardly live. They were so burned, almost to a crisp and covered with oil. Some of them were burned so bad that the bandages were all over their heads. Only their mouths were open. You just fed them in between the bandages." Dr. Benjamin Royal and his staff at Morehead City also tended to injured sailors, and although short-handed eventually became proficient in treating men suffering from burns, bullets, and exposure. The doctor had a large whistle mounted on the outside of the facility. When the staff spotted a boatload of survivors, he blew the whistle and local volunteers rushed to help. Eventually the government added some rooms and better equipment and assigned service doctors and nurses to aid the wounded.[21]

Strict wartime regulations about printing or broadcasting anything about submarine warfare existed in order to avoid widespread panic. The barrier island residents were more isolated than most, so the absence of facts and news about the war led to a flood of rumors. There was talk about German spies being caught with tickets from the Morehead City theater in their pockets, and locals reported German newspapers left under the seats in the movie house. Constant stories circulated about German submarines just off the coast and saboteurs landing on the beaches and melting into the population. Several citizens reported suspicious persons who "looked German." Locals talked of certain oil dealers smuggling gasoline to U-boats waiting offshore. Strange lights flashing from a water tower near Manteo were reported several times.

As far as is known, only two verified landings of German spies on the East Coast occurred. On June 13 four German agents/saboteurs came ashore on Amagansett Beach on Long Island. The English-speaking spies, armed with explosives and carrying U.S. dollars, had been charged by German Intelligence with blowing up bridges, railroads, munitions plants, and power plants. Just as the German agents struggled out of the surf, they were surprised by a coast guard lookout who raced back to his command post and reported the landing. The FBI became involved and barely one week later arrested the four men after Georg Johann Dasch turned himself in. On June 17, 1942, four more spies came ashore unobserved on Ponte Vedra Beach, Florida. Because of Dasch's defection, the FBI captured them as well. All of the enemy agents were tried and convicted. Two of them, including Dasch, received long prison terms; the other six were executed.[22]

The landings in Long Island and in Florida got national publicity and set off even more rumors on the North Carolina coast. The people in Ocracoke and other barrier islands who lived close to the ocean where enemy submarines lurked and enemy agents might be expected to appear experienced occasional bouts of near hysteria. Blanche Styron of Ocracoke reported that people "were frightened to death. And if we saw anything strange, any strange people, we would think they were Germans."[23] Several unfounded reports claimed that local fishers were assisting German subs by selling them supplies. Citizens with German names and backgrounds immediately came under suspicion. A schoolteacher of German descent on Ocracoke was suspected of being a spy. Well-intentioned citizens followed him around, waiting for him to rendezvous with the enemy. He was eventually forced to leave the island. A woman named Alice Hoffman, also of German descent, faced the same problem. The gossip about her was ludicrous. Some locals accused her of refueling German submarines from the dock of her home, where the water was approximately six feet deep. The FBI investigated some five hundred such reports, all of which were unsubstantiated.[24]

One of the more amusing incidents occurred when a car was reported to be flashing its lights in Morse code toward an unseen German U-boat off the coast. Two local men went to investigate and found a car with its red brake lights blinking on and off. The two intrepid and vigilant locals sneaked up on the car and discovered, to their chagrin, a young couple making love. In the heat of passion the young man's foot kept hitting the brake pedal, thus producing the blinking lights.[25] No German spies were found on this occasion. There is no indication that any submarine or German seamen (other than the eight spies) ever landed on American soil. Much of what authorities suspected might be enemy sabotage was a result of accidents, vandalism, imagination, or personal quarrels.

One of the more perplexing factors for the U.S. coastal defense was the public's ignorance of or unwillingness to adhere to blackout regulations. The shore lights unquestionably aided the-U-boats by putting the tankers in sharp profile against the night glow of city lights. The navy, the coast guard, and the state government constantly reminded citizens of their duty to restrict lighting at night. From 6:15 p.m. to 7:15 a.m. all citizens within twenty miles of the coast were required to turn off all outside lights, to use blackout curtains to limit light from within the home, and to black out their headlights when traveling at night. Some drivers used black tape to cover the headlamps, leaving only a small slit for light or used only parking lights while driving. Autos were warned to keep off the beaches at night.

The authorities, however, were very late in recognizing and reacting to the potential danger from the backlighting effect from shore lights. Four months after the Battle of the Atlantic began, numerous lights from the coast still helped the German U-boats spot their prey. Frank Dinwiddie, upset by the public's lax response to the lights, wrote Governor Broughton to complain:

> At the moment of the attack [the freighter *Byron B. Benson* was sunk just 7 ½ miles off of Currituck Banks], a number of bright lights were burning along the ocean front, particularly at the Nags Head Casino where a Saturday night dance was in progress. Numerous cars, coming to and from the casino, swung their headlights over the ocean in turning around. The lights of Manteo, more than four miles from the sea, produced a brilliant glow in the sky. Any of these light sources seemed sufficient to have brought a ship several miles at sea into clear silhouette as an excellent target for the enemy. Within a few minutes after the attack last Saturday night, the bright lights facing the sea were turned out and the casino thereafter showed dim blue lights; but I call that locking the barn after the horse is gone.[26]

Although the blackout regulations were difficult to enforce, numerous arrests were made in Beaufort and Morehead City. The mayor of Beaufort, acting as a civil defense official, often went to the shore to ensure that the lights from his town could not be seen from the water. Civil Defense workers constantly scrutinized the entire coastline to enforce compliance. An inspection trip by Civil Defense officials in May 1942 resulted in a recommendation to reduce the lights from the Wilmington shipyards (on a 24-hour work schedule), Camp Davis, Carolina and Wrightsville beaches, and cars on the highway.[27]

A major factor in forcing compliance with blackout regulations was the local population's determination to persuade or force transgressors to obey the law. The police arrested Edwin Williams of Fairmont, N.C., after he "unlawfully" refused to comply with blackout regulations by permitting his lights to burn after the air raid signal. Williams repeatedly rejected entreaties from neighbors and law enforcement officers to extinguish his lights and used "profane and indecent language" in refusing. A crowd of around fifty onlookers gathered at his house yelling at him and trying to make Williams obey the law. Due to public pressure, Williams was finally taken away and placed in jail. There were other examples of local vigilante action. Windows in two stores in Fayetteville were smashed by angry crowds when they noticed the lights on during curfew.[28]

The *Raleigh News and Observer* had an immediate response to the incidents in Fairmont and Fayetteville. In an editorial the paper denounced the man who defiantly refused to put out his lights. Williams deserved the public indignation and the charges filed against him by the police. The paper applauded those individuals who smashed out the lights of the store windows in Fayetteville. The owners of the stores had "their own carelessness of the community safety to thank for the property losses which they suffered." The *News and Observer* admitted that the blackout was just a test and that there was little likelihood of an enemy attack, but these displays of public indifference undermined public safety. Any man who willingly refused to turn out his lights "is in the same category as the man who poisons the community's drinking water. Indeed, his lights might lead as directly to the death of others."[29]

The newspaper's intolerant editorial reflected some of the shrill, excessively patriotic fervor that ignored political and social reality and condoned vigilante action. Fervent chauvinism could violate individual rights and lead to extreme behavior by some citizens. Since the blackout was a test and there was virtually no chance of an attack on Fairmont, comparing someone who refused to turn off his lights with someone who poisoned the city's water supply is unfair at best and dangerous at worst. The great majority of citizens cooperated fully with the blackout laws and encouraged their neighbors to do so.

In retrospect, it seems illogical for Civil Defense groups in the state to prepare the populace for a possible Nazi air raid. German airplanes could barely make the round-trip flight to bomb England: how could they possibly bomb any American target? It was prudent to enforce the blackout law on the coast and around military bases such as Fort Bragg, but there was no chance whatsoever that the Nazis would bomb Fairmont or Southern Pines. That conclusion did not deter Civil Defense officials.

The North Carolina Emergency War Powers Proclamation Number VI gave the state the authority to order blackouts and to initiate essential measures to ensure public safety. In almost every community Civil Defense workers enforced the blackout laws and quickly organized citizens to take steps to prevent a possible attack. While the defense initiatives might seem delusional, the groups argued that the activities gave citizens a sense of participation and increased an awareness of the duty and patriotism needed for the all-out effort to win the war.[30]

The Turnaround: Destroyers, Convoys, Civil Air Patrol, and the "Hooligan Navy"

State and local enforcement of blackout regulations helped significantly, but the United States needed to turn the tide against the U-boat threat after the virtually defenseless reaction to the great loss of life and cargo in early 1942. As the losses continued to mount and threatened an Allied victory, the U.S. Navy had to make a more effective response.

The responsibility for the defense of the Atlantic coast had been given to an experienced navy man, Rear Admiral Adolphus "Dolly" Andrews. From the beginning Andrews had an impossible task. He was expected to protect some 1,500 miles of coastline with limited assets. He set up headquarters in New York City with a communications center and a plotting room but little else. He commanded 20 ships, some of them no more than barges, and 103 obsolete aircraft. Early on Andrews requested that Admiral Ernest J. King, commander-in-chief of the U.S. Fleet, supply him with much needed help, because the navy had destroyers, cruisers and other ships operating out of Norfolk, Virginia. King did not want those forces used for coastal defense; he wanted the ships deployed in the North Atlantic, where he felt the U-boat threat was greatest. King told Andrews to make do with what he had. Andrews used his limited force to patrol important harbors and designated two army planes for daily sweeps over the ocean. But the planes had virtually no chance of ever spotting a submarine. Andrews had only one large antisubmarine ship, the *Dione*, to patrol the entire area around Cape Hatteras.[31]

Admiral Doenitz recognized that the United States deployed "antisubmarine patrols, but they were wholly lacking in experience. Single destroyers, for example, sailed up and down the traffic lanes with such regularity that the U-boats were quickly able to work out the timetable being followed. They knew exactly when the destroyer would return."[32]

As the devastating sinkings continued unabated, Governor Broughton made a personal visit to the coastal defenses. After reading "reliable" reports, he wrote a letter to Frank Knox, the secretary of the navy. Broughton contended that the defenses against submarines off the coast of North Carolina were "wholly inadequate and frequently inept and there is a shocking lack of coordination between army, navy, coast guard and air forces." He urged that a conference be held with those responsible for defense operations as a way to provide a more effective barrier to the German submarines. The governor wrote Knox that the U-boats were menacing the state's coastal waters with "impunity" and "causing tremendous tanker losses and overrunning the hospital and medical facilities on the eastern coast of North Carolina."[33] In addition to demanding better coastal defenses, Governor Broughton also rushed medical supplies, new equipment, and an ambulance to Southport to assist in the care of injured survivors of merchant ships.[34]

The navy slowly responded, partly due to the attitude of Admiral King. He still wanted to use his destroyers to protect vessels in the North Atlantic, claiming that he did not have enough destroyers to allocate to the U.S. coastal defense. King had accepted the advice of the British that the convoy system was the best method of protecting merchant ships in the Atlantic, but he thought the convoy system would not work on the American seacoast. Unlike the situation in the Atlantic, surface and air support on the east coast could be quickly summoned to the site of the attack and take care of the U-boats. What King overlooked was that the U-boats operated independently in the United States and would sink a ship and disappear before a distress signal could be sent. Even if a call for help occurred, the navy and coast guard had inadequate resources to respond and could not get there in time.

Despite limited resources and insufficient assistance from the U.S. Navy, the coast guard and local volunteer groups did the best they could. The coast guard created a mounted unit that patrolled the beaches between Wilmington and Jacksonville, North Carolina. These hard-riding horsemen were trained in observation techniques and in guerrilla warfare. The commander of the unit described their major function as follows. "We hope our beaches are never invaded, but if they are, mounted patrolmen are going to know how to put up a delaying fight which will enable civilians to evacuate the beaches and enable our armed forces to move in."[35]

Seaman First Class Billy Sutton had been posted by the U.S. Coast Guard to the beach south of Wilmington to search out submarines and prevent saboteurs. For six hours each day his mounted unit patrolled the beach fifty miles south and fifty miles north of Wilmington. Sutton reported that he was acutely aware of Wilmington's vulnerability, with its airfield, shipyard, and Ethyl Dow plant, and carried out his patrol with extreme caution.[36]

Another temporary expedient employed in shoreline defense was the organization of an emergency "civilian" navy—the Coast Guard Picket Patrol, also known as the "Hooligan Navy." Numerous civilians voluntarily deployed their pleasure boats to help in the fight against enemy raiders.

The group included amateur admirals, professors, college students, business people, deep sea charter operators, ex-bootleggers—anyone who could steer and handle a boat. To be eligible for the Picket Patrol, the private ships had to be able to be at sea at cruising speed in good weather for a period of forty-eight hours.

By April 1942 some seventy vessels were equipped with radios, direction finders, small arms, at least one machine gun, life rafts, and flares. The Picket Patrol initially carried four 300-pound depth charges, but the civilian captains were untrained in warfare. The navy cautioned them that depth charges should never be set to less than fifty feet, the speed of the boats should never be less than ten knots when the depth charge was dropped, and depth charges should never be dropped in water less than one hundred feet deep. It never wanted to get a message from its untrained Picket Patrol: "Sighted sub, sank self." After some unhappy experiences, the navy relieved the Picket Patrol of its depth charges. The concept of arming untrained skippers driving Chris-Craft boats was an untested and dangerous idea at best. Dropping depth charges from small pleasure craft would almost certainly never sink a sub but would invariably endanger the neophyte sailors.

The Coastal Picket Patrols operated out of thirty bases along the Atlantic Seaboard, each base commanded by a coast guard officer. The U.S. Coast Guard preferred experienced skippers manning fifty- to seventy-foot sailboats for the fleet, because the sailboats did not need fuel and could cruise noiselessly without vibration and thus would not attract the attention of the U-boats. One officer explained: "You could sneak up on 'Jerry' with a stitch of canvas."[37] The Hooligan Navy was of limited utility, but its members braved storms and infrequently rescued shipwreck victims and occasionally came up with an important sighting of a submarine or a shipwreck. Their main value was in keeping the U-boats underwater, where the subs' speed and maneuverability were strictly limited. On a number of occasions U-boats were seen diving at the first sight of a picket boat. The submarines knew they had been spotted and that their position would be relayed to the nearest destroyer, so they submerged and changed location.

The Coast Guard's Naval Air Station near Elizabeth City was an integral part of the defense structure. The coast guard pilots were assigned to search for U-boats on a daily basis and to report their findings back to the navy, which in turn would dispatch destroyers to the scene. The pilots accompanied merchant marine convoys and flew up and down the length of the convoy, reporting on U-boats, ships in distress, or any vessel that had wandered away from the convoy.

Perhaps the pilots' most valuable service was to search for survivors of torpedoed ships or ships in distress. It was extremely difficult to pick out small ships or lifeboats from overhead, especially when the sea was rough or in overcast conditions. When the aircraft spotted survivors, they would fly low to determine the status of the passengers and then report their findings to headquarters. The pilot stayed on site until help arrived. Occasionally an urgent rescue would lead to a landing by a seaplane and the transfer of food or medicine to those in need. If the landing was dicey, they could drop a packet known as a "food bomb." The rescue container included two rations of food, seven cans of water, several packs of cigarettes, a first aid kit, and, perhaps most important, a pint of whiskey.[38]

Desperate for help in combating the U-boat threat, the U.S. Navy even went so far as to establish a $6 million blimp base near Elizabeth City. The lighter-than-air dirigibles were helpful in sub chasing because they were able to hover over a certain territory, while airplanes had to fly past the target area.[39]

Another example of volunteer dedication and commitment in aid of coastal defense came from North Carolina's flying volunteers, the Civil Air Patrol (CAP). Established on December 1, 1941, the Civil Air Patrol organized the nation's civilian pilots, weaving them into the national defense as a type of "flying minutemen." The flying volunteers served in the state wing of the CAP under the control of North Carolina's Office of Civilian Defense. The CAP set up two patrol bases, first at Manteo then at Beaufort, helping close a gap in the navy's defense system. From 1942 to 1943 the North Carolina CAP became involved in escorting merchant vessels, antisubmarine patrol duty, and assisting sailors in distress.

CAP pilots served on a volunteer basis and did not receive draft deferments because of their assignment. The aviators used their own planes. When they were engaged in emergency services, the federal government reimbursed them for their time and use of fuel and equipment. Otherwise almost all other expenses were borne by the civilian pilots. The CAP required applicants to have a background check, to take an oath of allegiance, and to provide proof of citizenship. The North Carolina wing had 762 members and approximately 400 aircraft that flew in a two-plane formation, often only a few hundred feet above the waves. One of the Civil Air Patrol's major contributions was to force U-boats to submerge, thus restricting their range and operational capabilities.

Figure 5.1. Blimp on coast patrol. The U.S. Navy used blimps to help spot German U-boats. Courtesy of the State Archives of North Carolina.

Until the state CAP ceased to function on August 1, 1943, the pilots volunteered their time and skills, lent the military their expensive personal property, and risked their future to save lives and to help combat the U-boat danger.[40]

As the successful U-boat attacks reached a crescendo, newspaper agitation, pressure from the British, and letters from public officials such as

Governor Broughton forced Admiral King to relent and provide Admiral Andrews with seven fleet destroyers (although he had asked for fifteen). In the beginning, however, the destroyers were sent out on patrol rather than being used in a convoy. Because of the U-boats' speed and underwater capability, the destroyers were rarely able to make contact with the subs.

When losses became intolerable, the navy finally made some significant changes in the coastal defense structure. Shipping was restricted only to daylight travel and the vessels spent the night in protected anchorages such as Charleston and Cape Lookout. Submarine nets and Mark 6 contact mines were placed across the entrance to the harbor to prevent the U-boats from sneaking in at night. In this modified convoy system, known as the "Bucket Brigade," ships took four days to make the trip from Jacksonville, Florida, to New York. This strategy, while an improvement, also proved inadequate. In May 1942 the navy finally moved to a full-scale convoy system, with the average convoy being made up of twenty-one ships and five escorts. This simple convoy system eventually eliminated most of the U-boat threat to Allied shipping.[41]

The *Icarus*, the *Dione*, and the *YP389*

During the period from January to May 1942 the navy and the coast guard made a valiant effort to halt the U-boats' rampage. The *Dione*, the 165-foot coast guard cutter that had been built to combat smugglers in the Prohibition era, was constantly on patrol using sonar to locate subs. The ship spent most of its time rescuing crewmen from torpedoed tankers and protecting the Bucket Brigade. The *Dione* dropped tons of depth charges but never achieved its goal of sinking a submarine.

Its counterpart the *Icarus*, another sub chaser, was more successful. The German sub U-352, having spotted the *Icarus* on patrol, fired a torpedo at close range. Upon hearing the explosion of the torpedo, Captain Hellmut Rathke raised up his periscope and discovered to his horror that the torpedo had missed the *Icarus* and had exploded in the seabed in shallow water. The captain realized that he had been spotted when he saw a fast armed cutter coming directly for him. The U-352 submerged quickly but was in shallow water and had little room to maneuver. The cutter *Icarus* raced to the location of the last sighting of the sub and fired five depth charges. The explosions hit home, knocking out the submarine's instruments and the electric motors. The U-352 played dead, hoping that the cutter did not know the U-boat had been hit. The *Icarus* unleashed a second attack of three depth charges that ruptured the buoyancy tank. Seriously damaged and having few options, the U-352 surfaced.

When the U-boat emerged from the sea, Rathke opened the conning tower hatch. He saw that the tower bridge was badly damaged and that the U-boat was barely afloat. When the crew members scrambled out onto the deck, the *Icarus* opened fire with its machine guns and 3-inch deck gun, hitting and killing several Germans. The captain and the remainder of the crew dove into the water and swam away from the boat as the U-352 sank from view with twelve of its crew still aboard. The cutter's gunners continued firing while the Germans, flailing helplessly in the water, called for mercy. The *Icarus* finally ordered a cease-fire. But it did not have the authority to pick up prisoners, so the ship began to move away while radioing headquarters for instructions. The navy eventually gave Captain Maurice D. Jester permission to pick up survivors and take them to Charleston.

Captain Rathke, after asking that his wounded be taken in first, was the last of his crew on shore. He sternly cautioned his men not to speak with anyone and to maintain order and discipline. Rathke, a hard-core Nazi, refused to converse with the coast guard crew. He remained arrogant, proud, and unyielding until the day he was released at the end of the war. When the German prisoners left the ship in Charleston, Rathke marched them down the plank and had them stand at attention until American intelligence officers took them away for interrogation. These thirty-three combatants would be the first German POWs in America. Naval Intelligence learned very little from the crew, who refused to divulge any tactical, technical, or mechanical details except that the submarine had dived repeatedly to avoid patrol aircraft and that they enjoyed American jazz from U.S radio stations broadcast over the ship's loudspeaker.[42]

Another example of heroic action on the part of an undermanned defense force was the U.S. Navy's *YP389*, a Boston trawler pressed into service at the beginning of the war. Although equipped with a 3-inch gun on the deck, two .30-caliber machine guns, and four depth charges, it was totally inadequate as a warship. The *YP389* was slow, even by trawler standards, and had no underwater detection equipment. To attack a U-boat it would have to spot one, highly unlikely, and then try to catch it, virtually impossible. As a desperation measure, Admiral Andrews sent the *YP389* and its sister ship, *YP388*, to patrol off Cape Hatteras—perhaps they could locate a sub or rescue stranded seamen.

Captain Horst Degen and his U-701 crew lay in wait directly in the path of the approaching trawlers. Nauseated from diesel fumes and a summer temperature in the nineties, the U-701 crew was exhausted and morale was low. When Degen spotted the *YP389*, the frustrated captain decided to wipe out the little ship. He surfaced and opened up with his .30-caliber machine guns and his 88-mm guns. The guns tore up big chunks of the trawler's deck and wounded some of the crew. Captain R. J. Phillips gamely fired back but knew that he was outgunned. He tried to run for it, maneuvering frantically to prevent the U-boat from getting a clear shot, but the U.S. ship made only seven knots and the sub made eighteen knots. After dodging for about an hour, Phillips realized that the U-boat captain was intent on getting a kill at all costs. Phillips ordered the crew to abandon his badly battered ship and the *YP389* sank shortly thereafter. The eighteen surviving crew members (six had been killed) managed to stay alive until the morning, when they were picked up by a coast guard vessel. The *YP389* had been woefully unsuited to the task given it, but the ship's crew showed pluck and guts and fought back under withering fire.[43]

The *Bedfordshire* Incident

In February 1942, alarmed by the large number of its ships being sunk off the east coast of the United States, the British government offered to lend the U.S. Navy twenty-four antisubmarine corvettes that had been used in British home waters and were suitable for patrol. The U.S. Navy did not have enough patrol vessels, so it welcomed the British offer. While America had been providing Lend Lease supplies and fifty destroyers to England over the past two years, now the British had the opportunity to reciprocate.

At 170 feet long, the corvettes were about half the size of a destroyer, had a crew of four officers and thirty-three enlisted men, and were armed with a 4-inch deck gun, two .50-caliber twin machine guns, and approximately 100 depth charges. The ships arrived off the coast of North Carolina in April 1942 and spent the rest of April and May in endless patrolling in various locations from Cape Lookout, N.C., to Norfolk, Va.

In May 1942 two North Carolinians, including Aycock Brown of Ocracoke, met two officers of the *Bedfordshire* in a crowded restaurant in Norfolk. Brown admired the unusual gold watch and black onyx ring worn by the bearded sublieutenant, Thomas Cunningham. This chance encounter would add an unusual twist to the story of the ship and its ill-fated crew.

On May 10, 1942, the *Bedfordshire* left its dock at Morehead City for another routine patrol. The German U-558, under the command of Captain Gunther Krech, spotted the British ship. The submarine surfaced and attacked. His target was not a fat tanker with a load of oil, but U-boat commanders were rated on the tonnage they sank and any prey was a good one. Krech's first torpedo missed the *Bedfordshire* but the second one hit squarely amidships with a tremendous explosion, catapulting the ship into the air and sinking it almost immediately. No one survived the blast. The ship's fate would not be learned until after the war, when a study of the German U-boat records explained the mystery of its demise.

On May 14, while patrolling the shore at Okracoke Island, two coast guardsmen discovered the bodies of two unidentified British seamen washed on shore. Aycock Brown was called to help identify the bodies and instantly recognized the watch and ring and the bearded visage of sub-lieutenant Thomas Cunningham. The navy later identified the other body as telegraph operator Stanley Craig. The two men were given a military funeral by the U.S. Coast Guard. The funeral was solemn and respectful, honoring two brave men from another country who had come to protect American lives and property. The Union Jacks that draped the two coffins had been supplied earlier by Thomas Cunningham.

A week later two additional unidentified members of the *Bedfordshire* were discovered. The U.S. Navy decided to bury all four crew members in a small cemetery on Ocracoke. On December 27, 1942, the navy and the coast guard put up four white crosses to mark the graves and gave the British sailors a final farewell by firing three volleys and playing taps. The remains of the four British seamen's fellow crewmen still rest in the ship's underwater grave.

With the cooperation of the citizens of Okracoke and the United States government, the small burial plot was deeded to the British government and is now an official English cemetery, where the British flag flies continuously. A bronze plaque at the site pays tribute to all the British seamen who died defending America's coast. The plaque is inscribed with poet Rupert Brooke's memorable lines:

> If I should die think only this of me
> That there's some corner of a foreign
> field that is forever England.[44]

By August 1942, after a long and tortuous struggle with great loss of life and the destruction of precious tons of supplies, the U.S. Navy defeated the Nazi U-boat menace off the east coast of America. In July–August 1942 only one vessel was sunk and two German U-boats were sent to the bottom of the sea. Admiral Doenitz finally recognized that the battle in America had been lost and moved his U-boats to other war zones. Nonetheless, Operation Drumbeat had done considerable damage to ships plying their trade near the Barrier Islands. Numbers vary widely according to source, but somewhere between seventy-eight and eighty-seven merchant vessels and navy ships were sunk off the North Carolina shoreline.

The impact on the Allied war effort was devastating. Michael Gannon concluded in *Operation Drumbeat* that the U-boat assault in United States waters in 1942 "constituted a greater strategic setback for the Allied war effort than did the defeat at Pearl Harbor." He pointed out that the aircraft carriers were not at Pearl Harbor and that the other ships lost there had been quickly replaced. The loss of nearly 400 ships and cargoes, in the Battle of the Atlantic and off the eastern coast of the United States, "threatened to sever Great Britain's lifeline and to cripple American war industries." Gannon declared that it was difficult to replace the lost materiel on the merchant ships. If the onslaught had continued unchecked, it could have threatened the entire American war effort.[45]

Fortunately for the Allies, the navy, after a slow reaction to danger off the east coast, was able to bring its might to bear in the end. The U.S. Navy took advantage of assistance from the Civil Air Patrol, the Hooligan Navy, the mounted coast guard, the British corvettes, coast guard cutters and aircraft, blimps, and the formal installation of strict blackout regulations. The navy first adopted a limited convoy, the Bucket Brigade, with safe havens and finally went to what the British had advised from the beginning: a full convoy system. When the U.S. Navy had produced enough destroyers to constitute an effective defense system, the U-boats became less proficient.

By August 1942 life had not quite returned to normal on the Barrier Islands. The war was far from over, but the locals did not have to witness any more horrific explosions and view the bodies of badly burned survivors.

"MAKE DO WITH LESS"

RATIONING, WAR BONDS, AND VICTORY GARDENS

World War II did not change human needs and desires, but it significantly altered the way in which American citizens went through their daily lives. Military needs resulted in a severe metal shortage, depleting the country's inventory of automobiles, stoves, refrigerators, tires, and other durable goods. When the nation's demand for metal and other essential goods increased as the fighting continued, the War Production Board (WPB) took over control of rationing all strategic materials.

The WPB's decision to ration aluminum, tin, rubber, and oil led to a drastic reduction in the production of consumer goods from vacuum cleaners to cars to tin cans. The consumer industry, starved for raw materials necessary for production, had to commit to defense work, close down, or convert to alternative business options. Members of the buying public had to modify their choices and options. By the end of 1942 metals and numerous other goods that had been generally taken for granted were severely limited. America had now entered the age of national rationing.

The writer Paul Gallico described the changes that occurred in the spring of 1942. "That was the spring that women took to wearing slacks in the street . . . , old toothpaste tubes had to be turned in for new ones, men's trousers were commanded to be cuff less. . . . That was the spring we first heard about sugar rationing, with gasoline rationing to come. Ice cream was reduced to ten flavors and civilian suffering really hit its stride when the War Production Board banned the use of metal for asparagus tongs, beer mugs, spittoons, bird cages, cocktail shakers, hair curlers, corn poppers and lobster forks."[1]

While the Office of War Mobilization organized industry and labor to produce the goods needed to fight the war, the federal government had to manage the civilian economy. As the economy heated up and unemployment was reduced, the wartime government feared rampant inflation due to the scarcity of many essential products and the government's high demand for wartime purchases. Thus the federal government organized a bewildering variety of government agencies to extend controls over prices, wages, rents, resources, and spending in order to prevent an inflationary spiral.

President Franklin Roosevelt explained his proposed rationing plan to the people and the Congress in his "Cost Of Living" address on April 27, 1942. "It is obviously fair that where there is not enough of an essential commodity to meet all civilian demands, those who can afford to pay more for the commodity should not be privileged over others who cannot. I am confident that as to many basic necessities of life, rationing will not be necessary because we shall strive to the utmost to have an adequate supply. But where any important article becomes scarce, rationing is the democratic, equitable solution."[2]

Determined to avoid the economic mistakes of World War I, President Roosevelt created the National Defense Advisory Commission (NDAC). This agency, charged with retarding inflation while encouraging the production of goods, was authorized to begin the preliminary planning for price controls and rationing. The general plan was to control the allocation of strategic materials at the production level by disbursing scarce materials to industries involved in war production. At the consumer level the agency would establish price controls and a system for rationing scarce products.[3]

Management of the civilian economy would prove to be more difficult, and much more unpopular, than the control of war production. By regulating prices, wages, rents, and supplies, the concept of big government seemed to many to deny the fundamental American right to spend money without limit, to charge whatever rent the market allowed, and to determine the prices for their retail and agricultural goods and services. Americans perceived, often correctly, that any system of bureaucratic control would fall victim to favoritism, inequity, inefficiency, and violations of the law.[4]

In April 1941 Roosevelt established by executive order the Office of Price Administration and Civilian Supply (OPA). The avowed purpose of the agency was to prevent "price spiraling, rising costs of living, profiteering and inflation" as well as to limit any inequitable distribution of goods. The OPA had the power to establish and enforce price ceilings on all consumer goods as well as to establish a national system of rationing any consumer goods that were limited in quantities.[5] This level of government regulation was unheard of, but demand was exceeding supply and something had to be done. Citizens understood the need to control inflation and to allocate scarce goods, but this intrusion was far too Draconian for many individuals. The OPA was to have a controversial and complicated time in allotting goods and serving as an inflation fighter.

Prices

In the beginning ration boards were established in each of the forty-eight states. More than 30,000 volunteers were recruited to handle the extraordinary amount of paper work necessary to control the prices of 90 percent of the goods sold in more than 600,000 retail stores in the nation. In the introductory phase of rationing, the OPA issued a series of ration books to each man, woman, and child in the United States. By the end of the war, nearly every item eaten, worn, consumed, or lived in by Americans was rationed or regulated. "It was the most concerted attack on wartime inflation and scarcity in the nation's history and by and large, it worked."[6]

The agency implemented price ceilings on most goods and services (farm prices were exempted) in April 1942. The OPA set the ceilings so that the highest price for goods or services could not exceed the highest price for those goods in March 1942. From the outset the OPA found it difficult to stabilize price controls on consumer goods, as businesses found ways around the regulations by changing the packaging, style, or content of a product and claiming that it was new and thus did not fall under the price freeze.

Although the overall direction of policies came from Washington, the ration boards (the price panels) made decisions at the local level. These panels were composed of local business people who volunteered for the arduous task of issuing a series of ration books to all Americans. The OPA had a limited number of investigators at both the state and local level, but it was able to uncover violations partly because many of the illegal activities were reported by concerned citizens who resented their neighbors getting a product while they went without. To aid the process of keeping prices down, housewives were asked to take the Victory Pledge: "I will not buy anything above the ceiling price, no matter how much I want it."[7]

Local price panels in Charlotte held hearings on reported violations of the price ceilings and convicted scores of merchants and companies of disobeying the rules. When a violation occurred, the panel first tried to educate the offender about the need for price controls and appeal to the individual's sense of patriotism to rectify the situation. Next the panel asked the offending company to negotiate a settlement. If the violator refused, the panel had the authority to fine the miscreant or, in rare cases, close down a company. The price panel fined the owners of Raymond's Department Store $750 for selling nylon hose at $2.75 per pair, $1.10 over the ceiling price, and docked the Sanitary Grill $150 for selling cigarettes and chewing gum at pennies above the ceiling price.[8]

The heavy fines were mainly invoked to get the attention of other merchants and persuade them that the OPA was serious about punishing those who disobeyed the law. In reality, enforcement was impossible. There were too many merchants to watch and too many consumers who were willing to pay a higher price to get the goods that they needed and wanted. Black market activity was in full swing throughout the war, as in any such situation. Individuals looking to make a quick profit would purchase goods at the regular price and then resell the goods in their homes or on a street corner to those willing to pay the inflated price.

Wages

To control inflation across the board, an equitable policy toward wages was also needed. To offset the rise in living costs, the National War Labor Board allowed a 15 percent increase in hourly wage rates from January 1, 1941, until May 1942. Although wage increases were regulated after May 1942, laborers could increase income by working overtime and through incentive pay, job upgrades, and new fringe benefits. The formula helped curb the rise in wages. By 1943 the OPA had generally succeeded in bringing inflation under control, with the consumer price index increasing only about 4 percent from 1943 to 1945.[9]

Housing

One of the more difficult areas for the OPA to control was the housing market. Because of price controls and the scarcity of new civilian housing, a limited supply of rental housing was available. The influx of new workers coming to areas such as Wilmington, Fort Bragg, and other locations to work in shipbuilding, base construction, and war industries created a serious problem in terms of the lack of rental options. Prices rose steadily due to heightened demand, so the OPA intervened and ordered all prices frozen on May 18, 1942. All landlords were informed that the maximum rent that they could charge for any rental unit would be the price they charged as of April 1, 1942. Some rent controls were kept in place during the entire war, but from time to time when rental rates stabilized the OPA allowed the free market to determine prices.

The demand for rental housing grew steadily during the war. Despite homeowners' willingness to convert rooms and outbuildings to rental units, the requests outpaced supply. Landlords, who had to register with the Rent Control Office, bitterly opposed any rent controls and found various ways to subvert the regulations. Some landlords set up an illegal process whereby renters were asked to bid for units, with the highest bid winning. The OPA officials handled many complaints from renters about crooked landlords, including unwarranted evictions, overcharges, and a decrease in services. The OPA now and then succeeded in getting reimbursements for some renters in Charlotte and ordered a few rents to be lowered.[10]

In October 1942 Leon Henderson, the head of the OPA, decided to extend the rent control policy from defense areas to the entire nation. At the same time, the government cracked down on violators by placing restrictions on evicting tenants and forcing tenants to purchase units at exorbitant prices. Henderson said that the government was not going to permit "anyone to profiteer in rents at the expense of the defense workers, families of enlisted men, civilian personnel and local residents." Compliance with the government's rules meant that inflation would be held in check and that the cost of housing, usually the most important item in the family budget, would be kept stable through the remainder of the war.[11] The housing shortage never got any better until after the war ended, when the country experienced a huge housing construction boom.

Rationing

Throughout the war the governor, local politicians, administrators, and the military constantly repeated the mantra that victory in total war would require great sacrifices at home. According to Governor Brough- ton: "The American people and the people of North Carolina are willing to give their all to win victory over a cruel foe. It is going to take many sacri- fices, but we have a great tradition to uphold and we are going to uphold it."[12] Supreme Court justice Hugo Black and other speakers incessantly appealed to American pride and patriotism. Black repeated the view that in order to win the war the American people "must deny ourselves of daily necessities so that they can be donated to the services of those who so bravely fight on the battle fronts." Justice Black asked the citizens of the state to devote themselves to winning the war "ungrudgingly and with- out complaint."[13] Eleanor Roosevelt spoke at Lake Junaluska in July 1944 and reminded her listeners that the people of America could not shrink from their defense of democracy and their responsibility as the leading democracy in the world.[14] Many ordinary citizens agreed with the nation's leaders. Abel Warren wrote that complaining and criticizing the govern- ment during wartime amounted to insubordination and should not be tolerated. "We must shake off our complacency and indifference and settle down to the difficult task that is ahead."[15]

Helped significantly by positive comments from government officials and a generally supportive public, the OPA had good success with control- ling wages and rents, but its responsibility for rationing products proved to be more difficult and less popular. In 1942 the OPA implemented ten major rationing programs. The most important early decision was to ra- tion rubber supplies and gasoline. Later meat, coffee, sugar, butter, and shoes were rationed to meet military needs. These restrictions were espe- cially galling to many Americans because they involved some of the ba- sics of the good life—meat, sugar, and coffee. Americans were loath to do without these items that had always been abundantly available. Citizens now had money to spend for these products due to wartime employment, but the items were often not available. The average citizen was certain that any product shortages were due to foul-ups in Washington, OPA red tape, and the military's waste of goods.

Citizens objected to the confusing rules, regulations, and different types of rationing books and coupons. Members of the public often cir- cumvented the rules, especially when they observed others violating the law.[16] Hyman Katz from Wendell, N.C., typified the response of many citizens to the new regulations. Katz wrote to the *Raleigh News and Observer* that all citizens were willing to do their part in the prosecution of the war but complained that there were too many "loafers and expediters" and that price controls were unfair. He blasted the government bureaucracy for being "top heavy with long-haired professors from Harvard and Columbia" who were woefully lacking in common horse sense. Katz recognized the need for rationing to prevent inflation but noted that the people had a right to expect price controls based on equality and fairness.[17]

The penalties for violating rationing orders and regulations were severe and could go as high as $10,000 and ten years in prison. The ration books were not to be transferred and could be used only by the people to whom they had been issued. Any lost book was to be delivered to the nearest Ration Board. The more stringent penalties were seldom exacted, but the government recognized the need to provide some significant disincentives for potential violators of the law.[18]

The majority of individuals complied with government regulations on rationing most of the time, but some home-front Americans refused to go along at all. As expected, Americans tried various ways to circumvent the rules in their own self-interest. One effective way of overcoming ration restrictions was the widespread practice of hoarding. The government usually gave consumers a warning prior to rationing a product, so each warning led to panic buying as customers tried to purchase as much of the designated product as possible. When the OPA announced in Charlotte that shoes would be rationed, buyers went on a massive buying spree at downtown clothing stores. When President Roosevelt froze the production of silk, thousands of women mobbed department stores to purchase silk stockings. Lillian Spencer Steele of Greensboro remembered that "stockings made of nylon were so scarce that we would have to stand in line at Meyer's Department store to get two pair. If I got a run, I would take the stocking to a shoe shop . . . to get it repaired." Some girls, noted Steele, used leg paint to create the color of hosiery.[19] Although hoarding was not illegal, it violated the ethical aspects of rationing. Local officials condemned the "selfishness" of the hoarders and called on their patriotic impulses to resist panic buying.[20]

When rationing officially began in May 1942, all residents were required to divulge the amount of products (such as sugar) they had on hand. Stamps equivalent to the amount of the product that the consumer had on hand would be stripped from their ration books. Some individuals misrepresented the amount of sugar, meat, coffee, tires, gasoline, or shoes they had in order to avoid a shortage of the product.[21] Rather than lose ration stamps, citizens would simply not notify the authorities of the five pounds of sugar that they kept in the cupboard. Many did not see this as cheating because they had legally purchased the sugar.

John G. Thomas, reporting on the "ration front" for *State* magazine, roamed around North Carolina for three years observing the public's response to rationing. Thomas quickly learned that rationing was not liked by a liberty-loving public: "it is the only thing in the world that will turn the 'best' people into wartime violators of their country's regulations." He revealed the various ways in which citizens tried to circumvent the rules and get extra ration books. One farmer, reporting that a hog had eaten his gas rationing book, asked for a replacement. Some 200 citizens in Wilson claimed that they had never received their A books for gasoline because the books had been "lost in the mail."[22]

Naturally, it was difficult for the rationing boards to determine if the ration books had actually been destroyed or lost in the mail, because the holders had no proof of their loss. Some instances of neighborly favoritism and string pulling occurred, but the local Rationing Boards responded to requests for replacement of ration cards on a case by case basis, primarily making decisions on their opinion of the credibility and honesty of those making the claims. The hearings could be disruptive. On one occasion a wife in New York wrote a letter to the Ration Board asking it to reject her husband's request to replace a B gas coupon, because he only wanted the gas "to go out with other women."[23]

Black Market

Hoarding, however, was a minor issue as compared to the black market. With more spending money than in previous years, many consumers delved into the black market, where scarce products were illegally bought and sold. A black market developed for every rationed product, and huge profits could be made by enterprising and unscrupulous capitalists. Although any black market purchase was technically a violation of the regulations and a criminal act, millions of Americans took advantage of the opportunity to purchase goods that they could not otherwise obtain.

One study divulged that 25 percent of the population thought that black market activity was often justified. Purchasers convinced themselves that they were buying gas or sugar for the benefit of their family and thus that the activity was morally acceptable. While preaching patriotism and self-sacrifice, those who dabbled in the black market were selfishly undermining the system with their purchases. Small-scale violations were very common but usually limited in scope. Ration coupons were sold, traded, and counterfeited, while extra amounts of gas or food were purchased "off the books." Bribes were paid to grocers or store owners in order to get a very scarce item.[24]

There was a brisk black market in, of all things, Pullman reservations. With restrictions on gasoline and tires and with soldiers and their wives packing the trains, tickets were hard to come by. Some citizens, wallets bulging with war-stimulated greenbacks, wanted to vacation in Florida or to visit family and were willing to pay an inflated price for the opportunity. The black market even dealt in bubble gum and ice cream, as some parents were willing to pay more to keep their toddlers happy.[25]

With an unparalleled opportunity to make some easy money due to lax enforcement and customers willing to pay exorbitant prices, some large-scale crime flourished during rationing. Rings of thieves would steal or counterfeit massive numbers of coupons and easily dispose of them on the black market. Louis Williams, an ex-OPA employee and nine other men were convicted in Raleigh of brazenly stealing several thousand gas and sugar coupons from the local OPA office.[26] Although justice prevailed in this case, it was very difficult for the government to keep up with the large number of incidents. The OPA was most successful in capturing the criminals when someone turned in the lawbreakers.

The most fervent and frenzied black market activity was in gas and tires. The threat of long prison terms clearly did not deter the illegal trade. The FBI arrested a ring of twenty men in Charlotte for stealing gasoline intended for the army. The truck drivers carried full loads of gas for military use at Camp Sutton and Camp Mackall but delivered only part of their freight. The remainder of the fuel would be siphoned off for the black market. Thieves in the towns of Kenansville and Raeford stole gasoline coupons worth an astonishing $500,000 and sold them illegally.

The North Carolina State Bureau of Investigation lamented the fact that the illegal traffic in gasoline coupons in the state had become one of the largest in the country: the OPA named Raleigh as one of the most flagrant gasoline black market centers. The OPA called the counterfeiting of gasoline rationing coupons the "biggest criminal racket ever to blanket the country."[27] As time went on and war weariness set in, beating the system became common. One of the easiest ways to defeat the regulations was to obtain a friend or family member's unused coupons, a practice winked at by gas-station attendants because it produced no actual change in the amount of gas used.[28]

Because of the critical shortage of gas, the understaffed OPA turned to the FBI for help in stopping the counterfeiting and theft of gasoline coupons. The FBI helped stem the tide of criminal behavior. By the summer of 1944 about 1,300 persons had been convicted of black market activities in gas, some 4,000 gas stations had lost their licenses for being accomplices, and 32,500 motorists had their ration books revoked for using counterfeit or stolen coupons. Nonetheless, despite the FBI enforcement, officials estimated that some 25 percent of all gasoline sold in the nation was purchased with fake or stolen coupons.

Even more money could be made in tire theft. Drivers were willing to pay $50 for a new tire that had sold for $7. Penalties were severe: one thief, Eugene Alexander of Raleigh, received a fourteen-year sentence for stealing thirty-five tires.[29]

The rationing of tires was essential because the United States rubber supply from Malaysia and Borneo had been cut off. America had no synthetic rubber production. Tires wore out quickly in combat conditions, creating a huge demand by the military for more rubber. On January 5, 1942, the government declared that the general public could no longer purchase new tires for autos, trucks, or motorcycles. There were initially no restrictions on retreads, recapped tires, or used tires. Only people involved in essential services (doctors, nurses, police, and fire fighters) could buy new tires. Buses with ten or more passengers could purchase new tires, but not taxi drivers or traveling sales representatives. The crisis was so severe that the OPA even put a monthly quota on the sale of tires for essential vehicles. For the month of January 1942 a total of only 8,690 tires were allotted to the entire state of North Carolina.

Motorists could own five tires per vehicle. Anyone who had more than five tires was required to turn in all extra tires to the Rationing Board. As a result, recapping and retreading of tires became a booming business. Even so, car owners still had to get permission from the Rationing Board just to buy retreads.

The protests from traveling sales agents, cab drivers, and others dependent on automobile travel for their businesses were loud and vehement. They argued that driving a car was how they made their living and that without tires they would go bankrupt. Donald M. Nelson, head of the War Production Board, tried to quell the complaints by reminding citizens:

"We have just one job to do—to make enough war material to lick Hitler and the Japs and to do it in the shortest possible time."[30]

The drivers were not mollified by Nelson's statement and constantly lobbied Congress for a change in the rules. Traveling sales reps complained that they were engaged in the full-time selling of necessary products— food, medical supplies, fuel, clothing, farm equipment, and material for factories—and deserved more gas and tires. The group ended up hiring lobbyists and writing letters to Congress. As a result, the OPA agreed to provide commercial travelers a significant increase in gasoline and tires.[31]

As noted above, the profit on tires in the black market was so high that people risked long terms in jail for a big payoff. New tires were almost impossible for a thief to ignore. A wealthy woman parked her brand new car in a small town in eastern North Carolina but forgot to lock the door. She left her handbag, with a considerable amount of money and jewels, including diamonds, in plain view on the front seat. When she returned to her car, she found that her car had been stripped of her new tires, but her purse and jewelry were untouched. The thief left a scribbled note on the dash. "Lady: Roses are red, violets are blue, your diamonds sparkle but your tires are new."[32]

The traveling public suffered another setback when the sale of automobiles was rationed on February 2, 1942, but the real blow fell with the official imposition of a national plan for gasoline rationing. The government first restricted gasoline use in seventeen states on the east coast on May 15, 1942, and then set up rationing throughout the nation on December 1, 1942. The government stated that "it is clear beyond all argument that some curtailment in the use of gasoline for ordinary civilian purposes now is necessary." Consumers realized that cars could be repaired and one could occasionally find recapped tires, but without gasoline the car was useless.[33]

Prior to the inception of official rationing, the government encouraged drivers voluntarily to curtail their use of gasoline. The voluntary system failed miserably. Most Americans viewed the automobile as an essential part of the good life. People were willing to sacrifice in some areas, but not in the use of their cars. America was self-sufficient in oil and was a major exporter of oil products (the United States produced 64 percent of the world's crude oil) at the time, so people did not foresee a shortage of oil. Because of Americans' love of the car and what appeared to be an abundant supply of oil, citizens resented any controls on the sale of gasoline.

Due to vocal and active resistance to rationing, governmental restrictions and penalties had to be harsh. The country needed to get workers to factories and provide transportation for essential personnel to military bases and government offices. This goal could be met only if nonessential drivers were forced to limit their use of gas. The national speed limit was reduced to forty miles per hour to conserve fuel and tires (later reduced to thirty-five miles per hour). Each citizen in the seventeen state eastern zone (some 10 million drivers) was limited to an average of four gallons of gas per week, good for perhaps sixty miles of driving, a limitation that elicited further complaints.

There were initially five types of gasoline ration cards, allocated on the basis of the availability of gas and on the mileage driven by each operator. All drivers had to take their automobile registration card to the Rationing Board in order to receive a ration card. The basic A card went to most people, mainly those who drove less than six miles a week. An A card user could buy twenty-one gallons to use over a forty-seven-day period. If drivers could persuade the local rationing board that they had to have more fuel, they could be eligible for a supplementary ration card, the B card. B card holders, who drove from six to ten miles daily, got thirty-three gallons over the forty-seven-day period. When drivers received their gas coupon booklets, they were also given lettered windshield stickers corresponding to their official status—A, B, or C. At the gas pump the attendant would remove the appropriate number of coupons from the ration booklet and then write the car's license number on the coupons.

The most important and most coveted ration card was the C card, which allowed the unlimited use of gasoline. C cards were reserved for those involved in the war effort or doing work for the public welfare—such as doctors, nurses, and defense employees. The local ration board determined which individuals were eligible for the C card. The "emergency" category included police, fire fighters, and civil defense workers, along with a T ration for truckers. Although everyone yearned for a C card, about one-third of drivers got A cards. The rest were split between the B cards and the C cards. Buses, emergency vehicles, and other commercial vehicles were exempt from the rationing. All over America endless lines of streetcars, buses, and trains carried millions of passengers to engage in essential war work. These lines of transportation were vital for the war effort and had to be maintained at all costs.[34]

When rationing began in North Carolina (15,000 volunteers issued gas coupons to 650,000 drivers in the state), Governor Broughton urged all citizens to cooperate fully with government regulations.[35] The federal government produced a flood of posters and leaflets admonishing the public to adhere to the rules. In 1942 and 1943 most motorists complied with the regulations. Many drivers simply stayed at home, because there was not enough gas or tires for extra driving. Others rode bicycles and even horses, while some set up ride-sharing groups. Most working men and women walked, rode buses, or hired taxicabs to get around.[36]

With the demand for oil supplies at its highest level, on January 7, 1943, the government issued a fiat banning all pleasure driving on the eastern seaboard. Motorists were allowed to drive to such necessary activities as church, work, and school, but "Sunday" driving as well as driving to places of entertainment such as movies and ballgames was forbidden. Local police staked out theaters and movie houses and gave out thousands of tickets. The fine was significant: drivers lost their gas coupons. Banning pleasure driving was totally unenforceable, saved very little gas, and angered the driving public, who saw the fiat as petty and unfair. The ban was lifted after only three months.[37]

Overall the gas rationing system was probably as fair as could be expected. Despite some problems with illegal black market sales and often impenetrable red tape, the system worked fairly well. Civilian gas consumption fell 20 percent during 1942 and fell another 20 percent the next year. The number of miles driven from 1941 to 1943 had been reduced by one-third. Fewer cars were on the road, less rubber was being used, and the roads were safer with the lower speed limits. On August 15, 1945, with the war over, gas rationing came to an end. Chester Bowles, the last director of the OPA, told people that "you can take your gasoline and fuel oil coupons and paste them into your memory book." Now Americans could resume their love affair with the automobile. Many motorists had unpleasant memories of rationing, including one irate citizen who expressed his feelings in a poem.

> And when I die, please bury me
> Neath a ton of sugar, by a rubber tree.
> Lay me to rest in an auto machine,
> And water my grave with gasoline.[38]

Other rationing decisions affected the American people, of course, but none were more controversial or more of a threat to the pocketbook than gas and tire rationing. The OPA decided to ration shoes because civilians were buying shoes faster than manufacturers could make them and military personnel were wearing out shoes at an alarming rate. Every man, woman, and child was allotted three pair of shoes per year. The ban covered all shoes made of leather and all rubber-soled shoes. The government persuaded manufacturers to make only "sensible shoes" for civilian consumption. The shoes, when you could get them, came in only six colors, three of them a shade of brown.[39]

The complaints about shoe rationing were usually inconsequential, because most individuals did not have the resources to buy three pair of shoes per year. For one mother, however, the issue was a real problem. As ten-year-old Patricia Crumbley recalled: "My brother wore out his shoes so fast that she [her mother] was constantly trying to save enough coupons to buy him another pair and then would have trouble even finding them to buy." Members of the public accepted the limitations on shoes more easily but were constantly dissatisfied with the rationing of foodstuffs, especially sugar, butter, meat, and coffee.[40]

One of the more difficult decisions by the OPA was how to control the amount of badly needed food products available for civilian use. As with other items, the government wanted to hold down inflation and set up a fair and democratic distribution system. Regulators feared that wealthier citizens would rush in to buy up the food that others could not afford. If the poor were not adequately fed, they could not perform their work successfully. Inequities in the allocation system might lead to protests and social unrest.

Sugar was the first food product to be rationed, quickly followed by meat and other foods. A customer could buy one pound of sugar per week, but each person had to declare the amount of sugar on hand. If it was over two pounds, the excess had to be turned in to the OPA. Americans, innovative to the core, figured out how to live with less sugar. They baked less but also used saccharin, corn syrup, honey, and molasses as substitutes. America's insatiable desire for sweets never lessened. Americans in the 1940s literally consumed almost their weight in sugar—115 pounds per person, per year. Cagey retailers took full advantage of the situation. Some store owners required shoppers to purchase a certain amount of other grocery goods before they could buy sugar.

The government introduced a very complicated point system whereby each food item was assigned a point value that had been determined by demand and availability of the product. The OPA had a difficult job in juggling competing civilian, industrial, military, and governmental needs, but the voluntary boards generally functioned effectively by appealing to community spirit and patriotism. Citizens did not like government regu-

Figure 6.1. Rationing proved to be complex for some Americans. Here a local volunteer helps a customer. Note that the facility has run out of sugar. By permission of North Carolina Collection, UNC Library, Chapel Hill, N.C.

lation in any category but were angry and upset about control of such an important and personal commodity as food, especially sugar. Citizens accepted rationing as a necessary evil, but many thought that the government did not have the right to tell them what and how much to eat, even in wartime. This was especially true for meat and sugar, which were sources of energy, nutrition, and pleasure. A Gallup poll during the war asked Americans which one rationed product was the hardest to get along without. The top two items were sugar and meat.[41]

The government's control of meat distribution also brought widespread protests. In March 1943 Washington officials rationed meat, butter, cheese, edible fats, and oils. Each adult was limited to 2 ½ pounds of meat a week. The average family would get 4 ½ ounces of butter, 4 ounces of lard, 1 ⅓ ounces of margarine, 3 ounces of shortening, and 2 ounces of cheese for a week. The 1943 rationing decision left only a few nonrationed items—fresh fish, eggs, milk, cream, poultry, bread, cereals, fresh fruits, and fresh vegetables. In essence, the nonrationed items formed the bulk of the American diet during the war. As always, Americans made do and found acceptable substitutes for the foods that they could not get. The use of dried eggs in powdered form was a success: the mixture would not spoil and retained its nutritional value. Yellow coloring for shortening gave it the appearance of margarine, while bologna and Spam served as reasonable substitutes for red meat.

Spam, first introduced in 1937, is a precooked meat product made by Hormel Foods Corporation. Spam was a convenient meat option for the military because it was cooked in its own can and could be easily shipped. No refrigeration was necessary, because the canned Spam did not spoil in the tropical sun. Massive six-pound hams had been designed specifically for the military. Many families used Spam as the primary meat substitute because it was cheaper and more available than red meat. Various recipes provided cooks with options for a more delectable dish. One woman wrote her son that "Spam fried in butter makes a very tasty Easter dinner."[42] Many people who lived through the war found the use of Spam practical but had strongly negative views of the oft-derided item and refused to eat it ever again. One woman, after relying on Spam for too many nights, made a vow: "If this war was ever over, and rationing somehow became a thing of the past, and they could buy and eat whatever and however much they wanted, she would never, ever, eat spam again."[43]

But Patricia Crumbley, who recalled the war from the viewpoint of a ten-year-old girl, remembered how excited she was when her mother came back from the store with a can of Spam. "She would score the top, stick in a couple of cloves and bake it like a real ham. That was a great treat for the four of us for dinner. I still have a great fondness for spam." Crumbley also reminisced about her mother's constant quest for meat. When the family went grocery shopping, she seldom saw any meat in the display counter. "The store manager was a very fair man and would not hide meat for special customers, which we heard was done in some other stores." He would tell his customers when a meat shipment was arriving. On those days "my mother would make three or four trips hoping to get some meat. Sometimes she was lucky but often either the shipment did not come in or she missed it. It would sell out very rapidly."[44]

As was the case for many Americans, neighbors and friends were kind and helpful in an emergency. This support was especially true in case of a family illness or if children had to go without enough food. Everyone was in it together. Public concern for others, despite some selfish and criminal activities, was the standard form of behavior.

There was a public outcry when coffee was rationed and consumption was cut 25 percent in April 1942. Coffee was an essential part of daily life for most Americans, who had a difficult time facing the day without a jolt of java. Consumers had to declare the amount of coffee on hand. Each adult was allowed one pound of coffee every five weeks. Restaurants cut out refills and offered coffee only at breakfast. Americans could never determine why coffee had to be rationed: it was certainly not an essential foodstuff for the war effort, and there seemed to be plenty of coffee in Brazil. But, as in other instances, coffee drinkers made adjustments—they tried stretchers like chicory, rebrewed used grounds, and even utilized soybeans as a substitute.[45]

One coffee drinker expressed his views about the critical shortage of his favorite beverage. He was fine with gas and tire controls and was not upset about shoe rationing because he only used two pair each year. He did not eat much meat and the restriction on tin and canned goods was no problem, as his wife had put up plenty of goods at home. "But when they rationed coffee! Man! . . . Why couldn't we just trade our whiskey coupons for coffee? . . . Yours for an early victory and more coffee. B.T. Pickles, New Bern."[46] Apparently the government heard his plea: coffee rationing ended on July 29, 1943.

Despite all the rationing, most citizens in North Carolina carried on without much complaint. In fact, much of life went on as usual. A cursory glance at the *Raleigh News and Observer* on July 10, 1943, gives one a sense of some of the mundane events happening on that particular day. The Hudson-Belk department store had a sale advertised as "American Heroes Day." Despite gas restrictions, the North Carolina mountain counties advertised their beauty and nearness to large cities in the east. A sharp decline in automobile fatalities was reported. The number of weddings had increased during the past year. Hundreds flocked to the movie theaters to see the latest hit film. Churches had overflowing attendance, and preachers in pulpits all over town urged citizens to support the war.[47]

A critical issue for the federal government was how to pay for the most expensive war in history. By the end of 1941 the country had already spent over $64 billion, with most of the money going for munitions and equipment. A light tank cost $40,000; a medium bomber cost $250,000; one submarine cost $4 million; and the battleship *North Carolina* cost $70 million. The current revenue stream was obviously not sufficient. The question was whether to finance the war by taxes or by borrowing. Taxes would take money from the pockets of consumers and dampen purchasing power, thus keeping inflation in check. Borrowing, primarily through the sale of war bonds, would increase the nation's debt but would also siphon off some purchasing power. Roosevelt wanted to finance the war essentially through taxes, primarily on large personal and corporate incomes, but conservative reaction in Congress and opposition from business leaders forced him to relent and rely on both taxes and borrowing.

The first wartime tax in 1942 increased taxes on high personal incomes, corporate income, and excess profits while adding estate, gift, and excise taxes. By including taxes on incomes over $624, the nation increased the number of taxable incomes from 4 million to 28 million in 1942, with an additional increase to 43 million by 1945. Most full-time workers were paying income tax by then, which had not been the case prior to 1942, when very few Americans paid any income tax.

The initial revenue bill did not generate enough funds to finance the war, so FDR constantly asked Congress for additional allocations. Despite an urgent need to gear up for the war as quickly as possible, a conservative Congress provided less money than the president requested. Most of the early tax revenue came from large personal incomes that were taxed at a rather reasonable 12.2 percent. The government taxed the average wage earner at 3.4 percent. In July 1943, in an attempt to finance the war more efficiently, the federal government changed the way people paid their taxes with a pay-as-you-go withholding plan. Taxes were withheld from workers' pay each month, rather than having all the taxes paid at one time at the end of the year. This new option gave the Treasury better control of spending.

Other sources of revenue came from printing money, from savings plans, and from borrowing. The heavy borrowing increased the national debt from $49 billion in 1941 to $259 billion in 1945. This so-called deficit spending, or Keynesian economics, helped produce enough goods and services to win the war and also contributed to the full employment prosperity in place by the end of the war. The unemployment rate, 15 percent in 1940, had fallen to 1 percent in 1944.[48]

War Bond Drives

The United States Treasury launched its Defense Savings Program (later war bonds) on May 1, 1941, seven months before America's entrance into World War II. The government recognized that the cost of the inevitable war would be huge, so Congress raised the national debt limit and gave the Treasury broad authority to issue savings bonds. The objective for selling war bonds was first to fund the war and second to control inflation that would result from a rise in income and a shortage of consumer products. Rather than having citizens spend their money on consumer products, the government could dampen down the incipient inflation by taking money out of circulation with the purchase of war bonds.

The secretary of the Treasury, Henry Morgenthau Jr., chose bonds rather than taxes (by the end of the war 46 percent of the war cost had been funded by taxes and 54 percent by bond sales). Taxes were slow to collect and inequitably assessed, whereas the selling of bonds (in effect, borrowing money from American citizens) was immediate. Since all citizens would be encouraged to purchase bonds, the revenue would come from all groups, not just the wealthy. Morgenthau insisted that borrowing was voluntary, so it was a more democratic approach to paying for the war. The concept minimized inflation and gave the purchaser a sense of owning a piece of the war. Bond purchasers profited from the arrangement. The bonds would mature and provide interest on the investment, thus making the owner feel richer, while taxes made taxpayers feel poorer. Americans would realize that they not only were contributing to a national cause but were gaining financially.

The Treasury emphasized the ideological role that bond sales would play as a catalyst for national unity in a time of crisis and uncertainty. The bond sales would generate patriotic fervor for the war effort; buying bonds would become a symbol for "true Americanism." In essence, the bond sales would act as a physical reminder of the buyer's stake in winning the war and would demonstrate unity. The money invested in bonds would be the seed for postwar economic prosperity.

Defense bonds were issued in three series—E, F, and G. Each series varied slightly in the amount of interest returned and in the length of time until maturity. By far the most money came from the sale of F and G bonds, which were purchased in large quantities by banks and corporations. The bonds served as a safe haven for large businesses and banks to store cash until the end of the war.

The Series E bonds were designated for ordinary Americans. E bonds could be purchased only by individuals and could not be transferred or sold, thus eliminating speculation in these financial instruments. If lost or stolen, the bonds could be replaced. Issued in denominations of $25, $50, $100, $500, and $1,000 ($5,000 and $10,000 denominations came later), the E bonds were sold at 75 percent of their face value and earned a 2.9 percent annual interest rate. Thus a $25 E bond could be purchased for $18.75 and would be worth $25 when held to its full maturity of ten years. The bonds did not produce a significant profit, but the return was above the current bank rate and had the advantage of being a totally safe investment.

The Treasury also offered savings stamps to attract small investors, especially children, who could not afford the $25 bond. Available in denominations of 10, 25, and 50 cents and 1 and 5 dollars, the stamps were seen as a miniature version of a payroll savings plan. Citizens would purchase stamps until they accumulated a total of $18.75 and then convert the stamps into a $25 savings bond. The sale of savings stamps was never intended to raise much money; the purpose was to promote the war to children and teach them the advantages of thrift and sacrifice. Because anyone could afford to buy stamps, it made the war seem more inclusive as people were all doing their part.[49] All citizens, even the youngest, would be contributing to the common good.

The first Defense Loan Campaign began on May 1, 1941, but bond sales were sluggish until after Pearl Harbor. Once America entered the war, the Treasury Department stepped up its plan to sell more bonds by embarking on the "greatest mass selling achievement in history." The Treasury decided that seven separate and distinct bond campaigns would be the most effective approach to selling bonds. In each of the seven campaigns the Treasury established quotas for every conceivable entity—state, city, county, school, or factory. The idea of setting up quotas was a splendid idea, because various communities and businesses vied with each other to be the first to achieve their quota. When Meddybemps, Maine, with sixty people, became the first town in which all of its citizens had purchased bonds, the race was on for other towns to be 100 percent bond purchasers.[50]

The Treasury Department emphasized Payroll Savings plans as a key to increased bond purchases. Corporations, government entities, labor unions, and other groups encouraged their employees to buy bonds through the payroll savings plan. Each month a certain sum of money would be automatically withheld from the worker's pay check and applied to bond purchases. To make the buying of bonds relatively convenient, they could be purchased at places where citizens would normally convene—at banks, U.S. post offices, and some retail stores.

When the U.S. Treasury began its campaign to sell war bonds, it had significant advantages: full access to all national media, an unlimited promotional budget, and the largest list of potential customers in the world—the names and addresses of all the taxpayers in the country. The Treasury also assembled the largest sales force ever gathered—some 500,000 volunteers.

Advertising experts advised the government that the most effective way to sell bonds was through aggressive, direct, personal solicitation. Thousands of volunteers, supplied with a well-organized sales kit, went door-to-door to persuade individuals to sign a pledge that they would buy war bonds. The volunteers did not make sales; they were promoters. The buyer had to go to the bank or post office to complete the actual transaction. The Treasury Department infrequently used representatives from labor unions, teachers, and on one occasion New York bartenders as sales agents.

To get the message across, the Defense Savings staff used traditional advertising and promotion outlets—print, radio, and outdoor billboards. Patriotic posters appeared in virtually every public space. The catchy slogans on the posters emphasized sacrifice, national unity, and doing your part. Some of the slogans included: "Back the Attack," "You Buy 'Em, We'll Fly 'Em," "Buy a Share in America," and "All Together."[51]

Newspapers featured full-page advertisements by local businesses urging citizens to buy bonds. The ad sponsored by Eckerd's Drugstore in Raleigh reminded readers that it took thousands of planes and shells and tanks to win the war—and it took everyone, farmers, messengers, and bookkeepers, to raise the necessary money. "You don't *give* your money, you invest it for victory and for your own personal security." Another ad asked citizens to build their future "with the world's safest investment."[52]

Figure 6.2. Volunteers staff the war bond sales and display at the Boylan Pearce department store in Raleigh. Note the signs such as "Keep 'em Flying." North Carolina always exceeded its quota for the war bond drives. Courtesy of the State Archives of North Carolina.

The Defense Bond Committee realized that a war-weary public responded best to constant reminders of heroic patriotism and sacrifice by American troops. As the war dragged on, in 1944 a newspaper insert asked readers to purchase an extra war bond "when our country calls on you to do your all to help hasten the knockout blow. We know you won't fail America now."[53] On December 7, 1944, with the war effort now focused on Japan, another ad reminded citizens of the "infamous treachery" of Pearl Harbor and recalled the unspeakable cruelty demonstrated by the Japanese on the Bataan Death March. "We've got to stop them. We're *going* to stop them. We're going to teach all such fanatics a lesson. *They'll* remember Pearl Harbor, too." The war was not over. "Help scrap the Japs—with your bonds."[54]

One of the government's most successful strategies for selling bonds was by sponsoring national tours featuring movie stars and war heroes. Movie star tours proved to be tremendously popular. Celebrities such as crooners Bing Crosby and Frank Sinatra and such film legends as Humphrey Bogart, Gary Cooper, Cary Grant, and Judy Garland went from city to city to promote and sell bonds. Lana Turner, a blonde bombshell, single-handedly raised $5.25 million in bonds by selling 105 kisses for $50,000 each. The Treasury Department enlisted the professional skills of Eleanor Roosevelt, who made a series of national radio broadcasts. Even Norman Rockwell, the artist who had produced the famous Four Freedoms paintings, toured department stores in various cities. The Four Freedoms paintings were the centerpiece of a traveling war-bond sales drive.[55] Patriotic rallies for war bonds in Charlotte included film stars Jane Wyman (future wife of Ronald Reagan), Bob Hope, Tyrone Power, and Donald O'Connor. Later drives featured members of the armed forces demonstrating equipment purchased with bond proceeds. There were displays of paratroopers jumping from airplanes and C-47s flying low enough to snatch gliders off the ground.[56]

North Carolina enthusiastically supported the bond drives and had one of the best records for purchases per capita in the country. In May 1942 in Raleigh 1,411 volunteer canvassers and more than forty civic, fraternal, and other organizations turned out to spearhead a successful drive.[57] In the Second War Bond Drive the state's quota was $60 million; North Carolina sold over $65 million in Series E bonds. By the sixth drive, in January 1945, North Carolina had purchased $284 million in bonds, its largest total of the war.[58]

Examples of extraordinary bond purchases and contributions to various charities abounded. Many of these stories, publicized by the Treasury Department, inspired others to contribute. One couple purchased bonds with the $12,000 received in life insurance for their son who was killed in action in the Philippines.[59] A sailor stopped in front of the Red Cross War fund booth in the Sir Walter Hotel in Raleigh, pulled out his wallet, and contributed $20 to the Red Cross. One of the workers protested that the Red Cross was raising money for the troops and could not accept his contribution. The sailor responded that "when you've been in a hospital with injured and dying, and seen with your own eyes what the Red Cross is doing . . . then you begin to realize and appreciate what that symbol stands for." The crowd listened to the sailor's comments in silence and heard him say as he walked away that he did not need the $20, but the Red Cross did.[60]

Eight hundred women from the Civil Defense Organization, calling themselves the "Door Knockers," raised enough money in Charlotte to purchase a B-29 bomber.[61] Members of the General Federation of Women's Clubs of North Carolina were very successful in selling war bonds. In 1945 Ensign Bill Bragaw of Southport, North Carolina, the only Tar Heel in his unit, was called over by his squadron leader to inspect one of the new Hellcat fighters recently delivered. He was told that this plane would be assigned to him since "it's from the ladies of North Carolina." A closer inspection by Bragaw uncovered a small plaque on the plane: "This aircraft was bought through an equal amount in war bonds purchased by the Junior Woman's Club of Whiteville, N.C." The General Federation of Women's Clubs in North Carolina sold enough bonds to add nearly fifty bombers and fighters to the navy's arsenal.[62]

Schoolchildren were overwhelmingly supportive of the war effort and worked very hard in scrap drives and in Victory Gardens and by purchasing savings stamps. Patricia Crumbley remembered taking a dime to school each week to buy a savings stamp, which was pasted into her booklet. When the booklet was eventually filled, she could turn it in for a $25 savings bond.[63] In 1943 North Carolina schoolchildren bought enough Defense Savings Stamps to buy 2,080 jeeps.[64]

By the war's end, Americans had purchased 85 million war and victory bonds—a grand total of $185.7 billion, the largest amount of money ever raised for a war. The program had succeeded far beyond the government's expectations. "The greatest sales operation in history" had proved to be just that. The bond sales achieved their purposes by limiting inflation, helping to pay for the war, and creating a more unified nation. By combining personal aspirations, patriotism, and consumerism, the sale of war bonds offered all Americans a stake in the war and created, in Roosevelt's term, "one great partnership."[65]

Victory Gardens

In his book *Americans at War*, the distinguished historian Stephen Ambrose recalls that American patriotism was reflected in numerous activities by Americans to aid the war effort. His mother not only ran a Boy

Scout troop and worked eight hours a day in a pea factory but made a hot meal for her family every night and made certain that her boys planted a Victory Garden and collected scrap iron and newspapers. "How she did it I don't know. But I know that she did. So did millions of other American women. As much as the men, they made victory possible; more than the men, they held the American family together."[66]

Many American families, led by the women of the house, worked assiduously in Victory Gardens as the first line of defense. The objective was for families to grow their own fruits and vegetables to free the bulk of the commercially grown produce for the boys overseas. The Victory Gardens program was probably the most popular of all the civilian war efforts. At their peak in 1943, there were nearly 20 million Victory Gardens in America. Almost three-fifths of the population engaged in producing 40 percent of the vegetables grown in the country.

In addition, 4.1 billion jars of food were preserved at home and in community canning centers. The slogan was "Eat what you can and can what you can't." Canned foods made economic and practical sense. Cheaper than fresh produce, the canned goods could be kept year round without refrigeration and would be instantly available when needed.

Victory Gardens ranged from farms of several hundred acres, to small backyard plots in urban areas, to gardens in schoolyards and prisons, to a few tomato plants in a window box. Some cities and factories had communal gardens, but the most enthusiastic response came from individual landowners. Once again the federal government encouraged participation by appealing to patriotism and by the use of slogans: "Food Is a Vital Weapon of War" and "Behind every man with a gun stands a man with a hoe." Victory Gardens were important because everyone, especially children, could participate. Victory gardening combined recreation and patriotism and led to community cohesion in addition to supplying much-needed food.[67]

The state government of North Carolina wholeheartedly approved of Victory Gardens. Governor Broughton declared Victory Garden Week and announced that all agricultural, welfare, educational, and civic agencies were cooperating in the program. He made a statewide radio address to students around the state, telling them that whether they worked in Victory Gardens, collected tin foil, or invested pennies in defense stamps they were doing their part in helping America at a time of its greatest peril. The governor encouraged every farm family to grow extra crops and provide the necessary food for America's fighting forces.[68] The state government wanted state farms to be made more efficient in the production of food, as freedom from want was one of the Four Freedoms for which the country was fighting: "Vegetables for Vitality Needed for Victory in the War."[69]

Once again the state did its part to supply much-needed food. The successful Victory Gardens made a significant difference in food output. Raleigh alone had over 4,000 Victory Gardens within its city limits. The YMCA in Kannapolis plowed 200 acres into 300 separate plots, free for public use in planting fruits and vegetables. In Johnston County stores were closed on Wednesday afternoons for workers to go home and work in their gardens.[70]

Scrap and Clothing Drives

While applauding the nation's youth for planting Victory Gardens and purchasing stamps; the government called on the nation's young people for another important task: collecting scrap. The scrap drives accumulated badly needed materials such as rubber, copper, iron, newsprint, and other items. "In the barnyards and gullies of farms and in the basements and attics of homes is a lot of junk which is doing no good where it is but which is needed at once to help defeat the Japs and Nazis."[71] The government also intended for the scrap drives to help children develop a sense of common purpose and patriotism and prevent delinquency. These "great little scavengers" learned about volunteerism and community service by hauling wagons through neighborhoods picking up discarded items. They were admonished to join scrap drives by none other than the well-known comic strip character "Little Orphan Annie." She explained that she had "somethin' to do more important than playin.' We're doing war work. It's our war, just as much—or maybe more—than anybody else's." A successful national movement organized kids into a group known as the Junior Commandos and sent them scrambling through junk piles and knocking on doors all over the country. Henry Shavitz of Guilford County recalled collecting "scrap metal, grease and tinfoil. . . . We went door-to-door asking for them. Housewives donated old pots, pans, metal tableware and used cooking grease."[72]

The government's main focus was on children from ages six to thirteen. Older children and adults could collect more scrap in a shorter period than the children could, but the adults had more pressing tasks. There were simply not enough adult workers available to collect scrap. Teachers and local officials persuaded the youth of America to join in by making scrap

Figure 6.3. Schoolchildren stand behind their pile of collected scrap metal for the war effort. By permission of Carol W. Martin/Greensboro Historical Museum.

collecting fun, competitive, patriotic, and essential to victory. Some of the achievements were extraordinary. During the war the McDowell County schools collected 434 tons of scrap iron, 127 ½ tons of scrap paper, 13,700 pounds of waste fats, and 13,700 pounds of clothing.[73]

Rubber, always in short supply, was the most essential item that the government asked children to collect. President Roosevelt, after declaring a severe shortage of rubber, sent out an SOS to the American people to "Get in the Scrap." The kids were asked to pick up discarded tires, old rubber raincoats, old garden hoses, tennis shoes, bathing caps, bath mats, and gloves and take them to the local filling stations. Within a month 450,000 tons of scrap rubber had been turned in to gas stations. The gas stations paid a penny a pound for rubber and were reimbursed by the government at $25 a ton.[74]

Another essential item was scrap metal. The governor asked people to collect garden tools, stoves, metal beds, pots and pans, plumbing fixtures, doorknobs, knives, and metal pipes, and anything else made out of iron, steel, copper, and brass. Most of the scrap metal was remelted to make iron and steel. Children collected toothpaste tubes for the tin. In order to purchase a new tube of toothpaste, they had to turn in a used tube.[75] All scrap had to go through an independent scrap dealer, a vital cog in the war effort. The scrap dealers alone were qualified to segregate and grade the seventy-five classifications of scrap. The dealers had to build highly mechanized factories, inspected by the government, to process the material.[76]

Local organizations and newspapers encouraged their citizens to take part in the drives. The *Pilot* reminded its readers: "We are the most wasteful nation the world has ever seen. The city of Southern Pines has to learn not only to save, but to recover to the last possible pound, as much as possible of steel, iron, copper, aluminum and paper." One drive would not do. "It must be a continuous saving and salvage."[77]

The State War Salvage Committee printed a poem written by a marine in the Pacific:

And if our lines should form and break
Because of things you failed to make,
The extra tank or ship or plane
For which we waited all in vain.
And the supplies which never came
Will you come and take the blame?
For we, not you, will pay the cost
Of battles, you, not we, have lost.[78]

Citizens were bombarded with statistics about the value of salvage. One old tractor equaled two 37-mm antitank guns. Twelve worn-out lawnmowers could be used to build a three-inch antiaircraft gun. A worn-out iron could be converted to two steel helmets; a shovel into four grenades; one set of golf clubs into one .30-caliber machine gun; and silk and nylon hose into parachutes. One copper kettle could make eighty-four rounds of ammunition, and grease and cooking fats could be made into glyceride for gunpowder.[79]

By 1944 a paper shortage had led to an emphasis on collecting newspapers, used documents, files, and grocery bags. Boy Scouts sponsored "Paper Drives" during which they collected old newspapers. Most of the paper products were used to make cardboard containers to ship goods and supplies.

One youth recalled going to homes in his neighborhood and handing them a list of the items to be saved—mainly scrap metal, paper, grease, and cans. He reported a success rate of about 50 percent. Schools, churches, and local merchants all over North Carolina aided the cause. In Gastonia movie theaters held a "copper Matinee," where one copper pot would earn a ticket to see Walt Disney's *Bambi*.[80] State newspapers backed a scrap contest, "North Carolina's Scrap Can Beat the Japs." The county that produced the most scrap won a $1,000 prize. Government officials estimated that 30 million children brought in 1,500,000 tons of scrap metal, enough to build twenty-five Liberty ships.[81]

Some citizens went above and beyond the call of duty. R. S. Harris, a farmer in Chatham County, responded to a call for scrap with 50 pounds of scrap rubber and 14,000 pounds of scrap iron, including a 4,000-pound steam boiler. Farmer Harris was puzzled that some citizens had not responded in a more positive manner. "I can't understand it. We've got to beat those other countries to be able to keep on living here. The head man said we needed scrap to make guns and boats to fight the war with. I hope my scrap helps to plow the Japs under."[82]

The government never utilized significant portions of the scrap metal and newspapers collected. Many Tar Heels lost interest in the endeavor when the processing plants became overloaded with excess scrap and scrap iron lay piled in the schoolyard in great useless heaps. Nonetheless, the collection of used junk and rubbish in large quantities was important in supplying essential goods to the military. Equally important was the impact of the experience on the children and townspeople who had worked in a community project and had sacrificed for the commonweal.

In addition to helping raise scrap for America and its Allies, North Carolina demonstrated its generosity and commitment to human suffering all over the world. In 1943 the state government set up a clothing salvage program to distribute apparel through international relief agencies to residents of war-ravaged countries occupied by U.S. troops.[83] By the end of the war the state had contributed over 56,000 pounds of relief clothing and 11,000 pounds of food as well as shoes, books, carpenter tools, silverware, and 2,100 dairy cows.[84]

Propaganda, Censorship, and Internal Security

In wartime propaganda is essential to success. The U.S. government presented its objectives in a positive light and persuaded citizens that America's goals—the Four Freedoms (freedom from want, freedom from fear, freedom of speech, and freedom of religion)—were superior to those of the enemy and worth fighting for. The government promoted a propaganda onslaught designed to defame America's enemies, warning that an Axis victory would mean an end to Western civilization. America had to win the war at all costs, so the propaganda agencies often misled the public while keeping bad news of disastrous defeats and battlefield horrors from the American people. Always the goal was favorable publicity to win public support for the war.

In June 1944 President Roosevelt chose Elmer Davis, a highly respected newsman, as head of the Office of War Information (OWI). Responsible for both domestic and foreign programs, Davis's office coordinated the release of news from government agencies to the press, acted as a liaison between the press and government, prepared propaganda for overseas dissemination, and supervised the government's "war information program" in all the media, including motion pictures.[85]

To achieve its goals, the OWI presented Americans as a diverse and democratic people working together in a common cause in pursuit of a just peace. The OWI described Americans as fighting bravely to defeat the treacherous and beastly "Japs" and brutal Nazis. Billboards, posters, and pamphlets emphasized patriotism and inspired citizens to keep secrets and work hard. Anyone who was not doing his or her part was aiding the enemy.[86]

For millions of Americans in the 1940s, radio was the primary source of information about the war. War news became an increasingly important part of the daily broadcasts. By 1944 the National Broadcasting Company (NBC) was devoting 20 percent of its time to news, compared to only 3.6 percent in 1939. As Ese Baxley-Jarrett of Mount Gilead recalled: "We listened to the war news every night on WMFD in Wilmington. My parents wanted to know everything that was going on."[87] Journalists such as Edward R. Murrow, reporting from London during the Blitz, gave listeners a firsthand account of key battles, explaining what was happening and why. Some of the best reporting came from writers like Ernie Pyle, who vividly described what they witnessed on the battlefront. Nonetheless, the war was experienced at a distance by the public, and the news was filtered through a powerful and intrusive censorship machine.

OWI set up a Bureau of Motion Pictures (BMP) to advise Hollywood as to how film producers could help the war effort. The BMP voluntarily made and distributed its own films at no cost to the government. The most famous was the seven-picture indoctrination film *Why We Fight* directed by Frank Capra (the director of *It's a Wonderful Life*), seen by every soldier going overseas and also released to commercial theaters. One critic called the films cliché-ridden and filled with heroic posturing. But they were successful in fostering a spirit of can-do on the part of the American soldier.[88]

Hollywood actors, including a future president, made personal appearances for the agency and cooperated with the studios in producing educational and inspirational films and newsreels. Ronald Reagan had been called for duty in April 1942 but was disqualified for combat duty because of nearsightedness. Assigned to the First Motion Picture Unit of the Army Air Corps in Hollywood, he participated in making three of the most memorable of the training films.[89]

The OWI also set up a separate Office of Censorship, with authority over incoming and outgoing international communications, including film. The control of information shaped the perception of the war, so the Office of Censorship monitored American newspapers, photographers, journalists, and radio commentators. It issued a code of wartime practices for the media, encouraging "voluntary" censorship. Journalists were restricted in their movement and in access to information. The media should not publish anything that would disclose vital information. If asked to withhold negative information of a sensitive nature, newspapers and other outlets would usually cooperate with the government, as they knew certain information might help the enemy.

The military had its own censorship system and checked letters to and from GIs for any breach of security. There were 13,500 official censors, who monitored all letters, cables, and telephone conversations within America's borders. The censors were trained to look for any details about troop movements, strength and disposition of the military, naval and merchant shipping, and antiaircraft emplacements and defense fortifications. Radio announcers did not mention any weather data that might aid the enemy in assessing shipping conditions and troop movements. The censors opened suspicious messages and resealed them with the censor's number attached if they contained no problems.

When dangerous material was discovered, the letters were suppressed. One option would be to cut out the offending section and put the letter back into the mail with the least possible delay. Citizens complained that the censors violated their individual rights, objecting to the delays and what they considered senseless deletions from their mail. One young woman who had written a letter to her boyfriend informed the marine censor: "I love this Leatherneck and if you take out a single sweetie pie, I will never forgive you." Most Americans accepted the censorship because they knew that it was important for national security.[90]

Inevitable conflicts and tensions of course arose between freedom and national security. Nonetheless, there was always a sense that in a democratic society, even one at war, the concept of a free press had to be honored. American censorship, while strict, was less coercive and less intrusive than censorship in other belligerent nations. After all, freedom of speech was one of the freedoms for which the country was fighting.[91]

Americans in many areas of the country believed that a significant number of traitors, spies, and "fifth columnists" were actively engaged in espionage, sabotage, and subversive activities designed to cripple America's war effort. Fear and paranoia in Charlotte fueled a strong effort to identify and arrest those subversives. The *Charlotte Observer* took up the hunt for un-American activities, claiming that over 2,000 subversives were present in the area, and arguing that the U.S. Constitution did not protect anyone accused of Communist or Nazi sympathies. The paper chastised those who complained about FBI investigations as more concerned with civil liberties than with victory. The FBI investigated the paper's claims. The bureau examined a number of cases, including the rumor of a Nazi spy ring in Salisbury, and found no saboteurs. The ill-advised witch hunt came to naught.[92]

Some self-righteous patriots, motivated by anxiety and paranoia, became incensed over the most innocuous activity. Religious leaflets distributed by pacifists in Brevard, N.C., stated that "The Sword Was the Way of the Devil" and urged the United States to lay down its arms. Local citizens were outraged and denounced the leaflets, calling them a fifth column movement to undermine American morale.[93] Then there were the haters. Frank Buck, the "great white hunter" and author, announced that permanent peace and the survival of the white race would "depend upon the complete annihilation of the Japanese race through use of poison gas." Although Buck professed to believe in humanitarianism, he believed "in being humanitarian to our own race." He wanted to start gassing Japanese right away before they could kill any more white people.[94]

Movies and Entertainment

The American people found ways to ease the trials and tribulations of war and enjoy themselves while worrying about loved ones in combat, figuring out how to deal with rationing issues, and working hard to produce the goods and materials necessary to win the war. As the opportunities for travel were limited, the best escape for most Americans was going to the cinema. Movie attendance set new records during the war, rising from 85 million commercial moviegoers per week in 1939 to 95 million per week in 1945. Box office receipts surged from $1 billion to $1.5 billion. This number did not include military moviegoers, who were constantly hunkered down in front-row seats at base theaters. To meet the increasing demand of avid moviegoers, the number of movie theaters increased all over the state. Raleigh had six theaters, and other big cities in North Carolina had a comparable number.[95]

Filmgoers preferred escapism: adventure films, comedies, and musicals with themes that were familiar to their everyday lives. Many of the movie stars were crisscrossing the country to sell war bonds, so the American public became infatuated, even obsessed, with Hollywood royalty. Although many stars stayed in Los Angeles making films, a few joined the services. Jimmy Stewart was a colonel in the air force. Henry Fonda served in the South Pacific. When the heartthrob Clark Gable enlisted, women in America were heartbroken.

Most of the 2,500 films turned out during the war were entertainment for mass audiences, mainly musicals and comedies. But Hollywood did make several important war films. Commercial movie production became another war industry eager to cooperate with the government out of fear that it would be considered nonessential and would lose business. The common themes of war movies suggested teamwork, democracy, and diversity. Earlier films did not depict much war violence. After 1943, however, when Americans appeared to be overconfident about winning the war, films became more realistic and showed combat's harsh and terrible side. About 28 percent of the films made from 1942 to 1945 emphasized the war, with the peak production coming in 1943.

Most of the war movies featured overwrought tag lines designed to attract the customer. *So Proudly We Hail* was a film about nurses on the front lines. *Bataan* was advertised as "the blazing story of bedeviled Bataan." *Bombardier* was "the screen's mighty story of soldiers with wings, told in a blasting bomb run of romance and excitement."[96] Successful war films included William Wyler's *Memphis Belle* and John Wayne and Susan Hayward in *The Fighting Seabees*, marketed as "the thrilling story of America's supermen . . . men of heroic daring with exciting romance and dynamic courage." Navy and marine pictures included *The Fighting Lady*, the story of an aircraft carrier, and *To the Shores of Iwo Jima*. Stories about the army air corps included *Flying Tiger*; *God Is My Co-Pilot*, and *Thirty Seconds over Tokyo*, the saga of Jimmy Doolittle's daring raid, billed as "The Most Thrill Packed Half Minute in History."[97]

Eventually the public tired of war movies and their often strident messages. Moviegoers longed for films that portrayed American virtues—family, hard work, romance, beliefs, adventure, and the good life of abundant living.[98] Producers in Hollywood responded. An observer would be pleased with the variety of the films showing at the four largest movie theaters in Raleigh on March 28, 1943. The Capitol Theater featured Johnny Mack Brown in *Boss of Hangtown Mesa* for western fans and Claudette Colbert in the *Palm Beach Story* for sophisticates. The State featured *Kid Dynamite and the East Side Kids*, while *Once Upon a Honeymoon* with Cary Grant and Ginger Rogers was showing at the Colony. *Wake Island*, a war movie with "guns and grit and glory," was playing at the Wake Theater.[99]

Wartime movies of course included comedies by Bob Hope and light-hearted fare such as Betty Grable, the chorine with the famous legs, in *Pin-Up Girl*. Musicals were popular. Mickey Rooney and Judy Garland found success in *Girl Crazy*. Bing Crosby, the most famous crooner of the day, starred in *Holiday Inn*, where he sang perhaps the most popular song of the era, "White Christmas." Thousands of soldiers facing snowless Christmases in North Africa and Guadalcanal longed for home while listening to the words of the song: "I'm dreaming of a White Christmas, Just like the ones I used to know."[100]

Two of the best musicals of the war were *Yankee Doodle Dandy*, starring James Cagney, and *This Is the Army*, featuring seventeen Irving Berlin songs, including "This Is the Army, Mr. Jones," "Boogie-Woogie Bugle Boy of Company B," and "God Bless America." The most intriguing of the war films was Charlie Chaplin's *The Great Dictator*, a savage satire on Hitler (Adenoid Hynkel in the film). The audiences loved Chaplin's devastating imitation of the posturing, erratic, and often ludicrous Adolf. The classic film *Casablanca*, made in 1942, featured Humphrey Bogart and Ingrid Bergman trying to stay out of the clutches of the Gestapo.[101]

For the kids there were always serials, short comedy features, and the western B movies. At a typical Saturday matinee in small-town America in 1945, a youngster could get into the local theater for 10 cents. That entrance fee plus an extra nickel got the viewer a double-feature cowboy/adventure movie, a cartoon, a serial, and a Coke or a Mars Bar. The entire event often lasted over four hours, the cheapest babysitter a parent could get. Young cowboys, who fervently believed in the myth of the Old West, could live out their fantasies for three or four hours on Saturday and then go home and play cowboy with toy six-shooters. They watched a succession of cinema heroes—Roy Rogers, the Lone Ranger and Tonto, Hopalong Cassidy, Johnny Mack Brown, Gene Autry (the first singing cowboy), and John Wayne.[102] For many moviegoers, it did not matter much whether the movie was a western, an adventure story, a comedy or musical, or even a war film; it was all about escaping the pressures of wartime America for a few hours of pure fantasy.

Americans did not spend all their leisure time in darkened movie houses. There were always lots of sporting events, concerts, nightclubs, and church activities to attend. People who enjoyed the outdoors played baseball and tennis, went swimming, cycling, canoeing, and set out on long walks. Individuals often entertained themselves at home by listening to the radio or reading newspapers, the comics, magazines, and books (the war brought an increase in the publication of inexpensive paperback books). Music lovers listened to the recordings of hit songs on the Victrola and played cards (bridge, canasta, and gin rummy) and parlor games (such as Parcheesi) for the whole family.[103]

One of the more unusual sporting events of the war years was the January 1, 1942, Rose Bowl, played in Durham, N.C., the only Rose Bowl game played outside of California. In 1941 the unbeaten, untied Duke University football team was ranked number two in the nation. As was the custom in 1941, the Rose Bowl selected Oregon State as the host team. Oregon State, in turn, chose Duke University as its opponent. Duke quickly got permission from the other members of the Southern Conference to play in the game in sunny California.

The Japanese attack on Pearl Harbor on December 7, 1941, ended any chance of a game in California. Fearing a Japanese attack on southern California, the U.S. Army urged that the game not be played. The Rose Bowl committee concurred and cancelled the contest. Duke immediately offered to host the game. So Oregon State agreed to travel to Durham for the 1942 Rose Bowl. Duke borrowed bleachers from nearby universities and boosted the seating capacity from 35,000 to 55,000 spectators.

Although excited by the impending contest, the Duke student newspaper put things in perspective by reminding its readers that the war crisis superseded any other considerations. Some of the Duke football players, wearing blue football uniforms, would soon be clad in blue naval uniforms. The paper also advocated for a proper balance between athletics and academics. If Duke had a highly publicized football team, then the school "MUST have a nationally recognized medical center, law clinic, forestry school, engineering college and undergraduate school famous for its high scholastic standards. Otherwise, the school will be known by the epithet, 'football college.'" Unfortunately for the home team, the heavily favored Blue Devils lost to Oregon State by 20–16 on a cold, rainy day.[104]

The average American who stayed at home during the war was flexible and made do with whatever food and rationed items were available. The populace demonstrated its ingenuity and resourcefulness while facing shortages. The majority made the necessary sacrifices without complaint. A few Americans selfishly took advantage of the circumstances, but most citizens were loyal and patriotic and tried to do what was best for the country. Just about everyone understood what was at stake in the war and knew that America and the Allies had to win at all costs. Some censorship in the press and shortages of gas and tires were a small price to pay for freedom and liberty. Even with a lack of certain items and onerous restrictions, Americans understood that they were far better off than almost anyone else in the world. The inevitable griping and complaining were par for the course, but actual criminal acts were limited. Americans seldom offered any forceful opposition to the war. People stayed loyal, participated in scrap drives, knitted blankets for the troops, purchased war bonds, helped out neighbors, and worked hard at their jobs.

EDUCATION AND THE UNIVERSITY
OF NORTH CAROLINA
PRE-FLIGHT SCHOOL

As wars became global and lasted longer, all of the resources of the nation had to be called upon, especially skills developed by the educational system. With the demand for soldiers on the part of the military and the need for skilled workers in almost every phase of the economy, the nation's educational system had to adapt and adjust to the national crisis and the urgent need for enlightened citizens. Leaders at every level of instruction throughout the country were eager to place all their resources at the disposal of the government, but the initial guidance from Washington was vague and inconsistent.

The war impacted the educational system at all levels, especially higher education. The war effort made new demands on scholarly institutions, as the traditional programs of study had to conform to a new emphasis on science and vocational education. Schools had to prepare students not only for service in the military but also for technical work in war industries and other occupations designed to assist in the preparation for war. With the large withdrawal of male students into the armed forces, most universities and colleges, if they were to remain open, had to join with the federal government and provide new courses in technical fields and in military training. Some institutions bemoaned the decreased emphasis on traditional academic studies, but universities and colleges first had to contribute to winning the war. To preserve the future of American cultural and intellectual development, university faculties hoped to prevent a "blackout" of liberal education and continue the study of the humanities.

Schools at all levels were urged to emphasize health and physical fitness as well as training in skills and knowledge needed during wartime. Vocational training, whether as agricultural experts or in auto repair, became an essential function of the educational system, primarily at the secondary level.[1]

The mechanization of the military forces and the expansion of American industry required an increased emphasis on math, physics, and technical skills. America had to get up to speed in modifying its educational curriculum to adapt to the demand for more highly trained personnel in the sciences, especially medicine, dentistry, and pharmacy. The Defense Department provided loans to students and issued numerous grants to universities to develop new courses and new programs. In response to a request from the federal government, North Carolina State College added a course in diesel engineering training for naval officers.[2]

High schools in the nation faced transitional difficulties often greater than those at the college or primary level. Many senior high school students left school for military service or for jobs in industry. Most of these young men would probably not have gone on to college. But they were able-bodied and patriotic, so they wanted to take up some activity that would contribute to the war effort. As a result of the mass defection of students, the instruction in high schools could no longer be carried out in the traditional manner. Many teachers had been drafted or had opted for military service and defense work. There were simply not enough skilled teachers of math and science courses. Students had little other choice than to gravitate toward the vocational option.

Primary and secondary schools suffered significantly during the war, with reduced funding, shortened school terms, lack of trained administrators, and an insufficient number of teachers. There were shortages everywhere—books, transportation, fuel for heating, and money for teachers. Schools were forced to hire substitutes for talented teachers lost to defense jobs and the military. Many of the substitute instructors lacked proper qualifications, so institutions had to lower standards in order to find someone, anyone, to teach the students. Some experts indicated that it would take ten years to overcome the deficiencies (loss of funding, lack of books, inadequate teachers) that plagued the primary and secondary instructional system during the war. The fallout was particularly acute in rural sections of the country.

National and state leaders had a misplaced belief in the American instructional system as the best in the world. However, complacency, apathy, and the heavy burden of the Great Depression had undermined American education after World War I. The American system had not fulfilled its function of preparing a knowledgeable citizenry for participation in a democratic society and had failed to provide equality of educational opportunities for the poor and minorities. In 1940 almost 14 percent of all American citizens had fewer than five years of schooling.

The shortcomings of the public school system in North Carolina were amply demonstrated when the U.S. Selective Service rejected thousands of men in 1940 for mental or educational deficiencies. Of those registering for the draft in the state, 350,000 signed their names with a mark. The state had a high rate of illiteracy among whites. The percentage was much higher for blacks, who were the products of inferior schools, and for those living in nonurban areas. As the war began, it became clear that America lagged behind other Western nations in academic preparation.

The low economic status of teachers and the inability to provide for trained personnel in academic subjects crucial to meeting war needs placed a heavy burden on American education at the outset of the war.[3] Fortunately, the American people, state and federal governments, and educators quickly assessed the problems and made necessary adjustments. Effective cooperation among the federal government, the military branches, the state governments, and educational institutions made up for many of the previous deficiencies.

One of the best examples of the collaboration between the military and institutions of higher learning in North Carolina came with the development of educational programs sponsored by the U.S. Navy. As the *Raleigh News and Observer* noted, cooperation between the government and higher-education institutions in the state was essential. "Educators owe it to the good of the country to cooperate in such a way as to utilize the higher institutions of learning for the best training of youths in this all-out war." The paper went on to argue that "education as usual is out for the duration of the war. Colleges and universities should make such changes in their curricula and in shortening their courses as may be necessary. . . . The only business in America—in education and all other lines—is readiness and fitness for winning the war. All else should be adjourned for the duration."[4]

Eighteen months before Pearl Harbor, President Frank Porter Graham and the administration at the University of North Carolina recognized the developing crisis and the need to begin war mobilization on college campuses. Dr. Graham expressed the view that, although America had not yet entered the war, universities had to prepare their facilities "to help make the world freer and fairer to all men." Centers of learning "cannot be isolated from democracy, for democracy hurt anywhere is democracy hurt everywhere in the world." Universities, as Graham well knew, faced a harsh reality. With the beginning of hostilities and the departure of many students for the military or defense work, universities would have to either close the institutions or convert the campuses to war training facilities. Fortunately for higher education in the state, the military leaders quickly recognized the great potential of using university facilities for war training.[5]

After the war began, the mass exodus of male students from the University of North Carolina (UNC) resulted in a loss of $100,000 from reduced tuition, room rent, and limited use of the dining hall. UNC would have found it difficult to keep the doors open without government financial support. To make matters worse, the state legislature had cut the appropriations for the university by 10 percent. The critical financial situation made the university amenable to entering into contracts with the U.S. military. Eventually, the navy's spending in the V-5, V-12, and Pre-Flight School programs at UNC would enable the university to remain open and solvent.

In August 1940 the trustees of the Consolidated University of North Carolina (consisting of the University of North Carolina at Chapel Hill, North Carolina State College in Raleigh, and Woman's College in Greensboro), recognizing the need for war preparation, committed the university at Chapel Hill to military training, and required all physically able undergraduates to take fitness training. The trustees also asked that a Civil Aeronautics Department be established at State College and that $15,000 be made available for the purchase of an aviation field in Chapel Hill. By the end of 1940 the state had purchased land from Horace Williams and received a Works Progress Administration (WPA) grant to grade the runways and complete the airfield. At the newly established Horace Williams Airfield 180 students were trained for a civilian pilot's license from 1940 to 1943.

In 1940–41 the university at Chapel Hill set up a War Information Center located in the lobby of the university library. This center, containing maps, newspapers, articles, and books about the war, served as a resource available to faculty, students, and citizens of the state so that they might understand and stay abreast of military developments.[6]

In 1940 Chapel Hill was a bucolic village with some 3,500 townspeople and a student body of 4,000. As of this date the students and townspeople held ambivalent views about American entrance into the war. Most thought of the war as a faraway crisis and had hoped that the United States would never have to fight another war in Europe after World War I. Townspeople went about their business, generally unaffected by war clouds gathering in Europe. Students were more concerned about dates, dances, classes, and the next Duke-Carolina football game.[7]

Bill Snider, a student at UNC, recalled looking out of his window at Old East dorm to see what he described as a "disturbing sight." Several students had planted a series of small white crosses on the lawn of McCorkle Place. The crosses symbolized the graves of American boys who would be slaughtered if America entered the war to defend Great Britain. Snider initially agreed with the demonstrators that America should stay out of Europe's war, but after Hitler's invasion of France he realized the grave threat posed to Western democracies by the totalitarian powers. "Some things, I concluded, could be worse than war. Allowing democracy to die in Europe became one of them."[8]

President Graham and the state had already pledged its resources and energy to the war effort. Dr. Graham aligned the university with the group that proclaimed "this is our war." Graham believed that every person and institution had a part to play in stopping totalitarian dictatorships. "We favor immediate aid to the democracies, because the democracies, with all their injustices, frustrations and failures, give the world's people, including the German people, more hope of the opportunity to struggle for peace, freedom and democracy and humane religion as the basis of them all."[9]

On March 20, 1941, President Franklin Roosevelt appointed President Graham as a member of the eleven-member National Defense Mediation Board to reconcile disputes between government and labor. After Pearl Harbor, Graham continued his government service, working as a member of the War Labor Board, a committee designed to handle problems with industrial production. For almost three years Graham had two full-time jobs, running the university system and shuttling constantly between Chapel Hill and Washington to fulfill his duties on the War Labor Board.[10]

Everything changed after Pearl Harbor. The declaration of war jolted the university out of its sense of complacency and isolation. One student described his feelings immediately after the shock of the Japanese attack. "Out of the maze of changed plans and uncertain futures, there arose a feeling of unity which none of us will ever forget." Young men now had to give up their plans for a degree and go off to fight for their country, knowing that they might never return. Confused, frightened, and worried about the implications of Pearl Harbor, a large number of students and townspeople gathered at the president's home for advice and solace. Graham tried to put the situation in perspective, assuring his listeners that democracy would prevail in the end. The next day he called an emergency meeting of the students and repeated his view that the goal and mandate of the university was "to help our citizens equip and train themselves in the shortest possible time, to be of the greatest value to the nation, in its most critical crisis."[11]

V-12 Program

As the University of North Carolina began preparing for its new responsibilities, the navy began a long overdue redesign and expansion of its training programs. The navy created the V-12 program, as it was known, to grant bachelor's degrees to future naval officers. The navy hoped to train officers by combining a college education with basic naval discipline and navy classes. Once the candidates completed their baccalaureate program at a university, they would attend a U.S. Navy Reserve Midshipman (cadet) School. Upon graduation from the midshipmen's schools, they were commissioned as ensigns in the navy.

The V-12 course of study lasted four months. The navy paid tuition to the participating colleges for college courses that were taught by university faculty. The navy also contracted to use athletic fields, mess halls, classrooms, dormitory space, medical services, and administrative help. The V-12 program, established on July 1, 1943, eventually enrolled more than 100,000 men at some 137 colleges and universities, including UNC and Duke University.

The V-12 program was both physically and academically demanding. The men attended classes with civilian students and were allowed to participate in regular campus activities but were regulated and regimented by strict navy discipline: as cadets they had already been placed on active

Figure 7.1. Nancy Winn, a WAVE in the disbursing office, approaches the U.S. Navy Pre-Flight School administrative building in Chapel Hill, N.C. She is accompanied by two unidentified sailors. By permission of North Carolina Collection, UNC Library at Chapel Hill.

duty as navy seamen. One officer explained that the program was "to provide the men with training as nearly like normal college training as seems compatible with basic naval regulations."[12]

The course of study was essentially a liberal arts curriculum and in many ways was the equivalent of typical freshman courses. There were classes in math, English, the historical background of World War II, physics, engineering and geometry, naval organization, and physical training. The academic requirements, choice of professors, and standards of academic performance of the trainees were under the supervision of the university. Textbooks and teaching procedures were the prerogative of the faculty and the administration, although there was frequent communication between the administration and the naval officer in charge of the program. The cadets had an average course load of fifteen to seventeen hours a week, including at least one hour of drill each day. The navy staff took responsibility for teaching two courses on naval history and organization.

The initial group of 1,300 began their V-12 training at Chapel Hill on July 1, 1943. The university set aside several classroom buildings for study. Five dormitories, five sorority houses, and seventeen fraternity houses were used as living quarters for the trainees. Dr. Graham recognized a serious housing problem for all the new arrivals. There have been "so many demands on our space . . . the offices, rooms in town, university buildings that all the physical facilities are taxed to the utmost." UNC alleviated part of the problem by erecting two new brick barracks in back of the Carolina Inn and by renovating Swain Hall as the mess hall. The use of dorms by the navy meant that the civilian students had to find separate accommodations. The displaced students were often forced to bunk three or four to a room when they could find space.[13]

The Carolina Inn, a traditional facility on campus for many years, had been renovated and enlarged in January 1940. Due to the extreme housing emergency on campus, the UNC administration allowed navy officers to use sixteen of the thirty suites in the Inn. Because the navy had taken over Lenoir Hall and Swain Hall to feed their cadets, the Carolina Inn converted its ballroom into extra seating for a cafeteria to provide sustenance for the regular student body. By 1943 this cafeteria served 1,200 meals per day. The Carolina Inn continued to rent rooms to guests throughout the war. The rooms cost $3 for a single and $5 for a double. A full meal in the dining room was 75 cents.[14]

As soon as the trainees set foot on campus, the navy began its indoctrination. The navy placed a strong emphasis on physical training, so the V-12 program began recruiting physical training specialists for appointment as officers and petty officers. Most of these men had been college and high school coaches in civilian life. Some of these new instructors would end up coaching the navy's athletic teams at UNC, the Cloudbusters.

After July 1, 1944, as the number of pilots trained reached acceptable numbers, the navy began phasing out its V-12 programs but did not close any program completely. The reduction was done selectively across the board at all of the colleges and universities because the navy did not want to force undue hardship on some of the smaller schools that would have had to close their doors immediately. The last major intake of cadets occurred in July 1944. The V-12 program at UNC was absorbed into an expanded Naval Reserve Officers Training Corps (NROTC) program and ended on June 10, 1945. The navy reported that some 50,000 naval officers received part of their training at civilian colleges and universities throughout the nation. Navy records revealed that most of the students prepared in the V-12 program performed well during officer candidate training.[15]

Colleges and universities for women in the state were not as affected by the war as were colleges and universities for men. State institutions for women, particularly Woman's College (WC) of UNC at Greensboro, as well as private schools such as Meredith College, were not as concerned with finances and enrollments because fewer women than men dropped out of college for war industry work or for service in the military. The number of withdrawals did increase later in the war with the demand for the services of women in the WACs, WAVEs, and SPARs.

Woman's College at UNC was fairly typical of women's colleges in the state. WC followed a policy of unqualified support for the war effort while attempting to maintain student life at its highest level. The academic programs at WC-UNC remained essentially unchanged, but the college encouraged women to enter some form of war service, becoming nurses, teachers, industrial workers, secretaries, chemists, and accountants upon graduation. In spite of the war, academic enrollment at WC remained high.

WC's objective was to advise students on the activities and services that would be most beneficial for the war effort. The administration insisted that education *was* war training and that women who continued their education were preparing themselves for useful and long-term service to their country. The students at WC consistently contributed to the sale of war bonds, the Red Cross, and numerous voluntary efforts around the state. One unusual development on the Greensboro campus was the increase in the number of married students. Many young women married their sweethearts before they left for service, and some withdrew from school to follow their husbands. Most, however, stayed in school. The college had to amend its rule that married women could not live in the residence halls.[16]

Many of the state's private colleges, Davidson and Duke among them, played an important role in the education and training of military units. In May 1941, with world conflagration likely, President John R. Cunningham of Davidson appealed to the students to stay in school as long as possible because "men of education and Christian character are going to be the nation's dependence in the years ahead." The school faced a rapidly dwindling student population, from 691 in 1941–1942 to 245 in September 1943 and 162 in February 1945. Dr. Cunningham knew that the school could not pay its faculty or continue to operate with the income from student tuition so sharply curtailed. After he advocated for Davidson's advantage as a military training center, the college was approved for Aviation Cadet Training. Five hundred cadets had appeared on campus by April 1942. The college housed and fed the cadets and offered forty-eight hours of classroom work in math, physics, English, and geography. The campus had two colleges: the civilian college with regular Davidson students and the "war college," which served the war effort and kept the faculty together. By the end of the training on June 30, 1944, 1,500 cadets had trained at Davidson.[17]

V-5 Program

The building and preparation of the Horace Williams Airfield near Chapel Hill proved to be a wise decision, as the navy established a V-5 reserve program for aviation cadets from Duke University and the University of North Carolina at Chapel Hill. The eight-week program included 240 hours of ground work and 35 hours of flight training. The cadets studied math, physics, navigation, meteorology, military science, and civilian air regulations. After completing half of the requirements for a degree the cadets would go on active duty and would then attend one of the four Pre-Flight School programs in the country. After completing eight months in pre-flight and flight training, they would receive commissions in the navy.[18]

Navy Pre-Flight Program

The V-5, V-12, and other courses were significant for UNC, but the navy Pre-Flight School program brought the greatest changes to the UNC campus. After Pearl Harbor, the navy knew that it had to improve its training. The best way to do that would be to utilize the resources of colleges and universities around the country to the fullest. The navy simply had no time to build new training facilities, so the best option was to take advantage of classrooms, mess halls, and athletic fields already in place at selected universities. In desperate need of new pilots, the navy designed a national Pre-Flight School program to be "the most intensive, rigorous, comprehensive program of physical and mental training the world has ever seen." The Pre-Flight School programs ideally would train 30,000 pi-

lots a year until the end of the war and would emphasize academic preparation and military drills designed to develop the skills, stamina, and
strength needed in combat.[19]

The navy decided that the maximum number of cadets to be stationed
at one university would be 1,875. This meant that the site selected would
have to furnish sufficient classroom space, athletic fields, living quarters,
and mess facilities. Because of the difficulty of obtaining all the needed
space and qualified instructors at one site, the navy decided to establish
four Pre-Flight Schools in the nation. Seventy colleges and universities
applied for the designation. Originally the navy intended to have the four
institutions represent the West, Midwest, South, and East. The navy first
chose the University of Iowa in the Midwest then selected St. Mary's College in California in the West and the University of Georgia in the South.

With only one selection left and a school in the South already chosen,
UNC's chances seemed dim until some powerful North Carolinians ex-
erted their influence. Former secretary of the navy Josephus Daniels tele-
graphed current secretary of the navy Frank Knox and urged him to review
UNC's facilities. Dr. Frank Graham pointed out his close relationship with
Franklin and Eleanor Roosevelt and reminded Knox that he was currently
serving on the War Labor Board. Senator Robert Reynolds, chairman of
the Senate Military Affairs Committee, and Governor Melville Broughton
urged Secretary Knox to select Chapel Hill. In the end the political pressure helped, but the navy picked UNC because of its excellent facilities.

The selection committee liked Chapel Hill because it was a small, peaceful village without a lot of distractions. Thus the site would allow the cadets to concentrate on the difficult training regimen. The navy knew that
the mild weather would allow for participation in outdoor sports most
of the year and considered the housing, classroom, and library facilities
excellent. Lenoir Hall, which could seat 900 people, had one of the largest
seating capacities of any university dining hall in the country. The uni-
versity-owned Horace Williams Airfield was an asset, as were the athletic
facilities. Physical training, conditioning, and teamwork were essential
parts of the preparation for the pilots. Officials were impressed by the
university's athletic complex: Woollen Gym, Kenan Stadium, Bowman
Gray swimming pool, Emerson Stadium, the Tin Can, and many intramural fields.[20]

The official commissioning of the Pre-Flight School at Chapel Hill took
place on May 23, 1942. After the completion of the formal festivities, the
first class of 242 cadets arrived at the Durham bus station on May 28.

They were issued clothing, given a GI haircut, inoculated for diseases, and fed. Then they immediately began drilling. A contingent of 300 new cadets appeared in Chapel Hill every two weeks until the school achieved its full quota of 1,875. Most of the early arrivals, from Pennsylvania, New York, New Jersey, and New England, were charmed by the lovely village but had some difficulty in transitioning to the southern accent and the more sedate, slower way of life.[21]

In 1942 President Graham sent a letter to parents, students, and faculty of the university, explaining the momentous changes that had occurred to the "peaceful, freedom-loving village of Chapel Hill" since Pearl Harbor. First came the "speed-up" of graduation from college from four years to three. Then came Naval ROTC, V-5, V-12, and the Pre-Flight School programs. The university was happy to be chosen as one of the four "Annapolises of the Air" programs and accepted the "double responsibility of carrying out the regular functions . . . of a historic and progressive state University, and of cooperating to the limit of our capacity with our country in a total war."[22]

In order to accommodate the new Pre-Flight School trainees, the University of North Carolina leased ten dormitories to house navy personnel and cadets. UNC made all of its athletic facilities available, and Lenoir Hall served as the cadet dining hall. The administration reserved Memorial Hall exclusively for the Pre-Flight School program. Hill Music Hall was put aside for cadet Protestant and Catholic worship services on Sunday morning. The Chapel Hill Country Club permitted the area around its golf course to be used as a drill ground for the cadets.

During its time in Chapel Hill from May 23, 1942, until October 14, 1945, the navy built an armory, a swimming pool, an infirmary, two boxing pavilions, administrative barracks, a canteen, a post office, a tailor shop, a laundry building, and a new athletic field. By agreement, all of the new buildings were turned over to the university when the program ended.[23]

The Pre-Flight School cadets faced a rigorous and demanding schedule. Six days a week the trainees were awakened at 5:30 each morning. For all those who had been startled out of a deep sleep after an exhausting day of work, nothing could be more annoying than the sound of the dreaded bugle calling forth the cadets for another day of arduous labor. The cadets participated in fifteen minutes of calisthenics or road work and then had breakfast. After cleaning up their rooms, they were in class from 7 a.m. until noon, with a ten-minute break for chapel. The trainees were allowed forty-five minutes for lunch and began the afternoon regimen at 1:45 p.m. The emphasis was on physical fitness. For two hours the cadets participated in military and physical drills and then from 4:15 to 6:15 had to take part in compulsory varsity and intramural sports. They were at dinner by 6:45 p.m. then had either a study hall or a lecture or a film from 7:30 until 8:50. Lights were out by 9 p.m.

The sixteen-week course had four major divisions:

1. Academic: extensive work and tutoring in math, physics, meteorology, seamanship, engineering, navigation, and gunnery. Naval history included organization of the navy, regulations, ordnance, cockpit instruction, and tactics of naval aircraft. Cadets were not only graded on their academic work; the navy also evaluated their performance in physical and military drills.
2. Military conduct and close order drill.
3. Physical training: boxing, wrestling, swimming, and hand-to-hand combat. In the swimming pool cadets learned to swim long distances fully clothed. On occasion they worked at hard labor, including wood chopping, land clearing, and ditch digging.
4. Sports programs. All cadets had to learn ten required sports: basketball, football, gymnastics, swimming, tumbling, hand-to-hand combat, boxing, soccer, wrestling, and military sports. The idea was to develop aggressiveness, coordination, alertness, teamwork, endurance, and confidence through competition. Soccer taught agility and endurance, football emphasized teamwork and discipline, while boxing promoted aggressiveness and toughness.[24]

In addition to athletic and academic instructors, the Pre-Flight School staff consisted of dieticians, psychologists, a medical team, and a chaplain. The psychologists attempted to indoctrinate the cadets with love of country and a willingness to sacrifice their lives for the ideal of freedom and democracy. The psychological orientation emphasized love of combat, hatred of the enemy, pride in being a pilot, and a "reckless, devil-may care" spirit. The navy wanted not just fliers but fighters; not only officers but real leaders who could think in a flash and decide correctly; officers who not only could take punishment but who were schooled to win.[25]

The cooks and dieticians faced a monumental task feeding 1,875 cadets three meals a day. Because of the strenuous physical training, the cadets needed plenty of nutritious food and 5,000 calories a day (over twice the calories allotted for civilians) to maintain high energy and high morale.

The hungry guests had milk three times a day and ice cream six nights out of seven. On one typical day the cafeteria served 537 pans of smothered chicken, 22 pans of corn pudding, 1,000 dozen rolls, and 350 cherry pies for dessert.[26]

Overall the navy seemed pleased with the preparation and quality of the food, but in wartime even the navy had some difficulty in getting all the high-quality meat, milk, and other foods that the men craved. It was not easy to satisfy a large group of rowdy and ravenous men in an institutional setting. The cooks could not always live up to the navy's high standard for tasty and healthy food. On one occasion the commander complained to the comptroller about the food service in Lenoir Hall: "The stew is too greasy . . . water's too hot, ice cream melts, beef too stringy, dishes need washing. . . . The meat was not fit for human consumption, the only redeeming feature of it was the fact that it was not tainted or spoiled."[27]

Discipline was crucial to success of the Pre-Flight School training. The navy maintained a tight rein on trainees, keeping many of their activities separated from the regular campus. The naval officers tried to reproduce a "Spartan-like monastic lifestyle." The more the men concentrated on their duties and the less they were distracted by outside influences, the better. The hard-working cadets had very little opportunity for liberty. They were allowed to visit other parts of the campus or go into town only on Wednesday, Saturday, and Sunday afternoons and Saturday night. They were not allowed to ride in automobiles and were not permitted to leave Chapel Hill except for athletic contests.[28]

The military presence dramatically changed the campus. By the fall of 1943 some 3,500 of the 5,300 students were in uniform. Women were admitted in record numbers. In September 1943 about 900 of the 1,800 civilian students were women. Prior to the war women had been admitted to undergraduate programs only in unusual circumstances, but during the war the university offered six courses for women to assist them in qualifying for the WAVEs, WACs, or SPARs. Some male civilians still resided on campus. Critics said only cowards and the physically unfit were left, but many male students had deferments from the Selective Service, were studying essential subjects, or had physical disabilities that prevented them from serving.

The university community interacted closely with the Pre-Flight School organization, but inevitably conflicts arose. On occasion the cramped streets, crowded housing, and jammed restaurants tried the town's patience. Nonmilitary university students faced a lack of housing, limited eating facilities, and fewer academic courses. The male university students harbored some resentment about the cadets' success with the women and their so-called privileged position on campus. However, most civilian students and the town embraced the cadets.

The navy presence had positive benefits: the infusion of money and students kept the university open and the cadets were good for local businesses. The Pre-Flight School program invited the community to social and athletic events and tried not to get in the way of the university administration. Although the transformation affected every aspect of campus and community life and could be trying, most people were willing to cooperate, compromise, and communicate with the navy to reach solutions to vexing problems. The community accepted the navy's presence because it was all for the greater good.[29]

Although there were many restrictions, with gas rationing and beer shortages, both cadets and civilian students found ways to have a good time. For dances they depended on jukeboxes and local bands. And despite navy restrictions cadets were welcome to attend university social events. Local residents invited cadets to dinner during the holidays, while churches and civic clubs hosted parties for the naval trainees. Bert Bennett, the UNC student body president, reprimanded some students who had been rude to the cadets. "The cadets are our guests. [They] are undergoing . . . months of the most grueling existence" to prepare for war, and any discourtesy to them was a violation of the Carolina honor code. Bennett asked students to join with him "in seeing that our brothers in the Naval Air Corps shall find at UNC the highest type of southern hospitality."[30]

The cadets and navy personnel had a significant impact on the economy of Chapel Hill and Orange County. The influx of people led to the establishment of new retail and commercial businesses and the expansion of those already there. The Pickwick Theatre, Fowler's Food Store, the Carolina Bootery, Ledbetter-Pickard, and the Varsity Men's Shop, among others, saw a sharp increase in business. Navy personnel rented rooms and apartments wherever they could find them, and local residents earned extra cash from these rentals. Shoe shiners and dry cleaners had a booming business. Barbers worked around the clock to provide haircuts for the cadets. A significant increase in state sales tax receipts from Chapel Hill during the war years reflected the improved financial situation for local businesses. Business was so good that the town passed an ordinance allowing certain establishments (such as bookstores and bicycle rentals) to be open from 1 to 6 p.m. on Sunday—a dramatic shift from the traditional closing of all business on the Sabbath.[31]

While the Pre-Flight School program had a profound influence on campus events, the administration and faculty at UNC also made huge contributions to the preparation for and fighting of the war. Some 260 faculty members entered the armed forces, worked for the federal government, or labored in the defense industry. The university estimated that around 10,000 alumni and thousands of students were involved in some sort of war activity from 1940 to 1945, with a total of 348 UNC alumni making the ultimate sacrifice.[32]

North Carolina State College (NC State) in Raleigh had an easier time developing a military-technological curriculum: as a land grant college, military training had always been an essential part of the college program. NC State had long been in the business of training men for commissions in the army, so they merely expanded and intensified the ROTC program. Due to the high demand for engineers and technicians of all kinds, the college created new offerings in diesel engineering, state of the art technology, and design courses and increased the number of science and math offerings across the board. Because of faculty expertise, NC State was especially important in several critical fields during the war: engineering and the building of cantonments; the testing of war materials; the manufacture of machinery and textiles for war use; and helping farmers create an abundant food supply.[33]

U.S. Navy B-1 Band

Prior to 1941 the navy had been reluctant to integrate, limiting black seamen to mess, cooking, and steward duties. Cognizant of these shortcomings, President Roosevelt wanted to make a beginning in integrating the navy and determined that "good Negro bands" be selected for each Pre-Flight School program. On April 13, 1942, the navy ordered that the black bandsmen would be enlisted as musicians, second class. Promotions would be achieved as the men qualified for them.[34]

The forty-five-piece UNC Pre-Flight School Band recruited musicians exclusively from the state of North Carolina. The navy knew that there would be great social pressure on these black musicians working and playing in a white community. The bandsmen would be front-line pioneers in breaking the color barrier, and the navy wanted musicians who were intelligent and even-tempered. The musicians had to understand the rigid nature of a segregated society in the Jim Crow South and had to accept (at least in public) these social conventions as a way of life. One reason the navy limited members of the band to North Carolinians was that they had lived in and experienced a racially divided society and understood how to deal with insults and discrimination. The navy recruited young men who "knew how to act" in the South but were also excellent musicians and of good character. If the band members had been chosen from northern states, the navy feared that they might not have been willing to put up with the Jim Crow system and could have created racial problems that the navy did not need.

While racial tensions were heightened in the South by the infusion of black soldiers and sailors from the North, a somewhat enlightened leadership of state and university officials enabled a black band to succeed in Chapel Hill. Governor Broughton believed strongly in a segregated society, but he and Dr. Frank Graham wanted to improve race relations and were both proponents of a slow but steady progress toward integration. Graham and Broughton understood that wartime was not the time to push for integration and believed that racial progress was best promoted through cooperation rather than confrontation. The B-1 Band survived and prospered due to the cooperation of the state's governor, the black leaders of the band, the UNC administration, and the white and black community leadership of Chapel Hill. The attempt to put a black band at the University of Georgia, the southern site of the Pre-Flight School program, failed due to the vicious racism of Governor Eugene Talmadge and the rabid opposition of the Georgia state legislature.[35]

Bands had always been an integral part of the military, stimulating morale and increasing esprit de corps. Navy bands had a different role than did army bands. The navy was not just concerned with martial and marching music but focused on entertainment and ceremonial music. Thus navy musicians had to be proficient in a variety of styles: patriotic pieces, popular music, classical music, martial music, and jazz. As one of the B-1 Band members recalled, "the men that were recruited for the B-1 Band were the best. They were the men who knew music. We read it; we could arrange it. . . . We played the classics for the officers, the admirals, for dances, for the movie stars. We played concert music and marching songs."[36]

All the band members had a high school education and most had at least two years of college. They all had professional music experience. The new recruits agreed to join the band for a variety of reasons. One graduate knew that several of his friends were joining, which made it easier. Some

Figure 7.2. B-1 Band, the black band assigned to the U.S. Navy Pre-Flight School program in Chapel Hill, N.C. A group of band members gathered around a piano to showcase their mastery of several instruments. By permission of North Carolina Collection, UNC Library, Chapel Hill, N.C.

were attracted by the opportunity to play music in a top band, while others were more pragmatic. William Gibson said: "We figured it would be our best chance of survival in the war." Willie Currie chose the navy primarily because he wanted to stay out of the army at all costs. "They stayed outdoors all the time. I mean they *lived* outdoors." The recruits understood the importance of what they were doing. Calvin Morrow said: "We were aware of what was happening, of what we were doing by going into the Navy." Another band member said he knew that history was being made and wanted to be part of it. Nathaniel Morehead thought that it was just as big a deal to be headed to the white-only UNC campus as it was to break the color line in the navy.[37]

After six weeks of basic and band training, the forty-two bandsmen went sent on to Chapel Hill, a segregated town of 2,450 whites and 1,124 blacks. The new arrivals understood that they had to toe the line on segregation once they took up residence. The all-white police force made sure that segregation was enforced. The stores on Franklin Street did not welcome black shoppers. The members of the B-1 group knew that they could practice music in the university gym but had no access to the canteen or the dining halls. They were fed at the off-campus "Negro" Community Center. One band member recalled that the merchants "never did anything out of the ordinary for us. They hated those Pennsylvania whites from the pre-flight school, but they let them go into the drug store. They hated us worse." The musicians were acutely aware that they were heavily scrutinized at all times and that their leaders counted on them being smart enough to avoid any confrontations. They knew not to go into the drugstore and order food; although they did not like it, they understood that they were to sit in the back of the bus.[38]

The B-1 was given a warm welcome by the black community and also greeted with enthusiasm by the university administration. The navy renovated and expanded the town-owned Negro Community Center into a residence for the band. Embraced by the black community, the bandsmen became role models and local heroes. Their concerts and daily marches to campus were watched with great interest, pride, and enthusiasm.

Throughout its time in Chapel Hill, the B-1 Band became intimately involved in the black community: teaching music lessons, playing in the local churches, and giving concerts at the community center. John and Doug Clark were two youngsters in the community who were enthralled with the B-1 Band and followed it when it marched on campus. Inspired by the B-1 Band, Doug Clark would become the founder and leader of the famous party band known as Doug Clark and the Hot Nuts. UNC students for years would swing and sway to the band's raucous music.

The B-1 Band made its first entrance into Chapel Hill as part of a grand parade down Franklin Street. The band members' recollections of that first day varied widely. Some remembered racial slurs and rocks and mud being thrown, while others did not recall any hostilities. Regardless of the negative memories of some of the men, most citizens loved the music and greeted the band with respect. According to band members, the most exciting part of the band's experience in the Pre-Flight School program was performing with the Cloudbusters, the dance band that became a huge favorite in the area. Band members also enjoyed forming small and large ensembles and quartets, where they arranged their own music and wrote some original pieces.

The B-1 Band performed at special events such as regimental reviews, war bond rallies, football and basketball games, and concerts at area schools. It accompanied the renowned singer Kate Smith on her live radio show and played at a black war bond rally that raised $75,000. The band also appeared at visits by Henry Wallace, the vice-president of the United States; at a UNC commencement; and, most proudly, at the launching in Wilmington of the USS *Merrick,* named for a black man.

The B-1 Band members were eventually sent overseas to Hawaii in February 1944. But during their time in Chapel Hill they carried themselves with dignity and managed to endear themselves to the majority of the community, both black and white. The band members played a primary and significant role in moving the town and state toward integration. They were foot soldiers in the fight for racial equality and helped transform Chapel Hill into the enlightened and progressive community that it later became. The band members served without any major incidents, despite the Jim Crow system and provocation from some whites. They made a very small step toward equality, but it was an important step. They spent eighteen months working in a white community that had previously opposed any attempt toward equality for blacks.[39] The B-1 Band achieved success because its members had the courage to accept the reality of segregation and not fight back while at the same time demonstrating the absurdity of segregation by their musical skills and good behavior.

Sports and Celebrities

The navy had a significant number of sports stars and famous citizens participating in its programs. In May 1942 a young naval officer named Gerald R. Ford moved into a cottage on Burlage Circle in Chapel Hill. The future president of the United States had joined the navy after completing his law degree at Yale University. The navy assigned Ford, a star football player at Michigan, to the V-5 Pre-Flight School as a physical fitness instructor. Although Ford liked Chapel Hill, calling it a "beautiful, quiet but potentially well-organized campus," he did not like teaching physical fitness to cadets and yearned to see combat. "But there was a war going on and I desperately wanted to be a part of it, so I wrote letters to everyone I knew, pleading for a billet on a ship." Finally, Ford received orders to report to the USS *Monterey,* a light aircraft carrier, as the ship's athletic director and gunnery division officer. Ensign Ford saw action in the Pacific theater.[40]

While at Chapel Hill, Ford had taken flying lessons in a Piper Cub and was thus familiar with the local airport. During the 1945 football season Rear Admiral O. B. Hardison wanted to see the football game between UNC and Navy at Chapel Hill. Hardison was on an inspection tour of bases in the South and planned his visit so that he would arrive in time for the game. The plane carrying the admiral, accompanied by Gerald Ford, approached the Horace Williams Airport in the middle of a terrible storm. The airport had no landing lights, and the pilot landed on the wrong runway. Ford described the event. "Suddenly, the plane pitched forward, plunged down an embankment and crashed into a clump of trees. Stunned, we searched for the exits and scrambled out as fast as we could. Seconds after we escaped, the plane burst into flames. I got out with only the shirt on my back." Ford's political career had almost ended before it began. He survived his service in World War II and went on to become a congressman from Michigan then vice president and president of the United States.[41]

Another future president of the United States, George Herbert Walker Bush, was a cadet at the Pre-Flight Training School. A recent graduate of Andover prep school, Bush planned to go to Yale University. But when he turned eighteen, he told his father that he was adamant about joining the navy. His father reluctantly accepted Bush's decision. George H. W. Bush reported for duty at UNC on August 6, 1942. He lived at 317 Lewis Hall with three other roommates. Bush recalled: "I came out of a very sheltered background and woke up in Chapel Hill," where he "had a rude awakening from exposure to the rest of the world." Removed from his privileged and parochial world in Greenwich and Andover, young Bush was profoundly affected by the change in surroundings and responsibilities, both physically and emotionally.[42]

Bush thrived on the Pre-Flight School training. He grew to his full six feet two inches and improved his overall military fitness score by twenty-five points. Naval records indicated that he was excellent at baseball, soccer, and basketball and average at football and wrestling. The upbeat personality traits that made him popular at Andover were invaluable at Chapel Hill. Despite his young age, he became a strong leader. After leaving UNC, Bush went on to complete his flight-training course, becoming the youngest commissioned pilot in the naval air service.

When flying an Avenger off of the carrier *San Jacinto* in the battle for Guam in 1943, Bush's plane, the *Barbara*, was hit by antiaircraft fire, and the engine failed. Bush tried to make it back to the carrier but could not do so and had to ditch his plane into the ocean. He did not have time to jettison his bombs, so the twenty-year-old pilot had to make a tricky and skillful landing with 2,000 pounds of TNT under his wings. After a brilliant landing in the ocean, Bush was rescued by a passing destroyer.[43] George H. W. Bush went on to a distinguished political career as a U.S. congressman, head of the Central Intelligence Agency, U.S. envoy to China, ambassador to the United Nations, and vice-president and president of the United States. Both Ford and Bush, whose paths would cross frequently, almost died in plane crashes at a young age.

Other well-known visitors to the campus during the war period included the famous Jimmy Dorsey Band. Gene Tunney and Jack Dempsey, world boxing champions, came to UNC to demonstrate their expertise. Captain Eddie Rickenbacker, the World War I flying ace, and secretary of the navy Frank Knox visited Chapel Hill.[44] Perhaps the most unusual visit was by Lieutenant Philippe H. X. de Gaulle, son of the French general Charles de Gaulle. Philippe de Gaulle, along with thirty Free French naval officers, took a four-week pilot training course in Chapel Hill. The French cadets were the talk of the town and had great success romancing the UNC coeds. Several of the American cadets were jealous of the Frenchmen's success, complaining that it had taken them two months to build up as much goodwill with the coeds as the French had achieved in two days.[45]

Because of the emphasis on athletics and physical training at the Pre-Flight School, the navy recruited faculty, administrators, and cadets with exceptional coaching and playing experience. The cadre wanted the football and baseball teams, known as the Cloudbusters, to be top flight in regard to talent.

Sleepy Jim Crowley, one of the Four Horsemen at Notre Dame, was head coach of the football team. He was assisted by two Hall of Fame football coaches. In the 1942 season he was aided by John Vaught, later the coach at the University of Mississippi, and in 1944 the line coach was Paul "Bear" Bryant. With such future pro stars as Otto Graham at quarterback, the football team compiled a record of sixteen wins, eight losses, and three ties in three years of existence. In November 1944 the Bainbridge Naval Training Center of Maryland came to Chapel Hill for a game and brought with them a skinny nineteen-year-old running back named Charlie Justice. Justice played only ten minutes but made a 65-yard touchdown run. That run was a precursor to the legendary career that Justice would have at Kenan Stadium, where he became the most popular athlete in the history of the university.

Fans watching the Cloudbusters baseball team play at Emerson Field thought that they were watching a major league baseball game. All nine members of the starting lineup had played at one time or another in the major leagues. The Cloudbusters featured Johnny Pesky and Ted Williams of the Boston Red Sox and pitcher Johnny Sain of the Boston Braves. Ted Williams, the star of the team and the fans' favorite, had won the Triple Crown (best batting average, runs batted in, and home runs) in 1942 and has been touted as perhaps the greatest hitter in the history of the game.[46]

Long before the National Football League, baseball was America's national pastime and the nation's most popular sport. As a baseball superstar, Ted Williams was one of the best known public figures in the country. At the peak of his prowess as a player, Williams decided that he wanted to be a pilot and do his part in World War II. He quit baseball and joined the navy as a seaman second class in May 1942. He gave up a $30,000 a year salary to be paid $105 per month during cadet training. Williams served in the navy from 1942 until 1945 and missed what would surely have been his most productive years as a baseball player. By the time he retired from baseball in 1960, he had a lifetime batting average of .344 and had hit 521 home runs.

After completing the V-5 program, the navy assigned Williams to the Pre-Flight School program at UNC. "I'll never forget getting off the train in Chapel Hill, just at dusk, and marching up in front of the administration building with the other recruits," Ted recalled. "The cadets already there were hanging out the windows watching us, and as we passed, one guy hollered: 'OK Williams, we know you're there and you are going to be sorry.' I never was sorry. All of it was absolutely different from anything I had ever been through, and even the hairiest times were interesting."[47]

Williams's friend and teammate Johnny Pesky remembered the intense physical regimen in Chapel Hill. "They really ran us through the wringer there—up by the light of the moon, double time all day, and to bed with the owls." Pesky bemoaned the fact that they drilled

till your tongue bulged. . . . Sports, hikes, inspections, fatigue. We played all games to test us for versatility—boxing, football, wrestling, swimming, soccer and baseball. The object was to find if we had a nerve cracking point. Some did! A lot of guys, knowing Ted's reputation as a pop-off, waited for him to explode. But he never blew any fuses or got a single bad behavior demerit. If anything, he took a little stiffer discipline than the others, sort of stuff like, "Oh, you're the great Ted Williams, huh? OK, mister." Ted took it all.

The commander of the Pre-Flight praised Williams as "one of the finest young men we have in the entire school. He is liked equally well by the officers and the men."[48]

Rumor has it that Cadet Williams hit a home run his first time up at Emerson Field and that he had a special relationship with Lenoir Dining Hall, situated down the right field line. He dropped a few balls on the roof of the dining hall and allegedly could hit the side of the hall upon request. Williams left Chapel Hill in September 1942 to continue his pilot training. He completed his flight training at the Naval Air Station Pensacola and was commissioned as a second lieutenant in the Volunteer Marine Corps Reserve. He spent the rest of the war as a flight instructor in Pensacola. Although he did not see combat in World War II, he volunteered to serve his country at great expense to his professional career. He did serve as a pilot in the Korean War, where he flew thirty-nine combat missions.[49]

After the War

The formal decommissioning of the Pre-Flight School at UNC occurred on October 15, 1945. Students, faculty, former cadets, and townspeople attended a farewell ceremony to commemorate the friendly association the two schools had for more than three years. Since May 1942 the school had trained 18,700 cadets in the Pre-Flight School and V-12 programs, 360 Free French cadets, 78 French officers, and 1,220 Navy V-5 officers. When the navy withdrew, new buildings and additions worth $1,023,671.58, which cost the state only $127,000, were turned over to the university. Some of the physical structures, such as the navy hospital, which later became the student infirmary, remained as permanent reminders of the Pre-Flight School's impact on campus.

The navy and its support for the Pre-Flight School proved to be the economic savior of the university. Having lost over $100,000 in 1941–1942, the university badly needed the influx of funds that enabled it to overcome its losses and achieve a strong surplus. The construction of much-needed buildings by the navy saved the use of state funds, and the huge increase in the need for goods and services enabled the merchants of Chapel Hill to prosper.[50] UNC and the navy both benefited by the association.

More important than buildings and income was the important part that the University of North Carolina, with support from the state government, had played in the training of American pilots for the most difficult and devastating war in history. The civilian students at UNC, along with the townspeople, understood the gravity and the urgency of the moment and supported the military training with enthusiasm.

As the war came to an end, Dr. Frank Graham and University of North Carolina officials began to make plans for the veterans who would be returning to school. The university was "deeply conscious of its obligation and opportunity in working with all veterans." The university wanted to make certain that veterans could resume their educational careers where they left off. The university agreed to allow greater flexibility in choosing courses and agreed to schedule refresher courses for those who needed them. Former students would be welcomed back without any formal procedure for admission except registration.[51]

As expected, the returning veterans swelled enrollment and taxed housing facilities. Of the 6,802 university students in 1946, 4,800 were veterans. The university's extensive expansion during World War II took care of some of the overflow, but additional housing had to be provided. Students utilized Quonset huts, trailers, rooms, and apartments all over the county, even the Tin Can, the drafty old gym, as living quarters. There were thirty-six Quonset huts on campus—thirty reserved for living quarters, three for bathrooms, and three for study halls. One student lived in an 8 foot by 12 foot tent with wood flooring erected behind the journalism building. The university purchased surplus army housing from Fort Bragg and other bases and moved the prefabricated buildings to Chapel Hill, where they were converted into apartments for married students.

Married students had fond memories of a place that came to be known as Victory Village, a military-style encampment jammed with ex-GIs. The apartments were often unheated and walls were thin, but the rent was right. The ex-soldiers, some of whom had experienced the horrors of war, moved on with their lives without complaint. They wanted an education, worked hard to achieve their goals, and did not have time for beer drinking and social activities. Professors remembered these battle-hardened men as the most motivated students that they ever taught.[52]

Victory Village had a total of 352 apartments and houses. Sixteen prefabricated houses resembling narrow barracks were divided into individual apartments. The village featured twelve two-story former army barracks that would accommodate seventy-two families. Each apartment had a living room, one or two bedrooms, a fully equipped kitchen, and an icebox, stove, and heater. While a few complained about the accommodations, most were happy to have a place to live. Mr. and Mrs. T. L.

Crittenden thought the housing was wonderful, much nicer than they had expected.[53]

In 1942 President Roosevelt had authorized members of his administration to formulate plans to help returning veterans readjust to American life. As the result of these recommendations, in 1944 Congress unanimously passed the Serviceman's Readjustment Act, known as the GI Bill of Rights. The bill authorized the spending of $14 billion, an unheard-of sum at that time, for educational benefits, vocational training, medical treatment in Veteran's Administration Hospitals, and low-interest loans for building homes or for starting a business. Demobilized soldiers unable to find work received $20 a week (more than the minimum wage of 40 cents per hour) for up to one year. This program put spending money in the soldiers' pockets, gave them some sense of dignity, and enabled them to search for jobs while they returned to civilian life. Few Americans of moderate means could afford to attend college prior to 1941, but the GI Bill changed all that. The bill offered students in a college or a trade school $110 per month in living expenses plus additional money for tuition, books, fees, and even support for dependents.

The resulting increase of veterans in both public and private colleges had a profound and lasting impact on America. By the late 1940s over 2 million students, half of the total male enrollment at institutions of higher learning, were attending school on the GI Bill. Because of all the new students and crowded conditions, state legislatures were forced to fund public universities more generously—a decision that changed the educational landscape, particularly in the South and in North Carolina. The North Carolina state legislature approved a generous increase in funding for public education and appointed a new State Board of Education to oversee the disbursement of funds. The legislature also made school compulsory until the age of sixteen.

The GI Bill may well have been the best civilian investment that the government has ever made. Not only did it create a larger and more democratic educational system, but the professionals and technicians trained during these years ended up making greater salaries than unskilled laborers and thus enabled the government to recoup its outlay in increased tax revenues. The money given to those reentering civilian life and the increased salaries that they earned by educational achievement moved many Americans into the middle class and led to a dramatic increase in consumer spending. Instead of reverting to a recession after the war, the American economy, with all its pent-up demand, boomed.[54]

World War II had an enormous influence on southern colleges and higher education in North Carolina. The war brought southern schools into the national mainstream for the first time. North Carolina colleges now exhibited a diverse student body from all over the country, with different views and varied experiences. The university curriculum had been impacted by new educational concepts promulgated by the federal government and the military services. North Carolina, a state still trying to overcome large pockets of poverty, saw its college enrollments go up with expanded support from the state legislature and money from the GI Bill and with an increased demand for skilled and educated citizens. As state schools struggled to free themselves from the twin evils of segregation and poverty, they began to compete on a more level field with peer institutions throughout America.[55] The reputation of the University of North Carolina flourished in academic circles. Because of the fond memories of thousands of its visitors during the war, the charms of Chapel Hill became known all over the country.[56]

PRISONERS OF WAR IN
THE OLD NORTH STATE

Many citizens of North Carolina would be surprised to learn that there were some 3,000 Italian prisoners of war (POWs) and 10,000 German prisoners of war interned in the state from 1943 to 1946. During World War II 378,000 German POWs were held in 155 base camps and 511 branch camps in forty-six of the forty-eight states. The number of POWs brought into the United States increased after Allied victories in North Africa and in Europe. The prisoners needed to be removed from the battle areas to prevent their return to action. The overstressed economies of Britain and other Allied countries simply could not handle the cost of feeding and incarcerating so many enemy prisoners. Thus the United States, the country most able to handle a large influx of POWs, took on the responsibility of accepting the new detainees.

North Carolina became a logical site to house POWs because of the warm southern weather, farmers' demand for additional labor, and the presence of numerous military installations in the state. In addition to the German and Italian POWs, North Carolina hosted Czechs, Poles, and Austrians who had served in the armies of the Third Reich.[1] A few German and Japanese noncombatant enemies had been taken into custody by the Immigration and Naturalization Service when America entered the war. These Japanese and German families were housed, on separate floors, at the Assembly Inn in Montreat, North Carolina, for six months in 1942,

before the Japanese prisoners were transferred to an internment camp in
Texas.[2]

Germans were the most numerous prisoners (with eighteen German
POW camps in the state, six base camps, twelve branch camps) and the
most effective workers. It might be difficult to imagine Nazis picking
cotton in North Carolina, but prisoners labored in all sorts of economic
endeavors: they harvested peanuts and tobacco; labored on army bases,
cooking, cleaning, and constructing buildings; worked in hospitals; and
made important contributions to the lumber and pulpwood industries.
While the Germans had greater impact on the state, the Italians were the
first POWs to locate in North Carolina.

Throughout 1943 farms across the state, the Atlantic and North Carolina Railroad, and lumber mills implored Governor Broughton to supply
them with Italian POWs to help ease the critical labor shortage. The governor frequently requested that the War Department send "all the Italian
POWs that can be spared" to work in the timber and pulpwood industries
in the state.[3] Broughton's persistence paid off when the federal government assigned several thousand Italian POWs to North Carolina. Broughton was "confident that we will be able to use all the prisoners sent to this
state and that our experience with them will be equally satisfactory with
that of Texas and other states where prisoners are already being worked
and where the people are much pleased with the results." The governor
concluded that the best use of this new labor source would be to help harvest the peanut crop and to fill the silos of dairy farmers. He had already
requested that 200–300 Italian prisoners be used in construction work
on the Atlantic and North Carolina Railroad.[4] Local authorities around
the state welcomed the governor's decision. There was certainly no reason
why the POWs, under adequate safeguards, could not harvest farm crops
and perform other labor in exchange for their board and keep.[5]

Italian POWs

When the Italians arrived, the only incarceration facility available was at
Camp Butner, which had been activated on September 7, 1943. One day
later a POW train pulled into the Camp Butner siding, delivering a train-
load of recently captured Italians. As the prisoners filed off the train, the
armed guards lined them up and accompanied them to the internment
area. Once settled, they were assigned to their duties by the U.S. military.
Under the supervision of the War Department and the War Manpower

Commission (WMC), the prisoners would essentially work for the U.S. military but could be hired out to private contractors.

The post commander, Colonel Thomas L. Alexander, pointed out that the rules of the Geneva Convention would be followed to the letter and that the interned men would be treated as honorable prisoners of war. Alexander explained that humane treatment would make it easier to handle what might be a difficult situation. "That does not mean that we will pamper them, they will be given firm, but just, humane treatment." The Italians, uneasy and confused about how they would be treated, eyed their captors warily, but most were glad that their war was over. The prisoners were described as being "happy and jolly" about being brought to America.[6]

Colonel Alexander's commitment to adhere to the Geneva Convention reflected the U.S. government's promise to abide by the rules of that most important document. On July 27, 1929, forty-two nations, including the United States and Germany, signed and ratified the Geneva Convention Relating to the Treatment of Prisoners of War. It contained ninety-seven articles designed to protect prisoners of war from undue harshness or extreme cruelty by their captors. The Geneva Convention governed all aspects of military captivity: interrogations, privileges of rank, the quantity and quality of food, clothing, housing (the same amount of space allotted for U.S. soldiers), sanitary conditions, medical care, disciplinary measures, allowable work assignments, prisoner representation, and even mailing privileges. The document called for the segregation of different races and nationalities as well as separate compounds for officers, noncommissioned officers, and enlisted men.

The U.S. government attempted to keep a low profile on the POW system to avoid an intrusive press and a curious public. The military did not want the public to be frightened about Nazi prisoners in their midst and wanted the camps to be as covert as possible. The sequestration of the POWs would enable the military to adhere to the section of the Geneva Convention that protected prisoners from "insults and public scrutiny."[7]

The details of the Geneva Convention were posted in each camp so that prisoners would know their rights. No specific provision was made for enforcement of the Geneva Convention; that responsibility was left up to each country. The Geneva Convention called for International Red Cross inspections of the camps as well as frequent visits by a neutral power, usually Switzerland. Germany clearly violated the Geneva Convention on many occasions in its treatment of Allied prisoners and in the concentration camps. The American government hoped that humane treatment of German POWs in America in adherence to the Geneva Convention would provide protection for American POWs in German captivity. The Japanese essentially ignored the Geneva Convention and flouted the agreement with impunity.

Article 27 of the Geneva Convention was of specific concern to the North Carolina camps because it spelled out the guidelines for the employment of POWs. Officers did not have to work unless they specifically requested it, noncommissioned officers would work only in a supervisory capacity, and all the work would be done by the lesser ranks. Captors were forbidden to use prisoners if they were physically unfit for work or if a prisoner claimed that the work would be a threat to his health or well-being. Rank and privacy were respected, and outsiders were not allowed into the area without formal permission. Prisoners received the same clothing and food as the American soldiers. If prisoners were ill, competent medical care had to be available. For morale purposes, recreational facilities had to be provided.[8]

In October 1943, shortly after the Italian POWs arrived, a State Department visitor described the POW site at Camp Butner. The observer noted that the camp was in the middle of a general farming area specializing in corn, tobacco, and peanuts. The camp had a capacity of 2,950 men, housed in fortified tents, each one accommodating approximately 50 men. Eventually 2,897 Italian POWs, guarded by three companies of U.S. military personnel, took up residence at Butner.

Among the first group of war prisoners from Italy were farmers, artists, laborers, businessmen, and students. After a two-day period of processing, similar to the indoctrination that U.S. soldiers received, the internees were given anti-infection injections and warm clothing. They quickly settled down into the routine of POWs. Life was not difficult. After reveille at 6:45 a.m. and breakfast, the men cleaned up their quarters and prepared for work. The camp administration kept the prisoners constantly employed to keep them occupied and used the POWs to alleviate local agricultural labor shortages.

The POWs worked on nonessential jobs that did not directly aid the American war effort. The Italian internees were put to work building roads, clearing land, conserving soil, and farming. They primarily cut timber and harvested peanuts. On base they worked in the laundry and the shoe repair shop or as sign painters, tailors, and mechanics. All prisoners received $3 worth of canteen coupons each month that could be redeemed for the purchase of soft drinks, soap, tobacco, candy, and toilet articles. The prisoners had a library stocked with books in Italian, a soccer field, and their own newspaper. The internees had a form of self-government, with an overall representative to the camp administration and noncommissioned officers chosen by the prisoners to serve as barracks sergeant, mess sergeant, and duty sergeant.[9]

According to the War Manpower Commission (WMC), prisoners could be hired by civilian contractors to work outside the camp. The prisoners would be paid the prevailing wage for regular labor in that area and for that profession. For example, the prevailing wage for picking peaches in North Carolina was 22.5 cents per hour. The military utilized these prisoners without putting them into competition with free American labor. POWs were normally employed only where there was a severe shortage of labor. North Carolina farmers especially needed the help. They had been having a difficult time harvesting their crops due to the dramatic departure of many young men into military service and factory jobs.

In order to use POW labor, the civilian employer had to present a certificate of need to the U.S. Army. Potential employers then placed an order for workers to the U.S. Employment Service and the War Manpower Commission. If the WMC determined that civilian workers were unavailable, then a certificate for the use of POWs would be granted. Under a private contract, the POWs would get 80 cents a day in canteen coupons for their own use. The rest of the paycheck from the employer would go into the United States Treasury. The employment agreement was a win-win situation. Farmers got their workers, while the payment for POW labor earned significant money for the U.S. government. As of May 1944 the value of POW contracts around the country was over $11 million.

By October 1943 some 1,900 Italians were working for private contractors in North Carolina. Clad in blue uniforms with "PW" marked with orange on the back, 1,500 Italian POWs helped with the peanut harvest in Tarboro, Windsor, and Scotland Neck. Others were employed in fertilizer mills, were hired by pulp mills to cut timber, and were used as mess attendants at the Pre-Flight School at UNC. For employers, the use of POW labor was a great bargain, as the labor was cheap, available, and reliable. According to Colonel Alexander, private employers who used prisoner labor under contract had expressed great satisfaction with the POWs' work and praised them for their conscientiousness and efficiency. Many of the Italians had been farmers in their homeland and were eager to work at an occupation they liked and had followed for years.

When the internees worked adjacent to Camp Butner, the guards carefully checked them onto buses or trucks for the trip to the work site. The guards returned the prisoners to camp at the end of the day. In other areas farther from Camp Butner, such as Tarboro and Williamston, the workers set up temporary camps with tents and a mess hall. The Tarboro encampment was encircled by barbed wire and illuminated at night by large floodlights to discourage escapes. The guards were expected to keep a sharp watch over the prisoners, although escapes by Italian prisoners were infrequent.[10]

Unlike some of the conflicts between hard-core Nazi SS (Schutzstaffel) troops and less zealous German prisoners, the Italians had very few internal disagreements. In Williamston one fight broke out between northern and southern Italians. Apparently the cultures of the two groups were too far apart for them to be compatible. Eventually they had to be segregated and harmony was restored. The Italians, contrary to legend, were good workers and not lazy. One local newspaper praised the Italians for their good efforts in producing 71,245 stacks of peanuts while working for 181 local farmers.[11]

When they arrived at Camp Butner the Italians feared for their future, uncertain of their fate. After a short time, however, many picked up some English and quickly adapted to their new home. According to one report, the Italians seemed to be a contented, happy, and congenial group. They were thousands of miles away from the battle lines, with three meals a day along with recreational facilities, and their workload was not onerous. They tried to be patient during their captivity, as they understood that one day the war would end and they would be allowed to return home to their loved ones to begin their lives anew.

The owner of a peanut field in Scotland Neck had hired the Italians for a couple of days and was amazed to hear an operatic aria sung by one of the prisoners in a full, rich tenor. The rest of the prisoners joined in the chorus and sang exuberantly while they worked. During their time at Camp Butner, with few exceptions, the Italian POWs expressed nothing but praise for their captors. In May 1944 the Italian POWs were transferred from Camp Butner out of the state and were replaced by German POWs.[12]

German POWs

Of the eighteen German POW camps in North Carolina, the first and most important facility was located at Fort Bragg. The initial German prisoners

Figure 8.1. The first German POWs at Fort Bragg were the surviving crew members of the U-352, sunk on May 9, 1942. Courtesy of the State Archives of North Carolina.

at Bragg were men from the U-boat (U-352) sunk off the coast of North Carolina on May 9, 1942. The surviving thirty-two crew members were transported to a temporary "specially prepared Detention Camp" set up by the army at Fort Bragg. Fort Bragg served as a holding facility as other captured submariners passed through on their way to more intensive questioning at other bases.[13]

Although Italian prisoners had arrived at Camp Butner in September 1943, the War Department did not set up permanent POW camps for German prisoners until 1944. Perhaps due to the possible threat of Nazi escapees, the U.S. government initially decided to use German POW labor primarily on military reservations but later agreed to use the POWs as contract labor in the agricultural areas of North Carolina.

In February and March 1944 the first non-naval German POWs were allocated to four permanent base camps in North Carolina: Camp Davis, Camp Sutton, Camp Mackall, and Wilmington. In May 1944 the authorities designated two additional base camps at Fort Bragg and Camp Butner. From this initial organization, the government set up twelve smaller "branch" camps in Winston-Salem (276 POWs), New Bern (388 POWs),

Scotland Neck, Ahoskie (226 POWs), Williamston (451 POWs), Greensboro, Edenton, Whiteville, and Goldsboro at Seymour Johnson Field (241 POWs). Camp Butner organized and controlled most of the branch camps, while Fort Bragg supervised three base camps.

By April 1945 Camp Butner had become the largest of the base camps, with 2,562 prisoners at the main camp and 2,925 at eight side camps, for a total of 5,487. The authorities set up a separate compound at Butner for German prisoners who were members of the Nazi Party or who were disciplinary problems. The camp commandant also established the so-called United Nations Compound, made up of 782 Russians, Czechs, Austrians, Poles, French, and Belgians. These inmates were segregated from their German "comrades." The United Nations' POWs were treated differently from the German prisoners and were not required to work, because many of these men had been forcibly drafted into the German army (the Wehrmacht). The "UN prisoners" told the camp commanders that they were sympathetic to the Allied cause and would be willing to fight against the Germans. Some of these POWs were repatriated before the end of the war, and several went back to the front to fight against their former German allies.[14]

The facilities at Camps Mackall and Davis and at Fort Bragg were located within military installations. Unlike the situation in the branch camps, the prisoners usually worked on base, completing work normally done by civilian employees. On December 7, 1944, Camp Mackall received 249 German POWs, most of whom had been members of General Erwin Rommel's elite Africa Corps. The visitors were housed in fifty-two pyramidal sleeping tents with wooden walls up to shoulder height. Each tent had five to six beds. The mess halls and latrines were in wooden buildings. A guard contingent of U.S. Army soldiers, housed nearby in similar quarters, watched over the Germans. The stockade was surrounded by a seven-foot barbed wire fence manned by troops armed with submachine guns in open air guard towers.

Most detainees were employed to work at the camp, as the civilian workforce had been depleted by the draft and by departures for better jobs. The POWs' initial work assignments at Mackall were primarily maintenance jobs as carpenters and mechanics. Some worked as shoemakers and bakers to fulfill the needs of the U.S. military. Others did sanitation work. Small groups worked on neighboring farms, helping with peach crops, processing tobacco, harvesting and stacking peanuts, doing dairy work, logging timber, and harvesting corn.

The leadership at Camp Mackall stressed proper treatment for the POWs by both military personnel and civilians in the area. The commanding officer of the POW camp explained that "these men are honorable soldiers, captured while fighting for their country and must not be considered as criminals nor treated by military personnel or the public as such." Although contact with the public was mostly restricted to employers, the general consensus was that the POWs at Camp Mackall enjoyed good relationships with the civilian population.[15]

To maintain good morale at Camp Mackall, movies were shown twice a week and the POW orchestra provided regular concerts. The army offered educational courses in English and French, math, mechanics, and accounting. The men had a radio. Every two weeks both a Protestant minister and a Catholic priest came for religious services. An inspection visit by the Red Cross concluded that the POW camp at Mackall was well kept and that the morale of the prisoners was good. The Red Cross inspector noted that the officers and the prisoners collaborated effectively and "the discipline of the camp and the quality of the work may be considered excellent." The spokesman for the internees had no complaints about the facilities or the treatment of the prisoners.[16]

The POWs from Mackall worked at a variety of jobs. The Standard Fertilizer Plant of Aurora, N.C., was said to be one of the first industrial plants in the nation to use prisoner of war labor. The Germans also toiled extensively in harvesting peanuts and working in the pulp mill near Plymouth and logging in Bertie County. The contract for harvesting peanuts between the War Manpower Commission and the private contractor was very precise. The agreement called for a payment of 12 cents per stack of peanuts, with 25 stacks considered to be a day's work. The work day was fourteen hours, including travel time. The employers insisted that it was the duty of the guards, not the employers, to prevent escape and to ensure that the detainees worked a full day.[17]

A contract between a farmer in Martin County and the government was illustrative of the various chores requested of the prisoners. On August 18, 1944, the POWs put in eight hours of labor working in tobacco. On September 27 and October 5, 1944, seven POWs worked six and one-half hours in peanuts. On January 5, 1945, the owner had them helping with farming duties, and on January 18 and February 15 the laborers spent eight hours each day cutting wood. The last employment was June 26, 1945, when the POWs worked four hours in tobacco.[18]

From the Wilmington camp, the prisoners worked at a fertilizer plant, at sawmills, and on farms and dairies. At the fertilizer plant, where they worked at night, the POWs had to produce 200 tons of fertilizer in an eight-hour period. At the sawmills they had to cut 1,500 feet of wood each day. If the detainees did not finish their tasks, they had to stay at work until they completed their assignment.

The employers in the Wilmington area were pleased with the POWs, stating that their labor was superior to any they had ever had. One farmer said: "They are Germans and I hate them. But I have to admit they're the best help I have ever had." In addition to outside work, the German contingent cultivated fourteen acres of land and produced enough vegetables for themselves and a sufficient amount to feed the military personnel attached to the camps. The army estimated that the fresh produce grown by the POWs saved the government some $1,800 during the summer. The Germans primarily favored potatoes and bread as their staple diet, but the army encouraged them to eat more vegetables.[19]

Camp Sutton in Monroe, N.C., became a base camp on May 25, 1944. The new camp was better built and much more comfortable than the tented locations. The site included two mess halls, four buildings with toilets and showers, a recreation hall, a music building, a store, an infirmary, and a chapel. The work on the base was similar to work at other camps; Sutton used the POWs as mechanics, kitchen helpers, plumbers, and unskilled labor. At Camp Sutton military labor always took first priority.

The off-base work, still regulated by the War Manpower Commission and the War Department, was similar to the work at other camps. At Camp Sutton, however, there were several complaints that the POWs had been misused by greedy civilian employers. A brief examination of the situation determined that the charges had some truth to them. To resolve this issue the military tried to step up inspections of civilian employers. But so many units were scattered around the state that the army did not have the personnel to observe the working conditions of the prisoners in any satisfactory manner.[20] In one case German POWs in Wilmington had staged a sit-down strike because they thought that they had been worked too hard and had been unfairly punished for not finishing a very demanding task. The army officer in charge of the work group stated that he had asked twenty workers to handle 160 tons of fertilizer in eight hours, but they had not done so. He punished them by locking them in the compound and denying them any food for twenty-four hours. Shortly thereafter camp officials worked out a compromise. The POWs agreed to return to work and complete the task.

Despite occasionally harsh punishments of prisoners, the POWs had few complaints of mistreatment by the military. One German prisoner was favorably impressed with the treatment of POWs at Camp Sutton in regard to disciplinary matters and working conditions. He admitted that the Germans were disciplined for organizing small scams that enabled them to avoid work or for breaking camp rules. However, he considered the punishment of being forced to live outside of their tents for a brief period to be rather mild. This internee thought that in enforcing the rules of the camp the Americans were more considerate toward the POWs than toward their own soldiers.[21]

Camp Sutton was not far from Charlotte, the largest city in the state, so the camp assigned prisoners to a variety of tasks in the Queen City. They toiled as mechanics and maintenance men at the Charlotte Quartermaster Depot, as landscapers at Charlotte Memorial Hospital, and as metal workers at the Mecklenburg Iron Works. Although many of the German POWs continued to evince Nazi sympathies, had fought against American troops, and might have been responsible for the deaths of American soldiers, the civilian employers in Charlotte tended to like the "hard workers" and "nice boys" and treated them well.[22]

The Charlie Griffin family of Unionville, N.C., near Camp Sutton, used POW labor and were pleased with the results. The family remembered that the workers came with a ratio of one guard to approximately seven prisoners. Joe Griffin, a sixteen-year-old, recalled that the POWs were well fed and well treated. "They were fed better than we were. They took breaks and got snacks and ate lunch at noon. They even had hot coffee on portable stoves." Joe Griffin spoke of how friendly they were. "The Germans gave us candy and showed us pictures of their wives and children." Despite some name calling and many references to Adolf Hitler, the Griffins admitted that they actually admired those "dirty Nazis."[23]

Throughout the state a significant number of employees and guards befriended the Germans and in a few cases made lifelong friendships. German prisoners worked in the peach orchards near Southern Pines and on local dairy farms. June Bobbitt remembered that the German POWs "were very nice. They often ate dinner with us. We kept up a friendship with most of them for years after they returned to Germany." Watts Auman remarked that the POWs were friendly when they worked in his father's peach orchard. His mother had forbidden her children to eat candy, so the first candy bar that Watts ever enjoyed was given to him by one of the POWs. When it came time to pick the peaches, the family and the

POWs worked harmoniously late into the night, packing the peaches for shipment.[24]

Although the American guards warned bystanders to stay away from the "dangerous Nazis," a few citizens had an opportunity to converse with them for a brief period. One local farmer recalled that the Germans were hard workers, efficient and friendly.[25] When the Nazi POWs first arrived, there was a certain fear among the local populace that they might escape and terrorize the neighborhoods. Youngsters in Wilmington, naturally curious about their mysterious visitors, wanted to visit the POW encampment but had been instructed by their elders "not to get too close to the POW area." They were "never to smile, wave or show any friendliness toward the prisoners." Despite the warnings, the kids wandered down to the compound to bring the POWs candy and to try to talk with them. The Germans welcomed the attention.[26]

The general philosophy of the Germans at Camp Sutton was to live and let live, but there were constant differences and conflicts among the prison population. The spokesman for the POWs at Camp Sutton, Master Sergeant Frederick Glunz, revealed that he had to walk a fine line to please both the camp authorities and the men he represented. As a soldier his foremost duty was to see that the camp operated properly. When he insisted on a clean, disciplined, and well-ordered camp, his fellow inmates accused him of siding with the Americans. If he did not enforce the rules of the camp, he would draw the ire of the American authorities. He not only had to arbitrate disputes between the POWs and the U.S. Army but also had to reconcile the significant differences between the pro- and anti-Nazi factions in the camp.

As noted, the earliest German captives were members of the elite Africa Corps. They were hard-core Nazis, proud and arrogant. These unrepentant officers and NCOs tried to establish in prison the same kind of strict organization and mind control that existed in the Third Reich. As a result, occasional brutal confrontations occurred between those fanatical Nazi officers and those who opposed Hitler. At Camp Croft near Aiken, S.C., two Nazis killed a fellow POW for apparent disloyalty to the Third Reich. The two were later convicted of murder and hanged.

No such incidents took place at Camp Sutton, but the hostility between pro- and anti-Nazi groups always simmered just below the surface. There was a constant friction between the Germans and Austrians in the prisoner compound. The Austrians represented the majority of the anti-Nazi group but were a distinct minority in total numbers in the camp. Most

Austrian POWs had been anti-Nazi both before and during their captivity in America. The Austrians complained of oppressive and mean-spirited acts against them by the Nazi element and asked to be transferred to an all-Austrian unit. Some Austrians were transferred into the United Nations Camp at Camp Butner, while some of the more truculent pro-Nazis were sent to the so-called Nazi Camp at Camp Butner, reserved for troublemakers.

Commanders at the various camps, who were short of highly trained guards, in many cases felt they had no alternative than to defer to the Nazi hierarchy. The commanders preferred the Nazis to be in control because they wanted peaceful, disciplined, efficiently run camps without any problems. The Nazis often managed work details, the camp newspaper, and other aspects of camp life and took harsh measures against those prisoners that they deemed insufficiently loyal. Over time the camp regulators separated the more fervent Nazis from the rest of the prisoners in the compound and began a reeducation program for the hard-core believers. Toward the end of the war the newest German arrivals were older than the members of the elite units, were not members of the Wehrmacht, and were well aware that Germany was losing the war. Many hated Hitler because he was destroying their country. This later group of POWs was much easier to organize and control.[27]

In the winter of 1944 the American government initiated a program for prisoner reeducation because of concern about the influence of Nazi elements within some of the POW camps. The military leaders knew that they would eventually have to repatriate the prisoners and wanted to reeducate the Germans in the ways of democracy before returning them to their homeland. The goal of the program was to help Germans "understand and believe historical and ethical truth as generally conceived by Western civilization" and, "upon repatriation to Germany, . . . form the nucleus of a new German ideology which will reject militarism and totalitarian controls and will advocate a democratic system of government." Although the Geneva Convention forbade use of propaganda on prisoners, the Prisoner of War Special Projects Division went ahead with its reorientation program.[28]

The courses of study outlined by the Special Projects Division stressed competence in the English language and focused on American history and the American political system. The POWs saw American films, read American books, and listened to American radio shows, all generally favorable to the United States. In some camps officials showed prisoners newsreels of bombed-out German cities and graphic films delineating what had occurred in the concentration camps. The reeducation plan gained little traction at Camp Sutton. The POWs had limited interest in attending class, but some of the prisoners cooperated because they feared that they might not be permitted to return to their homeland if they did not profess allegiance to American ideals.[29] Overall the ill-advised program had little long-term influence on the thinking of the German POWs, most of whom had already rejected Nazism.

The government had begun phasing out the POW facilities by the spring of 1945; 73,000 German POWs in the United States had been repatriated by the end of November 1945. There was some opposition to returning POWs back to Germany for fear that the Nazi element would try to reorganize the Third Reich. Due to pressure from England, France, and some American political leaders, the United States government agreed not to repatriate 178,000 German prisoners immediately. The government designated 123,000 German POWs as British owned and 55,000 as French owned. Most of the early German detainees had been captured by the British or French in North Africa. The British and French could not house and feed them, so they became "temporary" wards of the United States.

After release from the United States, these prisoners were forced to work as POWs to rebuild the French and English cities and factories destroyed by Germany during the war. The desire of the French and British governments to punish those who had helped devastate their country is understandable, but the decision was a gross violation of the Geneva Convention, which required that prisoners be repatriated with "the least possible delay after the conclusion of peace." The United States should have adhered to the agreement to return the POWs to their homelands at the end of hostilities, but the British and French needed the labor to rebuild their war-torn countries and looked on this POW labor as a form of reparations.[30]

Matthias Buschheuer, a POW at Camp Sutton, was a victim of the decision to send certain POWs to England and France. He remembered his days as a prisoner at Camp Sutton as halcyon: he had been treated well and had been given adequate food, lodging, and medical care. When he left Camp Sutton, he expected to go home but ended up in France. After he had a difficult time working in four French POW camps, where they hated the Germans, the French finally released him in the summer of 1947. Despite his ordeal in France, he still had fond memories of his time in North Carolina. Over the years he came back for many visits to the state to see his former employers, the Hugh Harris family, for whom he had once picked corn.[31] The Harris family often visited Germany as guests of the Buschheuer family. Mary Elizabeth Harris reveled in the fact that the Harrises had "a home in America and one in Germany." The children of both families have maintained the friendships.[32]

Other prisoners established strong ties with American families. Prior to being repatriated, some German POWs in Wilmington did not want to leave but wanted to stay in America and become citizens. Jack McCarley, a dairyman, valued their work and friendship and kept in touch with many of his former POWs. He wrote to Max Speth in June 1948: "I often think of you boys that worked for me during the war and it makes me very happy when I hear from one of you and learn that you have arrived home safely. I only wish the conditions were much better for you. I sincerely hope that food supplies and everything will return to normal very soon."[33]

Escapes

One way of gauging prisoners' acceptance of their plight was the number of escape attempts. Being a prisoner of war was not easy, even under good conditions. As a rule, they all wanted to return home to their loved ones and resume their former lives. Many were ashamed that they had surrendered and were tortured by this failure for the rest of their lives.

The greatest difficulty for a POW in North Carolina was dealing with the boredom and lethargy of camp life. Other than work (and most officers chose not to work) the prisoners had very little to do. The inmates carried on endless conversations about home, wives, sex, food, Hitler, and the end of the war. They had music, a few movies, soccer, reading, and playing cards as pastimes but little else. Much time was spent sleeping and daydreaming. Some prisoners simply could not accept their fate and fell into deep depression. A few attempted suicide, but very few tried to escape.[34]

Chances of escape from an American POW camp were slim. Every camp had armed guards, guard dogs, and barbed wire. Extreme distances, language barriers, and the distinct possibility of being shot discouraged all but the most fanatic prisoners. They were not allowed to have money, only canteen scrip, so it would be difficult to raise enough money for an escapee to travel far from base. Their only decent chance would be if they had friends or family in the United States who would aid and abet the escape. Most German and Italian POWs accepted their fate. "Some of us thought it foolish to escape from a place where we were enjoying relative freedom and good care to return to a Germany where death, hunger and other dangers were still the rule of the day."[35]

Nationally 2,222 German POW escapes occurred from 1942 to 1946, from a prison population of 378,000. According to War Department statistics, 56 Germans were shot to death while trying to escape. Most were gunned down by guards, but on one occasion in a rural section of Tennessee a mountain woman killed an escapee who had wandered onto her property. Twenty-nine escape attempts took place in North Carolina. All but one attempt failed, and four tries resulted in death. With 10,000 German POWs in the state, this number reflected a very low attempt rate of 0.29 percent.

Werner Meier, a German prisoner who spoke English fluently, made a bid for freedom while working in a rural area. The guards called out for him to stop, but he was shot and killed when he continued running. His body was transported back to camp and buried with full military honors, because the Geneva Convention required the captors to uphold the honor and dignity of each combatant. Most escape attempts were kept from the public and the press, although Meier's bid for freedom ended up featured on the front page of the *Durham Morning Herald*.[36]

Fritz Teichman, because of his good English, functioned as an interpreter for the base chaplain and also founded a POW choir. During his time at Camp Butner he appeared to be a model prisoner, but the entire time he had been plotting his escape. His attempt was foiled when he was found with American cash (forbidden to prisoners). He was transferred to the Nazi compound on base.[37]

Helmut Haeberlein's attempt to escape was a more intriguing case. He left the stockade at Camp Davis apparently concealed in a garbage can. The army established an extensive roadblock around the area and the FBI distributed copies of a "wanted" circular, but the police agencies had little success in finding Haeberlein.

What made this case so interesting was the POW's reasons for leaving the camp, which he explained in a note to the camp commandant:

Mon Capitaine: According to the great philosopher Spinoza every man has to seek happiness. Having not found it in this camp of war prisoners, I must go some where [sic] else. As you are not supposed to give me a furlough, though, I am taking one myself. Once, one of your fellows told me "if you could live two weeks in the U.S.A. as a free man, you never would want to return home." Now I am going to try it and take way [sic] in search of happiness and freedom, which will cause you some troubles. I beg you to excuse and forgive me, after a certain lapse of time, if your authorities don't catch me before, I will return myself. Herewith I give you my parole, as a soldier, that I will not commit any act of sabotage, espionage, propaganda against the U.S.A. or any act of violence.[38]

Haeberlein made good on his escape but never got to live as a free man in the United States. On October 3, 1944, Haeberlein's body was discovered in the Hudson River in New York. Little is known of his activities from the time of his escape until October, so both his death and his romantic excursion from Camp Davis remain mysteries.

Gerd Roempke, a cocky, arrogant German who believed that he would never be caught, escaped three separate times from Camp Butner but was captured and returned each time. The only successful escape was by Kurt Rossmeisl, who left Camp Butner on August 4, 1945, and was never apprehended. He finally turned himself in to the FBI on May 10, 1959, fourteen years after the war ended. Rossmeisl, who spoke fluent English, caught a train to Chicago and lived there under an assumed name until he tired of worrying about the FBI arresting him and gave himself up.[39]

As would be expected, there was significant opposition in North Carolina and around the country to the "humane" treatment of POWs. This view was particularly prevalent toward the end of the war when the world learned of the atrocities at the Nazi concentration camps. Although the military had gone to great lengths to keep the public from finding out about the conditions in the POW camps, the American press discovered that the POWs had sugar, meat, bread, butter, vegetables, and other foods that were in short supply for Americans. After Allied forces rescued malnourished prisoners from Nazi brutality at Dachau, Buchenwald, and Matthausen, the American public learned that German POWs in America had not been mistreated; they had been coddled. For their two to three years of captivity in America, the POWs had access to decent living conditions denied to American soldiers and not always available to American civilians.

The new information about conditions in concentration camps led to a popular revulsion of all things German. Americans tended to view all POWs as Nazis. The press made numerous comparisons between the way the Germans treated American POWs and the contrasting indulgent treatment of German POWs in America. Photos of emaciated Americans being liberated from POW camps in Europe were contrasted with stories of "special menus" for German detainees. The public became upset about such activities as the POW sit-down strike in Wilmington over being worked too hard. One story that gained prominent exposure was an account of German POWs going on strike in Florida over a lack of cigarettes in their Post Exchange. The outcry from the American public was so great that the camps reduced food allotments for POWs, until the Red Cross protested that the decision was a breach of the Geneva Convention.[40]

Mrs. James O. Hall wrote a letter to the *Charlotte Observer* complaining about special privileges for the Germans. Her views were typical of many such letters written to newspapers all over the state:

> Why do our American people show so much concern for the German prisoners over here in giving them every comfort they can, while our own dear boys are being treated like a bunch of dogs in the various prison camps in Germany? . . . The German prisoners over here are being handled with kid gloves while our own boys are being treated like animals in that heartless, brutal, ungodly land. I have no tender spot in my heart for the German race for they have caused more broken homes and heartaches than any civilized nation that ever existed. May God grant that a day of reckoning may soon come when Hitler and all his clan will be wiped off the face of the earth forever.[41]

In April 1945 C. J. Williamson expressed similar views about the state's German guests. He had observed them shirking work and going off swimming in a creek and heard that they had a hot lunch of beefsteak and coffee carried to them in the field because they did not want to eat a cold lunch. Williamson charged that many of the POWs had escaped because they were not properly guarded and the government had to spend taxpayers' money to recapture them. "Treat prisoners like human beings (although they are not) but treat them like prisoners, not our equal or better. Think of our prisoners over there and the way they are being treated."[42] Another citizen became incensed when he discovered that amusement equipment and games had been shipped to a POW camp near Goldsboro. When he thought of how "our own boys had been treated, starved, tortured and murdered, it seems perfectly outrageous that we should be called upon to furnish members of the race of super fiends with entertainment."[43]

Although many farmers badly needed labor to harvest their crops, some farmers refused to use German POWs. One farmer said that "he wouldn't take a man on my farm who may have been shooting at my son at some time." On one occasion a local farmer took a German POW with him into a restaurant. The owners of the restaurant knew the farmer but refused to serve him as long as he had the German with him. These two cases were minor examples of the lingering fear and distrust of all "Huns," even when vouched for by a local farmer.[44]

The most caustic and bitter comments about the cushy life of foreign POWs came from American GIs who had seen combat. Robert Engstrom, who had recently returned from German captivity, became enraged when he encountered German POWs working in a kitchen where he took his meals. The emaciated Engstrom, who had dropped from 165 to 118 pounds, lost it when he saw the big, husky, well-fed Germans. "We were angry. They obviously had enjoyed more than enough to eat and we had not. They had been well treated and we had suffered." His buddies prevented him from carrying out any revenge on the POWs, but his reaction mirrored those of many returning servicemen.[45] A letter from Private Charlie H. Jenkins Jr., recovering from wounds received in the Tunisian campaign, maintained that he would gladly have traded places with the German POWs in America, because their conditions were far superior to the way in which U.S. prisoners had been treated by the Germans. He reminded those at home that the Germans in American camps were the "same Nazi followers who believed until their capture that they were the master race. . . . They're the same group of murderers who have killed and wounded thousands of American fellows who were buddies of mine—fellows who believed in democracy and fought until death believing that they could return to their wives, sweethearts, mothers." Jenkins thought that it was "hard for the average American to hate the POW, but it is essential that all of us must hate the Germans."[46] The anger toward the detainees was understandable, given the circumstances of wartime, but the indignation and resentment faded after hostilities ceased.

When all the discontent over the POWs surfaced, the U.S. government immediately began a campaign to douse the fires of protest by insisting that America had no choice but to adhere to the conventions of humane treatment for prisoners. A failure to conform to the Geneva Convention would result in retaliation against American POWs. The government published a series of articles explaining that enemy prisoners of war had not been pampered or given too much freedom. An investigation by the U.S. House of Representatives Military Affairs Committee failed to substantiate any of the rumors of excessively lenient handling of the POWs.

The army emphasized that the POWs were good workers and that their labor helped solve an acute manpower shortage. In order to be effective workers, the men had to have an adequate diet and proper rest; otherwise their labor would have been of little value.[47] Government figures indicated that civilian contractors paid the U.S. Treasury $22 million for POW labor in 1944. The government also saved $86 million by using prisoners to do civilian work on military posts, and POW labor preserved many crops essential for feeding the troops that otherwise would have been lost due to lack of adequate workers.[48]

Without question German POWs in North Carolina were fairly and decently treated. Except for a few occasions when prisoners were assigned to dangerous duty in sawmills, the United States strictly adhered to the Geneva Convention. The internees were properly fed and housed and were compensated for their work. For the most part the military kept the POWs separated from the general public except for limited interaction with civilian contractors. Americans expressed anger and frustration at the so-called cushy life of the prisoners, but little violence took place against the Germans or the Italians. Occasionally a few rowdies would throw rocks or hurl insults as the POWs were trucked to work, but surprisingly little physical damage was inflicted on these sworn enemies. There were twenty-nine escape attempts, some suicides, and internal conflict within the camps but no major discipline problems or significant riots among the prisoners. The camps were generally well run and competently organized and used the German and Italian labor in an efficient manner.

A study of the use of German POWs in the southern lumber industry concluded that the POWs usually worked hard, although they had very little monetary incentive to do well. The laborers produced somewhat below the output level of prewar civilian workers, but their work was critical and valuable in support of the war effort in essential industries.[49] Overall America profited from POW labor while demonstrating acceptance of universal standards in the treatment of POWs and exhibiting extraordinary tolerance for our wartime enemies.

THE DOUBLE V

RACISM DURING WORLD WAR II

The living conditions for African Americans in North Carolina on the eve of World War II were dismal at best. Black unemployment was approximately twice as high as white unemployment, and the median family income was one-third of white income. Two-thirds of black workers were in service or unskilled jobs. In North Carolina more than one-half to three-fourths of black women over the age of fourteen worked full-time as domestic servants, in personal service, or as agricultural workers—all at very low wages. Black women faced significant child-care needs of their own as well as trying to provide the necessary money to care for their families.

There was a high level of illiteracy among black people in North Carolina in 1948. One in ten had little or no schooling, and the average level of education was 5.9 years. Black schools were inferior, lacked books and qualified teachers, and were funded at a much lower level than the white schools. Black mortality rates were much higher than for whites. Black people had inadequate health care and suffered from pellagra, rickets, and other diseases of poverty. Black housing was segregated, overcrowded, and inferior in almost every respect. The Jim Crow system in North Carolina and the rest of the South left black people segregated by law and vulnerable to white power and prejudice. They were essentially disenfranchised and thus had little political recourse to affect the racial caste system that controlled their lives.[1]

The Federal Writers' Project on North Carolina in 1939 described the rather restricted and difficult life for black people during the Depression years. They had their own restaurants, hotels, and motion picture theaters but enjoyed only limited use of public facilities. Separate coaches, as well as separate waiting rooms, were provided on trains and use of the dining car by black passengers was prohibited. Streetcars and buses assigned black riders seats in the rear. The Writers' Project discovered that even educated black people found it difficult to register to vote. Black participation in civic affairs such as jury duty, holding office, and policing was practically nonexistent.[2]

The extent of racism that prevailed in wartime America cannot be exaggerated. While America fought a war for democracy and freedom, the subjugation of black citizens in the state and in America continued. Early in the war black Americans began to support what was known as the Double V campaign—victory over totalitarian forces abroad and victory over discrimination and racism at home.

Despite difficult economic and social circumstances, World War II presented black Americans with significant opportunities and led to circumstances that would eventually enable them to challenge the entrenched social order. They improved their financial situation, mainly by moving from rural to urban centers for better jobs and by taking positions in military base construction and in the shipbuilding industry. But black citizens still faced discrimination, as racial bias prevailed throughout the defense industry and in the federal government. Of 100,000 aircraft workers in the country during World War II, only 240 were black, most of them working as janitors. The work environment and the living and eating facilities at large industrial plants, in textile mills, and in tobacco warehouses remained segregated.

Black soldiers also encountered segregation and discrimination while serving their country in the armed forces. The discrimination began at the induction station. Some white physicians rejected black applicants because they simply did not want them in the military. On more than one occasion a recruiting station was designated for "whites only." Determined to do his duty for his country, John Hope Franklin, the distinguished black historian, volunteered for military service. A university professor at the time, Franklin told the recruiter that he knew how to type and run an office and had a Ph.D. from Harvard University. The sergeant denied Dr. Franklin admission to the military, indicating that he "had everything but color." The angry professor politely thanked the sergeant for his time and

left the recruiting station, vowing that he would never fight in an army
that discriminated in such a way.[3]

At the outset of the war the Marine Corps, the U.S. Navy, and the U.S.
Army Air Force would not accept black candidates. The Marine Corps
eventually formed the Montford Point Marines. The army air corps organized a separate flight school at Tuskegee, Alabama, that trained about six
hundred black pilots. Many of them saw action in Europe, but most were
denied combat experience. There were many examples of black applicants
who wanted to join a certain branch of the military but were turned away.
Ernest Henderson wanted to enlist in the army air corps. He was a good
student and in good health, "but they wouldn't let us in because of our
race. They thought black men didn't have the aptitude, technology or judgment to fly an airplane."[4]

Most of the military units remained segregated until the end of the
war and each military base had its "Little Harlem," with separate facilities. Except for the B-1 band members at UNC, black men who enlisted
in the navy were chagrined to learn that they would only be employed as
stewards and cooks. They wanted to fight not cook. Since many of them
spent their time shining shoes, making beds, washing dishes, and serving
officers at mealtime, they saw themselves not as navy men but as servants
under the control of white officers. As would be expected, their subservi-
ent position had a debilitating effect on morale.[5]

The largest number of black enlistees served in the army. Some signed
on because they recognized the military offered steady employment at a
time when civilian jobs were limited. Others hoped for an opportunity to
travel and to learn a useful skill. Segregation in the army remained firmly
entrenched in 1941, and military leaders in Washington fought any efforts
at desegregation. George C. Marshall, the army chief of staff, and others
claimed that trying to solve problems of social inequality during wartime
would affect American military efficiency, when winning the war was the
most important goal. Marshall explained that segregation was a well-
established custom and the educational level of most black recruits and
draftees was well below that of the white recruits. The army revealed that
more than 80 percent of black soldiers scored in the two lowest grades on
the Army General Classification Test. Nearly 50 percent of black soldiers
drafted between March 1941 and December 1942 scored in the lowest category, compared to 8.5 percent of white soldiers. The nation's military
leaders concluded that it would be more difficult and costly to train un-
educated black soldiers and that their numbers should be limited.

The black press and the National Association for the Advancement of Colored People (NAACP) refused to accept the army's explanation and backed a proposal for an experimental integrated military division made up of both black and white volunteers. The NAACP argued that racial segregation in the army was undemocratic and "dangerous to our national morale." Several prominent white southerners, including Dr. Frank Graham, endorsed this concept of integration. The War Department rejected the proposal, stating that the military "would not indulge in social experimentation in time of war."[6]

Late in the war the military made some much-delayed gestures toward integration. With the need for additional troops, the army created some all-black units, but they were usually trained for noncombat roles. Reserve Officer Training Corps (ROTC) courses were established at primarily black universities, including North Carolina Agricultural and Technical College, but many of the new officers worked in a segregated military and were often officers in name only. The military eventually introduced blacks into the Army Air Corps and provided equal and integrated training for officers and combat soldiers in all branches.

By the end of the war over 700,000 black soldiers were serving in the army and nearly 6,000 had become officers. The army air force employed 678,000 black airmen and over 1,000 officers. Black women had been accepted in the WACs and the WAVEs. More than half a million black people served in uniform in Europe, Africa. and the Pacific, although most still worked in labor or service units. While the military remained essentially segregated at the end of the war, these limited steps at improving the status of black soldiers would ultimately lead to the desegregation of the armed forces.[7]

One example of a successful all-black military unit was the 555th Parachute Infantry Battalion, the "Triple Nickels." In an army that had traditionally relegated black soldiers to menial jobs, the 555th succeeded in becoming the nation's first all-black parachute unit. Although trained as combat soldiers, the members of the 555th still had to use "colored" toilets and water fountains in railroad stations and sit in segregated sections of the theaters. Officers' clubs on post were closed to black officers. Despite the restrictions, they were determined to show black pride by being the best-trained, toughest, and bravest parachute unit in the army.

The 555th began its training on July 17, 1944, at Camp Mackall. Members of the battalion spent five months engaged in serious unit combat training and received high marks for their skill and dedication to duty. They had high morale and felt that they could take on any task and do as well as any other unit. They expected to be posted to the European front to replace the large number of paratroopers lost in the Battle of the Bulge. Although they were combat ready and alerted for European duty, they were disappointed to learn that they had been assigned to parachute in to fight forest fires in Oregon. While members of this unit did not get into combat, they had pride in what they had accomplished as the first black paratroopers.[8]

Perhaps the most volatile and most relevant issue for all black Americans was their full-scale participation in defense production. In January 1941 A. Philip Randolph, head of the Brotherhood of Sleeping Car Porters, the leading black union, organized the Negro March on Washington Committee to dramatize job demands. The proposed march was an attempt to mobilize the black masses to appeal for direct action to achieve greater economic opportunities. The idea was to force President Roosevelt and the federal government to accede to their demands by awakening public anger at the injustices of racism.

President Roosevelt sympathized with the goals of the black workers, urged defense contractors to hire blacks, and demanded "immediate steps to facilitate the full utilization of our manpower." But he consistently viewed domestic reform, including civil rights, as secondary to the main goal of winning the war. He also feared agitating southern Democrats who could block some of his legislative initiatives in Congress. Roosevelt tried to appease Randolph with platitudes and vague promises, but Randolph wanted something concrete and tangible. He demanded an end to discrimination and segregation in the armed forces, in government, and in hiring.[9]

Roosevelt, fearing a national embarrassment if the march took place, held a series of meetings that produced a presidential directive against discrimination. Executive Order 8802, issued on June 25, 1941, barred "discrimination in the employment of workers in defense industries or Government because of race, creed, color or national origin." The order forbade discrimination by either management or labor in government agencies, job training programs, and defense contracts and set up a Fair Employment Practices Committee (FEPC) to investigate complaints and enforce the edict. No reference was made to segregation in the armed forces. The FEPC had the power to disseminate information and to investigate complaints but no power to enforce any order or to cancel defense contracts. It lacked staff, money, federal support, and enforcement power, while often accommodating its policies to white public opinion.[10]

The FEPC was never an effective agent of change, especially in the South, as it could do little to prevent any company from hiring a white-only workforce. In Charlotte, for example, only a few of the largest employers had nondiscriminatory hiring practices for any entry-level job. Still, the order was an important document that calmed the racial waters. For the first time since Reconstruction, the federal government had taken decisive action in behalf of equal rights for black citizens.

The FEPC clearly did not intend to challenge the legal status of segregation. Southern employers generally ignored or flouted Executive Order 8802. Southern newspapers denounced the FEPC as an example of federal socialism run amok and the beginning of a communistic dictatorship. Due to active resistance to the FEPC, wartime gains for black people came slowly. Discrimination in hiring continued.

In some places, however, like the North Carolina Shipyard in Wilmington and other defense plants, black workers did make gains. Due to mounting labor shortages, not Executive Order 8802, companies in increasing numbers turned to black workers, who were paid less than white workers. Most of the blacks were hired for what were called "H" jobs: hot, heavy, and hard. Blacks in the North Carolina Shipbuilding Company, while grateful for their jobs, recognized that most new positions were menial labor, requiring few skills. All of their bosses were white, they had very few benefits, and segregation prevailed from the front gate to the restroom. Black workers made few gains in professional, managerial, or white-collar jobs. The number of black workers in government and the military rose by 20 percent during the war, however, and there was an important increase in defense work for blacks.[11]

Over 700,000 black civilians moved all over the country during the war, seeking improved working opportunities. More than 2 million southern blacks traveled to northern and western industrial centers such as Detroit and Chicago. Black soldiers also spread out across the country, often into military bases in the South. All of these transfers brought increased chances for better pay but also brought potential trouble. Wartime migration put intolerable strains on housing, transportation, and social services. The black migrants faced antipathy from hostile white people who resented their incursion into their territory and the loss of defense jobs. In the South they were greeted by legal segregation, educational inequality, restricted voting, and harassment by local officials and police who resented their presence. It seemed inevitable that rising black demands and increasing white resentment would produce a high potential for racial disturbances.

As the war progressed, racial attitudes among the more educated and militant blacks began to change. In North Carolina and elsewhere the new way of thinking was reflected in the subtle but frequent challenges to segregated seating on public transportation, in railroad dining cars, and at soda fountains. While black citizens overwhelmingly supported the war, contributed to war bond drives, and volunteered for active military service, they remained dissatisfied with their economic and social status. With the March on Washington and the Double V Campaign, black protests became far more frequent and visible.[12] As one black North Carolinian, who recognized the evil of Hitler but also the evil of segregation at home, expressed it: "No clear thinking Negro can afford to ignore our Hitlers here in America. As long as you have men like Talmadge [Eugene Talmadge, segregationist governor of Georgia, 1933–1937, 1941–1943] in Georgia we have to think of the home front whether we want to or not."[13]

There were many examples of long-term and ingrained discrimination against blacks in the military. When nine black soldiers boarded a train in Kentucky, they were refused service at a restaurant stopover and were not allowed into the dining car, going hungry for the entire trip. The *Carolina Times*, a black newspaper in Durham, was outraged. "We are fighting for equal rights and for equal treatment. Yet within our own borders and within our own allied forces we allow conditions of shocking inequality." The paper continued: "What possible justification can there be for treating these men, who are ready and willing to give their lives for their country, in that way?"[14]

North Carolina had long prided itself as a bastion of racial tranquillity characterized by mutual respect between the races. In a letter to Margaret McCullough at Fisk University, a black institution in Nashville, Tennessee, Governor Melville Broughton insisted that the "race situation in North Carolina, while not free from some serious problems, is quite harmonious and satisfactory." Of course things seemed satisfactory to the white elite, not to the black community, which faced serious problems of discrimination and poverty. Although Broughton surely knew that racial relations were not harmonious, he argued incorrectly that the black health programs, schools, and social services offered the same quality of service given to the white people. Broughton believed that both races accepted segregation as a sound and sensible policy and that black leaders in the state had recognized that cooperation would accomplish more than agitation.[15] Broughton would quickly change his paternalistic views as militant black leaders in the state began an active campaign for equal rights and became increasingly bold in their demands.

As black North Carolinians began to press for first class citizenship, the NAACP took charge of organizing protests and boycotts in the state. During the war, with the Double V program as the focus, the number of branches doubled and membership increased to 10,000. Ella Baker, a graduate of Shaw University in Raleigh, became the director of NAACP branches in the state and a vocal leader for progress. She was supported by an aggressive black press.

Louis F. Austin, editor of the black newspaper *Carolina Times*, demanded an end to any discrimination in the military, higher wages for domestic workers, equal access to the ballot box, an increased number of defense jobs, and adequate housing for black citizens. He repeatedly declared that black citizens wanted to fight and denounced radical propaganda that implied that they would be better off under fascism. He insisted that many black Americans who were willing to fight against fascism abroad also wanted to fight the Hitlers here in America.[16] Austin constantly attacked Governor Broughton for perpetuating a system that accepted inferior black schools, lower wage scales, police brutality, discrimination in jobs, poor housing, and "a thousand other injustices." Broughton, in turn, denounced the "violent and radical Negro press" for "incendiary articles" that were "the greatest menace to race relations in the nation today."[17]

America's leaders, in an untenable moral position over race, were faced with a dilemma. Forced to denounce Hitler's racial policies in order to gain public support for the winning of the war, the United States had to admit the reality of racial discrimination in America. Black supporters took advantage of the contradiction in public policy to press for their rights.[18] The forceful demands of the black press and the NAACP along with increased racial tension led to a white backlash. Jonathan Daniels, FDR's chief advisor on race relations, feared that the insistent black demands for equal rights might lead to "bloodshed at home" and worried that any racial conflict would provide material for anti-American propaganda abroad.[19]

Rumor mills went into overtime, fabricating tales of violence in public transportation, warning that blacks intended to "take over" white women and that they were "gathering ice picks" for a mass insurrection.[20] Louis

Austin of the *Carolina Times* called on both black and white people to end such rumors during a national crisis. He defended black citizens as loyal to America and repeated his contention that they simply sought the same rights as everyone else.[21]

Whites in North Carolina and the South became alarmed that a burgeoning black rights movement would undermine loyalty to the war. Fears of black sedition and disloyalty led FBI director J. Edgar Hoover, obsessed with the possibility of Communist and fascist influence among black groups, to designate some "Negro Organizations" as subversive. Although no black Americans were ever prosecuted for subversion, they were constantly under suspicion. Stephen Dew pointed out that black people in Charlotte were not trying to subvert the United States but were attempting to undermine Jim Crow. For some white Charlotte residents, however, an attack on Jim Crow was an attack on the United States.[22]

In May 1943 fears of a black uprising increased when the *Charlotte News* published a letter from Leander Derr, a black insurance salesman from Monroe, N.C. Upset by attempts to disenfranchise blacks, Derr posed the question: "What are blacks fighting for?" In his letter he alleged that blacks were "fighting to make it safe for the white man to take away our right to vote—to discriminate against us, to exploit us, to 'keep the nigger in his place?' . . . I know not what opinion others may have, but as for me, to hell with the USA." Upset by Derr's letter, white people in Monroe thought that his comments were insulting to the United States. Due to public outrage and threats on his life, the Monroe police apprehended Derr and put him in protective custody. The police ultimately determined that he was not a threat and released him. Events such as this escalated racial fear among white people, but extensive FBI investigations of alleged black seditious activities in Charlotte and elsewhere in the state "met with negative results." Black leaders in Charlotte proclaimed again and again that the overwhelming majority of black Americans were patriotic. Black churches in Charlotte demonstrated their commitment to the war by sponsoring a "Loyalty Sunday."[23]

In general, there was broad black support for the war effort. In addition to work in defense plants and volunteering for military service, black Americans demonstrated their loyalty and patriotism by purchasing a significant number of war bonds. Walter White of the NAACP, the great jazz musician Duke Ellington, and other black leaders went around the county urging blacks to buy war bonds. Joe Louis, the heavyweight boxing champion of the world, joined the army as a private and traveled 21,000 miles across America, giving exhibition boxing matches, making patriotic speeches, and asking black Americans to join the military. [24]

The *Carolina Times* frequently printed full-page ads for the Treasury Department, asking black Americans to buy war bonds: "It's Your Move Now. The More Bonds You Buy, the More Planes Will Fly." A letter to the editor of the *Carolina Times* reiterated black support for the national defense program: "This country is the best country in the world for the Negro. It is our home and we ought to protect it with everything we have." Austin, while continuing his criticism of a racist society, maintained that black Americans would remain loyal to the cause.[25]

Despite numerous attempts to persuade the white population that they were loyal, black citizens were constantly harassed in public and vilified in the press by white people who resented their challenge to segregation during wartime. In a typical rant by a white supremacist in the state, O. C. Walters wrote the *Raleigh News and Observer* that he was "fed up" with the letters the paper continued to print from black people belly-aching about "equality." It is about time, pontificated Walters, that they were told that they could not have social equality. He argued that black people had not produced any great men and that what little they knew they picked up by imitating white people. "If the Negro had any pride of race he wouldn't try to force himself on a race that doesn't want him. We want no mulatto United States and if the Negro had any pride neither would he. . . . This is a white nation and please God it'll remain one."[26]

Attacks on black leaders and citizens came from all directions. Mississippi's segregationist senators Theodore Bilbo and James O. Eastland publicly accused "nigra soldiers" of having low intelligence and being deserters, cowards, quitters, and violaters of white women. A few southern newspapers defended black troops and indicated that Bilbo and Eastland had gone too far in their comments. Van T. Barfoot, a native Mississippian and holder of the Congressional Medal of Honor, said that he had done some fighting in the war and that the black soldiers had done as well as the white soldiers. "I've changed my ideas a lot about colored people since I got into this war and so have a lot of other boys from the South." He continued: "I've fought with colored men, why shouldn't I eat with them?"[27]

Military leaders praised the achievements of black soldiers in the war. General Jacob L. Devers, a former commander at Fort Bragg, said that black troops under his command had "done a splendid job . . . under diverse and difficult conditions."[28] A few white people sent letters to the paper praising black Americans. Festus L. Woodall wrote that the "negro has proven himself just as patriotic in time of war as his white neighbor. . . . When called upon to defend the flag of his country, he goes forth willingly." He believed that blacks were 100 percent patriotic when called upon to give to a worthy cause, such as the Red Cross. "The Negro, if given a chance, makes a good citizen."[29] These encomiums were few and far between, however, and most white people continued to exhibit anger and resentment about the insistent black claims for equality.

Throughout the war black Americans continued to work vigorously for equal rights, but some moderate leaders advocated a less confrontational manner during wartime. In October 1942 the Southern Conference on Race Relations, made up of prominent black business leaders, clergy, and college presidents, met at the North Carolina College for Negroes in Durham. Fifty-nine black representatives from ten southern states drew up a "new charter for race relations in the South." The group purposely excluded northern black leaders to avoid excessive agitation on the segregation issue. After two months of deliberations, the group issued a document: "A Basis for International Cooperation and Development in the South," which came to be known as the "Durham Manifesto." The conveners admitted that the war had "increased racial tensions, fears and aggressions" but stated that it had also reopened "the basic questions of racial segregation and discrimination, Negro minority rights and democratic freedom." The proposal called for cooperation between "the better class of southern whites and blacks." The manifesto did not demand the abolition of segregation but called for a "wartime victory in both arms and ideals."[30]

By not challenging Jim Crow laws, the framers of the manifesto committed themselves to gradualism and goodwill. The document asked for complete voting rights for black citizens and an end to white primaries and voter intimidation. It urged equalization of teachers' salaries and school facilities for both races and insisted on equal access to all jobs and public services. The Durham Manifesto was a measured and conciliatory series of demands that represented a significant departure from previous such documents, bypassing the NAACP. Some black leaders, like Louis Austin, thought that the manifesto was entirely too conservative, especially since the NAACP had not been represented.

Governor Broughton, hoping to avoid racial acrimony, praised black leaders for being "conservative and reasonable." He reminded citizens that progress would continue if the state was spared "outside interference and the agitation . . . stimulated by the radical Negro press." Broughton's op-

Figure 9.1. The Montford Point Marines, the first all-black unit in the U.S. Marines, underwent rigorous training at Camp Lejeune. Courtesy of the State Archives of North Carolina.

timistic view of the racial situation in North Carolina and the publication of the Durham Manifesto demonstrated just how far apart white rhetoric and black aspirations remained. Things may have seemed calm on the surface, but many black citizens in the state were angry and frustrated at the slow progress toward civil rights.[31]

Now that black soldiers had taken up arms for their country and northern black soldiers were coming in large numbers to military bases in the state, it was inevitable that black demands for equality would collide with the traditions of a rigid Jim Crow society. For example, Fort Bragg had only three black doctors and fourteen black nurses. Black soldiers constantly complained about inadequate and inferior medical care.[32] Racial enmity in North Carolina had increased after 1942 due to the volatile rhetoric of the black press and the increasing white anxiety that some sort of black insurrection would occur. Discrimination, along with the strict enforcement of segregation in on-base facilities such as theaters and post exchanges, led to some racial violence in and around the camps. Although in uniform, black soldiers still had to adhere to Jim Crow laws, ride in the back of the bus, and sit in segregated sections of local theaters. They were often harassed and attacked by a few belligerent white people who were outraged at seeing a black man in a military uniform and were willing to do anything to preserve the color line.[33]

Although numerous racial incidents took place, fewer than twenty riots or major racial brawls were reported from 1941 to 1945. And some of those fights had nothing to do with racial conditions. While many black soldiers experienced inferior training and facilities and faced abusive behavior by hostile military police, most accepted their lot.

Militant protests never entirely abated during the war, but the needs of the war came first. Young black people who might have been out protesting reveled in their new jobs and newfound economic status. The more conservative of them hoped that the future success of black Americans would rely on legal redress, education, and collaboration with the white leadership.

Some violent confrontations between the races, however, captured newspaper headlines all over the state. On August 6, 1941, a gunfight near Fort Bragg left one black soldier and one white military policeman dead. The fight erupted after a dispute over seating arrangements on the bus transporting black soldiers from Fayetteville back to their base at Fort Bragg. A black soldier named Ned Turman refused to sit in a segregated section of the bus and became disorderly, according to the MP report. When approached by the military police from Fort Bragg, Turman grabbed an MP's gun, shot and killed him, and also wounded two other MPs before being gunned down. A reinforced group of angry white MPs then forced all of the black soldiers off the bus. They were searched, cursed, and occasionally beaten by the MPs. Later the provost marshal ordered all black soldiers who were not in their barracks to be rounded up and forced into the base stockade, although they had nothing to do with the episode on the bus.[34] The military, realizing the great potential for trouble, tried to cover up these incidents while consistently maintaining that black and white troops had no serious disagreements.

Some camps had more racial episodes than others. Clashes between the races were commonplace at Camp Sutton. One black observer, Frederic Morrow, called Camp Sutton a "racist hellhole." He recalled that MPs beat black soldiers because they were suspected of being rapists or had been seeking some form of equality. Blacks had to be kept in their place. Black soldiers at Camp Sutton finally grew tired of being harassed by white officers and the Military Police and on September 22, 1943, they fought back. When MPs tried to arrest a black soldier at the Negro Service Club, a group of black soldiers battled the MPs, shouting, "We may as well die here as over there." Once again, military leaders played down the incident, saying that the problem lay with the volatility of the "general Negro situation." Local newspapers placed the blame for unrest on agitators trying to amalgamate the races. Throughout the war at Camp Sutton, black soldiers continued to resist the debilitating influence of segregation.[35]

These hostile interactions did not always pit servicemen against one another. Some quarrels were reminiscent of altercations between white people and black people who had been challenging Jim Crow laws for many years. In Kershaw, N.C., a black army sergeant went to the police department to ask about the arrest of one of his men. The sergeant's attitude apparently angered a white police officer, who threw him into a jail cell then hit him and shot him in the leg. Local papers bragged that this occurrence proved that white people could easily handle such "bad eggs."[36]

The most destructive race riot in the state occurred in Durham on July 9, 1945. Black private Booker T. Spicely boarded a Durham city bus driven by Herman L. Council. Spicely and his companions took seats directly behind the bus driver. When two white soldiers approached the bus at the next stop, Council ordered Spicely and his friends to move to the rear of the bus. Spicely refused to give up his seat, saying that he should be allowed to sit wherever he pleased. Council reminded him of the North Carolina segregation law and angrily told him to move to the back. Spicely approached the two white soldiers and demanded to know whether he was not "just as good to stop a bullet as they were." Why should he have to give up his seat? "I thought I was fighting this war for democracy." The white soldiers apparently agreed: they moved to the rear to sit in the black section. Having observed an arrogant black soldier defy his order and white soldiers supporting him, the embarrassed and angry bus driver unleashed a torrent of profanity at Spicely.[37]

Spicely then made a critical error in judgment. He announced to the passengers in a loud voice that if the bus driver had not been 4-F, unfit for service, he would not be driving the bus. A black man not only had challenged the driver's authority but had insulted his manhood. To be shamed by a black man was too much for Council. Spicely recognized that he had gone too far in criticizing the bus driver and apologized for his actions before he left the bus. His apology came too late: the visibly upset Council grabbed a .38-caliber revolver and shot Spicely twice in the chest, killing him almost instantly.

Word of Spicely's death spread quickly and unleashed a blind rage among members of the black community. Within minutes much of down-town Durham's warehouse district was in flames. The *Durham Morning Herald* described the scene: "Great clouds of flame and smoke shot hun-dreds of feet into the air." When the fire fighters, servicemen, and civilian volunteers finally put out the fire, four large warehouses, several private homes, a stable, a car company, and a restaurant had been destroyed in the blaze. The destruction in Durham reminded one reporter of a European city after an enemy air raid. One white woman complained that "those niggers burned down a whole block of downtown Durham."[38] As usual, white newspapers blamed the riot on outside agitators, mainly black sol-diers from the North and white officers who did not understand the cul-ture of the South.

Racial occurrences were not limited to the South. Across the nation racial disorders broke out sporadically in cities full of wartime employees, most spectacularly in Detroit in 1943. Black people aggravated by hous-ing problems, discrimination in hiring, dislocation, poor education, and wartime anxieties finally vented their anger. On a crowded downtown on a hot day, fighting began as black people and white people jostled for posi-tion at the bath houses, the casino, and refreshment centers. By 11 p.m. 5,000 people were fighting in the streets. After much looting and burning, the Military Police and the local police were able to quell the violence, but not until the situation had resulted in 34 dead, 700 injured, over $2 mil-lion in property losses, and a million man hours lost in war production.[39]

Governor Broughton, frightened by the severity of the Detroit riot, feared a similar outbreak in North Carolina. On July 11, 1943, the gover-nor made a major speech on race relations in Wilmington at the launching of the Liberty vessel named for the noted black business leader John Mer-rick. The governor praised the achievements of Merrick, who had been born a slave but though hard work and ingenuity became "the foremost Negro in North Carolina." Merrick founded the North Carolina Mutual Life Insurance Company, which had become the largest black-owned busi-ness in the world by 1943. The governor declared that Merrick's life and philosophy offered "lessons of great value to this troubled time." Brough-ton hoped that in the light of Merrick's wholesome philosophy and suc-cessful career the state would find a "path of harmony, success, victory and peace through mutual respect and honest cooperation."[40]

Repeating his oft-expressed view that North Carolina had established a record of racial harmony; the governor nonetheless viewed the serious race riot in Detroit and outbreaks in other parts of the North with deep concern. Broughton once again denounced "certain inflammatory news-papers and journals" for "dangerously fanning the flames of racial antag-onism." He charged that black editors and activists were using the war emergency to support racial theories that, if followed to their ultimate conclusion, would "result in a mongrel race." In a thinly viewed threat, the governor told those editors and activists that "they should watch their step."[41]

The governor's grandiloquent and misguided comments on racial con-ciliation, designed to allay the fears of his white constituents, flew in the face of reality. According to Broughton and the white supremacists in the state, there would be peace and harmony so long as the blacks stayed in their proper place and made no overt challenges to white domination. Once black Americans slipped their bonds, then the state would have to assert its superiority to quell any unrest that would threaten the status quo and the war effort.

Nonetheless, for black citizens in the state and nation World War II was a watershed and a long-term turning point in the fight for equality. The war provided realistic chances for black people to oppose legalized seg-regation. Many blacks, led by A. Philip Randolph, the NAACP, and other organizations, challenged Jim Crow on numerous occasions. The riots and disruptive acts by defiant individuals helped draw attention to the plight of black Americans. During World War II, black people in the state and the nation began the long process of breaking away from the old Uncle Tom acquiescence in and acceptance of white supremacy. With a realistic but new and more hopeful attitude, they set out on the long movement of social activism that would ultimately lead to the end of segregation in America. The political, economic, social, and cultural events during the war encouraged black activism, protest, and rising expectations.

The United States Supreme Court made a vital contribution to minority rights and democracy with a series of decisions. In *Smith* v. *Allwright* in 1944 the court ruled that black citizens could no longer be excluded from voting in Democratic Party primaries. The Democratic Party had argued that political parties were private clubs and that membership was subject to the rules promulgated by the leaders of the club. The Democratic Party controlled elections in the South, so black citizens had been effectively de-nied the right to vote.[42] This decision encouraged minority voting drives. Ultimately the court would address the issue of segregation in a series of cases, culminating in *Brown* v. *Board of Education* in 1954.

The federal government, through the FEPC and ultimate integration of the armed forces, improved racial conditions somewhat by taking a stronger position with regard to discrimination. The FEPC did not end discrimination in defense industries, however, and most of the military remained segregated until the end of the war. Thus the Double V concept had limited success. Clearly black Americans made significant progress in economic opportunity and in access to industrial jobs previously closed to them. Black organizations like the NAACP flourished, and black workers made limited inroads into labor unions. But the record of discrimination cannot be dismissed just because of these improvements during the war. The nation would have greatly benefited if black Americans had been used to the fullest extent in jobs and in the military. Prejudice cost the country in job production and underused soldiers. Beyond the physical loss was the moral cost. As a democratic nation fighting the tyrannical forces of fascism around the world to achieve freedom for all people, America had a difficult time explaining why it had not provided equal justice and opportunity for all its citizens at home.[43]

On a visit to North Carolina in March 1945 Eleanor Roosevelt brought out another important aspect of the war for minorities. When asked by a reporter what the black Americans would get out of the war, she replied that she thought that they would get a feeling of satisfaction from the knowledge that they had participated in the war effort as far as they were allowed to. "Everywhere I have seen functioning Negro troops, I have been just as proud of them as of our other troops." Presciently, she added: "This time the Negro has had obligations to perform that he never was allowed to perform before, and he has done them well. I think this will mean more after the war than we realize now."[44]

"This Is My War, Too"

Women at War

Judy Litoff's essay "Southern Women in a World at War" discusses the significance of World War II for women in the South. During the war women from North Carolina and other states in the South joined with women from all over the nation "to plant victory gardens, roll bandages for the Red Cross, contribute to war bond drives, seek war jobs, volunteer for military service and write millions of morale-boosting letters to loved ones and friends stationed far from home. They got married, had children, crisscrossed the continent as they followed their husbands to distant postings, agonized about loved ones stationed at 'far flung fronts,' planned for the postwar world and became stronger, more self-reliant individuals in the process."[1]

World War II could not have been won without the support and participation of women. Most histories of the war focus on military activities and battles in combat zones. While historians cover the home front in America, too little emphasis has been placed on the extraordinary benefits that the nation derived from women's activities during the war. Many observers understood that women could not win the war by themselves but that it could not be won without them. The nation needed all the help that women could give. Without women's determination, commitment, resourcefulness, and patriotic spirit, winning the war in four years would have been virtually impossible.

Since the beginning of the nation women had been primarily relegated to a place in the home as mothers and wives, not as wage earners. Women had not been given enough opportunities in skilled manual jobs, important legislative offices, and leadership positions in business enterprises. Women did not get the right to vote in a national election until 1920. In many cases, especially in the South, women's legal status was inferior to that of their husbands and other males. As late as November 8, 1944, the North Carolina Supreme Court ruled by a 5–2 vote that women were not eligible to serve on juries in the state because the constitution specifically stated that a jury consisted of "good and lawful men."[2] The status of women would change after December 7, 1941.

One key to eventual victory in World War II was war production. With most men either in the service or already gainfully employed it fell to women to help build the tanks and ships needed for victory. Women in the workforce increased from 24 percent in 1940 to 36 percent at war's end. The knowledge gained from that productive labor changed their lives. Women's experience working for the government, on farms, and in war industries gave them a sense of self-confidence that they had not often experienced. They became more self-reliant and more assertive as they recognized the major contributions that they made to the war effort. After many years of work as housewives, women during the war embraced the challenges of new kinds of employment and the interaction with new friends.

The women who left their homes for the first time to earn a salary and the intrepid ones who joined the armed forces made up only a small part of the American woman's contribution to the war effort. Women who stayed at home and continued their traditional roles as housewives and mothers made significant efforts at promoting the success of the war by working on scrap and bond drives, volunteering their time and skills with the Red Cross and USO clubs, writing letters to service members, knitting sweaters and gloves, and managing their homes.

Many young mothers whose husbands were in the military had to raise children on their own, often with inadequate funds. In 1942 the federal government initiated an allotment system whereby each mother received a total of $50 per month. The U.S. Treasury contributed $28 and deducted $22 from the husband's paycheck. If the family included children the allotment increased. Most women were grateful for the government's largesse. But, as always, a few women took advantage of the allotment system. Known as "Allotment Annies," they contrived to marry as many lonely servicemen as they could before their husbands went off to battle and then lived off the allotment checks.

The marriage rate went up substantially during the war, partly due to new and more lucrative jobs and increased prosperity. Young men wanted to be married to avoid the draft or to secure the blessings of marriage prior to leaving for duty. The husbands at war could take comfort in knowing that they had a loved one at home waiting for their return, which gave them some peace of mind while they were away.

Many children, known as "good-bye babies," were conceived prior to the husband's departure for the military. Fathers wanted a child to carry on their name and legacy if they perished in battle and also wanted the wives to interact on a daily basis with a living symbol of their marriage. Many babies were produced accidentally, out of wedlock, when boyfriends had one last passionate encounter with their sweethearts.

Once their husbands were off to war, the young war brides had to learn how to make home and auto repairs, figure out the best way to adjust to the often confusing rationing laws, open their own checking account, and adjust to the loneliness and the worry of their loved ones in harm's way. Some mothers had to move in with their parents or their husband's parents to help with child-raising, especially if they were working.[3] Florence Hollis, left alone by her husband's departure for the front, expressed some of the anxieties felt by other young mothers. "We must learn to wait. To endure the slow trickle of time, from hour to hour, from day to day, for weeks in anguish and suspense. And then wait for some message, a letter sent from far off—a small scrap that tells something of how he was, sometime ago."[4] Despite the hardships, these new and unanticipated responsibilities enabled many young women to achieve a greater level of independence and a sense that what they were doing, no matter how small, was important in winning the war.

Military Service

In addition to Rosie the Riveter and other women in the workforce, some 350,000 pioneering women served their country by joining one of the women's branches of the military: the army (WACs), the navy (WAVEs), the air force (WASPs), the coast guard (SPARs), or the women marines. More than 7,000 of these women came from North Carolina. Those who joined the armed forces immediately changed the stereotypical view of southern womanhood. North Carolina women drove trucks, built planes and ships, worked as welders, tended to bloody and life-threatening wounds on the battlefield, flew planes, and worked in numerous jobs heretofore considered off limits or "unfit" for women. They held many kinds of jobs—control tower operators, parachute riggers, mechanics, pharmacists, photographers, spies, cryptographers, and many more. To the surprise of many, sometimes even the women themselves, they performed their tasks as well as or better than men did. These new opportunities gave women a new appreciation of their abilities and a chance to show the doubters what they could do.

WAACs

At the outset of the war the idea of women in the military was frowned upon and in many cases dismissed as a foolish idea. As the war progressed and many men were sent overseas, however, some innovative thinkers proposed that women hired in clerical and administrative positions could replace men and free them up for combat roles. No one entertained the idea of putting women in combat roles.

The decision to create a Women's Auxiliary Army Corps had significant precedents. Great Britain already had female military organizations such as the WRENs (Women's Royal Navy Service), and British women were eligible for the draft. In Russia women not only served in the military in large numbers but also fought in combat units.

Congresswoman Edith Nourse Rogers proposed the bill establishing the WAACs, arguing that "there are innumerable duties now being performed by soldiers that can actually be done better by women." The War Department backed the bill, which eventually passed despite some significant opposition. One New York congressman thought that the idea of a woman's army to defend the United States was the silliest piece of legislation that he had ever seen. "Think of the humiliation. What has become of the manhood of America, that we have to call on our women to do what has ever been the duty of men? The thing is so revolting to me, to my sense of decency, that I just cannot discuss it." By creating the WAACs as an auxiliary branch rather than allowing women to be full-fledged members of the army (meaning that the WAACs did not have full military status and the same benefits as the men), the War Department overcame strident opposition to the bill. President Roosevelt signed the bill on May 15, 1942, creating a volunteer corps of women and an organization quickly dubbed the "Petticoat Army."[5]

The initial concept was to select 150,000 WAACs between the ages of twenty-one and forty-five who were without dependents and in good physical condition. Senator Bob Reynolds of North Carolina, the former isolationist, came out strongly in favor of the bill. He noted that women were playing a more and more significant part in the life of the nation and pointed out that vast numbers of women had been utilized to great advantage in Britain and Russia. Reynolds insisted that America would need every bit of human power it could obtain and that women would be very useful in filling the gaps in noncombat duties.[6]

The *Raleigh News and Observer* had already come out in favor of a volunteer auxiliary army of women. The idea is "so sound and sensible that it is difficult to see how there could be any argument about it. Indeed, in this day when women are doing and doing well so many different kinds of jobs it would seem as logical that women be subject to selective service just as men are." The paper conceded that the idea of women in arms had upset many southerners' idea of chivalry, but times had changed and those notions were outmoded and naive.[7]

Oveta Culp Hobby, a thirty-seven-year-old newspaper executive, was named as the director of the WAACs with the rank of major. The new director determined that WAAC recruits would not be armed and would not receive combat training but would be taught the fundamentals of military discipline and close order drill. Volunteers would be given the title of "auxiliaries," which would correspond to the rank of private. Initially they were to be paid $21 a month, but that figure would later be raised. The WAACs could be assigned to noncombat service with the army anywhere in the world and would replace enlisted men currently performing certain types of duties such as clerks, lab technicians, postal clerks, and telephone operators.[8]

Regular army recruiting stations handled the recruiting process to select WAAC officers for training. Those applying for officer status had to have a high school diploma or the equivalent. Students completing the training course with the highest grade would be commissioned as officers, while those whose work was satisfactory would be assigned to the noncommissioned ranks. The officers would then be detailed to train the new members of the corps.[9]

On May 22, 1942, about 13,000 enthusiastic women inundated the 440 recruiting stations around the country, eager to be one of the first women to sign up as a WAAC. The women who signed up did so for many different reasons. Some wanted employment security and decent pay. Educational benefits motivated some women, while others were moved by patriotism. Several enlistees just wanted an adventure, a new place to live, or a new lifestyle. A common theme for the new inductees was a desire to help in the war effort and make a better life for themselves. A few wanted to escape the dull existence of small-town America. And there was always the possibility of meeting a future husband while in the service. One enlistee reflected the attitudes of many women: "If a man can give up his life for his country, certainly a woman can give up her time."[10] Katherine Katopes, who had recently joined the WAACs, wrote her brother to explain her choice: "Perhaps I am doing a fool thing but the only way to find out is to do it. . . . At least I will be doing my part in the war effort and probably acquire a novel experience in the bargain."[11] By joining the military, most of the new enlistees saw themselves as pioneers and trailblazers.

Dorothy Hinson Brandt's story was similar to others who joined the army. When the army recruiting officer opened the office in Charlotte in February 1944, he found Brandt sound asleep against the entry door. She was so anxious to sign up that she had stopped by the recruiting office after completing her eight-hour shift at a defense plant.

Brandt wanted to join the WAACS partly because her family had a long history of military service and she had four brothers in service. She thought that enlisting in the army was the patriotic thing to do. Her parents objected because she was only sixteen and they did not want to risk losing their only daughter. Determined to cast her lot with the WAACs, Brandt persuaded a neighbor to sign an affidavit stating that she was twenty-one years old. The ploy worked: she entered the army at Fort Bragg. Her parents expected her to fail and be home in a week, but she stuck it out and completed her basic training.

Brandt actually enjoyed basic training and made several lifelong friends. She described her extraordinarily diverse group of bunk mates at basic training: "A Powers model from New York, a woman lawyer from Oregon, a minister's daughter, a showgirl from Las Vegas, a set of twins and a mother-daughter combo from Virginia." Brandt loved her experience in the WAACs and ended up making a career in the military.[12]

Most of the early enrollees were young, but Vesta K. Joyner, a grandmother, joined the WAACS in Winston-Salem. On the first day for applications in Raleigh the first three recruits for officer candidate school included a female psychologist, a partner in a law firm, and a construction firm personnel director. These were not giddy teenage girls looking for an occasion to leave town or avoid strict parents but professionals who saw the opportunity to break down a barrier and achieve something that had been always denied to women in America—joining the army.[13]

Many men were outraged at the thought of women in uniform and assumed that anyone who joined would be a lesbian, a prostitute, or a person of low moral character seeking a liaison with a soldier. Military leaders did not want women coming into their ranks to distract the men and foul up their routine and discipline. The general sense of the military brass was that America was in the midst of a difficult war and that women would just get in the way.

Some women also opposed the idea of females in the military. Ruth E. Peters wrote an article for the *American Mercury* entitled: "Why I Didn't Join the WACS." A hostess in a USO club, she reported that 99 percent of the men she knew did not want their girlfriends and wives leading a GI's life. Peters concluded that the general view of the public was that any woman who joined the army was crazy or a young kid or an "old maid" seeking adventure and romance. Peters thought it ridiculous to try to make soldiers out of women who were unprepared, not motivated to be a soldier, and not allowed to fight anyway. In any event she refused to join the army partly because she could not abide the strict discipline and loss of freedom.[14]

Several Catholic priests strenuously objected to subjecting innocent and impressionable women to the temptations found in the army. Bishop James Cassidy warned female parishioners that to join the WAACs would be to oppose the teachings of the church. Cassidy disapproved of the WAACs because the organization would break down the traditional values of American society by "bringing back the pagan goddess of desexed lustful sterility." It is unclear what he meant by this, but the bishop clearly did not want women in the military. The National Catholic Welfare Conference worried that the state would use the war as an excuse to assume control of children by removing their mothers from the home for military service.[15] However, a Gallup poll taken as early as September 10, 1942, showed that 81 percent of those polled favored drafting women over drafting married men.[16] The general public not only accepted the concept of women in the military but supported including them in the draft.

In June 1942 the army sent the first contingent of 400 WAAC officer candidates to Fort Des Moines, Iowa. The idea was that an eight-week training course would prepare women to do army jobs in the army way— jobs that they could do as well or better than men. The officer candidates, "soldiers in skirts," underwent disciplined and rigorous training. *Time* magazine revealed that those who evaluated the newly inducted WAACs found them to be intelligent, hard-working, and very adaptable to the military way of life.[17]

When the candidates reported for duty they were issued three brassieres, two girdles, cotton and flannel pajamas, rayon panties, wool panties, three slips, four pair of cotton stockings, an apron, sunglasses, and a hand mirror. The WAACs could wear "inconspicuous make-up, girdles if they were plump and civilian clothes off duty." All candidates wore army uniforms, received army pay ($21 a week), and were subject to army discipline.[18]

The women were up at 6 a.m. every day and attended class for five hours a day. They had close order drills for an hour, physical training for an hour, and study hall for two hours in the evening. Lights were out at 11 p.m. One of the more sensitive problems faced by the training cadre was how to train female voices to issue clear and audible commands—what one officer called a "guttural roar."[19] Adeline LaPointe wrote her parents from Fort Des Moines, complaining of the hard work and little free time. She had discovered that the best way to succeed was to do what was asked without breaking down. She reported that the army had clamped down on long hair. She did not like the short haircuts, "inasmuch as we look mannish enough."[20]

Once their training ended, the newly minted officers were posted to forts and offices all over the country, performing a variety of jobs as clerks, machine operators, telephone and telegraph operators, pharmacists, dieticians, librarians, cooks, and stewardesses. To no one's surprise, the WAACs did these jobs much better than men.[21] Anyone who had observed men trying to do laundry or pecking away at a typewriter with one finger immediately realized the huge boost in unit efficiency generated by the WAACs. Although these jobs were still considered "women's work," the WAACs understood that by entering the military they had overcome an obstacle that had restricted women in the past.

Despite hard-core resistance to integration in the other branches of the military, forty black women were included in the first class of WAAC officer candidates. Hobby, a southerner, had promised to recruit black women in proportion to their percentage in the population. True to her word, the first WAAC officer graduating class had thirty-six black women, 10 percent of the class. Jim Crow prevailed in training: the black WAACS were segregated into separate barracks, ate at separate tables, and were assigned to "All-Negro platoons."[22] Millie Veasey, a black woman from Raleigh, was one of the first to sign up for the WAACs. She noted that only three out of twenty-one women in her group passed the intelligence test. After she took her physical, she began to have second thoughts about committing to the WAACs, but the army told her that it was too late to back out. She eventually served with the first black women's unit to be sent overseas.[23]

Ruth Lillian Gaddy, a black woman from Charlotte, signed up for the WAACs because she had an "extremely patriotic feeling." Despite her father's objections, she was sworn in on October 10, 1942, at Fort Bragg. As part of the first black group at Fort Des Moines, trained by black sergeants, Ruth learned early on that she was now "a part of a bigger human picture and that you're going to have to roll with the flow." She realized that if she did not perform she would be "sent home in a body bag or you'll be sent home in a straightjacket." Overall Ruth saw her army experience as very worthwhile because it afforded her the chance to travel and see and do things that she would never have experienced on her own.[24] The black WAACs were acutely conscious of winning the war against fascism and were willing to sacrifice to win the victory but were hopeful that they could also achieve a victory over discriminatory racial policies at home, the Double V.

One year after it was established, the WAAC corps had 58,100 enrollees. After a sensational start, enrollment fell off dramatically due to apathy and the army's failure to grant WAACs formal recognition as members of the military with full benefits. Unlike the WAVEs and women marines, the army designated the WAACs as auxiliaries, so they received less pay than men, no retirement, and no life insurance. Another factor for the downturn in recruiting was unrelenting male resistance to the concept of women in uniform.[25]

By mid-1943, due to inept advertising and a drop-off in enthusiasm, the army admitted that it had signed up only a little over 60,000 enlistees and would not be able to meet the initial quota of 150,000. Some women understood the dire need for clerical skills and wanted to help but did not like marching and doing kitchen patrol (KP). They also resented the strict discipline and restrictions on whom they could date and with whom they could socialize.

WAAC director Oveta Culp Hobby, determined to attract more women, renewed local recruitment drives with assistance from women's clubs and organizations. General George C. Marshall asked the nation's governors to help, but the real impetus to persuade more women to join up came from commanders in the field. WAACs had already proved their worth; by 1943 the demand for WAACs had exceeded the supply. Army officers, skeptical in the beginning, had come to value the performance of the WAACs and asked for more.[26]

Colonel Hobby and the army accelerated the recruitment effort, so the new push met with considerable success. A typical newspaper ad in April 1943 called on the women of Raleigh to "Look to the Future with the WAAC." The ad told women: "This chance to take an active part in the fight for victory is now offered for the first time in our history. Never before had your government called on you to help in this way, and never before have women had the privilege of being thus allied with the armed forces of the Republic." WAACs, the ad emphasized, were learning new skills and would speed the end of the war by taking the place of men so that they could fight. Their efforts would preserve a better world for their children.[27]

A major step toward successful recruiting came in July 1943, when Congress changed the Women's Army Auxiliary Corps to the Women's Army Corps (WAC). The corps began as an experiment, so it was initially thought best to bring women in as auxiliaries. But as time passed women became a real and valued part of the army. With the new bill the women were no longer auxiliaries but had full membership in the army.[28] Now that the military had accepted the WACs as an official part of the army, enlistments increased substantially.

The second round of enlistments attracted younger women like Margaret Lewis. She wanted to join the navy, but her mother vigorously opposed the decision and "threw a fit" when her daughter threatened to run away. Margaret tried lying about her age to get in, but navy personnel discovered that she was too young. So Margaret altered her birth certificate and signed up with the WACs.[29]

When Oveta Culp Hobby resigned as director of the WACs, she was succeeded by Colonel Westray Battle Boyce, a native of Rocky Mount, N.C. Colonel Hobby said that she was leaving her post because the WACs had been accepted by the American public and were now an integral part of the army. The new director, Colonel Boyce, had joined the WAACS in August 1942 and a year later transferred to North Africa as theater WAAC director on the staff of General Dwight D. Eisenhower. She was responsible for the health and welfare of over 2,000 women in the North African and Mediterranean theaters. She was the first woman in the military to be honored with a Legion of Merit. Her citation noted her "maximum utilization of WAC personnel" and her contributions to increasing the morale of the women under her command. A personal letter from General Eisenhower praised Boyce for accepting the "responsibility of proving that an active theater of operations had a definite need for women soldiers." Colonel Boyce presided over the reduction in strength of the WAC at the end of the war and its ultimate dissolution in 1948.[30]

WASPs

Jackie Cochran, a famous aviator with five national and international speed records to her credit, set up the WASPs (Women Air Force Service Pilots), a group of trained female pilots who would be used to ferry planes around the country. On August 5, 1943, the government formally established the WASPs as a civilian agency, with Cochran as the director. The War Department suggested that the WASPs be attached to Colonel Hobby and the WACs. Cochran wanted to run her own outfit and exclaimed that she would not "serve under a woman who did not know her ass from a propeller." The fiery Cochran won that battle. From 1943 until late 1944 the WASPs ferried and flight-tested military planes, towed shooting targets for artillery gunners, and transported passengers and cargo. Some 1,074 women served with the WASPs during the war, 38 of whom lost their lives.[31]

With airplane production increasing at unprecedented levels (from 19,000 in 1941 to 96,000 in 1944), it was necessary to increase not only pilot training but also the ferrying of airplanes from the factory to their final destination. General H. H. "Hap" Arnold, commanding general of the army air force during World War II, quickly realized that with the increasing shortage of trained pilots due to losses in combat it was necessary to use WASP pilots to transfer the aircraft. Arnold, an innovative commander, had both the imagination and the confidence to establish and deploy the WASPs despite widespread protest among male pilots and the public in general.

Responding to General Arnold's plea for help, Jackie Cochran signed up 1,830 women with at least thirty-five hours of logged flight time. The women had to be at least eighteen years of age and at least five feet half an inch in height. Of the 1,830 women who entered the program, 1,074 earned their wings, with a dropout rate comparable to that of male pilots. The WASPs underwent the same rigorous training regimen as the male pilots, rising every morning at 6:45 a.m. to begin their work. Most of these so-called Petticoat Pilots were independent and strong willed and relished the challenges of flight school.[32]

The young women who signed up for the WASPs had broken away from their traditional roles as housewives, secretaries, and teachers. The initial volunteers had the will, determination, and moxie to do something completely unprecedented. They were not sorting mail or doing clerical work; they were embarking on a much more dangerous mission—flying powerful military planes and towing targets for antiaircraft gunners firing live ammunition. The WASPs flew planes, primarily the new P-51s, from factories to shipping docks around the country. Dora Dougherty Strother McKeown explained why she enrolled in the WASPs. "It was a magnificent opportunity. I think that aside from the thrill of it, anytime that any of the women flew anyplace, they felt they were representing women worldwide and for generations to come. We knew we were breaking barriers, and we had to fly our best." Kate Lee Harris Adams joined up because of her life-long fascination with flying. She ended up flying seventeen different single-engine planes. She loved her experience in the WASPs except for some male resistance to women flyers. "Our safety record was a little bit better than the males. But still, men didn't think women could fly and resented us generally."[33] Adams and her cohorts proved the men and a disbelieving nation wrong by their exploits.

Subject to military training and authority, WASPs remained Civil Service employees, earning less than male flyers. They had to pay for their own uniforms and part of their room and board. The enlistees came from all over the nation and from varied backgrounds. The first training group included teachers, bookkeepers, a magazine writer, a parachute rigger, and six married women.

When the first group of twenty-five WASPs reported to Camp Davis, N.C., in July 1943, they moved in with 50,000 men already in camp. After much ogling and flirtation from the male inhabitants, the WASPs settled into their jobs. There was always some hostility in camp from pilots who saw the WASPS as threats to their jobs and were offended by the intrusion of females into what had always been a male bastion. One commander disliked the idea of women pilots so much that he told them to go home and knit socks for the troops.

In the first two months at Camp Davis two WASPs died in plane crashes and a third was severely injured. These events did not discourage the flyers, as it was part of the risk they had accepted when they signed up. Instead of succumbing to fear they learned from the crashes. Marion Hanrahan remembered the circumstances when they learned that Mabel Rawlinson had died in a fiery crash. "We were in the dining room when we heard the

Figure 10.1. Three intrepid WASP pilots prepare to tow targets for the U.S. Navy artillery. Courtesy of the State Archives of North Carolina.

siren that indicated a crash. When we ran out on the field we saw the front of her plane engulfed in fire and could hear Mabel screaming. It was a nightmare." Cornelia Fort, the first woman pilot to die in military service, understood the risks and rewards of flying. "If I die violently, who can say it was before my time. I want no one to grieve for me. I was happiest in the sky—at dawn when the quietness of the air was like a caress, when the noon sun beat down, and at dusk when the sky was drenched with the fading light. Think of me there and remember me, I hope, as I shall you."[34]

By the end of 1943 the two groups assigned to Camp Davis primarily worked at flying tow targets for antiaircraft gunners. Ground crews had to practice repelling attacking enemy planes. How else could they gain this experience than by shooting at flying targets? The antiaircraft gunners had to improve their accuracy in order to be more effective and thus use less ammunition.

The work proved to be not only arduous but tension filled and dangerous. The tow target was a cloth sleeve about twenty feet long, towed behind the plane on a cable. The target was usually from 2,000 to 2,400 feet from the rear of the plane; but if the gunners were careless, the flight could be perilous. One female pilot had her tail section shot up while pulling a target. The WASPs flew the planes at between 5,000 and 10,000 feet, varying altitude to allow the 90-mm and 40-mm guns to adjust to the target. The WASPs also flew night missions for the antiaircraft artillery searchlight battalions, who needed practice in picking up enemy raiders in the dark.

One WASP pilot described her experiences towing targets: "While towing a target sleeve, it was sobering to realize that the queer round blots of smoke outside the window were live ammunition exploding a bit ahead of the target. Some airplanes came back with holes in them." She discussed the difficulty of flying the searchlight missions. "This was essentially instrument flying. If you looked outside at the blinding light you lost your night vision and you could not even read the instruments."[35] The WASP pilots liked the challenges and the work at Camp Davis but complained about male opposition to their work. All of the pilots disliked the ever-present mosquitos at Camp Davis. "They say the mosquitos fly formation—two come in and pull the covers off and two more do the stinging. They are fast too. You can't swat them."[36]

Many of the women who joined the WASPs had always dreamed of being a pilot and were confident that their service had made a difference to the war effort. Dorothy Hoover, who grew up in Asheville, had been dazzled by Charles Lindbergh's achievements and from an early age had a desire to fly. Aware that some male pilots resented women flyers, Hoover did not care "as long as they let me fly."[37] Ann C. Waters of Wilmington signed up for the WASPs. Although the "men were fighting us left and right, didn't want us there," she persevered and was proud of her effort as a pioneer. "I felt fortunate that somebody opened the door for me because a lot of others had the door slammed in their face."[38]

The army air force ignored the program's attempt to win military status. It remained an auxiliary part of the army air force at war's end. General Arnold deactivated the WASPs on December 20, 1944, acknowledging that the women had exceeded all expectations. But after hostilities ended, like many other women in the military and in war industries, WASPs were dismissed from the service for fear that they would take the jobs of male pilots returning home from the war. Victory was in sight, and female pilots were expendable.

The army air force's decision was a terrible blow to the morale of the women pilots who had discovered that they loved their job and had a real passion for flying. One WASP complained: "They taught us how to fly, now they send us home to cry, 'cause they don't want us anymore."[39] As the

WASPs were about to be disbanded in 1944, Betty Emanuel praised their work in a letter to the *Raleigh News and Observer*. She was upset that very little had been said about their accomplishments and that they were undervalued and underpaid. WASP pilots had "sacrificed the luxury of civilian life in order to do their part in the field of aviation." They were given civilian status and had to pay "their own living expenses, transportation [and] have difficulty obtaining insurance. In other words, they live a complete GI life with none of the compensation." Emanuel worried about the young women who had just been released from duty and feared for the future of women's rights. "What then are these young women to do—women whose talent is flying and whose very lives are aviation? Are we back in the age of women suffragettes? Will we have to argue, and parade and shout to make a place for ourselves? Obviously that is the only way, and believe me, we will fight for the right to fight for our country."[40]

The WASPs had achieved their goals without adequate compensation and with their accomplishments virtually unrecognized, a shameful failure by the U.S. government. They left the service with no medical care, no insurance benefits, no burial subsidy, no military funeral honors, and no Gold Star if a daughter died in service to her country. The WASPs did achieve veteran status in 1977. But when WASP pilot Elaine Harmon died at ninety-five in 2015, the military refused to allow her ashes to be laid to rest at Arlington National Cemetery alongside those of her fellow veterans.[41] Despite these snubs, the WASPs overcame the various barriers to success. After having their abilities and stamina questioned, these women proved that they could fly just as well as the men.

WAVEs

The navy picked a great acronym, WAVEs (Women Accepted for Emergency Voluntary Service), for their new women's organization. When possible inductees saw the term "WAVEs," they thought of the navy. The birthing problems of the WACs had taught the navy that it would be much better to avoid the concept of an auxiliary unit, so from the beginning the WAVEs had full military status but not a pension or retirement. Once the WAVEs were in service, real equality was an ephemeral goal, as women were assigned lower ranks than men and their job opportunities were often limited. Frequently the navy did not use women's skills wisely and assigned them to basic jobs below their skill level.

Unlike the contentious debate over forming the WACs, the federal legislation organizing the WAVEs quickly passed Congress. The navy wanted highly skilled and educated women and advertised for those who majored in engineering, electronics, physics, math, statistics, and foreign languages, leading to higher admission standards than in the WACs. The women had to be twenty years old and possess a college degree or two years of college work and two years of professional business experience. Most of the WAVEs were college graduates. The navy envisioned a total of 150,000 "sailorettes" in the service to relieve men for seagoing duty. The original bill establishing the WAVEs included a ban on overseas duty. The WAVEs could serve outside the United States but only in the Western Hemisphere and were not to be selected for combat duty.

The navy, having learned from the overcrowded conditions at WAC training centers, developed a different concept in training WAVEs. The brass decided that the WAVEs would receive both their basic training and specialty training at colleges. The navy conducted boot training for enlistees at Hunter College in New York and officer training at Smith College in Massachusetts. Women learning to be radio operators were sent to the University of Wisconsin or Miami University of Ohio; supply clerks were assigned to Indiana University or Georgia State College for Women. Aeronautical training took place at the Massachusetts Institute of Technology, and a few WAVEs took advanced training in supply at the Harvard Business School.[42]

Approximately 560 women from North Carolina served in the WAVEs. They had a much different military experience than did their comrades in arms, the WACs. While the WAVEs had to wear uniforms, drill, and adhere to military discipline, their college-based experiences were dramatically different from the training that the WACs underwent in army camps. Most WAVEs did not live in barracks. Officers and even some enlisted women had their own rooms (and in a few cases officers had maid service). Unlike WACs, WAVEs were allowed to entertain men in their recreation centers. Overall the WAVEs fared better than the WACs, because most were college educated and had the opportunity of working in highly trained, skilled positions.[43]

SPARs

The United States Coast Guard Women's Reserve (SPARs) came into existence later than the WACs (May 15, 1942) and WAVEs (July 30, 1942). Not until November 22, 1942, did the coast guard set up its women's organization. Like the WAVEs, the acronym was important to attract new members. "SPAR" stood for the coast guard's motto *Semper Paratus* (Always Ready). The enlistment criteria were much lower than for the WAVEs. SPARs had to be between twenty and thirty-six years of age, but the coast guard required only a high school education and some business experience. SPARs received the same pay, ratings, and safeguards as did male members of the coast guard. Enlisted SPARs had their basic training at Palm Beach, Florida. By 1943, of the 2,000 SPARs who had completed training, 50 percent were employed as typists, 20 percent were storekeepers dealing with payroll and supplies, and 10 percent worked with radio equipment. A few worked as pharmacist mates and lab technicians and one even as a chaplain.[44]

The coast guard made history when thirteen women were admitted to the U.S. Coast Guard Academy at New London, Connecticut, the first time a government military institution had opened its doors to women. Barbara Gouge of Hickory joined the SPARs and quickly learned that they meant business. "The leaders in the Coast Guard were not fooling around. They made sure we kept on a schedule and followed all the rules." Gouge committed to the coast guard because she "needed to feel like I was accomplishing something and not just sitting back not taking an active part. It was the best thing I could have done."[45]

Marine Corps Women's Reserve

While the army, navy, army air force, and coast guard accepted female recruits, the traditionally conservative Marine Corps was reluctant to welcome women into its ranks. After significant losses of marines at the battle of Guadalcanal, however, senior brass realized that it was necessary for the corps to free up as many males as possible for combat duty. When the Marine Corps finally accepted women, they were given full military status. On January 28, 1943, the corps set up its women's branch with a typical, no-nonsense attitude. They used no acronyms (such as Marinettes), they were simply women marines. As of early 1943 all branches of the U.S. military included women.

The marines were very successful in their early recruitment efforts. When the enlistees were asked why they took on the challenge of being a marine, most cited patriotism. But others joined the marines to complete their education, and a few did it for the adventure and for the challenge of becoming a marine.[46] The experience turned out to be more of an adventure than many expected. Unlike the WAVEs, women marines did not get their training in cushy colleges. They were sent to the notorious boot camp at Camp Lejeune, N.C. In order to accommodate the women marines (officially the Women's Reserve) the Marine Corps built new barracks, complete with mess halls and other support facilities. The cantonment was physically separate from that of the male marines.

A total of 525 women, a new class every two weeks, underwent six weeks of basic training. The corps did not relax its traditional standards for admission. Officer candidates had an attrition rate of almost 30 percent. The marine cadre at Lejeune imbued women with the same esprit de corps, discipline, and core values as their male counterparts. The training was not as rigorous as that planned for the men, but it was difficult enough. The women were also indoctrinated in marine combat training, although they would not be in combat. The corps wanted them to learn as much about their job and equipment as possible. The women marines lived up to their motto, "Free a Marine to Fight"; without their contribution in filling noncombat roles, it would have been more difficult to find the manpower to organize the 6th Marine Division, which played a key role in the battle for Okinawa in 1945.[47]

To no one's surprise, the marines had a difficult time accepting women on their sacred ground at Lejeune. Despite the unwelcome attitude, the women were ready for the rigors of marine boot camp. In the first weeks the recruits learned the history of the Marine Corps and the customs, courtesies, and organization of the corps. The trainers observed that the women learned more quickly than the men, but the drill instructors (DIs) had great trouble keeping them perfectly still at attention; they were reportedly a bit too fidgety and their eyes wandered. Their commanders, however, praised the women marines for their work ethic and attitude. "I must say that you never saw such an eager bunch of people to do everything they're told. We can't seem to give them enough work. They are deeply conscientious and serious about this career of serving in the Marine Corps. Eager is certainly the word."[48]

By the end of the war a total of 23,145 women marines had enlisted, of whom 965 were commissioned as officers. They worked primarily in motor transport, aviation-related fields, and the Quartermaster Corps. Eugenia Lejeune, daughter of the general after whom the base was named, was one of the 17,672 women who trained at the camp. Women did their jobs so efficiently that the early prejudice against women in the corps turned to admiration. After the war the leadership considered women marines expendable and discharged the entire reserve force on March 13, 1946. The Women's Armed Forces Integration Act of June 12, 1948, reestablished the presence of women on active duty, however, and females were once again inducted into the Marine Corps.[49]

Volunteers

Without American women who devoted literally millions of hours of their free time in myriad volunteer organizations, the American economy and the prosecution of the war would have suffered. The most popular and prestigious of the volunteer organizations was the Red Cross, a quasi-governmental agency. The Red Cross, with 10,000 permanent employees, had a sterling reputation for helping with disasters. The organization had an efficient and effective bureaucracy that offered serious training courses. The Red Cross was divided into the Home Service, which dealt with the problems faced by service members and their families; Production, which made items such as bandages and surgical dressings; Nurses' Aides and Gray Ladies, who helped in overcrowded hospitals (an important effort due to the shortage of nurses all over the country); First Aid, which

Figure 10.2. The USO Travelers Aid helped soldiers and their families arrange travel and lodging. By permission of Carol W. Martin/Greensboro Historical Museum.

trained women in a number of life-saving courses; the Motor Corps, which ferried the sick to hospitals and delivered blood; and the Blood Bank. The Red Cross made an extraordinary contribution to the war effort.

While the Red Cross sponsored canteens for the troops, the primary emphasis was always on health. Participation in Red Cross activities often awakened women to the horrors of war and the urgent need for their services. One woman who had a husband fighting in the Pacific donated blood on five separate occasions. After she arrived home from her fifth visit, she learned that her badly wounded husband's life had been saved by five successive transfusions of Red Cross blood, a dramatic and personal example of how her sacrifice had paid off.[50]

Many other women's volunteer organizations made a significant effort to improve living conditions during the war. The General Federation of Women's Clubs refocused its energy and efforts to center on the war effort. The Women's Ambulance and Defense Corps of America, whose motto was "The Hell We Can't," trained women to serve as security guards, air raid wardens, and couriers for the armed forces. The American Women's Voluntary Services provided both land and air ambulance services. Volunteer groups among working women included the WIRES (Women in Radio and Electric Service); WAMs (Women Aircraft Mechanics); and WOWs (Women Ordnance Workers).[51] The commitment and effort of all of these volunteer organizations not only gave women a sense of purpose but also helped America win the war.

Nurses

Women nurses served nobly in all theaters in World War II, including major combat areas. Nurses, both civilian and military, had professional status and a tradition of service and, unlike WASPs and WACs, did not threaten established gender norms. They found ready acceptance and real opportunities in the armed forces.[52]

From the outset of the war there was a critical shortage of nurses. In 1944 the Public Health Service announced that it needed 66,000 nurses for military service and 300,000 for civilian duty. The Red Cross and the Office of Civilian Defense pleaded for another 100,000 volunteers. Although the government provided some funds to the Public Health Service for nursing schools, the authorities tended to rely on volunteers and recruitment to fill the ranks. By January 1945 President Roosevelt, recognizing the continuing shortage of nurses, proposed a bill to draft nurses into the military. "It is tragic that the gallant women who have volunteered for service as nurses should be so overworked. It is tragic that our wounded men should ever want for the best possible nursing care." Congress was about to pass the Nurses Selective Service Act of 1945, which would require nurses to register for a draft. When the war in Europe ended, Congress decided that the bill was no longer needed. If the fighting in Europe had lasted a little longer, women (only nurses) apparently would have been drafted—an extraordinary change in the status of women in American society.[53]

The shortage of nurses had several causes. The military branches did not want to use male nurses, resisted using black nurses, insisted on single women only, and often excluded women over thirty. The military was reluctant to use women doctors. There were not many female doctors to begin with, as most medical schools limited their enrollment to 5 percent of the class. The War Department feared that female doctors would be too emotional and male patients would be embarrassed by them, although they seemed to have no problem with female nurses.[54]

North Carolina produced the first woman to be commissioned directly into the Army Medical Corps, Margaret D. Craighill, of Southport, N.C. She graduated Phi Beta Kappa from the University of Wisconsin and took her medical degree at the Johns Hopkins University. Major Craighill was assigned to the army's division of preventive medicine and took a 56,000-mile tour of war zones, reporting on the health and living conditions of army nurses. Dr. Craighill was awarded the Legion of Merit for her service.[55]

The troops considered nurses operating in combat zones to be angels of mercy. When Allied troops landed in North Africa, some 200 nurses set up hospitals while being bombed and strafed. Understaffed and overworked, the nurses had a difficult and demanding job but rarely complained. In the end they saved countless soldiers and comforted thousands of dying men. Although not trained for combat, occasionally nurses ended up having to fight their way out of an enemy trap. Some spent time in concentration camps. Praising their performance in combat zones, the army surgeon general commented that he did not see fear in their eyes, only kindness and certainty.

In an area where fierce fighting was going on, nurses had to concentrate on the job at hand and had to learn to deal with pain and suffering on a daily basis. Despite working in the midst of death and destruction, they seldom broke down. One nurse expressed her feelings about serving in a shooting war: "War is now an Awful Actuality and not something we hear about on the radio. Our friends are being killed—those gay young lads we danced with last week; those fine young men who told us their plans for the future when this is all over and the world has stopped being mad. We don't discuss their deaths; we pat each other on the shoulder and say, 'Well, he's had it.'"[56]

Two communities in North Carolina organized Army General Hospitals to serve in Europe. Duke University sponsored the 65th General Hospital, made up of volunteers and staffed by skilled doctors and nurses trained at Duke. The unit received high praise from both patients and higher headquarters and was commended for saving "lives that only skill and care could possibly have saved."[57] Virginia Reavis of Onslow County was assigned to the 65th in December 1943. The unit learned that D-Day was approaching. "It was a sickening feeling knowing what was going to happen. We went in five days after D-Day and took in supplies and loaded up the injured. There were so many head injuries, it was horrible. They left home as strong young men. I thought to myself, this is worse than death."[58]

Recruited almost entirely from volunteers from the medical staffs of Charlotte hospitals, the army's 38th Evacuation Hospital Unit's more than 600 staff members served behind the lines in Africa and Italy. A number of the exploits of the 38th made national news. A painting of Lieutenant Martha Pegram Mitchell, a nurse in the hospital, appeared on the cover of *Life* magazine, which later published a lengthy article about the hospital. Ernie Pyle, the famed war correspondent, wrote about some of the 38th Evacs' activities in North Africa. Richard Tregaskis, the author of *Guadalcanal Diary*, lauded the 38th for saving his life after he suffered a severe head wound.

The evacuation hospitals dealt with traumatic wounds and lived a precarious existence, having to move on a moment's notice as the battle lines changed. Lieutenant Martha Mitchell reflected on her experience in the 38th Evac: "I wanted to help with the war effort. Word got around Charlotte that the 38th Evac was looking for nurses so I signed up. The hardest part was seeing the casualties. These were young men our age and they were coming to us after being hit with mortar shells. I remember one young man who had been hit so hard, he had abdominal wounds and his hip bones were shattered. He had so many holes we just had to put him back together. We had to collect blood from our unit in order to give him enough transfusions, but he made it."[59]

Nurses back home in North Carolina faced less trauma, but their medical responsibilities were similar. Their emotional response to wounded soldiers was comparable to those of nurses working on the battle front. Margaret Rose Ensley, a nurse at Moore General Hospital near Asheville (a 1,520-bed hospital for burn victims), nursed seriously wounded troops who had been returned to the States. "The wounded were brought in by special train. . . . A party was planned for their arrival and USO girls were called. You always wore your prettiest long dress and a smile on your face. Sometimes it was hard to smile when you saw their wounds and agony. At the dances you talked to them and danced with them if they felt up to it."[60] No matter where they worked, nurses had to have strong wills and boundless energy in order to care for their charges.

The war focused public attention on nursing activities as never before and gave a great boost to the profession. As a result of the war, nursing schools expanded while improving standards and organizing specialized training. Until 1941 patients tended to use hospitals only in case of emergencies, but after 1946 the public began to demand their right to decent medical care. As the number of hospitals increased, nurses were attracted to the profession by greater pay and a professional status. Nurses selflessly did their job during the war. Those whom they helped and those whose lives they saved remembered the nurses' sacrifice and their desire to do what nurses had always done—to heal and to comfort.[61]

Employment

As noted, women did every job imaginable during World War II. They operated cranes, worked as ordnance testers, flew planes, built ships and planes, and worked on railroads. Women were employed as clerks, communications experts, filling station operators, taxi drivers, and schoolteachers. They fought fires, planted trees, delivered mail, and worked as police officers, cowgirls, farmers, lumberjacks ("lumberjills"), hydraulic press operators, welders, bus drivers, and train conductors.

As World War II evolved and more men went into military service; America's need for skilled and unskilled labor increased. There was some discussion that Congress should consider a bill that would require compulsory war work for women in critical industries in order to prosecute the war successfully. The government decided to rely on voluntary recruitment—a wise choice. Millions of women voluntarily left their kitchens and menial jobs for better pay in defense industries, in the military, and even in unskilled jobs that paid more than their previous work. Women eagerly answered the call. The number of working women jumped from 12 million in 1940 to 19 million in 1945, when they made up 36 percent of the civilian workforce—up from 24 percent in 1940.

It should be pointed out that the overwhelming number of women remained homemakers or continued to work in traditional women's jobs. Most women did not work outside the home and did not have industrial jobs. But those who decided to work in critical industries made an important difference in the increased production levels of the country.[62]

The hiring of women in skilled work came slowly and grudgingly. The war years saw great change and expansion as employers realized that women worked as well as or better than men and would be paid less. Women sought out challenging jobs because they wanted to help win the war, for adventure and travel, for education and personal advancement, and very often for emancipation from financial worries. War brides did not get enough money from their husbands' allotment to pay for all the family expenses. Many of the new workers were single women who liked living in new places, enjoyed challenging work, and looked forward to meeting new people, including possible husbands. A sizable proportion of female workers were older married women who reveled in their freedom from what some saw as the drudgery, repetition, and isolation of housework.[63]

The most dramatic change in women's work came in the defense industries, where women took jobs previously limited to male workers. Some 1.7 million females worked in major industries: steel, machinery, aircraft, shipbuilding, and automobile production. Women made up 45 percent of the workforce at the Douglas Aircraft plant and 47 percent of the employees in the Boeing plant. "Every time I finish a piece for a bomber," declared a woman who had lost a son at Pearl Harbor, "I feel that we are that much closer to winning the war." Female workers were particularly proficient at the dangerous job of manufacturing munitions. They usually had small hands that could squeeze into tight places necessary for welding jobs and could handle precise instruments more easily than males. Munitions manufacturing required excellent quality control, a steady hand, caution, precision, and an awareness of safety regulations. The workers knew that their work had to be exact and that the lives of soldiers depended on how well they did their job.[64]

Factories converted from peacetime to wartime production and from "lingerie to camouflage netting; from baby carriages to field-hospital food carts; from lipstick cases to bomb fuses; . . . from ribbons and silk goods to parachutes; from beer cans to hand grenades; . . . from vacuum cleaners to gas-mask parts." Female workers flocked to these factories, while the number of women in clerical, sales, and service jobs declined. Women felt fortunate that so many new opportunities had opened up in industries heretofore unavailable to them and took full advantage of their good fortune. To publicize the contributions of women in industrial production, the government used Rosie the Riveter as the symbol of the hard-working woman. The American public began to appreciate the effectiveness of women workers and loved seeing newsreels of women making a V for Victory sign as they drove a tank off the production line.[65]

Eighteen-year-old Alice McGuire, a native of Piney Creek, N.C., had been hired on an experimental basis for the difficult job of testing weapons at the Aberdeen Proving Ground in Maryland. After so many men left for military service, the military was desperate for help and turned to McGuire and other women, including one grandmother.

Firing a 75-mm antiaircraft gun, McGuire was so accurate that she would hit the bull's-eye six out of seven times. She said that she learned her marksmanship potting skunks and rabbits on her family's farm in North Carolina. "It's just pie for me. I just reckon I was born knowing how to shoot. . . . It just seemed natural for me to get a job firing these guns for the government." The stocky McGuire, who allowed she was so tough that "the boys wouldn't let me play on their football team," fired everything from tank guns to carbines. She summed up her experience testing weapons and the changing status of women with wisdom beyond her years. "I reckon this isn't rightly what you'd call women's work but I don't know where you'll find any real woman's work in this war. Seems like you can't tell man's work from woman's anymore."[66]

Women joined the workforce in Charlotte in ever increasing numbers. They took many jobs previously held by men only, as electricians, welders, and woodworkers. One manufacturer appreciated the hard work that his female employees put in, noting: "If it were not for the ladies, I don't know what we'd do." Another observer, Rex B. White, concluded: "They use their brains more effectively than men."[67] In the small town of Sanford there were many calls from local retailers and manufacturers for women to work in plants producing wartime materials. The city went so far as to reserve places for fifteen women in a class to train machinists.[68] The situation in Sanford demonstrated that many of the job opportunities were not just in large plants like Boeing or in the auto industry but in local manufacturing units all across the state.

War and societal change from 1940 to 1945 had a tendency to sweep aside old prejudices and habits of thought, but some of the changes were limited and transient. Stereotypes persisted, as some men clung to the traditional view of women's place in the world and resented women taking "men's jobs." T. J. Martin Jr. wrote that he wanted the federal government "to see to it that no woman, who has a husband to support her, be allowed to do the job that some man can do."[69]

While women had new and better jobs, male employers still unfairly discriminated against them. The bosses often assigned women the more difficult and onerous jobs in a plant. Although they should have received equal pay for equal work, women received less pay than men—in some cases 40 percent less. Female workers often were passed over for promotion and suffered from male sexual harassment. Women were frequently limited to clerical work or semiskilled labor. Labor unions were not excited about allowing women into their ranks. The facilities in plants and factories were not designed for female workers. Many workplaces lacked an adequate number of clean toilets, child-care facilities, and adequate medical care for women. Not until later in the war did some employers remedy these inequities.[70]

Not all of women's work during the war occurred in manufacturing, as there were significant openings in agriculture. The government needed to increase the amount of food grown. To achieve this goal the state recruited women to work on farms. By the first summer of the war women farmworkers across the country had risen from 1 percent to 14 percent. In North Carolina the figure increased from 8 percent to 22.4 percent. The state's tobacco farms were an important source for decent-paying jobs for women. These women farmers worked in burning heat in the summer, with calloused hands from chopping cotton, pitching hay, and harvesting potatoes. They put up with sore muscles, poison ivy, pesticides, and other discomforts to do the job. Farmers were initially a bit skeptical about women in the fields but soon praised them as diligent, reliable, and capable workers. Women were much less likely than male farmworkers to get drunk, get into fights, and miss work. In the summer of 1943 the U.S. Department of Agriculture began organizing female farmworkers by setting up the Women's Land Army, which ultimately employed over a million female farmworkers.[71]

While white women in North Carolina faced gender discrimination, black women suffered from both racial and gender intolerance on the part of petty-minded white males. War gave black women the chance to get out of domestic work and led to increased income, but the gain for black female workers was not as great as for white women. Black women in manufacturing increased from 50,000 in 1940 to 300,000 in 1944. Overall the number of black women workers expanded by one-third. Although there were opportunities in defense plants in the North and West, the crippling legacy of racial discrimination in North Carolina resulted in lower levels of education and experience for black women and thus were major factors in lack of job opportunity.

Good jobs were available in the tobacco factories. A few black women, approximately one in thirty, managed to get white-collar jobs such as clerks and secretaries. But black women did not have nearly as many options as white women. Except in local black enterprises, very few black females were hired as saleswomen. Most of them found work in commercial and domestic service—cooking, cleaning, and serving in offices, hotels, and restaurants. Black women generally were hired in the least appealing and poorest-paying jobs. Even when they had decent jobs, they still faced prejudice and bias from white males and white females. Black women were used to this kind of treatment, but like other minorities they hoped that America would eventually embrace the concept of the Double V for victory.[72]

As the war came to an end, women workers faced an uncertain future. Many of the industrial jobs disappeared as production ended and the economy shifted from making wartime goods back to service industries. As factories retooled from producing tanks to making cars, both men and women were idled. During the first nine months after V-E Day the number of women in the workforce decreased by 4 million. When the rehiring began, a veteran's right to a job became an inviolable rule. Although women had sacrificed much and had committed themselves to the war effort, many women in skilled jobs were now shunted aside for men, the traditional breadwinners of the family. Women who had done their patriotic duty were in effect asked to return home where they "naturally belonged" and give their jobs back to the men who had done the fighting.

A significant number of women, tired of trying to raise a family and work at the same time, were happy to return to their roles as wives and homemakers. Other women had discovered a new world of work. They loved the challenges and the opportunities that skilled labor offered and wanted to continue in their newfound careers. Although women were discriminated against in the postwar job market, there were many opportunities for nurses and teachers. More jobs were available that would be considered naturally suited to women. An expanding federal government offered career jobs in numerous categories. Women's employment began to rise in 1947; and by 1950 more women were working than in 1944.[73] Nonetheless, career women who had achieved economic success during World War II resented their removal from wartime jobs. They considered the loss of a professional opportunity to be a rather ungrateful response for their hard work during the war.

Overall the war had been a difficult four years for women, who had to balance their time as mothers and homemakers with work in a factory or in volunteer pursuits. Many were young, often war brides without a husband or enough allotment money to pay the bills. Economic worries and the need for child care led to many anxious moments. But perhaps the most difficult times were when wives and mothers had to wait, fearful and frightened, for the telegram that no one wanted to receive ("The War Department regrets to inform you"), notifying them that their husband, son, or brother had perished in the war.

The military protocol for contacting the next of kin about a soldier's death usually involved notification by a telegram, followed by a letter. Occasionally the Red Cross or military officials made a visit to the home— a personal touch that might have made the news a little easier to bear. Women and other family members dreaded the appearance of telegraph messengers or mail carriers for fear of the devastating news that they might be carrying. On more than one occasion the mother or wife would refuse to answer the door or would not admit the carrier in hopes of somehow postponing the sad news.

Mozell Page Cobb from Caswell County remembered how she received the news that her husband had been killed. "I opened a telegram for me from the Army. Pvt. Melvin Wilson Baker—my Melvin,—had been killed in action on December 2 in Germany. I started screaming and Minnie May Wilson, a neighbor came running outside. That telegram, not even hand-delivered, was telling me my life would never be the same. How can I stand this, I wondered. Left alone with a little baby [her parents had died]. I felt like my world had come to an end that day." Like many others who received news of the devastating loss of a loved one, she realized she had to carry on for the sake of her daughter, Carol. "I knew I had to put aside all those sad and bad feelings and think of the good times we had together. I was lucky to have Carol, a part of him. We both loved her so much. Death can take away your loved ones. But thank the Lord, it can't take away your memories." Mozell Cobb later remarried and had another daughter.[74]

A few mothers and wives had a positive outcome after receiving the terrible news that their loved one was missing in action. Ann Spratt Wilson of Polk County received a telegram saying that her husband, a B-24 pilot, had been shot down and was assumed dead. Her reaction was sadness, disbelief, and denial. "How could he be missing? I thought there must be some mistake. This couldn't be happening. I'd received a V-mail letter from him only yesterday. . . . I relayed the news to our parents and both mothers came right away. I was still in a state of shock and disbelief." Despite the ominous telegram, Ann Wilson was certain that he was not dead. "I rationalized that I was much too young to be a widow. It couldn't be true. We had a child to raise together—so many dreams and plans. I prayed a lot and never gave up on my belief that he would come home." Fortunately, word came that Jim Wilson was a prisoner of war in Germany. Eventually he was released from the German prison and returned to the United States in June 1945. He arrived home by bus to surprise his wife. As he approached the house he saw a little girl in a stroller being pushed and cared for by a nurse. He asked the nurse: "Whose little girl is she?" She answered that the girl was Mrs. Wilson's daughter. Jim Wilson smiled. "She's mine too."[75]

In *The Girls of Atomic City* Denise Kiernan described the difficult times that mothers and wives faced while waiting for the latest news about their loved ones:

Small flags of remembrance, a star for each loved one, marked the homes of those affected by the war. So many stars hung in so many windows, stitched carefully by nervous mothers, sisters and sweethearts. No matter the town, a walk down any residential street was sure to turn up blue-star banners waving alone in living room windows, requesting silently to passers-by to pray for the safe return of the brother, father or husband that each five-pointed fabric material signified. And every Blue Star mother lived in fear that her star's color might one day change, might be rendered gold by an unwarranted telegram or a knock at the door, that what once hung as a sign of support and concern would be transformed into a symbol of mourning.[76]

The Blue Star Service banner, designed in World War I, signified that the family had a loved one serving in the armed forces. The banner was to be displayed in the front window of the family's home. Often large numbers of service members came from one family, and some Blue Star Banners had up to five stars. The family placed the banner in the window to express pride in the loved one who was in the service. The government approved the Blue Star Banners because it wanted the world to know about those who gave so much for liberty. If the individual recognized by the Blue Star was killed, then a Gold Star was superimposed on the banner.

A poem to the Gold Star Mothers expresses the sorrow borne by mothers all over the country:

TO MOTHERS OF THE GOLD STAR
His country called and he was gone,
That little boy of yours.
Who overnight became a man
And sailed for foreign shores;
No shadow marred his happiness
The day he said good-bye,
For valiantly you smiled to hide
The tear drop in your eye.
Now Mother Earth holds to her breast
Secure from all alarms,
The one who only yesterday
You cradled in your arms;
And tho' the nation tenders you
Its gratitude untold,
Within your lonely window shines
A bright new star of gold.[77]

Conclusion

Women made huge contributions to America's fight against fascism, but the War Department and business leaders, while providing excellent opportunities for many women, failed to overcome gender prejudice. Like manufacturers and farmers, they had not taken full advantage of women and their skills. Had women and black citizens been employed in full measure in the military and war industries from 1940 on, the war might have been over sooner. Nonetheless, the commitment and achievements of those women who had the fortitude to join the military services were exemplary. The women who volunteered for the Red Cross, worked in Victory Gardens, toiled on farms and factories, and maintained the home fires helped the nation achieve a momentous triumph.

During the war women had succeeded in many areas and had grown in maturity and self-confidence. One aircraft worker explained why her wartime work experience was so important for her: "For me, defense work was the beginning of my emancipation as a woman. For the first time in my life I found out that I could do something with my hands besides bake a pie. . . . I had the consciousness raising experience of being the only woman in this machine shop and having the mantle of challenge laid down by the men, which stimulated my competitiveness and forced me to prove myself."[78] It was also significant that many men who had doubted women's ability in numerous areas changed their views. Men now recognized women's skills and applauded the investment that they had made in giving of their time and energy. This new view of women's place in a changing society undermined but did not replace the old definition of women's work and women's status in America.[79]

North Carolina women were profoundly affected by their experiences in civilian or military roles during the war. They were proud of their patriotic efforts to help win the war and knew that victory would not have been possible without the aid and support of women. During the war women achieved some success in the fight for women's rights. Judy Litoff argued that the war "served as a major force for change in their lives. The war transformed the way women thought about themselves and the world in which they lived, expanding their horizons and affording them a clearer sense of their capabilities." Despite women's return to a traditional role, life would never be the same for those who had lived through such a traumatic time. According to Litoff, "with fortitude and ingenuity, they had surmounted the challenges posed by total war. As the women of a wartime generation are quick to acknowledge. 'We knew that if we could overcome the trials and tribulations of the war years, we could do anything.'"[80]

TAR HEEL HEROES

As noted earlier, the state of North Carolina sent approximately 372,325 men and women to serve their country in World War II. Roughly 7,100 of all veterans from the state lost their lives in the conflict. Throughout history, wars have been fought with dramatic stories of individual courage and service above and beyond the call of duty. Seven North Carolinians received the nation's highest military award, the Congressional Medal of Honor: Jacklyn H. Lucas, Henry F. Warner, Max Thompson, William D. Halyburton Jr., Charles P. Murray Jr., Ray E. Eubanks, and Rufus G. Herring. Three of these citations were given posthumously.

The most colorful of those receiving the Medal of Honor was Jacklyn (Jack) Lucas, a native of Plymouth, North Carolina. He was barely seventeen when he became the youngest U.S. Marine ever to win the honor. Lucas, a strapping, athletic young man, was five feet eight inches tall and weighed 185 pounds on his fourteenth birthday. According to his own account, he "resented a lot of things because I became a real mean kid." Because he was so rambunctious, his mother sent him to a military academy, where adherence to the disciplinary code straightened him out. He became a cadet captain at thirteen. When Pearl Harbor was attacked, Lucas was still in school and underage but was determined to join the Marine Corps and fight the enemy. In later years, when he was asked why he wanted to fight the Japanese at age fourteen, he gave a simple answer: "Because they attacked my country."[1]

Defying his mother's wishes, Lucas went to the Marine Corps recruiting office in Norfolk, Virginia, and told the recruiters that he was seventeen, although he was really fourteen at the time. Because of his muscular build and his experience in military school, he convinced them that he was old enough to fight. Lucas passed all the exams, forged his mother's signature on his enlistment papers, and was sworn into the Marine Corps on August 6, 1942. He went through boot camp at Parris Island, S.C., qualifying as a heavy machine gun crewman, but was assigned to training duty. Lucas had not signed up to train other marines. He wanted to fight. When the rest of his unit transferred to San Diego to prepare for overseas duty, Lucas stowed away in the back of the train. Although without orders, he accompanied his unit when it sailed to its staging area in Pearl Harbor. At this point the Marine Corps discovered that Lucas's true age was fifteen. Although he was not discharged from the marines, the corps determined that he would not be allowed to go into combat.

Thwarted in his desire to fight, Lucas became more frustrated as the war drew to a close and feared that he might miss his chance altogether. He learned that men who got into trouble spent time in the brig and were frequently transferred to a combat unit. So Lucas, who had always been a scrapper and handy with his fists, decided that he would stir up enough trouble to get transferred into a combat unit. "I provoked a fight anytime I could and was locked up a number of times. I mashed up a sergeant and was sentenced to thirty days on bread and water."[2]

When this ploy did not work, Lucas left his unit without authorization and sneaked aboard the USS *Deuel*. The ship carried marines of the 5th Marine Division, part of an invasion force bound for Iwo Jima. With help from his cousin, Lucas hid in a landing craft and slept on the weather deck for twenty-nine days. Knowing that he would be declared a deserter after a thirty-day absence without leave, he turned himself in to the company commander. He did not tell the officer that he was just sixteen but repeated his strong desire to be allowed to go into combat. The colonel said to Lucas: "I'd like to have a whole shipload of Marines that want to fight as bad as you." The marines issued Lucas a rifle and gear and assigned him the 1st battalion of the 26th Marines. He celebrated his seventeenth birthday while at sea and hit the beach at Iwo Jima five days later, on February 19, 1945.[3]

Lucas later described the exhilarating and frightening experience of finally getting into combat: "Shells were flying, people were being blown apart and bullets were everywhere. This was just where I wanted to be. I was as anxious as ever to fight and kill as many of the enemy as I could." On the second day of a fierce battle he and his fire team entered an enemy trench and encountered eleven Japanese soldiers. After he had killed two of them, Lucas's rifle jammed. At that moment two Japanese grenades landed in the trench next to him. With no time to throw them back, Lucas leaped on top of one and pulled the other one beneath his body. "I was there to fight and we were there to win. You do what you have to do to win. It was not in me to turn and run."[4]

The blast blew Lucas's body off the ground, but miraculously he was still alive. Fortunately one of the grenades was a dud. Severely injured by the shrapnel, he was abandoned by his buddies because they thought he was dead. "The volcanic ash and the good Lord saved me. If I'd been on hard ground, that thing would have split me in two." The grenade punctured Lucas's right lung. He had shrapnel in his thigh, neck, chin, head, chest, and right arm and hand, but he never passed out. By risking his own life and falling on the grenades, Lucas had saved his comrades from serious injury and possibly death.[5]

The only part of his body that Lucas could move was his left hand. He kept waving it feebly in the air, hoping that someone would realize that he was still alive. A navy corpsman spotted him and began giving him medical aid. Lucas had been extraordinarily fortunate to have survived this far, but his rescue was far from over. The initial attempt to extricate him was delayed by a mortar barrage. While carrying him on a stretcher, one of the bearers stumbled and dropped the stretcher. Lucas split his head open on a rock. The medics nearly dropped him in the sea as they tried to hoist him on board an LST (tank landing ship), but someone caught his leg and pulled him aboard.

The navy finally evacuated Lucas from Iwo Jima to the hospital ship USS *Samaritan*, where the attending surgeon said: "Maybe he was too damned young and too damned tough to die." Lucas would then undergo twenty-two separate operations to repair the damage caused by the enemy grenade. For the rest of his life he would carry some 200 pieces of shrapnel in his body, some the size of .22-caliber bullets, frequently setting off airport metal detectors. The feisty Lucas later discussed his experience at Iwo Jima. "I had fought for my country and I felt a great deal of pride in that. My only regret was that I didn't get to stay there longer to kill more Japs."[6]

Jack Lucas received the Congressional Medal of Honor as well as a Purple Heart from President Harry S. Truman on October 5, 1945. The citation was for conspicuous gallantry above and beyond the call of duty. "By his inspiring action and valiant spirit of self-sacrifice, he not only protected his comrades from certain injury or possible death, but also enabled them to rout the Japanese patrol and continue the advance. His exceptionally courageous initiative and loyalty reflect the highest credit upon Private First Class Lucas." When Lucas was receiving his medal, President Truman said to him: "I would rather be a Medal of Honor winner than President of the United States." The irrepressible Lucas grinned and said: "Sir, I'll swap with you." Lucas later wrote an autobiography about his exploits entitled *Indestructible: The Unforgettable Story of a Marine Hero at the Battle of Iwo Jima*. Jack Lucas, who loved to regale listeners with stories of his exploits, lived a long and full life, passing away on June 5, 2008, at age eighty.[7]

The other Medal of Honor winners from North Carolina were perhaps not as colorful as Lucas, but their courage and achievements live on in the annals of warfare. Corporal Henry F. Warner, from Troy, N.C., was a 57-mm antitank gunner with the 2nd Battalion in the First Infantry Division. He won the award for his heroism in Belgium on December 20, 1944, after twenty German tanks overran the American defensive line. Ignoring the intense cannon and machine-gun fire, Warner destroyed two German tanks. Unable to reload his antitank gun, he pulled out his pistol and killed the German tank commander of a third tank that was menacing his position. On the following day the German tanks again broke through the battalion line. After scoring a direct hit on one of the oncoming tanks, Warner was killed by enemy machine-gun fire.[8]

On October 18, 1944, army technical sergeant Max Thompson singlehandedly repelled a German attack near Haaren, Germany. After a German infantry battalion, supported by tanks, overran the American lines, Sergeant Thompson repeatedly entered the battlefield under withering fire to rescue several of his wounded comrades. He then became a one-man army. As the German infantry poured through a gap in the lines, Thompson took charge of a machine gun and fired at the advancing enemy until a shell blew the gun from his hands. Shaken and dazed, he picked up a Browning automatic rifle (BAR) and fired burst after burst into the advancing enemy, halting the leading elements of the attack and dispersing the German troops. In stopping the attack Thompson had killed at least twenty-three of the enemy and wounded many more. When his BAR jammed, he found an abandoned rocket gun and destroyed an enemy tank. As if he had not done enough for one day, that night he was given orders to dislodge the enemy from three pillboxes. Once again acting alone, Thompson crawled to within twenty yards of one of the pillboxes and began hurling grenades. Although wounded by return fire, he continued to throw grenades until the enemy vacated their position. The Congressional Medal of Honor citation lauded his personal effort and courageous leadership that inspired his men and enabled them to hold an important hill position.[9]

William D. Halyburton Jr. from Canton was a medical corpsman attached to a marine rifle company in the battle for Okinawa. While exposed to enemy fire, Halyburton rushed to the aid of a wounded marine. He shielded the fallen marine with his own body. Although constantly menaced by Japanese fire, Halyburton continued to minister to the injured marine until he himself sustained mortal wounds and died.[10]

Charles P. Murray Jr. graduated from Wilmington's New Hanover High School and was in his third year at the University of North Carolina when he was drafted into the U.S. Army. Lieutenant Murray arrived in northeastern France as a company commander of an infantry regiment. While leading a platoon-size group on a reconnaissance mission, he discovered 200 German SS troops. In a remarkable example of courage and tenacity under intense fire, Murray single-handedly attacked the enemy, sending ten rifle grenades into the German lines. He began firing a Browning automatic rifle into the SS ranks, killing twenty Germans and setting a truck on fire. Next he got one of his unit's 60-mm mortars and blasted the fleeing Germans.

A short time later Murray charged into enemy foxholes, capturing ten German prisoners. The eleventh German, pretending to surrender, hurled a grenade at Murray. The explosion knocked him to the ground, sending eight pieces of shrapnel into his left leg. Although suffering and bleeding profusely, Lieutenant Murray organized his unit into a defensive position before relinquishing command and seeking medical attention. His single-handed attack on an overwhelming force stopped a counterattack and provided an inspiring example for the men of his command.[11]

Sergeant Ray E. Eubanks of Snow Hill, N.C., saw combat in Dutch New Guinea. On July 23, 1944, unaided, he assaulted a Japanese-held ridge with his BAR, yelling at the Japanese to "get up and fight." Although he was wounded and his weapon was disabled, he continued his charge, using his gun as a club to kill four Japanese soldiers until he himself was killed. His bravery encouraged his men to take and occupy the Japanese position.[12]

Rufus G. Herring, a native of Roseboro, N.C., and a graduate of Davidson College, commanded an LCI (landing craft infantry) in the invasion of Iwo Jima. Guiding his ship close to shore, Herring drew devastating fire from the Japanese coastal defense guns. He directed his 40-mm and 20-mm guns against the hostile beaches until he was struck down and wounded by an enemy shell that set his boat on fire. Upon regaining consciousness after the explosion, he continued firing his guns. He was critically wounded when a Japanese mortar hit the LCI. Upon recovering the second time, Herring took the helm of the badly damaged vessel and carried on valiantly until relief arrived. When he was no longer able to stand, he propped himself up on shell cases, rallied his men, and continued firing his 20-mm guns. The Medal of Honor Citation noted his "aggressive perseverance and indomitable spirit against terrific odds."[13]

The seven North Carolinians who won the nation's highest honor for bravery demonstrated an extraordinary, almost unbelievable, display of courage and fortitude. We can only wonder what mind-set enabled Charles Murray to charge a large enemy force alone or Ray Eubanks to do the same against insurmountable odds. What would the average person do if placed in similar circumstances? Would others, like William Halyburton, leap out of a protected foxhole and rush to the aid of a wounded comrade? It is hard to imagine what possessed these brave men to engage in such exemplary military action. Whether it was love of country, the desire to save a comrade, or eagerness to defeat the enemy that inspired them, all of these men were willing to give their lives for their country. Warner, Halyburton, and Eubanks paid the ultimate price. The other four heroes were badly wounded but continued to fight despite the odds.[14]

These seven men won the Medal of Honor, but other Tar Heels also excelled in the war and brought great credit to their state and nation. Major George E. Preddy, a P-51 Mustang pilot and a Greensboro native, was the highest-ranking ace in the European theater, with twenty-seven kills in 1943 and 1944. Major Preddy won the Distinguished Service Cross, the Air Medal, the Distinguished Flying Cross, a Silver Star, and a Purple Heart. Preddy wanted to be a pilot from an early age but was short (five feet five inches) and had curvature of the spine. After being rejected three times by the navy because of his failure to pass the physical, Preddy took bodybuilding courses to help his back. On his fourth try he passed the physical. Like Jack Lucas, Preddy wanted to fight and would not be denied. He was assigned to the 352nd Fighter Group in England.

According to observers, Preddy was a very aggressive fighter and predator behind the stick of his P-51. General John C. Meyer said that Preddy

Figure 11.1. Major George E. Preddy and his plane "Cripes A'mighty." Preddy, a P-51 Mustang pilot, was the highest-ranking ace in the European theater of war with twenty-seven kills, once shooting down six German planes in five minutes. By permission of Greensboro Historical Museum Archives.

"was the greatest fighter pilot who ever squinted through a gun sight; he was the complete fighter pilot." On August 5, 1944, Preddy's unit was charged with protecting a group of B-17s on a bombing mission. During the flight to the target, his group spotted more than thirty German Messerschmidt 109 fighter planes closing in on the B-17s. Preddy immediately attacked and in an incredible feat of skill and marksmanship shot down six planes in less than five minutes. "I just kept shooting and they just kept falling." Preddy refused to return home when his tour of duty was up. He asked for and got several extensions. On Christmas Day in 1944 Preddy again tangled with the Luftwaffe in the Battle of the Bulge but was shot down and killed by friendly antiaircraft fire. His brother Bill, also a pilot with three kills, was shot down by enemy ground fire and died a few days later. A local newspaper, in a memorial to the brothers, printed the following editorial: "In the AAF's Hall of Fame, the Preddys will be a symbol and a legend among fighter pilots, and to the advancement of aviation, having given their youth and talent to help recapture the lost peace."[15]

William C. Lee, a native of Dunn, N.C., graduated from N.C. State College, where he participated in the ROTC program. After fighting in World War I, Lee was assigned as a peace-time observer in Germany. Excited and intrigued by Adolf Hitler's development of airborne forces for the German military, Lee constantly urged the United States to develop a similar program. Superior officers shut him down. His commanding officer told Lee: "I'm sick and tired of hearing your nonsense about airborne warfare. No American soldier is ever going to have little enough sense to jump out of an airplane even in a parachute and I don't want to hear the word airborne spoken in this office again."[16]

One individual, however, had been reading about the German airborne program and wanted more information. The interested person was none other than President Franklin D. Roosevelt. He ordered Lee to Washington to brief the president on what he had seen in Germany. FDR, impressed with what he heard, asked Lee to begin planning and training for an airborne unit as soon as possible. Lee then organized and established the Airborne Command at Fort Bragg, N.C. By exceptional ability and force of character, General Lee built the framework of what would become a powerful striking force, the 82nd Airborne Division. He helped organize the D-Day drops into Normandy on June 6, 1944, and planned to jump with his men but suffered a heart attack and was ordered back to the states. Military leaders and historians have praised General Lee's innovative contribution to American war strategy as the "Father of the Airborne."[17]

At 8:15 a.m. on August 6, 1945, Major Thomas Ferebee pushed a lever in his B-29 bomber, the *Enola Gay*, and unleashed the first atomic bomb that the world had ever seen. Although Major Ferebee had a distinguished military career that lasted from World War II to Vietnam, it was that single day, August 6, 1945, that ensured him a place in history.

Born on a farm outside of Mocksville, N.C., Ferebee enlisted in the army air corps in 1941 and was assigned as a B-17 bombardier upon completion of flying school. The following year he and a friend from flight school, Theodore "Dutch" Van Kirk, a navigator, were assigned to the same B-17 bomber crew in England. That bomber, piloted by Paul Tibbetts, flew the first daylight American bombing mission over Europe. By 1944 Ferebee had flown sixty-three missions, an unusually high number for a combat airman.

When the army air force selected Colonel Paul Tibbetts to fly history's most significant bombing mission—the dropping of the first atomic bomb, his first decision was to pick Dutch Van Kirk as the navigator and Ferebee as the bombardier. The three men had flown together many times and worked well as a team. Tibbetts called Ferebee "the best bombardier who ever looked through the eyepiece of a Norden bombsight." He described Ferebee as "an old hand at dropping bombs with the wind, against it or in a crosswind. From long experience, he knew what a falling bomb would do under almost any wind condition and he knew how to crank all the right information into his Norden bomb sight."[18]

When the twelve crew members of the *Enola Gay* (named after Tibbetts's mother) set out on their top secret mission on August 6, 1945, they knew it was an important assignment but did not know that they would be dropping an atomic bomb. The crew members also were unaware that prior to departure Colonel Tibbetts had been given twelve capsules with a lethal dose of cyanide, one for each crew member in case they were shot down and captured. At the first sign of trouble, Tibbetts was to give the men a choice: they could blow out their brains with their pistol or commit suicide by poisoning.

After a thirteen-hour flight the *Enola* Gay, a stripped-down B-17, arrived at the target, Hiroshima, Japan, a mere seventeen seconds after their scheduled time of arrival. Hiroshima had been chosen as one of five possible targets because it was an important military and communications center. Tibbetts decided on Hiroshima because the weather was good and the skies were clear. Ferebee announced "bombs away" as he watched a single 9,000-pound uranium bomb, known as "Little Boy," fall on Hiroshima. Forty-three seconds after the release of the bomb, the sky erupted in a dazzling light and a huge mushroom cloud hovered over the city. Ferebee told the press that "there are no words to describe how bright the flash was. The sun doesn't compare at all."[19]

Immediately after jettisoning the bomb, the *Enola Gay* made a 155-degree diving turn to the right with a 60-degree bank to escape the aftershock of the bomb. The shock wave from the explosion, which took a minute to reach the plane, struck with violent force. One crew member said it felt as if some giant had slammed the plane with a telephone pole. Ferebee thought they were under attack until he realized that it was the blast effect. Once the plane had weathered the powerful shock wave, Colonel Tibbetts calmly announced over the intercom: "Fellows, you have just dropped the first atomic bomb in history." Tibbetts and the other crew members were aware of the obvious devastation that they had wrought and were sobered by the knowledge that the world would never be the same because of the new technology.[20]

As the plane flew away from the bomb site, the crew witnessed a "giant purple mushroom cloud" that was "boiling upward like something terribly alive. It was a frightening sight." The cloud rose to a height of 45,000 feet, over three miles above the plane's altitude. While the crew looked down at the burning and devastated city, Hiroshima completely disappeared under "an awful blanket of smoke and fire."[21]

"Little Boy" hit directly above the Shima Institute, a medical center. "The stone columns flanking the entrance . . . were rammed straight down into the ground. The entire building collapsed. The occupants were vaporized." The temperature reached several thousand degrees centigrade at ground zero. The flash heat started fires a mile away and burned human flesh two miles away. Of the estimated 320,000 citizens in the city, 80,000 were killed instantly. Several thousand Japanese soldiers, who made up one-third of the death toll, were standing out in the open near the epicenter. "They were incinerated, their charred bodies burned into the parade ground." Out of a total of 90,000 buildings, 62,000 were destroyed. All utilities and transportation services were eliminated.[22]

Scientists were well aware of the devastation that would be caused by the concussion of the bomb and the firestorm but were less sure about the long-term consequences of radiation. The experts later determined that radiation would have killed 95 percent of the people within a half mile of the center. Even if the citizens of Hiroshima had not died by burns or blast effects, they had absorbed enough radiation to kill them. "The rays simply destroyed body cells. . . . Many people who did not die right away came down with nausea, headache, diarrhea, malaise and fever which lasted several days." After time passed, patients suffered from a high fever up to 106 degrees, hair falling out, and a dramatic drop in white corpuscles. The body could no longer fight an infection. Over a longer period, radiation poisoning led to miscarriages, sterility, and some genetic abnormalities in later generations.[23]

The dropping of a second bomb, "Fat Boy," on Nagasaki on August 9, 1945, led to the surrender of Japan on August 14. The formal peace treaty was signed on September 2, 1945, ending World War II. After the war Ferebee flew B-47s during the Cold War and B-52s during the Vietnam War, retiring from the air force in 1970. His decorations included two Distinguished Flying Crosses, the Silver Star, and the Legion of Merit. He died on March 16, 2000, at the age of eighty-one. Ferebee was always convinced that the dropping of the bomb ended the war and thus saved many American and Japanese lives. He never apologized for the part that he played. The crew members were just doing the job they had been trained for. Ferebee said: "I'm sorry an awful lot of people died from that bomb and I hate to think that something like that had to happen to end the war" but felt no guilt about his part in the bombing. He merely expressed the hope that it would never happen again.[24]

Another famous North Carolinian, Robert K. Morgan, pilot of the iconic B-17 *Memphis Belle*, was born in Asheville, N.C., on July 31, 1918. Morgan joined the army air corps in February 1941. After basic flight training and advanced B-17 training, he flew his new plane, bomber number 448, a B-17 Flying Fortress, to Bassingbourn, England, home of the 91st Bomb Group.

Nose art (the naming and decorating of planes) was one of the great fads of World War II. The name and an illustration chosen by the crew were painted on the nose and fuselage of the aircraft. According to Morgan, the naming of a plane was a great morale booster. "It's a way of holding on to our individuality or sense of humor, in a war that was overwhelmingly vast, mechanized and brutal." Morgan persuaded the crew to name the ship the *Memphis Belle* after his current girlfriend, Margaret Polk of Memphis. The nose art featured the "Belle" as a comely young woman in a bathing suit. On one side of the plane she was attired in a red bathing suit; on the other side she wore a blue bathing suit.[25]

Morgan thought that naming the plane after his girlfriend would accomplish two purposes. It would give the crew a sense of pride and might seal his romance with Margaret Polk. What Morgan could not have anticipated was that the decision to name the plane the *Memphis Belle* would be the beginning of one of the most-publicized romances of World War II. The press loved the story of the whirlwind courtship between Margaret Polk and Morgan that had been interrupted by the war. Thousands of couples went through a similar experience, but the military success of the plane and the sexy illustration of the Memphis Belle emblazoned on the nose of the plane made this couple famous. But Bob Morgan never married Margaret Polk. They broke up shortly after he returned to the United States from combat duty.[26]

When the Allied daylight bombing began in Europe, the army air force had little experience in high-altitude strategic bombing. The commanders had to figure out a strategy as they went along. In the early days 80 percent of the U.S. bombers were shot down. Morale was very low, so as an incentive the generals set twenty-five missions as the number to be flown before the crew could return home. The *Belle*, both very good and very lucky, became the first B-17 heavy bomber in the Eighth Air Force to complete twenty-five missions with the same crew.

From November 7, 1942, until May 15, 1943, the crew flew about 20,000 miles and dropped some sixty tons of bombs on military and industrial targets in Belgium, France, and Germany. The risks were enormous, and many of their buddies did not return to base after a mission. Once over the target they faced a horrendous amount of antiaircraft fire (flak) and had to fend off attacks from enemy fighter planes. The *Belle* was hit on many occasions. By the end of its run almost every major part of the plane had been replaced at least once. On one occasion the plane landed with eighty-one holes in the fuselage and one engine knocked out. Despite all the damage during combat, the crew always made it home and suffered no injuries. The plane earned sixty-one decorations for bravery, and each member of the crew received a Distinguished Flying Cross and an Air Medal.

Bob Morgan described the great relief he felt when landing safely after a long, perilous mission. He said it did not matter whether it was the first or the twenty-fourth mission. What mattered, recalled Morgan, was that you were down from the sky and had brought your crew back to the base. It felt good "to have turned loose of that yoke. You've held on to it for maybe six, eight hours, knuckles white, keeping thirty-two tons of bomber steady at 25,000 feet, your hands wrapped around that shuddering yoke, your feet tensing against the rudder pedals. Your margin of error is down to feet, from the wingtips of the bomber on your left and the bomber on your right. All this with deadly antiaircraft fire and cannon and machinegun rounds from hostile fighter planes."[27]

Colonel Morgan tried to explain why the *Belle* had survived so many dangerous missions when many of their comrades had perished. According to Morgan, the desire to survive and the focus on achieving the mission somehow melted down the crew's individual personalities, blended all of the different skills, and turned the crew into "a single functioning organism of war. . . . It was intelligence and it was instinct and it was alertness and it was technical prowess and it was superhuman concentration and it was a way of setting fear aside and it was interdependence—a way of knowing at every instant under extreme duress what the other fellow's function was, and how he was handling it—and it was faith."[28]

After completing twenty-five missions, the *Memphis Belle* returned to the United States and began a thirty-city tour, including Asheville, to raise money for war bonds. Morgan could have been assigned to desk duty for the remainder of the war, but he wanted to fly. In October 1944 he deployed to Saipan with his new B-29, *Dauntless Dotty*, named for his current wife, Dorothy Johnson.

On November 24, 1944, Morgan led the first B-29 bombing raid on Tokyo. The Allies attacked Tokyo with 325 planes armed exclusively with incendiaries (magnesium and napalm). Flying at night and at a low altitude, the B-29s surprised the Japanese and devastated the city. The firestorm created by the bombs consumed sixteen square miles of the city. The temperature at the heart of the firestorm caused the water in the canals to boil. Over 267,000 buildings, many of them flimsy wooden structures, were destroyed; 89,000 Japanese citizens died, a death total greater than at Hiroshima. Morgan described how the fires depleted all the oxygen and created fire winds of up to hundred miles an hour. The air was too hot to breathe. Those trying to escape the fires were either incinerated or asphyxiated.[29]

After completing another twenty-five missions in the Pacific, Colonel Morgan finally came home in April 1945. He lived the remainder of his life in Asheville and visited the *Memphis Belle* at least once a year. He died on May 15, 2004, at the age of eighty-five. Married three times and engaged several times, Bob Morgan was a swashbuckler of the first order and an extraordinary American hero who risked his life again and again to help win the war.

Several North Carolina natives had influential governmental leadership positions. Kenneth C. Royall of Goldsboro, a graduate of UNC and Harvard Law, was commissioned as a colonel in the U.S. Army in 1942. He served as a special assistant to the secretary of war and later became the undersecretary of war. Royall served as the last secretary of war when that position was abolished. He became the first secretary of the army from September 1947 to April 27, 1949.[30]

Jonathan Daniels, the scion of a famous North Carolina family, also made major contributions to the war. His father, Josephus Daniels, had been secretary of the navy under President Woodrow Wilson. The assistant secretary at the time was Franklin D. Roosevelt. Josephus Daniels was the publisher of the influential *Raleigh News and Observer* and a powerful force in state politics. In early 1942 Jonathan Daniels joined the war effort as assistant director of the Office of Civilian Defense, in charge of civilian mobilization. He carried out special assignments for President Roosevelt and in 1943 became one of only six administrative assistants to the president, focusing on race relations. In March 1945 Daniels became

FDR's final press secretary. He was a trusted advisor to the president during a critical time in the nation's history.[31]

One of the best-known names and voices during World War II belonged to North Carolina native Edward R. Murrow. A celebrated American correspondent and possibly its greatest broadcast journalist, Edward Murrow was born in Polecat Creek, a small Quaker community near Greensboro, N.C., on April 25, 1908. Although his family moved to the state of Washington when he was five, Murrow always proudly viewed himself as a Tar Heel from Guilford County.

Charles Kuralt, another accomplished newsman and a North Carolina native, believed that Murrow, despite his many years in London and New York and Washington, always belonged to Guilford County. "I am southerner enough to believe that there really is something born into a man that helps determine what he will become and if that is so, then there was a century of good earth and hard work and woods and creeks and wild flowers born into Edward R. Murrow. And a Scotch-Irish and English Quaker dignity and decency and respect for the truth."[32]

In 1937 the Columbia Broadcasting System (CBS) sent Edward R. Murrow to London to report on the growing tensions on the European continent. Murrow assembled a dedicated and highly qualified team of reporters, known as "Murrow's Boys." The group featured important journalists such as Eric Sevareid, Charles Collingwood, William L. Shirer, and Howard K. Smith. Murrow, with compelling and heart-rending stories, described the horrors of war both on and off the battlefield. His radio broadcasts from the rooftops of London during the German blitz and the Royal Air Force's Battle for Britain would make his voice and name well known all over America.

By 1940 Murrow was a living link between America and the besieged island of England. He wanted his listeners to know how Londoners reacted to the horrors of war and what it felt like to suffer through the fire bombings of London. Murrow described "those black-faced men with bloodshot eyes . . . fighting fires" and "the policeman who stands guard over that unexploded bomb." He frequently depicted the tragic sight of soldiers in graphic images, with their backs bent, digging in the bombed-out rubble of London's streets, searching for victims of the blast.[33]

Murrow not only described the devastation of war but allowed his audience to hear the air raid sirens, the measured marching of Londoners descending into the underground shelters, the moans and groans of injured citizens, and the sounds of the German Luftwaffe dropping bombs on the city. Throughout his stay in London he denounced America's outdated isolationism and urged Americans to mount a strong and highly organized battle against the evils of Nazism and Hitler's barbaric expansion into Europe. Murrow's voice not only inspired millions but kept the nation informed in real time of exactly what was happening on the war front.

Perhaps Murrow's most poignant and disturbing reporting came when he visited the Nazi concentration camp at Buchenwald. Appalled, sickened, and angry at what he witnessed, Murrow tried to convey the unspeakable horror of the camps to a disbelieving public. "There were two rows of bodies stacked up like cordwood. They were thin and very white. Some of the bodies were terribly bruised, though there seemed to be little flesh to bruise. . . . I tried to count them as best I could and arrived at the conclusion that all that was mortal of more than five hundred men lay there in two neat piles." Murrow concluded his broadcast: "God alone knows how many men and boys have died there during the past twelve years. . . . I was told that there were more than 20,000 in the camp. There had been as many as 60,000. Where are they now?"[34]

After the war Murrow became a key correspondent for CBS television, hosting programs such as *I Can See It Now,* where he challenged the Red-baiting Senator Joe McCarthy. Murrow won several Emmys for programs about important issues in America. In 1961 President John F. Kennedy appointed him as head of the U.S. Information Agency, charged with telling America's story to the world. Edward R. Murrow died of cancer in New York on April 27, 1965.[35]

Some forty-one naval vessels (one battleship, three cruisers, and thirty-seven transports, gunships, and seaplane tenders, usually named after North Carolina counties) represented North Carolina during World War II. The most important vessel was the battleship USS *North Carolina,* known as the "Showboat." It was one of ten new battleships to enter service in June 1941. As the first battleship to incorporate new shipbuilding technology, the *North Carolina* combined high speed with powerful armaments. Some experts declared it "the most powerful ship afloat." In July 1942, when the ship arrived in Pearl Harbor, Fleet admiral Chester W. Nimitz recalled the moment. "I well remember the great thrill when she arrived in Pearl Harbor during the early stages of the war—at a time when our strength and fortunes were at a low ebb. She was the first of the great, new battleships to join the Pacific Fleet and her mere presence in a task force was enough to keep morale at a peak. Before the war's end she had built for herself a magnificent record of accomplishment."[36]

During forty months and 307,000 miles of service in the Pacific theater, the ship earned twelve battle stars and lost only nine men despite several hits from torpedoes and enemy aircraft. In numerous key battles— Guadalcanal, the Gilberts, Tarawa in the Marshall Islands, New Guinea, Iwo Jima, and Okinawa—the *North Carolina* was credited with downing twenty-four Japanese planes, sinking one merchantman, and unleashing tons of explosives on Japanese strongholds.[37]

Before Christmas of 1943 the chaplain of the ship came up with a unique plan to improve ship morale during the holidays. After raising $2,400, the chaplain wrote Macy's department store in New York, enclosing the funds and requesting that Christmas presents be purchased and mailed to all 729 sons, daughters, brothers, and sisters of the crew. "We know we are asking a great deal, but . . . you will be adding greatly to the happiness of our children and to our own Christmas out here in one of the war zones." Macy's not only purchased, wrapped, and shipped all of the presents but invited all the mothers and children who could get to the store to come and open them there. The store then filmed the children opening the gifts and sent the film to the *North Carolina*. The chaplain showed the film on Christmas eve. "The effect of that flickering black and white newsreel—the high, excited voices and sweet laughter of youngsters, the loving smiles and longing eyes of a spouse—in a darkened hold of a ship, on a Christmas eve is hard to picture. A longing too deep to describe, a homesickness too great to express, a surprise too joyous to forget."[38]

Decommissioned on June 27, 1947, the *North Carolina* languished in dry dock until a large number of North Carolinians, led by former governors Luther Hodges, Terry Sanford, and the U.S. Navy, raised $250,000 to save the ship from destruction. Much of the *North Carolina*'s former glory lives on at the battleship memorial in Wilmington, N.C. The ship, dedicated on April 29, 1962, is a permanent war memorial to heroism.[39]

The state of North Carolina, with seven Congressional Medal of Honor recipients, heroes in the air, and stalwart leaders in the military hierarchy and in Washington, made notable contributions to America's success in World War II.

CONCLUSION

The initial years of World War II had been costly and difficult for the Allies, but by the end of 1943 an overwhelming superiority in technology, manufacturing, and the best-equipped troops in the world enabled the Allied High Command to envision a favorable end to the war. The successful invasion of Normandy on D-Day, June 6, 1944, permitted the Allied forces to begin the final difficult push into Germany. After intense fighting in the Battle of the Bulge and elsewhere, American troops met Russian troops at the Elbe River, signaling the beginning of the end of the war against Germany. On April 28, 1945, Italian partisans captured Benito Mussolini. The dictator and his mistress were lined up against a wall and shot. His body was then hanged upside down by a meat hook and stoned and reviled by the Italians, whom he had led into a disaster.

Meanwhile Adolf Hitler, not yet fifty-six years of age, hunkered down in his bunker beneath the Wilhelmplatz in Berlin. His face gray and ashen, the Führer suffered from tremors and fits of rage, but he continued to give orders that could not be obeyed. On April 30, 1945, realizing that the end was near, Hitler committed suicide. The bodies of Hitler and his lover Eva Braun were soaked with gasoline and burned. Hitler's "Thousand Year Reich" had come to an ignominious end. The entire German command surrendered unconditionally on May 8, 1945 (known as Victory in Europe Day: V-E Day). After five years, eight months, and seven days of horrendous conflict, the guns fell silent at 6:01 p.m. The war in Europe had ended.[1]

The *Gastonia Daily Gazette* ran a banner headline: "*FULL GERMAN SURRENDER.*" The paper reported that the citizens of Gastonia were jubilant but took the victory news in a calm spirit.[2] Other state newspapers displayed similar headlines. The *Charlotte News* printed an extra edition with the bold headline: "THE WAR IS OVER IN EUROPE." The paper announced that the citizens of Charlotte had a happy but subdued reaction to the conclusion of the fighting in Europe. Most of the state observed the news in a quiet, thankful, and prayerful manner as citizens began to turn their thoughts and actions to winning the war in the Pacific.[3] Fire and air-raid sirens sounded and horns were blown in some towns, but most continued their work in the state war industries. Governor R. Gregg Cherry reminded citizens not to relax but to prosecute the war with renewed effort. An editorial in the *Raleigh News and Observer* called the victory a triumph of democracy over totalitarianism. In a war waged for conquest and inspired by greed, the forces of freedom and liberty had prevailed. "If the Axis powers had won, there would have fallen on the earth another era of the Dark Ages, the light of learning would have been extinguished and the glory of Christianity submerged into the worship of Military Power."[4]

President Franklin D. Roosevelt, the architect of victory, did not get to witness the hard-won military triumph. He died of a cerebral hemorrhage in Warm Springs, Georgia, on April 12, 1945. America was devastated and shocked at the passing of its great leader. As Roosevelt's funeral train made its way back to Washington, tens of thousands of mourners lined the tracks to express their grief in an unprecedented display of emotion. Their numbers were astonishing. Some guessed that close to 2 million people came to the tracks and train stations to pray and sing hymns and weep unabashedly. People waited reverently for hours at the small depots and crossroads. Through his fireside chats and his leadership during the war, FDR had created a special bond with the American people. Many of the poor and common people saw him as their savior. The grieving citizens who came to pay their respects loved and admired FDR as the president who had forged the New Deal, had led them out of the Great Depression, and had now brought them to the brink of victory in the most destructive war in history. For some younger Americans, he was the only president they had ever known, the only man elected to the office four times. Many people saw him as the ultimate casualty of the war. General Alexander M. Patch said that the president had "just as surely given his life in the service of his country as any soldier on the far-flung battlefronts."[5]

The train took twenty-five hours to make the slow journey to Washington, D.C. Roosevelt's coffin, flanked by a military guard, was in the last car of the train. Eleanor Roosevelt had asked that the curtains be opened and the lights kept on for the entire trip so that mourners could view the coffin as it passed. A saddened crowd waited at the Southern Railway Station in Charlotte for the train's expected arrival at 6 p.m. The train did not arrive until 10:45 p.m., but 10,000 Charlotteans still lined the tracks waiting to express their condolences.[6]

North Carolina flew its flags at half-mast. Special memorial services were held in every hamlet and town, especially at the military bases, as FDR was laid to rest at Hyde Park, New York. The *Raleigh News and Observer* praised FDR for his sterling leadership as president and for his foresight in planning for the postwar peace with the formation of the United Nations. "His loss will be mourned throughout the world, but the inspiration of his leadership lives and in that inspiration we can thank God and take courage." Expressions of sorrow came from all the leaders of the world and from the U.S. military, which had lost its commander-in-chief. Lieutenant General Jacob L. Devers, commander of the Sixth Army Group, said: "No greater loss, no grief more profound could come to the civilized world than the death of the man whose foresight, leadership and courage was primarily responsible for the inevitable defeat of the Axis powers."[7]

The loss of Roosevelt was a heavy blow to the Allied cause, but President Harry Truman promised to take up the fallen leader's banner and win the war in the Pacific. It took over a year of bitter clashes in such remote islands as Iwo Jima and Okinawa, where Allied forces suffered grievous losses, for victory to be won. Japan's fanatical defense made the invasion of the Japanese homeland a potential nightmare. After several years of research the Manhattan Project had developed two atomic bombs for use against Japan. On August 6, 1945, the *Enola Gay* dropped the first atomic bomb in history on Hiroshima with devastating results. Although President Truman warned the Japanese that they should surrender or face "complete and utter devastation," Japan refused to give up. On August 9 a second bomb was dropped on Nagasaki. Peace negotiations began, resulting in an agreement for Japan to surrender on August 14, 1945. The Japanese signed formal documents of surrender on the battleship *Missouri* on September 2, 1945. The deadliest war in history had finally come to an end.[8]

The announcement of Japan's surrender and the end of World War II led to an explosion of joy: people greeted the news with shouting and hurrahs. The *Winston-Salem Journal's* headline was "JAPAN SURRENDERS." The *Durham Morning Herald* trumpeted: "PEACE—IT'S OVER—JAPS GIVE UP."[9] As the word of the end of hostilities began spreading throughout the state, citizens from Manteo to Murphy voiced their feelings. The *Greensboro Daily News* recorded the event: "Four years of pent up tension burst forth in wild shouts, blaring horns, and jangling cowbells as half the population of Greensboro congregated on Elm Street within two minutes after President Truman's announcement last night that the Japanese have accepted Allied surrender terms."[10] Scenes of rejoicing were repeated everywhere. Parades, prayers of thanksgiving, and memorials were held in every city.

Chapel Hill experienced a tremor of excitement: "suddenly the village was in a frenzy. From houses, from the university campus, from business buildings, people came flocking to the central block on Franklin Street. Shouting and laughter added to the pealing of the bells and the blasts from the sirens, roused such a din as had never been heard in Chapel Hill."[11] Raleigh held the wildest celebration in a generation, with 20,000 inhabitants swarming through downtown streets. Charlotte had the worst traffic jam in history, as thousands of drivers, horns blowing, tried to get into the center of town. The manager of Roses department store on Main Street in Burlington gave away all the U.S. flags that he had in the store. Thousands of soldiers from Fort Bragg joined thousands of civilians in the streets of Fayetteville to cheer the news.[12]

Margaret Parker was listening to the radio when the announcement was made: "And I don't know, I just stood there and the tears started rolling." All of the neighbors gathered in the front yard, saying how wonderful it was that it was all over. Then the group started saying things like it was too late for so and so and too late for one of the neighbors. "And it sort of took all the joy of the occasion out."[13] *The Daily Tar Heel* provided a final eloquent comment: "The black night studded with a billion stars furnished the setting for one of the greatest nights in Carolina history . . . a night with war behind and peace ahead."[14]

After the war had ended, things slowly returned to normal. Social events and weddings proceeded as usual, tobacco prices were very good, the baseball pennant races created much interest, and Governor Cherry was about to crown Miss North Carolina. Gasoline rationing and censorship ended, travel restrictions were lifted, and the reconversion director rescinded controls on the production of automobiles, refrigerators, and other consumer items. The goal was to get privately owned plants back into peacetime operations as soon as possible. Although the government began cutting military contracts and many workers were temporarily laid off, people had high hopes for future jobs in the private sector. Major shortages of gasoline, sugar, meat, and other foodstuffs still existed. But war production had now turned to manufacturing consumer goods, so the country would soon be close to prewar conditions.[15]

The process of demobilizing American troops was a complicated, controversial, and a daunting task for the government. Soldiers wanted to get home as soon as possible to resume their former lives and see family and friends. Wives, children, and parents wanted to welcome their husbands, fathers, and sons home immediately. The army set up a system whereby a soldier could return to the United States if he accrued eighty-five points. A soldier got one point for each month of service and another point for each month of overseas service. Each soldier got five points for combat duty, five points for any wound, and five points for decorations. Twelve points were awarded for every child under eighteen. Those who earned the Congressional Medal of Honor were eligible for immediate discharge. The system applied equally to officers and enlisted men.[16]

The discharge was fairly efficient; the difficulty was in finding the necessary transportation to get soldiers not only to America from overseas but also back to their hometowns. The bureaucratic procedures took much longer than anticipated and evoked some serious grumbling and numerous complaints about the long, involved process. Nonetheless, the troops finally came home to a hero's welcome. When a family welcomed its warrior home from the war, the occasion was joyous, emotional, and poignant. Norman Rockwell's painting *Homecoming GI* beautifully captured the enthusiastic embrace of the soldier's family, including his dog and his girlfriend, as he returned home.[17] Unlike other wars, such as Vietnam, people had no doubt about the rightness of the cause and the courage and success of American troops. Even today, as the World War II veterans pass away in increasing numbers, the American public still has a special fondness for them because of the price they paid and the sacrifices they made.

President Harry Truman paid homage to the 12,000,000 men and women who defended America. "To you who answered the call of your country and served in its Armed Forces to bring about the total defeat of the enemy, I extend the heartfelt thanks of a grateful Nation. As one of the nation's finest, you undertook the most severe task one can be called upon to perform. Because you demonstrated the fortitude, the resourcefulness, and calm judgment necessary to carry out that task, we now look to you for leadership and example in further exalting our country in peace."[18] The *Raleigh News and Observer* noted that for the first time in almost eight years the world was free from war and all the tragedies that accompanied the greatest of scourges. "All honor and glory to the courage of the noble fighting men whose bravery made possible the peace we have always carried in our hearts and all will bow to the many who made the supreme sacrifice that freedom should not perish from the earth." The paper also recognized that the war could not have been won without the generosity and selflessness of those on the home front.[19]

A British memorial to troops who died in the Battle of Kohima in Burma in World War II best expressed the view of those soldiers who fought and died for their country.

> When you go Home
> Tell them of us and say,
> For your tomorrow
> We gave you our today.[20]

World War II changed America and North Carolina in fundamental ways. The war ended the Great Depression and led to the return of prosperity. It increased living standards, uplifted a new and growing middle class, and strengthened and diversified the economies of the South. Wartime technology produced radar and the atomic bomb as well as new wonder drugs, synthetic materials, and the computer revolution. The growth of large corporations and labor unions changed the business climate. Big business and the military would dominate Washington in the future. The wartime government expanded far beyond any expectations, and after the war most Americans accepted the idea of big government.

The significant expansion of government services was coupled with a bewildering variety of government agencies to oversee the economy, the military, and the nation's health. The war expanded the power of the commander-in-chief. In the future the president would wield great influence on Congress and the military. World War II reshaped the global role of the United States. At the end of the conflict America was the world's most powerful nation, with an industrial capacity greater than that of the rest of the world combined. American leaders saw the remainder of the century as the period of the Pax Americana: the United States would rule the world and maintain the peace.

World War II profoundly affected the availability and distribution of goods and services and changed the nature of employment and the nature of the workforce. Partly as a result of the war, there would be a huge population growth in the Sunbelt states and a move toward urbanization as rural residents moved to cities for defense jobs and other economic and social opportunities. This internal and external migration helped break down regional prejudices and provincialism. The South, long isolated from the impact of the flood of immigrants to America, became something of a melting pot during the war. The influx of northern GIs, many immigrants or children of immigrants, provided southerners with a different view of the world. Religious views and beliefs began a metamorphosis. Many rural North Carolinians had never seen a Catholic or a Jew. After the war the Baptist and Pentecostal congregations began to challenge the Presbyterians and the Episcopalians for influence. Tar Heels in the military had not only seen Paris, Rome, and London; they had fought and traveled in distant parts of the world previously known only to a select few. These experiences altered their myopic and ethnocentric worldview as no other events could. Embarrassed by their backwardness and cultural isolation, southerners began to exhibit a more tolerant, less homogeneous mind-set than in the past.

The state's educational institutions had been significantly affected by the war. The large number of students from diverse backgrounds helped modify a conservative view of who should be educated and how they learned. The government made education a national priority and provided the funds and the means for ordinary citizens to pursue a higher education. The development of educational democratization altered the outlook and the future for those who could never have afforded a college degree.

The economic consequences of the war altered the practices and beliefs of many educational, scientific, and economic institutions and led to a shift away from ruralism, poverty, and apartheid. The South and North Carolina, historically hostile to new ideas and criticism, now embraced the emphasis on modernism and industrialization as well as the concept of integrating the state and local economies into a national and global world market. Significantly, from 1940 to 1945 the region's large rural population declined by nearly 3.5 million inhabitants, a drop of more than 20 percent. In 1939 farmworkers outnumbered production workers 3 million to 1.4 million. By 1945 farmworkers had declined to 2.6 million, while production workers had risen to over 2.2 million. The shift from farm work to factory work narrowed the per capita gap between farm and industrial workers, helping fuel the economic surge after the war.[21]

Despite continuing gender and racial discrimination, arguably more pronounced in the South than elsewhere, the world conflict opened new doors and improved the status of minorities and women. By questioning the conventional wisdom about the place of women and black people in society, the war helped pave the way for the postwar civil rights and women's rights movements.

The conclusion of the war on August 14, 1945, found North Carolina drastically different than it had been when the fighting started on December 7, 1941. While the state had lost 7,000 of its sons and many more had suffered serious injuries, North Carolina was much better off than it had been before the war. After the federal government poured $2 billion into the state, average wages had risen, and its citizens enjoyed an increased standard of living. With modernization and new technology North Carolina's farmers entered a period of prosperity and expansion.

The state could take pride in its contributions to the war effort. Over 350,000 Tar Heels had served directly in the armed forces. Its citizens had done their part on the home front with Victory Gardens, scrap and bond drives, and aid to the Red Cross. Farmers had exceeded their production levels in almost every category in helping feed the nation and the armed forces. The state's manufacturing plants had provided an extraordinary variety of essential supplies from blankets to artillery shells that were necessary for winning the war.

The war led to a more important role for state government and an increase in government services. North Carolina had accumulated a large budget surplus during the war and began to use those funds to improve education and health care and to pave new roads. Higher education received an important boost with the introduction of the GI Bill. The state's citizen-soldiers could look forward to a free college education and a more promising future. Many of the airfields built during the war, such as Raleigh-Durham and Charlotte Douglas, were purchased by the state from the federal government as war surplus and turned into commercial airports. Many of the World War II bases, especially Fort Bragg and Camp Lejeune, would remain and be expanded. Today North Carolina remains integral to the defense of the nation, and military spending continues to be a critical part of the state's economy.

Almost every family in North Carolina had been affected by the war in one way or another. Families had lost sons and daughters, fathers and mothers, and brothers and sisters, some families more than one. Tar Heels were relieved that they had survived the long months of rationing, shortages, sacrifices, and hardships. They were sad for the human losses but happy for those who returned. North Carolinians looked forward eagerly to the future, free of the bonds in which they had been held for four years, anxious for a new way of life. World War II, despite all the sacrifices and dislocations, had helped move North Carolina toward its goal of becoming a more modern, diversified, and highly industrialized state.[22]

NOTES

Introduction

1. Terkel, *The Good War*, p. 14.
2. Egerton, *Speak Now against the Day*, pp. 327–328.
3. Fussell, *Wartime*, pp. ix, 3–13, 87 (quotations).
4. Jeffries, *Wartime America*, pp. 5–15.
5. Sosna, "Introduction," pp. xiii–xix.
6. Brunsman, *Census of Population, 1950*, pp. 33–49; Link, *North Carolina*, 369–378; Moss, *The Rise of Modern America*, p. 286.

Chapter 1. Prelude to War: The Years 1931–1941

1. Keegan, *The Second World War*, pp. 31–36.
2. Moss, *The Rise of Modern America*, pp. 284–286; Keegan, *The Second World War*, pp. 36–38; Olson, *Those Angry Days*, pp. 32–33.
3. Pleasants, *Buncombe Bob*, pp. 87, 101.
4. Moss, *The Rise of Modern America*, p. 286.
5. Keegan, *The Second World War*, pp. 36–40, 41–47; Olson, *Those Angry Days*, pp. 13, 32–34; Buchanan, *The United States and World War II*, pp. 6–9; Moss, *The Rise of Modern America*, pp. 286–289; Dallek, *Franklin Roosevelt and American Foreign Policy*, p. 171.
6. Dew, *The Queen City at War*, pp. 7–8.
7. Buchanan, *The United States and World War II*, pp. 6–9; Moss, *Rise of Modern America*, pp. 286–289 (quotation on p. 288).
8. Keegan, *The Second World War*, pp. 65–102; Moss, *The Rise of Modern America*, pp. 293–297.
9. Moss, *The Rise of Modern America*, pp. 296–297.
10. Pleasants, *Buncombe Bob*, p. 193.
11. Moss, *The Rise of Modern America*, pp. 297–299.
12. Dew, *The Queen City at War*, pp. 9–11.
13. Burns, *Roosevelt: The Soldier of Freedom*, p. 28.
14. Pleasants, *Buncombe Bob*, pp. 202–205; Lemmon and Midgette, *North Carolina and the Two World Wars*, pp. 131 (quotation)–133.

15. Hastings, *Inferno*, pp. 113–126, 127–148; Keegan, *The Second World War*, pp. 173–184.

16. Moss, *The Rise of Modern America*, p. 301.

17. Ibid., pp. 302–305; *Raleigh News and Observer*, December 8, 1941.

18. Keegan, *The Second World War*, pp. 245–250; *Raleigh News and Observer*, December 3, 6, and 7, 1941.

19. Hastings, *Inferno*, pp. 188–197; Keegan, *The Second World War*, pp. 240–250; Moss, *The Rise of Modern America*, pp. 306, 311.

20. Keegan, *The Second World War*, pp. 251–261; Moss, *The Rise of Modern* America, pp. 309–313 (quotations); Hastings, *Inferno*, pp. 192–197; Lord, *Day of Infamy*, p. 19 and passim; *Raleigh News and Observer*, December 9, 1941.

21. *Raleigh News and Observer*, December 8, 1941.

22. *Raleigh News and Observer*, December 8, 9, and 11, 1941; *Asheville Citizen*, December 8, 9, 1941; Pleasants, *Buncombe Bob*, pp. 220 (quotation)–221.

23. *Charlotte Observer*, January 14, 1941.

24. Dew, *The Queen City at War*, pp. 57–59; *Raleigh News and Observer*, December 8, 1941.

25. Interview with James Waynick by Ken Samuelson, January 13, 2005.

26. Interview with Robert Collen Thomas by Ken Samuelson, May 21, 2003.

27. Interview with William E. Riggs by Ken Samuelson, November 17, 1999.

28. *Sanford Herald*, December 11, 1964.

29. Pike, "Some Memories of World War II as Recalled in 1988."

30. *Pilot* (Southern Pines, N.C.), December 12, 1941.

31. *Raleigh News and Observer*, December 19 and 26 (quotation), 1941.

32. *Raleigh News and Observer*, December 11, 1941.

33. Duvall, *North Carolina during World War II*, p. 10.

34. Bigger, ed., *World War II*, pp. 13–14.

35. Eleanor Peck to "Poppy," December 12, 1941, Eleanor K. Peck Papers.

36. *Raleigh News and Observer*, December 8, 1941.

37. *Raleigh News and Observer*, December 11, 12, 13, and 14, 1941.

38. *Sixteenth Census of the United States, 1940*, pp. 5–8, 9, 24–25, 71; Brunsman (preparer), *Census of Population, 1950, Part 33, North Carolina*, pp. 573–586; *Raleigh News and Observer*, September 5, 1941.

Chapter 2. A Call to Duty: The Selective Service Act of 1940

1. Leuchtenburg, *Franklin D. Roosevelt and the New Deal*, pp. 306–307; Larrabee, *Commander in Chief*, pp. 114–115.

2. Davis, *Experience of War*, p. 33; O'Neill, *A Democracy at War*, pp. 85–87; Larrabee, *Commander in Chief*, p. 115; King, *Selective Service in North Carolina in World War II*, pp. 12–24.

3. Burns, *Roosevelt: The Soldier of Freedom*, p. 120.

4. Larrabee, *Commander in Chief*, pp. 117–118; O'Neill, *A Democracy at War*, pp. 30–31; Davis, *Experience of War*, p. 74.

5. Link, *North Carolina*, p. 356.

6. Jeffries, *Wartime America*, p. 171.

7. Interview with Manfred T. Blanchard by Ken Samuelson, August 23, 2002.

8. *Garner (N.C.) News*, November 7, 2012.

9. Interview with William D. Lashley by Ken Samuelson, September 5, 1997; Dew, *The Queen City at War*, pp. 16–18.

10. *Raleigh News and Observer*, December 19, 1943.

11. King, *Selective Service in North Carolina*, pp. 13–50.

12. Dew, *The Queen City at War*, pp. 16–17; King, *Selective Service in North Carolina*, pp. 50–90.

13. Interview with William A. Stansfield by Ken Samuelson, August 6, 2003 (quotation); King, *Selective Service in North Carolina*, pp. 50–87.

14. "Order to Report for Induction," in the military collection, Charlotte Mecklenburg Library Archives, Charlotte, N.C.

15. King, *Selective Service in North Carolina*, pp. 96–146 (quotation on p. 123).

16. Ibid., pp. 69–72, 109–115.

17. *Raleigh News and Observer*, April 12, 1942.

18. King, *Selective Service in North Carolina*, pp. 305–307.

19. Interview with James Waynick by Ken Samuelson, January 13, 2005; King, *Selective Service in North Carolina*, pp. 192–198.

20. King, *Selective Service in North Carolina*, pp. 197–201.

21. Ibid., p. 213.

22. Salemson, "Conscientious Objection," pp. 276–277.

23. King, *Selective Service in North Carolina*, pp. 213–217.

24. Dew, *The Queen City at War*, pp. 18–19.

25. King, *Selective Service in North Carolina*, pp. 349–350.

26. FBI Report #25-29799, July 31, 1943; FBI Report #61-7497-27, January 17, 1941; FBI Report #100-693, October 16, 1941; J. Edgar Hoover to Special Agent in Charge, Charlotte, N.C., November 15, 1943; in Joseph Andrew Felmet Papers #04513.

27. *Raleigh News and Observer*, March 3, 1943.

28. *Raleigh News and Observer*, April 13, 1943, and June 1, 1945.

29. Bigger, ed., *World War II*, p. 180.

30. *Raleigh News and Observer*, January 21, 1942; *Asheville Citizen*, August 28, 1941 (quotation).

31. Bigger, ed., *World War II*, p. 181.

32. Chapman and Miles, *Asheville and Western North Carolina in World War II*, pp. 46–47.

33. Bigger, ed., *World War II*, p. 182.

34. *Raleigh News and Observer*, March 5, 1942.

35. King, *Selective Service in North Carolina*, pp. 309–312.

36. Jeffries, *Wartime America*, pp. 142–143.

37. *Raleigh News and Observer*, May 27, 1942.

38. *Raleigh News and Observer*, November 2, 1942.

39. *Raleigh News and Observer*, February 12, 1943.

40. *Raleigh News and Observer*, August 7, 1943.

41. *Raleigh News and Observer*, September 19, 1943.

42. Bigger, ed., *World War II*, pp. 199–200.

43. King, *Selective Service in North Carolina*, pp. 218–290; *University of North Carolina News Letter*, 31, no. (March 14, 1945). It should be noted that the numbers for the various rejections vary markedly depending on what figures are used and how they are interpreted. I have relied primarily on King's book on selective service in North Carolina.

44. *Raleigh News and Observer*, November 26, 1944.

Chapter 3. A Call to Arms: Military Preparedness

1. *Raleigh News and Observer*, January 10, 1941.

2. Tindall, *The Emergence of the New South*, p. 695.

3. Duvall, *North Carolina during World War II*, pp. 3–4, 41–44; Lemmon, *North Carolina's Role in World War II*, pp. 11–14; *Raleigh News and Observer*, December 27, 1942.

4. *Charlotte News*, October 10, 1942.

5. Bell, "Lake Lure Rest and Redistribution Center," p. 659.

6. Chalker, "Blimps over Elizabeth City," p. 28; Duvall, *North Carolina during World War II*, pp. 68–69; Lemmon and Midgette, *North Carolina and the Two World Wars*, pp. 138–145; Billinger and Williford, "World War II."

7. *Fayetteville Observer*, January 4, 18, and 20, 1941.

8. Parker, *Cumberland County*, p. 134.

9. *Fayetteville Observer*, August 4, 1994.

10. Parker, *Cumberland County*, pp. 11–137; Parker, "Fort Bragg"; Duvall, *North Carolina during World War II*, pp. 68–69.

11. *Raleigh News and Observer*, December 28, 1941 (quotation), and November 1, 1942.

12. Parker, *Cumberland County*, p. 136.

13. *Raleigh News and Observer*, March 4, 1943.

14. *Raleigh News and Observer*, January 10, 1942.

15. Corbitt, ed., *Public Addresses, Letters and Papers of J. Melville Broughton*, pp. 406–407.

16. Hegarty, *Victory Girls*, pp. 6–7, 165–166.

17. Ibid., pp. 6, 167–168.

18. Winchell, *Good Girls, Good Food, Good Fun*, pp. 109–112.

19. Hegarty, *Victory Girls*, pp. 8, 13–16.

20. *Raleigh News and Observer*, June 19, 1942.

21. Hegarty, *Victory Girls*, pp. 38–41; *Raleigh News and Observer*, July 23, 1942.

22. *Raleigh News and Observer*, September 22, 30, and November 4, 1942.

23. *Raleigh News and Observer*, January 21, 1942, and May 2, 1943.

24. *Raleigh News and Observer*, January 28, 1942; *Fayetteville Observer*, January 29, 1942.

25. *Raleigh News and Observer*, July 26, 1942.

26. *New York Times*, August 28, 2003.

27. Hargrove, *See Here, Private Hargrove*, pp. 7, 27, 36, 81.

28. Ibid., pp. 36, 81.

29. Simon, *Biloxi Blues*, p. 22.

30. *New York Times*, August 28, 2003.

31. Bigger, ed., *World War II*, pp. 256–257.

32. MSNBC report, April 9, 2014.

33. Blazich, "The Relationship between Hoffman, N.C. and Camp Mackall," p. 15.

34. Ibid., pp. 1, 6, 26, 32–33.

35. Ibid., pp. 28, 29, 30–35; Stevens and MacCallum, *Camp Mackall*, pp. 41–45.

36. *Pilot* (Southern Pines, N.C.), November 19, 1943; *Raleigh News and Observer*, November 7, 1943.

37. Stevens and MacCallum, *Camp Mackall*, p. 53; Blazich, "The Relationship between Hoffman, N.C. and Camp Mackall," p. 28.

38. Stevens and MacCallum, *Camp Mackall*, pp. 7, 8, 25–32, 56; Blazich, "The Relationship between Hoffman, N.C. and Camp Mackall," p. 44.

39. Stevens and MacCallum, *Camp Mackall*, p. 107.

40. Ambrose, *Band of Brothers*, pp. 15–16 (quotation), 35–39.

41. Stevens and MacCallum, *Camp Mackall*, pp. 75–80, 87 (quotation).

42. Lowden, *Silent Wings at War*, pp. 21–22.

43. Stevens and MacCallum, *Camp Mackall*, p. 159.

44. Blazich, "The Relationship between Hoffman, N.C. and Camp Mackall," pp. 6, 27, 31 (quotation), 34, 42, 48–53 (quotation on p. 49).

45. Smith and Patrick, *Voices from the Field*, pp. 17, 165, 167.

46. Ibid., p. 169.

47. *Raleigh News and Observer*, August 4, 1942.

48. *Raleigh News and Observer*, April 6, 1944.

49. Smith and Patrick, *Voices from the Field*, pp. 187, 191–198; *Raleigh News and Observer*, June 14, 1942.

50. Smith and Patrick, *Voices from the Field*, pp. 181–182; no author, "A Camera Trip through Camp Butner," 1943, first-person account in possession of the Camp Butner Society, Butner, N.C.

51. *Raleigh News and Observer*, February 6, 1945.

52. Smith and Patrick, *Voices from the Field*, pp. 208–219.

53. Merryman, *Clipped Wings*, pp. 2–45.

54. Stallman, *Echoes of Topsail*, pp. 87–106; *Raleigh News and Observer*, October 31, 1943, August 13, 1944, July 21 and July 28, 1945; *Greensboro News Record*, April 14, 2003; *State*, 8, no. 53 (May 31, 1941): 6–9; *Camp Davis Military News*, January 22, 1944; *AA Barrage News*, September 2, 1944.

55. *Raleigh News and Observer*, January 5, 1945; Dew, *The Queen City at War*, p. 352.

56. *Union Observer* (Monroe, N.C.), February 22, 1944; *Raleigh News and Observer*, January 5, 1943; Ben Taylor, "Camp Sutton, Gone But Not Forgotten" and "Camp Sutton, Monroe, NC: 1942–1945," in the Union County Public Library, Monroe, N.C.

57. *Raleigh News and Observer*, January 29, February 8 and 16, 1941; Watson, *Onslow County*, pp. 133–135.

58. Carraway, *Camp Lejeune Leathernecks*, pp. 5–25; Breant, "The New River Camp Lejeune Is Corps East Coast Combat College"; Farnham, "Camp Lejeune," p. 166.

59. Watson, *Onslow County*, p. 135.

60. Interview with Marlene Blake, UNC-TV, 2010.

61. Carraway, *Camp Lejeune Leathernecks*, pp. 5, 39–41; Farnham, "Camp Lejeune," p. 166; *Raleigh News and Observer*, November 10, 1942.

62. Arthur, "Camp Lejeune—The Early Days."

63. *Raleigh News and Observer*, September 18, 1944.

64. Mrs. Wilson Hall to the editor, *Raleigh News and Observer*, September 12, 1944.

65. *Raleigh News and Observer*, September 18 (quotations) and 21 and October 1, 1944.

66. *Raleigh News and Observer*, September 28, 1943.

67. *Raleigh News and Observer*, June 27, 1943.

68. *Raleigh News and Observer*, December 20, 1944.

69. Interview with William D. Lashley by Ken Samuelson, September 5, 1997.

70. McLaurin, *The Marines of Montford Point*, pp. 5–7; Carraway, *Camp Lejeune Leathernecks*, pp. 51–53.

71. McLaurin, *The Marines of Montford Point*, p. 1.

72. Ibid., pp. 7–10; Carraway, *Camp Lejeune Leathernecks*, pp. 51–53.

73. McLaurin, *Marines of Montford Point*, pp. 25–26 (quotation), 31.

74. Ibid., pp. 47–50 (quotation), 74.

75. Ibid., p. 96.

76. *Raleigh News and Observer*, June 28, 2014.

77. *Raleigh News and Observer*, August 20, 2012.

78. Carraway, *Camp Lejeune Leathernecks*, pp. 55–58; *Raleigh News and Observer*, September 27, 1942, and February 5, 1944; Putney, *Always Faithful*, pp. 1–44, 155–224 (quotations on pp. 165, 181–182).

79. Carraway, *The United States Marine Corps Air Station*, p. 13.

80. *Raleigh News and Observer*, November 10, 1942 (quotation); Carraway, *The United States Marine Corps Air Station*, pp. 3–37.

81. Catlett, *Army Town*, pp. 5–19; Arnett, *Greensboro, N.C.*, p. 413.

82. *Raleigh News and Observer*, May 15, 1943; Catlett, *Army Town*, p. 27.

83. *Ten-Shun* (weekly newspaper for Basic Training Center), #10, March 27, 1943, p. 1.

84. *Ten-Shun*, May 15, 21, and 28 and October 15, 1943.

85. *Ten-Shun*, May 21, 1943.

86. *Ten-Shun*, May 15, 1943.

87. *Ten-Shun*, June 18, 1945.

88. *Ten-Shun*, September 7, 1945.

89. Dew, *The Queen City at War*, p. 29.

90. *Morris Code*, April 21, 1942, p. 5.

91. Dew, *The Queen City at War*, pp 23–31, 39–43; Howard, "Morris Field," p. 767; "The Home Front: Morris Field"; *Morris Code*, April 21, 1942, p. 5.

92. Dew, *The Queen City at War*, pp. 33–37.

93. Bigger, ed., *World War II*, p. 179.

94. Dew, *The Queen City at War*, pp. 33–37.

95. Price, "Seymour Johnson Air Force Base"; *Goldsboro News Argus*, February 13, 1974; "Seymour Johnson Air Force Base," historical marker text, North Carolina Department of Cultural Resources; "History of Seymour Johnson Air Force Base," Fact Sheet, 4th Wing Public Affairs Office, Seymour Johnson Air Force Base, January 1995.

96. Baker, *Mrs. GI Joe*, pp. 1, 2, 8, 9, 22–23, 31, 47, 139, 153, 165, 207, 242.

97. "Laurinburg-Maxton Air Force Base," Historical Marker, North Carolina Department of Natural and Cultural Resources.

98. *Maxton Times*, October 5, 2008; *Raleigh News and Observer*, November 10, 1942, October 27, 1944; Stevens and MacCallum, *Camp Mackall*, pp. 35–39, 93–94; "Laurinburg-Maxton Air Force Base," Historical Marker, North Carolina Department of Natural and Cultural Resources.

Chapter 4. Arsenal of Democracy: The Economic Impact of the War

1. Corbitt, ed., *Public Addresses, Letters and Papers of J. Melville Broughton*, pp. 110–112.

2. Egerton, *Speak Now against the Day*, pp. 201, 206 (quotations); Lemmon, *North Carolina's Role in World War II*, pp. 20–21.

3. Tindall, *The Emergence of the New South*, p. 701.

4. Ibid., pp. 694, 700.

5. Jeffries, *Wartime America*, pp. 16–26.

6. Lemmon, *North Carolina's Role in World War II*, p. 23–24.

7. Mobley, ed., *The Way We Lived in North Carolina*, p. 487.

8. Interview with Orion Blizzard, UNC-TV, 2010.

9. Interview with Lauch Faircloth by Joe Mosnier, July 16, 1975, pp. 4–5.

10. Interview with Thomas Fuller by Brent D. Glass, October 9, 1975.

11. Jeffries, *Wartime America*, pp. 69–80; Egerton, *Speak Now against the Day*, p. 208.

12. Corbitt, ed., *Public Addresses, Letters and Papers of J. Melville Broughton*, p. 446.

13. Ibid., pp. 261–262.

14. Bigger, ed., *World War II*, pp. 163–164.

15. Coates, "Guide to Victory," pp. 152–153; *Charlotte Observer*, July 27, 1941; *Raleigh News and Observer*, September 21, 1941.

16. *Raleigh News and Observer*, July 5, 1942.

17. Interview with Thomas Snipes by Tony Nace, December 2, 1978, pp. 25–28.

18. *Raleigh News and* Observer, July 12, 1942 (quotation), and December 7, 1942.

19. *Greensboro Daily News*, January 2, 1943; Lemmon, *North Carolina's Role in World War II*, pp. 23–24.

20. Corbitt, ed., *Public Addresses and Papers of Robert Gregg Cherry*, p. 246.

21. Tilley, *The RJ Reynolds Tobacco Company*, pp. 214–217; Yeargin, "Tobacco"; Link, *North Carolina*, p. 360.

22. Interview with Lauch Faircloth by Joe Mosnier, July 16, 1975, pp. 4–6.

23. Jeffries, *Wartime America*, pp. 76–81; interview with Lauch Faircloth by Joe Mosnier, July 16, 1975, pp. 4–6. *Raleigh News and Observer*, May 11, 1942 (quotation).

24. Jones, *J. A. Jones Construction Company*, pp. 39–41.

25. Ibid., pp. 46, 50.

26. Ibid., pp. 47–57 (quotation on 53); Dew, *The Queen City at War*, p. 139.

27. Interview with Gordon Berkstressor, April 29, 1986, pp. 9–10.

28. Mobley, *The Way We Lived in North Carolina*, pp. 496, 502; *Raleigh News and Observer*, June 24, 1942.

29. Interview with Paul Edward Cline by Allen Tullus, November 8, 1979.

30. Interview with Ethel Faucette by Allen Tullus, November 16, 1978, pp. 19–35.

31. Interview with Murphy Y. Sigmon by Sharon P. Dilley, July 27, 1979, pp. 9–19.

32. Glass, *The Textile Industry—North Carolina*, p. 82; Mobley, *The Way We Lived in North Carolina*, p. 496; Troxler, "Burlington Industries."

33. Vandenburg, *Cannon Mills and Kannapolis*, pp. 104–107; Cherry, "Cannon Mills."

34. *Raleigh News and Observer*, July 1, 1942.

35. Corbitt, ed., *Public Addresses, Letters and Papers of J. Melville Broughton*, pp. 355–357, 385.

36. *Our State*, January 2015, p. 36.

37. J. S. Dorton to R. Gregg Cherry, May 2, 1945 (a complete list of 62 different war items produced in the state), J. S. Dorton Papers, 5353-Z.

38. Mills, *Randolph County*, pp. 4–6.

39. Interview with Alda Womack, UNC-TV, 2010.

40. *Charlotte Observer*, July 14, 1942.

41. Bigger, ed., *World War II*, p. 146; "The Shell Plant"; *Charlotte Observer*, February 18, 1943, and February 28 and March 7, 1950.

42. Bigger, ed., *World War II*, pp. 149–151 (quotations on 151); *Charlotte Observer*, March 5, 1981.

43. *Charlotte Observer*, March 5, 1981.

44. J. S. Dorton to R. Gregg Cherry, J. S. Dorton Papers; Dew, *The Queen City at War*, pp. 135–138.

45. *Raleigh News and Observer*, August 18, 1945; Duvall, *North Carolina during World War II*, pp. 24–26.

46. *Raleigh News and Observer*, March 7, 1942.

47. *Raleigh News and Observer*, December 9, 1943 (quotations); Bolden, *Alamance: A County at War*, pp. 8, 9, 33, 46–47, 56, 74, 79–80.

48. Interview with Dock E. Hall by Brent Glass, June 5, 1980, pp. 16–42.

49. J. S. Doughton to R. Gregg Cherry, May 2, 1945, J. S. Dorton Papers; *Raleigh News and Observer*, September 21, 1941, and December 7, 1942; *Charlotte Observer*, October 5, 1941; Catlett, *Army Town: Greensboro*, p. 24; Lemmon, *North Carolina's Role in World War II*, p. 23; *Sanford Herald*, September 23, 1943.

50. *Raleigh News and Observer*, June 14, 1942.

51. *Raleigh News and Observer*, December 23, 1941.

52. Glass, "Fontana Dam"; "Fontana Dam Safety News," June 1943 to July 1944.

53. *Raleigh News and Observer*, September 21, 1941; King, *Selective Service in North Carolina*, p. 150; Corbitt, ed., *Public Addresses, Letters and Papers of J. Melville Broughton*, p. 152.

54. *Raleigh News and Observer*, December 7, 1942, and July 18, 1943; Marshall, "Furniture"; Bell, "Broyhill Furniture Company"; J. S. Dorton to R. Gregg Cherry, May 2, 1945, J. S. Dorton Papers.

55. King, *Selective Service in North Carolina*, pp. 154–155; J. S. Dorton to R. Gregg Cherry, May 2, 1945, J. S. Dorton Papers; *Raleigh News and Observer*, January 2, 1943.

56. Kennedy, "Seaboard Airlines Railway."

57. Kennedy, "Atlantic Coast Line Railroad."

58. Dew, *The Queen City at War*, pp. 141–144; J. S. Dorton to R. Gregg Cherry, May

2, 1945, J. S. Dorton Papers; *Charlotte Observer*, July 27, 1941; Duvall, *North Carolina during World War II*, p. 23; "A History of Wachovia," pamphlet published by Wachovia Bank, n.d. (quotation), in interview with John Medlin by Joe Mosnier, May 24, 1999.

59. "A History of Wachovia," in interview with John Medlin by Joe Mosnier.

60. Dew, *The Queen City at War*, pp. 142–144; *Raleigh News and Observer*, June 6, 1944; Covington, *Belk: A Century of Retail Leadership*, pp. 138–141.

61. Bigger, ed., *World War II*, p. 168.

62. Scott, *The Wilmington Shipyard*, pp. 9–14; Tindall, *The Emergence of the New South*, pp. 696–702.

63. *Raleigh News and Observer*, November 8, 1942 (quotation, citing *State*); Duvall, *North Carolina during World War II*, pp. 22–23.

64. Scott, *The Wilmington Shipyard*, p. 34; Duvall, *North Carolina during World War II*, p. 23.

65. Cecelski, "The Voice of the Shipyard," p. 52.

66. Meyer, *Journey through Chaos*, pp. ix–xiii, 222–229 (quotations on p. 223).

67. Duvall, *North Carolina during World War II*, p. 23; Scott, *The Wilmington Shipyard*, p. 36.

68. Scott, *The Wilmington Shipyard*, pp. 40–43.

69. "Women Doing Excellent Work at Jobs in the Yard," p. 3.

70. Scott, *The Wilmington Shipyard*, pp. 37–39; Duvall, *North Carolina during World War II*, pp. 23–24.

71. *Colored Shipbuilder* 1, no. 1 (July 1944): 4, 22 (quotations); *Raleigh News and Observer*, July 11, 1943; Scott, *The Wilmington Shipyard*, p. 37.

72. *Colored Shipbuilder* 1, no. 1 (July 1944): 11–30.

73. *Raleigh News and Observer*, December 5 and 7 (quotation), 1941, and September 5, 1943; Lillard, "Liberty Ships"; Duvall, *North Carolina during World War II*, p. 23.

74. *Raleigh News and Observer*, August 7, 1942, and June 24, 1944; Scott, *The Wilmington Shipyard*, pp. 99–100.

75. Jeffries, *Wartime America*, pp. 23–25, 54–57; *Raleigh News and Observer*, February 10, 1944.

76. *Raleigh News and Observer*, June 7, 1944.

77. *Raleigh News and Observer*, July 1, 1943.

78. *Raleigh News and Observer*, June 1 and 7, 1942.

79. *Raleigh News and Observer*, February 15 and 16, 1945.

80. Chapman and Miles, *Asheville and Western North Carolina in World War II*, p. 55.

81. *Raleigh News and Observer*, May 21, 1945.

82. Jeffries, *Wartime America*, pp. 55–57.

83. Interview with Roy Lee Auton by Jackie Hall, February 28, 1980, p. 9.

84. Interview with Murphy Y. Sigmon by Sharon P. Dilley, July 27, 1979.

85. Jeffries, *Wartime America*, pp. 44–49.

Chapter 5. Torpedo Junction: Submarine Warfare off the North Carolina Coast

1. Link, *North Carolina*, pp. 6–7.

2. Branch and Barefoot, "Submarine Attacks"; Gannon, *Operation Drumbeat*, p. xvi;

Hickam, *Torpedo Junction*, p. 1; Lemmon and Midgette, *North Carolina and the Two World Wars*, pp. 187–191.

3. Keegan, *The Second World War*, pp. 10–13; Davis, *Experience of War*, pp. 44–55; Smith, *The Secrets of Station X*, pp. 90–100.

4. Gannon, *Operation Drumbeat*, pp. xvi–xvii; Hickam, *Torpedo Junction*, pp. 1–2.

5. Gannon, *Operation Drumbeat*, xvii–xxii; *Raleigh News and Observer*, January 12, 1947.

6. Hickam, *Torpedo Junction*, p. 9.

7. Cheatham, *The Atlantic Turkey Shoot*, pp. 14–15 (quotation); Hickam, *Torpedo Junction*, pp. 145–146.

8. Interview with David Best by Ken Samuelson, August 20, 2003, pp. 1–12. See also Hickam, *Torpedo Junction*, pp. 11–13; Gannon, *Operation Drumbeat*, pp. 244–247.

9. Cheatham, *The Atlantic Turkey Shoot*, pp. 12–14, 26–27; Hickam, *Torpedo Junction*, p. 84 (quotation).

10. Gannon, *Operation Drumbeat*, pp. 256–258; Hickam, *Torpedo Junction*, p. 14.

11. Duffus, *War Zone*, pp. 66–69.

12. Ibid., pp. 89–90.

13. *Raleigh News and Observer*, January 12, 27, 1942; Hickam, *Torpedo Junction*, pp. 20–22; Gannon, *Operation Drumbeat*, pp. 270–271; Duffus, *War Zone*, pp. 89–90.

14. *Raleigh News and Observer*, March 16, 1942.

15. Hickam, *Torpedo Junction*, pp. 69–76.

16. *Raleigh News and Observer*, March 28 and April 3, 1942 (quotations); Hickam, *Torpedo Junction*, pp. 140–144; Duffus, *War Zone*, pp. 162–176. Where the number of crew members, the number of survivors, and the number of ships sunk were listed, the numbers almost always vary widely. The newspapers stated that 83 people were rescued from the *City of New York*, while Hickam cites the number as 69. It is almost impossible to get an accurate number, but the purpose here is to give the details of the story and use approximate numbers when necessary.

17. Duffus, *War Zone*, p. 121.

18. Ibid., pp. 121–122.

19. Ibid., p. 120. Cheatham, "Memories of the U-Boat War," p. 2.

20. Ibid., p. 148.

21. *Winston-Salem Journal*, August 27, 1972; Cheatham, "Memories of the U-Boat War," pp. 1–10; Duffus, *War Zone*, p. 150 (quotation).

22. Gannon, *Operation Drumbeat*, p. 379; Hickam, *Torpedo Junction*, pp. 248–252.

23. Duffus, *War Zone*, p. 132.

24. Cheatham, "Memories of the U-Boat War," pp. 1–7; *Winston-Salem Journal*, August 27, 1972; Lemmon and Midgette, *North Carolina and the Two World Wars*, pp. 188–190.

25. Duffus, *War Zone*, p. 142.

26. Ibid., p. 103.

27. Lemmon, *North Carolina's Role in World War II*, pp. 50–51; Cheatham, "Memories of the U-Boat War," p. 3; *Raleigh News and Observer*, March 12 and May 12, 1942.

28. *Raleigh News and Observer*, January 15, 1942.

29. *Raleigh News and Observer*, January 16, 1942.

30. *Pilot* (Southern Pines, N.C.), January 9, 1942.

31. Hickam, *Torpedo Junction*, pp. 4–5.

32. Duvall, *North Carolina during World War II*, p. 15.

33. Corbitt, ed., *Public Addresses, Letters and Papers of Governor J. Melville Broughton*, p. 530.

34. *Raleigh News and Observer*, March 20, 1942.

35. *Raleigh News and Observer*, December 7, 1942.

36. Interview with Billy Sutton, UNC-TV, 2010.

37. Gannon, *Operation Drumbeat*, p. 353. See also Hickam, *Torpedo Junction*, p. 159; Duffus, *War Zone*, pp. 208–211.

38. *Raleigh News and Observer*, December 6, 1942.

39. *Raleigh News and Observer*, April 2, 1942.

40. Blazich, "North Carolina's Flying Volunteers," pp. 399–422.

41. Cheatham, *The Atlantic Turkey Shoot*, pp. 26–34.

42. Hickam, *Torpedo Junction*, pp. 186–198; *Raleigh News and Observer*, January 12, 1947; Gannon, *Operation Drumbeat*, pp. 380–85.

43. *Raleigh News and Observer*, February 15, 1948; Hickam, *Torpedo Junction*, pp. 261–266.

44. Naisawald, *In Some Foreign Field*, pp. 12–14, 20, 35–37, 50–52, 57–85 (quotation); Hickam, *Torpedo Junction*, 203–208; Cheatham, *The Atlantic Turkey Shoot*, pp. 9–11.

45. Gannon, *Operation Drumbeat*, p. xviii; Blazich, "North Carolina's Flying Volunteers," p. 409 (quotations); Duvall, *North Carolina in World War II*, p. 19.

Chapter 6. "Make Do with Less": Rationing, War Bonds, and Victory Gardens

1. Lemmon and Midgette, *North Carolina and the Two World Wars*, p. 155 (quotation); Dew, *The Queen City at War*, pp. 106–107.

2. Bentley, *Eating for Victory*, p. 14.

3. Dew, *The Queen City at War*, p. 103.

4. Jeffries, *Wartime America*, p. 27.

5. Lingeman, *Don't You Know There's a War On?* p. 234; Dew, *The Queen City at War*, p. 104 (quotation).

6. Lingeman, *Don't You Know There's A War On?* p. 235.

7. Ibid., p. 235; Dew, *The Queen City at War*, p. 104 (quotation).

8. Dew, *The Queen City at War*, p. 105.

9. Jeffries, *Wartime America*, pp. 28–29.

10. Dew, *The Queen City at War*, pp. 106–107.

11. *Raleigh News and Observer*, March 3 (quotation) and October 5, 1942.

12. *Raleigh News and Observer*, January 9, 1942.

13. *Raleigh News and Observer*, July 15, 1942.

14. *Raleigh News and Observer*, July 26, 1944.

15. *Raleigh News and Observer*, January 4, 1942.

16. Jeffries, *Wartime America*, p. 30.

17. *Raleigh News and Observer*, June 5, 1943.

18. Ration book belonging to Mrs. C. J. Emmett, in the Rachel Bailey Collection, Box 195, Private Collections, State Archives of North Carolina, Raleigh.

19. Bigger, ed. *World War II*, p. 215.

20. Dew, *The Queen City at War*, p. 116.

21. Lingeman, *Don't You Know There's a War On?* p. 242.

22. Best, ed., *North Carolina's Shining Hour*, p. 122.

23. Sears, "How Americans Met the First Great Gasoline Crisis," p. 13.

24. Dew, *The Queen City at War*, pp. 116–117.

25. Lingeman, *Don't You Know There's a War On?* pp. 241, 254.

26. *Raleigh News and Observer*, May 29, 1945.

27. *Raleigh News and Observer*, December 2, 1942 (quotation); Sears, "How Americans Met the First Great Gasoline Crisis," p. 15.

28. *Raleigh News and Observer*, March 15, 1944; Sears, "How Americans Met the First Great Gasoline Crisis," p. 15.

29. Dew, *The Queen City at War*, pp. 117–119; Lingeman, *Don't You Know There's a War On?* pp. 241–244.

30. *Raleigh News and Observer*, December 19, 1941; January 1 and 15 (quotation) and February 19, 1942; Dew, *The Queen City at War*, p. 110.

31. Dew, *The Queen City at War*, p. 112; *Raleigh News and Observer*, December 6, 1942.

32. *Pilot*, January 9, 1942.

33. *Raleigh News and Observer*, March 15, 1942.

34. *Raleigh News and Observer*, March 15 and May 9, 1942; Sears, "How Americans Met the First Great Gasoline Crisis," pp. 5–13.

35. *Raleigh News and Observer*, July 9, 1942.

36. Sears, "How Americans Met the First Great Gasoline Crisis," p. 13.

37. Dew, *The Queen City at War*, p. 113; Sears, "How Americans Met the First Great Gasoline Crisis," p. 15.

38. Sears, "How Americans Met the First Great Gasoline Crisis," p. 17.

39. *Raleigh News and Observer*, February 8, 1943.

40. Crumbley, "Memories of World War II."

41. Bentley, *Eating for Victory*, pp. 15–26, 86, 95; *Raleigh News and Observer*, February 7 and 12, 1942.

42. *Raleigh News and Observer*, July 27 and October 4, 1942; March 13 and April 6, 1943; O'Neill, *A Democracy at War*, pp. 248–249 (quotation).

43. Kiernan, *The Girls of Atomic City*, p. 219.

44. Crumbley, "Memories of World War II."

45. *Raleigh News and Observer*, April 28 and November 10, 1942; Lingeman, *Don't You Know There's a War On?* p. 246.

46. *Raleigh News and Observer*, April 28, 1943.

47. *Raleigh News and Observer*, July 10, 1943.

48. Jeffries, *Wartime America*, pp. 31–36.

49. Samuel, *Pledging Allegiance*, pp. 10–21.

50. Ibid., p. 50.

51. Ibid., pp. 46–51.

52. *Raleigh News and Observer*, September 6, 1942.

53. *Raleigh News and Observer*, February 3, 1944.

54. *Raleigh News and Observer*, December 7, 1944.

55. Samuel, *Pledging Allegiance*, pp. 58–59, 66–67; Soloman, *American Mirror*, pp. 212–214, 233–235.

56. Dew, *The Queen City at War*, p. 161.

57. *Raleigh News and Observer*, May 3 and 4, 1942.

58. *Raleigh News and Observer*, April 16, 1943; February 16, 1944; January 7, 1945.

59. Samuel, *Pledging Allegiance*, p. 71.

60. *Raleigh News and Observer*, April 3, 1943.

61. Dew, *The Queen City at War*, p. 162.

62. Bigger, ed., *World War II*, pp. 25–26, 36.

63. Crumbley, "Memories of World War II."

64. Best, ed., *North Carolina's Shining Hour*, p. 128.

65. Samuel, *Pledging Allegiance*, pp. xiv–xvii, 72.

66. Ambrose, *Americans at War*, p. 145.

67. Bentley, *Eating for Victory*, pp. 114, 117, 121, 127, 128, 131 (quotations); Lingeman, *Don't You Know There's a War On?* pp. 251–252.

68. *Raleigh News and Observer*, February 9 and 11, 1942; Corbitt, ed., *Public Addresses, Letters and Papers of J. Melville Broughton*, pp. 181–184.

69. *Sanford Herald*, January 9, 1942.

70. Best, ed., *North Carolina's Shining Hour*, p. 125.

71. *McCormick Messenger*, August 6, 1942.

72. Bigger, ed., *World War II*, p. 174. See also Dew, *The Queen City at War*, pp. 122–123.

73. McDowell County, in County Collections, World War II Collection, Box 62, North Carolina Department of Archives and History, Raleigh; Kirk, "Getting in the Scrap," pp. 223–225.

74. Kirk, "Getting in the Scrap," pp. 223–225; *Raleigh News and Observer*, January 9, 1941.

75. *Raleigh News and Observer*, January 24, 1941, and March 4 and 5, 1942.

76. "War Salvage," p. 19.

77. *Pilot*, January 9, 1942.

78. "War Salvage," p. 1.

79. Coates, "Guide to Victory," pp. 142–143; Dew, *The Queen City at War*, pp. 120–121.

80. Duvall, *North Carolina during World War II*, p. 27.

81. *Raleigh News and Observer*, October 9, 1942.

82. *Raleigh News and Observer*, June 14 (quotation) and October 15, 1942.

83. *Raleigh News and Observer*, May 2, 1944.

84. *Durham Morning Herald*, July 21, 1946.

85. Jeffries, *Wartime America*, pp. 174–177; Lingeman, *Don't You Know There's a War On?* pp. 297–298.

86. Jeffries, *Wartime America*, pp. 180–181; Kiernan, *The Girls of Atomic City*, p. 163.

87. Best, ed., *North Carolina's Shining Hour*, p. 132; see also Lingeman, *Don't You Know There's a War On?* pp. 223–226.

88. Jeffries, *Wartime America*, pp. 174–179; O'Neill, *A Democracy at War*, p. 257.

89. Cannon, *Reagan*, p. 57.

90. *Raleigh News and Observer*, January 17, 1943; O'Neill, *A Democracy at War*, pp. 250–259; Kiernan, *The Girls of Atomic City*, p. 154 (quotation).

91. Jeffries, *Wartime America*, pp. 174–181; Lingeman, *Don't You Know There's a War On?* pp. 173, 188–189; O'Neill, *A Democracy at War*, pp. 140–142.

92. Dew, *The Queen City at War*, pp. 61–67.

93. *Raleigh News and Observer*, January 3, 1942.

94. *Raleigh News and Observer*, January 25, 1945.

95. *Raleigh News and Observer*, August 1, 1943; Jeffries, *Wartime America*, pp. 182, 188–189.

96. *Raleigh News and Observer*, August 1, 1943, and October 3, 1943.

97. *Raleigh News and Observer*, March 6, 1944, September 3, 1944, and June 3, 1945; Dick, *The Star-Spangled Screen*, pp. 125–139.

98. Jeffries, *Wartime America*, p. 182.

99. *Raleigh News and Observer*, March 28, 1943.

100. *Raleigh News and Observer*, December 26, 1943; June 18 and September 3, 1944.

101. Dolan, *Hollywood Goes to War*, pp. 39–45.

102. Horowitz, *They Went Thataway*, p. 2.

103. Jeffries, *Wartime America*, p. 189.

104. Lemmon and Midgette, *North Carolina and the Two World Wars*, pp. 156–157; *Raleigh News and Observer*, January 1, 3, 5, 11, 14, 15, and 18, 1941; King, "The Durham Rose Bowl, 1942," p. 139 (quotation).

Chapter 7. Education and the University of North Carolina Pre-Flight School

1. Kandel, *The Impact of the War on American Education*, pp. 3–11, 17, 28.

2. Ibid., pp. 128, 135, 145, 147, 151.

3. Ibid., pp. 40–46, 52–63, 77–85.

4. *Raleigh News and Observer*, September 13, 1942.

5. Baker, "The Sky's the Limit," p. 122.

6. Coates, "Guide to Victory," p. 160; Wilson, *University of North Carolina under Consolidation*, pp. 105–107; Baker, "The Sky's the Limit," pp. 3, 7, 8.

7. Baker, "The Sky's the Limit," pp. 4–8.

8. Snider, *Light on the Hill*, pp. xiii, 127–128.

9. White, *Defense for America*, p. 10.

10. Snider, *Light on the Hill*, p. 228; Ehle, *Dr. Frank*, pp. 104–106.

11. Baker, "The Sky's the Limit," pp. 9–10 (quotations); Ehle, *Dr. Frank*, p. 107; Brown, "The War Years," p. 161.

12. Baker, "The Sky's the Limit," p. 47.

13. Ibid., pp. 9–25 (quotation on p. 21); Brown, "The War Years," pp. 161–163.

14. Zorgry, *The University's Living Room*, pp. 50–56.

15. Cardozier, *Colleges and Universities in World War II*, pp. 52–73; *Raleigh News and Observer*, June 13 and July 4, 1943; June 10, 1945; Wilson, *University of North Carolina under Consolidation*, p. 109; *Greensboro Daily News*, August 21, 1942.

16. Wilson, *University of North Carolina under Consolidation*, pp. 113–115; Kandel, *The Impact of the War on American Education*, pp. 165–170.

17. Beaty, *A History of Davidson College*, pp. 322–325.

18. Cardozier, *Colleges and Universities in World War II*, pp. 12–13.

19. Baker, "The Sky's the Limit," pp. 10–12.

20. Ibid., pp. 20–23.

21. Ibid., p. 25; *Daily Tar Heel*, May 28, 1942, p. 1.

22. Barefoot, ed., *Hark the Sound of Tar Heel Voices*, p. 157.

23. Wilson, *University of North Carolina under Consolidation*, p. 108; Baker, "The Sky's the Limit," pp. 44–45.

24. Henderson, *The Campus of the First State University*, pp. 312–314; Baker, "The Sky's the Limit," pp. 26–32; *Asheville Times*, July 13, 1942; *Washington Star*, July 16, 1942; *West Palm Beach Times*, July 24, 1942.

25. *Raleigh News and Observer*, May 23, 1943.

26. *Raleigh News and Observer*, July 5, 1942, and May 23, 1943; Baker, "The Sky's the Limit," pp. 37–38.

27. Brown, "The War Years," p. 162.

28. Baker, "The Sky's the Limit," pp. 31–32.

29. Ibid., pp. 49–50, 57; Brown, "The War Years," p. 162.

30. Baker, "The Sky's the Limit," pp. 72–73, 86; *Daily Tar Heel*, May 29, 1942 (quotations).

31. Baker, "The Sky's the Limit," pp. 103–105.

32. Wilson, *University of North Carolina under Consolidation*, p. 110; *Raleigh News and Observer*, November 1, 1942.

33. Wilson, *University of North Carolina under Consolidation*, pp. 111–112.

34. Albright, *The Forgotten First*, p. 57.

35. Albright, *The Forgotten First*, pp. 10–13, 36–43.

36. Ibid., pp. 42–55, 61 (quotation).

37. Albright, *The Forgotten First*, p. 57 (quotations); see also pp. 56–61; *Winston Salem Journal Sentinel*, July 12, 1942.

38. Albright, *The Forgotten First*, p. 75.

39. Ibid., *The Forgotten First*, pp. 18–19, 73–95.

40. Ford, *A Time to Heal*, pp. 57–58 (quotations); Baker, "The Sky's the Limit," pp. 1, 120; Greene, *The Presidency of Gerald R. Ford*, p. 2.

41. Ford, *A Time to Heal*, pp. 60–61.

42. Parmet, *George Bush*, p. 46.

43. Ibid., pp. 45–54.

44. Baker, "The Sky's the Limit," pp. 110–112.

45. Ibid., pp. 110–111; *Raleigh News and Observer*, August 4, 1945.

46. Baker, "The Sky's the Limit," pp. 35, 108–109; *Raleigh News and Observer*, July 10, 11, 13, 14, and 15, 1943.

47. Bradlee, *The Kid*, p. 225; see also pp. 213–230.

48. Ibid., pp. 226, 229.

49. Bradlee, *The Kid*, pp. 230–231.

50. Baker, "The Sky's the Limit," pp. 113, 114, 122; Brown, "The War Years," pp. 168–169.

51. *Raleigh News and Observer*, August 29, 1945.

52. Snider, *Light on the Hill*, pp. 229–230; Brown, "The War Years," p. 168.

53. *Daily Tar Heel*, September 19, 1946.

54. Schaller et al., *Present Tense*, pp. 50–53; Maney, *The Roosevelt Presence*, pp. 176–177.

55. Mohr, "World War II and The Transformation of Higher Education," pp. 52–55.

56. Snider, "Light on the Hill," p. 230.

Chapter 8. Prisoners of War in the Old North State

1. Link, *North Carolina*, p. 362.

2. Chapman and Miles, *Asheville and Western North Carolina in World War II*, p. 26.

3. *Raleigh News and Observer*, July 13 and October 6, 1943 (quotation).

4. *Raleigh News and Observer*, July 14, 1943.

5. *Wilmington Star*, July 26, 1943.

6. *Raleigh News and Observer*, July 29 and September 9, 1943 (quotations); January 23, 1944.

7. Billinger, *Nazi POWs*, p. 122.

8. Billinger, *Nazi POWs*, pp. 39, 40, 122; Carlson, *We Were Each Other's Prisoners*, pp. xxi–xxii; *Raleigh News and Observer*, January 23, 1944.

9. *Raleigh News and Observer*, January 23 and May 29, 1944; Billinger, *Nazi POWs*, pp. 58–59.

10. *Durham Herald-Sun*, October 3, 1943; *Raleigh News and Observer*, May 29, 1944, and May 19, 1963; Billinger, *Nazi POWs*, pp. 58–59, 75.

11. *Williamston Enterprise*, November 14, 1943; Billinger, *Nazi POWs*, pp. 75–76.

12. *Raleigh News and Observer*, October 6, 1943, and January 23, 1944; *Durham Herald-Sun*, October 3, 1943; Billinger, *Nazi POWs*, pp. 59–60.

13. Billinger, *Nazi POWs*, p. 21.

14. Billinger, *Nazi POWs*, pp. 32–34, 58–69.

15. Stevens and MacCallum, *Camp Mackall*, pp. 139–142 (quotation on p. 140); *Rockingham Post-Dispatch*, February 2, 1944; Billinger, *Nazi POWs*, pp. 27–34.

16. Billinger, *Nazi POWs*, p. 29.

17. Manning and Booker, *Martin County History*, pp. 107, 226.

18. "Martin County," Military Collection, County Collections, Box 67, State Archives and History, Raleigh, N.C.

19. *Raleigh News and Observer*, May 7, 1945.

20. Billinger, *Nazi POWs*, pp. 35–39. See also Billinger, "Behind the Wire," pp. 492–497.

21. *Raleigh News and Observer*, March 23, 1945; Billinger, *Nazi POWs*, p. 45.

22. Dew, *The Queen City at War*, pp. 131–132.

23. Bigger, ed., *World War II*, pp. 252–254.

24. Woodruff, *Tap Roots*, pp. 122–123.

25. Dew, *The Queen City at War*, pp. 131–132.

26. Jones, *A Sentimental Journey*, pp. 130–138.

27. Carlson, *We Were Each Other's Prisoners*, pp. 155–160; Billinger, *Nazi POWs*, pp. 43–48.

28. Billinger, *Nazi POWs*, p. 142.

29. Ibid., pp. 141–155.

30. Ibid., pp. 169–172.

31. Ibid., pp. 4–5, 175, 191.

32. Jones, *A Sentimental Journey*, pp. 139–141; Billinger, *Nazi POWs*, p. 191.

33. Jones, *A Sentimental Journey*, pp. 139–141.

34. Carlson, *We Were Each Other's Prisoners*, pp. 59–66.

35. Ibid., pp. 128–133.

36. *Durham Morning Herald*, July 13, 1944; Billinger, *Nazi POWs*, pp. 39–40, 122–124; Carlson, *We Were Each Other's Prisoners*, p. 131.

37. Billinger, *Nazi POWs*, pp. 7–11.

38. Billinger, *Nazi POWs*, pp. 126–127.

39. *Raleigh News and* Observer, July 5, 1944, and August 5, 1945; Billinger, *Nazi POWs*, pp. 133–139.

40. Billinger, *Nazi POWs*, pp. 156–160.

41. *Charlotte Observer*, April 5, 1945.

42. *Raleigh News and Observer*, April 28, 1945.

43. *Raleigh News and Observer*, April 26, 1945.

44. *Raleigh News and Observer*, August 16, 1945.

45. Carlson, *We Were Each Other's Prisoners*, p. 232.

46. *Rockingham Post Dispatch*, January 24, 1945.

47. Billinger, *Nazi POWs*, pp. 160–166.

48. *Raleigh News and Observer*, March 12, 1945.

49. Fickle and Ellis, "POWs in the Piney Woods," p. 722.

Chapter 9. The Double V: Racism during World War II

1. Jeffries, *Wartime America*, p 108; Crow et al., *A History of African Americans in North Carolina*, p. 147; James, *The Double V*, p. 169.

2. *Federal Writers' Project: North Carolina*, pp. 55–57.

3. Sitkoff, "African American Militancy," p. 255; interview with John Hope Franklin, UNC-TV, 2010 (quotation).

4. Bigger, ed., *World War II*, p. 191.

5. Jeffries, *Wartime America*, pp. 110–114; Tindall, *The Emergence of the New South*, p. 716.

6. James, *The Double V*, pp. 144–147.

7. Jeffries, *Wartime America*, pp. 108–109; Tindall, *The Emergence of the New South*, pp. 711–712; James, *The Double V*, pp. 152–166.

8. Biggs, *The Triple Nickels*, pp. 35–73.

9. Tindall, *The Emergence of the New South*, p. 713.

10. Ibid.

11. Tindall, *The Emergence of the New South*, pp. 714–716; Jeffries, *Wartime America*, pp. 108–113; Dew, *The Queen City at War*, pp. 128–129; Egerton, *Speak Now against the Day*, pp. 216–217; Jones, *A Sentimental Journey,* pp. 210–213.

12. Jeffries, *Wartime America*, pp. 114–116; Crow et al., *A History of African Americans in North Carolina*, p. 147.

13. Jeffries, *Wartime America*, pp. 113–114 (quotation).

14. *Carolina Times*, May 23, 1943.

15. Broughton to Margaret C. McCullough, October 2, 1943, Corbitt, ed., *Public Addresses, Letters and Papers of J. Melville Broughton*, pp. 546–550.

16. *Carolina Times*, March 14, 1942; Crow et al., *A History of African Americans in North Carolina*, pp. 152–153.

17. *Carolina Times*, March 14, 1942 (quotation); Albright, *The Forgotten First*, p. 33; Corbitt, ed., *Public Addresses, Letters and Papers of J. Melville Broughton*, p. 546 (quotation).

18. Sitkoff, "African American Militancy," pp. 256–257.

19. Eagles, "Two Double V's," p. 255; Sitkoff, "African American Militancy," p. 257 (quotation).

20. Tindall, *The Emergence of the New South*, p. 717.

21. Crow et al., *A History of African Americans in North Carolina*, p. 148.

22. Dew, *The Queen City at War*, p. 69; Steele, *Free Speech in the Good War*, pp. 174–177.

23. *Carolina Times*, May 16, 1943 (quotations); Dew, *The Queen City at War*, pp. 64–67.

24. Egerton, *Speak Now against the Day*, pp. 420, 441.

25. *Carolina Times*, January 5 and 24, 1942; Samuel, *Pledging Allegiance*, pp. xviii, xix, 152–153, 178–183, 204–205, 210–211.

26. *Raleigh News and Observer*, June 1, 1943.

27. Egerton, *Speak Now against the Day*, pp. 326–327.

28. *Raleigh News and Observer*, July 8, 1945.

29. *Raleigh News and Observer*, April 3, 1943.

30. Crow et al., *A History of African Americans in North Carolina*, p. 151.

31. Crow et al., *A History of African Americans in North Carolina*, pp. 153–154 (quotation; see also pp. 151–152); Sitkoff, "African American Militancy," pp. 79–80.

32. Gladys Irene Giles papers, World War II Private Collections, North Carolina State Archives, Raleigh.

33. Albright, *The Forgotten First*, p. 35.

34. *Fayetteville Observer*, August 6, 7, 1941; Sitkoff, "African American Militancy," p. 259.

35. Sitkoff, "African American Militancy," pp. 259–260.

36. Ibid., p. 261.

37. Ibid., pp. 266–267; *Durham Morning Herald*, July 10, 11, 1944 (quotations); Albright, *The Forgotten First*, pp. 37–38.

38. Sitkoff, "African American Militancy"; *Raleigh News and Observer*, June 22 and 23, 1944; *Durham Morning Herald*, July 10 and 11, 1944 (quotations).

39. *Raleigh News and Observer*, July 12, 1943; Sitkoff, "African American Militancy," pp. 268–270.

40. *Raleigh News and Observer*, July 12, 1943.

41. Ibid.

42. *Smith v. Allwright*, 321 US 649 (1944); Eamon, *The Making of a Southern Democracy*, pp. 13–14.

43. Sitkoff, "African American Militancy," pp. 270–271; Jeffries, *Wartime America*, pp. 116–119; Eagles, "Two Double V's," p. 269.

44. *Raleigh News and Observer*, March 7, 1945.

Chapter 10. "This Is My War, Too": Women at War

1. Litoff, "Southern Women in a World at War," p. 69.

2. *Raleigh News and Observer*, November 9, 1944.

3. Lingeman, *Don't You Know There's a War On?* pp. 90–93; Litoff, "Southern Women in a World at War," pp. 64–69.

4. Interview with Florence Hollis, n.d., UNC-TV.

5. Weatherford, *American Women and World War II*, pp. 28–31.

6. *Raleigh News and Observer*, April 8, 1942.

7. *Raleigh News and Observer*, January 2, 1941.

8. *Raleigh News and Observer*, May 16, 1942; *Time*, June 8, 1942.

9. *Raleigh News and Observer*, May 27, 1942.

10. Weatherford, *American Women and World War II*, pp. 32–33.

11. Katherine Katopes to Charlie Katopes, August 13, 1942, Katherine G. Katopes Papers.

12. Dorothy Hinson Brandt papers, Vertical Files, Military Collection, North Carolina State Archives, Raleigh.

13. *Raleigh News and Observer*, July 15, 1942.

14. Peters, "Why I Didn't Join the WACS," 293–297.

15. *Time*, June 15, 1942.

16. Weatherford, *American Women and World War II*, p. 36.

17. *Time*, August 24, 1942 (quotation); *Collier's*, September 5, 1942, pp. 38–39.

18. *Nation*, July 27, 1942.

19. *Nation*, July 27, 1942 (quotation); *Newsweek*, March 30, 1942, p. 33.

20. Adeline LaPointe to parents, October 5, 1942, Adeline LaPointe Papers.

21. *Nation*, July 27, 1942; *Newsweek*, March 30, 1942, p. 33.

22. Weatherford, *American Women and World War II*, p. 40.

23. Best, ed., *North Carolina's Shining Hour*, p. 93.

24. Interview with Ruth Lillian Gaddy by Eric Elliott, June 23, 2001.

25. *Time*, May 10, 1943, pp. 55–56.

26. Weatherford, *American Women and World War II*, pp. 32–39.

27. *Raleigh News and Observer*, April 4 and 14, 1943.

28. *Newsweek*, July 12, 1943; Weatherford, *American Women and World War II*, pp. 84–85.

29. Interview with Margaret Lewis by Ken Samuelson, May 6, 2005.

30. *Raleigh News and Observer*, July 13, 1945; Dwight D. Eisenhower to Colonel Boyce, March 14, 1947, citation for Legion of Merit and biographical essay, Westray Battle Boyce Papers (quotations).

31. Stallman, *Women in the Wild Blue*, p. xvii.

32. Merryman, *Clipped Wings*, pp. 2–45; Stallman, *Women in the Wild Blue*, pp. xi, xii, xv, xvii, 5, 104.

33. Stallman, *Women in the Wild Blue*, p. 137 (quotation); Bigger, ed., *World War II*, pp. 193–194.

34. Stallman, *Women in the Wild Blue*, pp. xviii, 92, 102–103 (quotation), 125 (quotation).

35. Ibid., pp. 52–56, 96 (quotations).

36. Ibid., p. 78.

37. Best, ed., *North Carolina's Shining Hour*, p. 92.

38. Interview with Ann C. Waters by Eric Elliott, June 2000.

39. Merryman, *Clipped Wings*, pp. 35–45; Stallman, *Women in the Wild Blue*, pp. 9, 197 (quotation).

40. *Raleigh News and Observer*, September 18, 1944.

41. *New York Times*, February 22, 2016.

42. *Raleigh News and Observer*, April 17, 1942; Weatherford, *American Women and World War II*, pp. 31–32, 53, 80–81, 85; Cardozier, *Colleges and Universities in World War II*, pp. 161–162.

43. Weatherford, *American Women and World War II*, pp. 57–58, 85, 99; *Raleigh News and Observer*, February 21, 1944.

44. *Raleigh News and Observer*, April 16, August 8, and November 21, 1943; Weatherford, *American Women and World War II*, pp. 32, 37, 54.

45. Weatherford, *American Women and World War II*, pp. 55, 86; Best, ed., *North Carolina's Shining Hour*, p. 95 (quotation).

46. Weatherford, *American Women and World War II*, pp. 33–35.

47. Ibid., pp. 53–54.

48. *Raleigh News and Observer*, November 14, 1943.

49. Carraway, *Camp Lejeune Leathernecks*, pp. 47–50; "Women Marines," North Carolina Highway Historical Marker.

50. Weatherford, *American Women and World War II*, pp. 230–231, 239, 244.

51. O'Neill, *A Democracy at War*, pp. 132–134.

52. Jeffries, *Wartime America*, p. 100.

53. Weatherford, *American Women and World War II*, pp. 16–20.

54. Ibid., pp. 16–21.

55. *Medical Women's Journal* 58, no. 2 (March–April, 1951): 33–34; *New York Times Biographical Service* 8 (July 1977): 927.

56. Weatherford, *American Women and World War II*, p. 10.

57. *Raleigh News and Observer*, April 2, 1945.

58. Best, ed., *North Carolina's Shining Hour*, p. 105.

59. Ibid., p. 107 (quotation); *Life*, February 21, 1944, pp. 88–95; Dew, *The Queen City at War*, p. 20.

60. Chapman and Miles, *Asheville and Western North Carolina in World War II*, pp. 70–71.

61. Weatherford, *American Women and World War II*, pp. 22–23.

62. Ibid., pp. 120–125.

63. Jeffries, *Wartime America*, pp. 93–95; Lingeman, *Don't You Know There's a War On?* pp. 148–149.

64. Weatherford, *American Women and World War II*, pp. 128–141 (quotation on p. 134); O'Neill, *A Democracy at War*, pp. 242–245.

65. Weatherford, *American Women and World War II*, p. 128 (quotation); Lingeman, *Don't You Know There's a War On?* pp. 150–151.

66. *Raleigh News and Observer*, October 1, 1942.

67. Dew, *The Queen City at War*, p. 127.

68. *Sanford Herald*, April 3, 1942.

69. *Raleigh News and Observer*, September 24, 1944.

70. Jeffries, *Wartime America*, pp. 96–97; Lingeman, *Don't You Know There's a War On?* pp. 149–157.

71. Weatherford, *American Women and World War II*, pp. 220–223; Link, *North Carolina*, p. 358.

72. Jeffries, *Wartime America*, pp. 98–99; Lingeman, *Don't You Know There's a War On?* p. 165; Litoff, "Southern Women in a World at War," pp. 61–62.

73. Weatherford, *American Women and World War II*, pp. 186–187, 307–308; Jeffries, *Wartime America*, pp. 102–105.

74. Bigger, ed., *World War II*, pp. 301–303.

75. Ibid., pp. 246–248.

76. Kiernan, *The Girls of Atomic City*, p. 6.

77. *State*, September 15, 1945.

78. Jeffries, *Wartime America*, p. 97.

79. Ibid., p. 106.

80. Litoff, "Southern Women in a World at War," p. 69.

Chapter 11. Tar Heel Heroes

1. Jackson and Jackson, *America's Youngest Warriors*, 2:139 (quotation); interview with Jack Lucas by Julian M. Pleasants, November 19, 2003.

2. Ibid., p. 140.

3. Ibid., p. 141.

4. Ibid.

5. Ibid.

6. Ibid., p. 142.

7. Jackson and Jackson, "Jacklyn H. Lucas," pp. 142–143 (quotations); Lucas and Drum, *Indestructible*, pp. 11–140.

8. *Raleigh News and Observer*, July 3, 1945.

9. *Raleigh News and Observer*, May 2, 1945.

10. Chapman and Miles, *Asheville and Western North Carolina in World War II*, p. 108.

11. *Raleigh News and Observer*, June 9, 1945.

12. *Raleigh News and Observer*, April 6, 1945.

13. Congressional Medal of Honor Society: http://www.cmohs.org.

14. On a point of privilege, I have had the honor of meeting and talking with fifteen or so Congressional Medal of Honor winners, most of them from World War II. I had the opportunity to spend a considerable amount of time with the colorful Jack Lucas and Charles Murray Jr. What impressed me most about all of these men who had acted above and beyond the call of duty was their modesty and constant assurance that they

did what anyone would have done. Not so. And that is why a grateful nation recognized their exploits. They considered themselves ordinary men, but they did extraordinary things. They all told me that they were not the heroes. The real heroes were those who did not return home.

15. *Raleigh News and Observer*, March 30, 2008 (quotations); Arnett, *Greensboro, N.C.*, p. 412; Duvall, *North Carolina during World War II*, p. 43; "George Preddy," Preddy Memorial Foundation, http://www.preddy-foundation.org/preddy-bios/george-preddy/.

16. "William C. Lee."

17. Ibid.

18. *New York Times*, March 18, 2000.

19. *Raleigh News and Observer*, March 15, 2007 (quotation); Thomas and Witts, *Enola Gay*, pp. 287–288.

20. *New York Times*, March 18, 2000; Tibbetts, *Return of the Enola Gay*, pp. 192–234 (quotation on p. 232); interview with Thomas W. Ferebee by LeGette Blythe, October 16, 1966.

21. Tibbetts, *Return of the Enola Gay*, p. 233; *New York Times*, March 18, 2000 (quotations); Thomas and Witts, *Enola Gay*, pp. 316–317.

22. Thomas and Witts, *Enola Gay*, pp. 313–314.

23. Hersey, *Hiroshima*, p. 98.

24. *Charlotte Observer*, August 6, 1995 (quotation); *New York Times*, March 18, 2000; *Raleigh News and Observer*, March 15, 2007.

25. Morgan and Powers, *The Man Who Flew the Memphis Belle*, p. 97.

26. Ibid., pp. 99–100.

27. Ibid., p. 5; see also pp. 122–211.

28. Ibid., p. 13; see also pp. 5–15.

29. Ibid., p. 312; Keegan, *The Second World War*, p. 576.

30. *Goldsboro News Argus*, May 26, 1971.

31. "Jonathan Daniels," in Powell, ed., *Dictionary of North Carolina Biography*, p. 12; *Raleigh News and Observer*, March 30, 1945; Daniels, *White House Witness*; Eagles, *Jonathan Daniels and Race Relations*, pp. 253–255.

32. Kuralt, "Edward R. Murrow," p. 170.

33. Sperber, *Murrow*, p. 179.

34. Sperber, *Murrow*, p. 251; see also pp. 157–197 (quotations on p. 179), 249–253; Kuralt, "Edward R. Murrow," p. 161.

35. Kuralt, "Edward R. Murrow," p. 168; Sperber, *Murrow*, pp. 249–253.

36. Gorell and Roberts, *USS North Carolina*, p. 6.

37. Mobley, *USS North Carolina*, pp. 1–14; *Raleigh News and Observer*, February 18, 1946.

38. Kelly, "Christmas to Remember," p. 142.

39. Mobley, *USS North Carolina*, pp. 1–14; *Raleigh News and Observer*, February 18, 1946; Gorell and Roberts, *USS North Carolina*, pp. 1–6.

Conclusion

1. Davis, *Experience of War*, pp. 620–623; *Raleigh News and Observer*, May 9, 1945.

2. *Gastonia Daily Gazette*, May 7, 1945.

3. *Charlotte News*, May 8, 1945.

4. *Raleigh News and Observer*, May 9, 1945.

5. *Raleigh News and Observer*, April 14, 1945.

6. Egerton, *Speak Now against the Day*, pp. 329–330; Dew, *The Queen City at War*, pp. 191–192; *Charlotte News*, April 13, 1945.

7. *Raleigh News and Observer*, April 13 and 14 (quotations), 1945.

8. O'Neill, *A Democracy at War*, pp. 421–427.

9. *Winston-Salem Journal*, August 15, 1945; *Durham Morning Herald*, August 15, 1945.

10. *Greensboro Daily News*, August 15, 1945.

11. *Chapel Hill Weekly*, August 16, 1945.

12. *Raleigh News and Observer*, August 15 and 16, 1945; Dew, *The Queen City at War*, pp. 198–199; Covington, *The Good Government Man*, p. 203; Bolden, *Alamance*, p. 115.

13. Interview with Margaret Parker by W. Weldon Huske, March 7, 1976.

14. *Daily Tar Heel*, August 16, 1945.

15. *Raleigh News and Observer*, August 15 and 16 and September 21 and 25, 1945.

16. *Raleigh News and Observer*, May 11, 1945.

17. *Saturday Evening Post*, May 26, 1945.

18. *Raleigh News and Observer*, December 21, 1945.

19. *Raleigh News and Observer*, August 15, 1945.

20. Reynolds, ed., *We Remember*, p. xvi.

21. Sosna, "Introduction"; Cobb, "World War II and the Mind of the South."

22. Jeffries, *Wartime America*, pp. 58–59, 194–197; Ambrose, *Americans at War*, pp. 142–143; Dew, *The Queen City at War*, pp. 1–3; Duvall, *North Carolina during World War II*, pp. 59–61.

BIBLIOGRAPHY

Primary Sources

Bailey, Rachel. Papers. North Carolina State Archives, Raleigh.

Baker, Mary Lane. "The Sky's the Limit: The University of North Carolina and the Chapel Hill Community's Response to the Establishment of the U.S. Naval Pre-Flight School during World War II." M.A. thesis, Department of History, University of North Carolina, 1980.

Biser, Jennifer Marie. "Homefront Heroines: Contributions of the North Carolina Federation of Women's Clubs to the Defense of Democracy in World War II." Honors thesis, Department of History, University of North Carolina, May 2007.

Blazich, Frank A., Jr. "The Relationship between Hoffman, N.C. and Camp Mackall, from September, 1942 to September, 1945." Honors thesis, Department of History, University of North Carolina, May 2004.

Boyce, Westray Battle. Papers. North Carolina State Archives, Raleigh.

Brandt, Dorothy Hinson. Papers. North Carolina State Archives, Raleigh.

Brunsman, Howard G., preparer. *Census of Population, 1950, Part 33: North Carolina.* Washington, D.C.: Government Printing Office, 1952.

Cameron, D. C. Diary, 1944–1945, 5451-Z. Southern Oral History Program, University of North Carolina, Chapel Hill.

Corbitt, David Leroy, ed. *Public Addresses and Papers of Robert Gregg Cherry, Governor of North Carolina, 1945–1949.* Raleigh: Council of State, 1951.

———. *Public Addresses, Letters and Papers of J. Melville Broughton, Governor of North Carolina 1941–1945.* Raleigh: State Department of Archives and History, 1948.

Crumbley, Patricia. Papers. North Carolina State Archives, Raleigh.

Daniels, Jonathan. Papers. Southern Historical Collection, University of North Carolina, Chapel Hill.

Daniels, Josephus. Papers. Southern Historical Collection, University of North Carolina, Chapel Hill.

Dorton, J. S. Papers. Southern Historical Collection, University of North Carolina, Chapel Hill.

Eure, Thad. *North Carolina Manual, 1943*. Raleigh: Secretary of State, 1943.

————. *North Carolina Manual, 1945*. Raleigh: Secretary of State, 1945.

Federal Writers' Project: North Carolina. Chapel Hill: University of North Carolina Press, 1939.

Felmet, Joseph. Papers. Southern Historical Collection, University of North Carolina, Chapel Hill.

Giles, Gladys Irene Giles. Papers. World War II Private Collections, North Carolina State Archives, Raleigh.

Horn, Jerold Ira. "The Late Awakening: North Carolina Economic Development since World War II." Thesis, Princeton University, 1963.

Katopes, Katherine. Papers. University of North Carolina–Greensboro Archives.

LaPointe, Adeline. Papers. University of North Carolina–Greensboro Archives.

Martin County Collection. Papers in the North Carolina State Archives, Raleigh.

McDowell County Collection. Papers. North Carolina State Archives, Raleigh.

North Carolina Agricultural Statistics. No. 83. Raleigh: North Carolina Department of Agriculture, November 1942.

Parker, John J. Papers. Southern Historical Collection, University of North Carolina, Chapel Hill.

Peck, Eleanor K. Papers in the University of North Carolina–Greensboro Archives.

Salm, Margaret. Papers. Southern Historical Collection, University of North Carolina, Chapel Hill.

Sixteenth Census of the United States, 1940. Washington, D.C.: Bureau of the Census, Government Printing Office, 1943.

Smith v. Allwright, 321 US 649 (1944).

Swain County Collection. Papers. North Carolina State Archives, Raleigh.

"War Salvage: A Manual for Volunteer Workers." Raleigh: State Salvage Committee, 1945.

Interviews

Howard Allred. "World War II Experience." University of North Carolina Television. Chapel Hill, 2010.

Jere C. Austin. "World War II Experience." University of North Carolina Television. Chapel Hill, 2010.

Horace Barbee. "World War II Experience." University of North Carolina Television. Chapel Hill, 2010.

Ray Barber. "World War II Experience." University of North Carolina Television. Chapel Hill, 2010.

Marlene Blake. "World War II Experience." University of North Carolina Television. Chapel Hill, 2010.

Orion Blizzard. "World War II Experience." University of North Carolina Television. Chapel Hill, 2010.

Don Bolden. "World War II Experience." University of North Carolina Television. Chapel Hill, 2010.

Russell K. Bond. "World War II Experience." University of North Carolina Television. Chapel Hill, 2010.

Roger Casey. "World War II Experience." University of North Carolina Television. Chapel Hill, 2010.

Warren L. Coble. "World War II Experience." University of North Carolina Television. Chapel Hill, 2010.

Marie Colton. "World War II Experience." University of North Carolina Television. Chapel Hill, 2010.

Virginia Russell Davis. "World War II Experience." University of North Carolina Television. Chapel Hill, 2010.

Philip Dresser. "World War II Experience." University of North Carolina Television. Chapel Hill, 2010.

Tom Easterling. "World War II Experience." University of North Carolina Television. Chapel Hill, 2010.

John Hope Franklin. "World War II Experience." University of North Carolina Television. Chapel Hill, 2010.

William Friday. "World War II Experience." University of North Carolina Television. Chapel Hill, 2010.

Everett "Bud" Hamilton. "World War II Experience." University of North Carolina Television. Chapel Hill, 2010.

Mattie Donnell Hicks. "World War II Experience." University of North Carolina Television. Chapel Hill, 2010.

Stephen L. Houser Jr. "World War II Experience." University of North Carolina Television. Chapel Hill, 2010.

Eleanor Kennedy. "World War II Experience." University of North Carolina Television. Chapel Hill, 2010.

Robert Morgan. "World War II Experience." University of North Carolina Television. Chapel Hill, 2010.

Hubert Poole. "World War II Experience." University of North Carolina Television. Chapel Hill, 2010.

Troy Rouse. "World War II Experience." University of North Carolina Television. Chapel Hill, 2010.

Walter Schackleford. "World War II Experience." University of North Carolina Television. Chapel Hill, 2010.

W. J. Simmons. "World War II Experience." University of North Carolina Television. Chapel Hill, 2010.

Helen Wyatt Snapp. "World War II Experience." University of North Carolina Television. Chapel Hill, 2010.

Billy Sutton. "World War II Experience." University of North Carolina Television. Chapel Hill, 2010.

Alda Womack. "World War II Experience." University of North Carolina Television. Chapel Hill, 2010.

Interview with Dorothy Austell by Herman Trojanski, January 29, 1999. Betty H. Carter Women Veterans History Project. Special Collections, University of North Carolina–Greensboro.

Interview with Roy Lee Auton by Jackie Hall, H-108, February 28, 1980. Southern Oral History Program, University of North Carolina, Chapel Hill.

Interview with Gordon Berkstressor by Patricia Raub, H-0263, April 29, 1986. Southern Oral History Program, University of North Carolina, Chapel Hill.

Interview with David Best by Ken Samuelson, August 20, 2003. In possession of the interviewer.

Interview with Manfred T. Blanchard by Ken Samuelson, August 23, 2002. In possession of the interviewer.

Interview with Ernest Chapman by Mary Murphy, H-016, June 4, 1979. Southern Oral History Program, University of North Carolina, Chapel Hill.

Interview with Paul Edward Cline by Allen Tullus, H-0239, November 8, 1979. Southern Oral History Program, University of North Carolina, Chapel Hill.

Interview with Lauch Faircloth by Joe Mosnier, I-70, July 16, 1975. Southern Oral History Program, University of North Carolina, Chapel Hill.

Interview with Frances Pruitt Falls, first-person account. In Bigger, ed., *World War II*, pp. 149–151.

Interview with Ethel Faucette by Allen Tullus, H-0020, November 16, 1978. Southern Oral History Program, University of North Carolina, Chapel Hill.

Interview with Thomas W. Ferebee by LeGette Blythe, October 16, 1966. Southern Oral History Program, University of North Carolina, Chapel Hill.

Claude E. Pike. "Some Memories of World War II as Recalled in 1988." Pamphlet in World War II Private Collection, Box 116, North Carolina State Archives, Raleigh.

Interview with Thomas Fuller by Brent D. Glass, H-269, October 9, 1975. Southern Oral History Program, University of North Carolina, Chapel Hill.

Interview with Ruth Lillian Gaddy by Eric Elliott, June 23, 2001. Betty H. Carter Women Veterans History Project. Special Collections, University of North Carolina–Greensboro.

Interview with Dock E. Hall by Brent Glass, H-0271, June 5, 1980. Southern Oral History Program, University of North Carolina, Chapel Hill.

Interview with Florence Hollis. "War Bonds: The Songs and Letters of World War II," n.d. University of North Carolina Television: http://www.unctv.org/content/war-bonds/letters#a.

Cedric H. Jones, first-person account. In Bigger, ed., *World War II*, pp. 199–200.

Interview with William D. Lashley by Ken Samuelson, September 5, 1997, in possession of the interviewer.

Interview with Margaret Lewis by Ken Samuelson, May 6, 2005, in possession of the interviewer.

Interview with Jack Lucas by Julian M. Pleasants, November 19, 2003, in possession of the interviewer.

Interview with John Medlin by Joe Mosnier, I-0076, May 24, 1999. Southern Oral History Program, University of North Carolina, Chapel Hill.

Interview with Margaret Parker by W. Weldon Huske, H-0278, March 7, 1976. Southern Oral History Program, University of North Carolina, Chapel Hill.

Interview with Charlene Regester, K-0216, February 23, 2001. Southern Oral History Program, University of North Carolina, Chapel Hill.

Interview with William E. Riggs, by Ken Samuelson, November 17, 1999, in possession of the interviewer.

Interview with Murphy Y. Sigmon by Sharon P. Dilley, H-142, July 27, 1979. Southern Oral History Program, University of North Carolina, Chapel Hill.

Interview with Thomas Snipes by Tony Nace, H-100, December 2, 1978. Southern Oral History Program, University of North Carolina, Chapel Hill.

Interview with William A. Stansfield by Ken Samuelson, August 6, 2003, in possession of the interviewer.

Clarence Ray Thomas, first-person account. In Bigger, ed., *World War II*, pp. 180–182.

Interview with Robert Collen Thomas by Ken Samuelson, May 21, 2003, in possession of the interviewer.

Interview with Ann C. Waters by Eric Elliott, June 2000, Women Veterans History Project. Special Collections, University of North Carolina–Greensboro.

Interview with James Waynick by Ken Samuelson, January 13, 2005, in possession of the interviewer.

Interview with Lacy Wright by William R. Finger, E-0017, March 10, 1975. Southern Oral History Program, University of North Carolina, Chapel Hill.

Magazines

AA Barrage News
American Mercury
Camp David Military News
Collier's
Colored Shipbuilder
Leatherneck Magazine
Life
Medical Women's Journal
Morris Code (magazine for Morris Air Field)
Nation
Newsweek
North Carolina Shipbuilder
Saturday Evening Post
State
Tenshun (camp newspaper/magazine for the American Air Force Replacement Center in Greensboro, 1941–1943)
Time

Secondary Sources

Articles and Miscellaneous

The Archives of the United States Navy Pre-School, Chapel Hill, N.C., 1942–1943. Pamphlet. Philadelphia: Merin Balaban Studios, 1943.

Arthur, Billy. "Camp Lejeune—The Early Days." *Leatherneck Magazine* (November 1982): 31, 69.

Bell, John L. "Broyhill Furniture Company." In Powell, ed., *Encyclopedia of North Carolina*, p. 151.

———. "Lake Lure Rest and Redistribution Center." In Powell, ed., *Encyclopedia of North Carolina*, p. 659.

Billinger, Robert D. "Behind the Wire: German Prisoners of War at Camp Sutton, 1944–1946." *North Carolina Historical Review* 61, no. 4 (October 1984): 481–504.

Billinger, Robert D., and JoAnn Williford. "World War II." In Powell, ed., *Encyclopedia of North Carolina*, pp. 1230–1234.

Blazich, Frank A., Jr. "North Carolina's Flying Volunteers: The Civil Air Patrol in World War II, 1941–1944." *North Carolina Historical Review* 89, no. 4 (October 2012): 399–442.

Boyce, Westray Battle. *Medical Women's Journal* 58, no. 2 (March–April 1951): 33–34.

Branch, Paul, and Daniel Barefoot. "Submarine Attacks." In Powell, ed., *Encyclopedia of North Carolina*, pp. 1089–1091.

Breant, Harold A. "The New River Camp Lejeune Is Corps East Coast Combat College." N.d. Historical Marker, World War II Collection, North Carolina State Archives, Raleigh.

Brown, David E. "The War Years." In *27 Views of Chapel Hill: A Southern University Town in Prose and Poetry*, pp. 160–169. Hillsborough: Eno Publishers, 2011.

Cash, W. J. "Close View of a Calvinist LHASA." *American Mercury* 27 (April 1933): 444, 449.

Cecelski, David S. "The Voice of the Shipyard: Arthur Miller in Wilmington, N.C., 1941." *North Carolina Literary Review* 23 (2014): 48–59.

Chalker, Stephen D. "Blimps over Elizabeth City." *Tar Heel Junior Historian* (Spring 2008): 5–8.

Cheatham, James T. "Memories of the U-Boat War in World War II off the Outer Banks." Paper presented to the North American Society for Oceanographic History, Washington, D.C., April 24, 1992. North Carolina Collection, University of North Carolina, Chapel Hill.

Cherry, Kevin. "Cannon Mills." In Powell, ed., *Encyclopedia of North Carolina*, pp. 169–170.

Coates, Albert. "Guide to Victory." *Popular Government* 9, nos. 1–4 (May 1943). Chapel Hill: Institute of Government.

———. "What the University of North Carolina Means to Me." Chapel Hill: UNC Law School, n.d. North Carolina Collection, University of North Carolina, Chapel Hill.

Cobb, James C. "World War II and the Mind of the South." In McMillen, ed., *Remaking Dixie: The Impact of World War II on the American South*, pp. 3–20. Jackson: University Press of Mississippi, 1997.

Crumbley, Patricia. "Memories of World War II." Patricia Crumbley Papers, World War II Private Collection. North Carolina State Archives, Raleigh.

Daniel, Pete. "Goin' among Strangers: Southern Reaction to World War II." *Journal of American History* 77 (December 1990): 886–911.

Eagles, Charles W. "Two Double V's: Jonathan Daniels, FDR and Race Relations during World War II." *North Carolina Historical Review* 59, no. 3 (July 1982): 252–270.

Emerson, W. Eric. "The *USS Asheville* and the Limits of Navalism in Western North Carolina." *North Carolina Historical Review* 89, no. 3 (July 2012): 301–330.

Farnham, Thomas J. "Camp Lejeune." In Powell, ed., *Encyclopedia of North Carolina*, pp. 166–167.

Federal Bureau of Investigation Report (FBI). Number 25. July 31, 1943. Joseph Felmet Papers. Southern Historical Collection, University of North Carolina, Chapel Hill.

———. Number 61-7497-27. January 17, 1941.

———. Number 100-693. October 16, 1941.

Ficklen, Ames E., and Donald W. Ellis. "POWs in the Piney Woods." *Journal of Southern History* 56 (November 1990): 695–724.

"Fontana Dam Safety News." June 1943 to July 1944. In "A History of Fontana Dam." Proctor Revival Organization, 2010. County Collection, World War II Collection. North Carolina State Archives, Raleigh.

Glass, Brent. "Fontana Dam." In Powell, ed., *Encyclopedia of North Carolina*, pp. 449–450.

Howard, Joshua. "Morris Field." In Powell, ed., *Encyclopedia of North Carolina*, p. 767.

Jackson, Ray D., and Susan Jackson. "Jacklyn H. Lucas." In *America's Youngest Warriors*, pp. 139–143. Vol. 2. Conroe, Tex.: Veterans of Underage Military Service, 1996.

Kelly, Susan Stafford. "Christmas to Remember." *Our State* (December 2015): 140–142.

Kennedy, George A. "Atlantic Coastline Railway." In Powell, ed., *Encyclopedia of North Carolina*, p. 72.

———. "Seaboard Airlines Railway." In Powell, ed., *Encyclopedia of North Carolina*, pp. 1014–1015.

King, William E. "The Durham Rose Bowl, 1942." In *If Gargoyles Could Talk: Sketches of Duke University*. Durham, N.C.: Carolina Academic Press, 1997.

Kirk, Robert M. "Getting in the Scrap." *Journal of Popular Culture* 29 (Summer 1995): 223–233.

Kuralt, Charles. "Edward R. Murrow." *North Carolina Historical Review* 43, no. 2 (April 1971): 161–170.

"Laurinburg-Maxton Air Force Base." Historical Marker. North Carolina State Archives, Raleigh.

Lillard, Stewart. "Liberty Ships." In Powell, ed., *Encyclopedia of North Carolina*, p. 671.

Litoff, Judy Barrett. "Southern Women in a World at War." In McMillen, ed., *Remaking Dixie*, pp. 56–69.

Marshall, Patricia. "Furniture." In Powell, ed., *Encyclopedia of North Carolina*, pp. 483–486.

"Martin County." County Collection, World War II Collection, Box 67. North Carolina State Archives, Raleigh.

"McDowell County." County Collection, World War II Collection, Box 62. North Carolina State Archives, Raleigh.

Medal of Honor Citations. U.S. Army Center of Military History. Fort McNair, Washington, D.C.

Mohr, Clarence. "World War II and the Transformation of Higher Education." In McMillen, ed., *Remaking Dixie*, pp. 33–55.

"Morris Field." The Charlotte Mecklenburg Story (collection). Charlotte Mecklenburg Library. Charlotte, N.C.

MSNBC News Report, April 9, 2014.

Parker, Roy, Jr. "Fort Bragg." In Powell, ed., *Encyclopedia of North Carolina*, pp. 457–458.

Peters, Ruth E. "Why I Didn't Join the WACS." *American Mercury*, September 1943, pp. 293–297.

Pike, Claude E. "Some Memories of World War II as Recalled in 1988." Pamphlet in World War II Private Collection, Box 116. North Carolina State Archives, Raleigh.

Preddy Memorial Foundation. "George Preddy." http://www.preddy-foundation.org/preddy-bios/george-preddy/.

Price, Eugene. "Seymour Johnson Air Force Base." In Powell, ed., *Encyclopedia of North Carolina*, pp. 1020–1021.

Salemson, Daniel J. "Conscientious Objection." In Powell, ed., *Encyclopedia of North Carolina*, pp. 276–277.

Sears, Stephen W. "How Americans Met the First Great Gasoline Crisis." *American Heritage* 30 (October–November 1979): 4–17.

"Seymour Johnson Air Force Base." Fact sheet, January 1995. 4th Wing Public Affairs Office, Seymour Johnson Air Force Base, Goldsboro, N.C.

"Seymour Johnson Air Force Base." Historical Marker, North Carolina State Archives, Raleigh.

"The Shell Plant." The Charlotte Mecklenburg Story (collection), Charlotte Mecklenburg Library, Charlotte, N.C.

Sitkoff, Harvard. "African American Militancy and Interracial Violence in North Carolina during World War II." In Tyson and Cecelski, eds., *Democracy Betrayed: The Wilmington Race Riot of 1899 and Its Legacy*, pp. 253–274.

Sosna, Morton. "Introduction." In McMillen, ed., *Remaking Dixie*, pp. xiii–xix.

Taylor, Ben. "Camp Sutton: Gone But Not Forgotten." In *Camp Sutton: Monroe, N.C., 1942–1945*. Monroe, N.C.: Union County Public Library.

Troxler, George. "Burlington Industries." In Powell, ed., *Encyclopedia of North Carolina*, p. 158.

UNC News Letter 31, no. 5, March 14, 1945.

U.S. Navy. *A Panorama of the U.S. Navy Pre-Flight School in Chapel Hill, N.C.* Philadelphia: Merin Balaban Studios, 1942.

"William C. Lee." Pamphlet. William C. Lee Airborne Museum, Dunn, N.C.

"Women Doing Excellent Work at Jobs in the Yard." *North Carolina Shipbuilder*, January 1, 1943, 1.

"Women Marines." Historical Marker, December 17, 2007. North Carolina State Archives, Raleigh.

Yeargin, W. W. "Tobacco." In Powell, ed., *Encyclopedia of North Carolina*, pp. 1120–1123.

Books

Albright, Alex. *The Forgotten First: B1 and the Integration of the Modern Navy*. Fountain, N.C.: R. A. Fountain, 2013.

Ambrose, Stephen E. *Americans at War*. Jackson: University Press of Mississippi. 1997.

———. *Band of Brothers*. New York: Simon and Schuster, 1992.

———. *To America: Personal Reflections of a Historian*. New York: Simon and Schuster, 2002.

American Tobacco Company. *The American Tobacco Company Story*. Durham, N.C.: American Tobacco Company, 1960.

Arnett, Ethel Stephens. *Greensboro, N.C.: County Seat of Guilford County*. Chapel Hill: University of North Carolina Press, 1955.

Autry, Jerry. *General William C. Lee: Father of the Airborne*. N.p.: Airborne Press, 1995.

Baker, Blanche Egerton. *Mrs. GI Joe*. Raleigh: Graphic Press, 1951.

Barefoot, Daniel W. *Hark the Sound of Tar Heel Voices: 220 Years of UNC History*. Winston-Salem: John F. Blair Publisher, 2008.

Barringer, Edwin C. *The Story of Scrap*. Washington, D.C.: Institute of Scrap Iron and Steel, 1954.

Beaty, Mary D. *A History of Davidson College*. Davidson: Briarpatch Press, 1988.

Bentley, Amy. *Eating for Victory: Food Rationing and the Politics of Domesticity*. Urbana: University of Illinois Press, 1998.

Best, Mary, ed. *North Carolina's Shining Hour: Images and Voices from World War II*. Greensboro: Our State Books, 2005.

Bigger, Margaret G., ed. *World War II: Hometown and Home Front Heroes*. Charlotte: A. Borough Books, 2004.

Biggs, Bradley. *The Triple Nickels: America's First All-Black Paratroop Unit*. Hamden, Conn: Archon Books, 1986.

Billinger, Robert D., Jr. *Nazi POWs in the Tar Heel State*. Gainesville: University Press of Florida, 2008.

Billy, George J. *Merchant Mariners at War: An Oral History of World War II*. Gainesville: University Press of Florida, 2008.

Birnbaum, Jonathan, and Clarence Taylor. *Civil Rights since 1787: A Reader in the Black Struggle*. New York: New York University Press, 2000.

Blythe, LeGette. *38th Evac: The Story of the Men and Women Who Served in World War II with the 38th Evacuation Hospital in North Africa and Italy*. Charlotte: Heritage Printers, 1966.

Bolden, Don. *Alamance: A County at War*. Burlington: Times News Publishing Company, 1995.

Boston Publishing Company, eds. *Medal of Honor: A History of Service Above and Beyond*. Boston: Zenith Press, 2004.

Bradlee, Ben, Jr. *The Kid: The Immortal Life of Ted Williams*. New York: Little, Brown and Company, 2013.

Brinkley, David. *Washington Goes to War*. New York: Ballantine Books, 1988.

Buchanan, Russell. *The United States and World War II*. Vol. 1. New York: Harper and Row, 1964.

Budiansky, Stephen. *Battle of Wits: The Complete Story of Codebreaking in World War II*. New York: Simon and Schuster, 2000.

Burns, James McGregor. *The Lion and the Fox*. New York: Harcourt, Brace and World, 1956.

———. *Roosevelt: The Soldier of Freedom*. New York: Harcourt Brace Jovanovich, 1970.

Campbell, D'Ann. *Women at War with America*. Cambridge, Mass.: Harvard University Press, 1984.

Cannon, Lou. *Reagan*. New York: G. P. Putnam's Sons, 1982.

Cardozier, V. R. *Colleges and Universities in World War II*. Westport, Conn.: Praeger, 1993.

Carlson, Lewis H. *We Were Each Other's Prisoners: An Oral History of World War II American and German Prisoners of War*. New York: Basic Books, 1997.

Carraway, Gertrude S. *Camp Lejeune Leathernecks: Marine Corps' Largest All-Purpose Base*. New Bern: Owen G. Dunn Company, 1946.

———. *The Flying Marines*. New Bern: Owen G. Dunn Company, 1946.

———. *The United States Marine Corps Air Station, Cherry Point, North Carolina*. New Bern: Owen G. Dunn Company, 1946.

Catlett, Stephen J. *Army Town: Greensboro, 1943–1946*. Greensboro: Greensboro Historical Museum, 1994.

Chambers, John Whiteclay, II, ed. *The Oxford Companion to American Military History*. New York: Oxford University Press, 1999.

Chambers, John Whiteclay, II, and David Culbert, eds. *World War II Film and History*. New York: Oxford University Press, 1996.

Chapman, Reid, and Deborah Miles. *Asheville and Western North Carolina in World War II*. Charleston, S.C.: Arcadia Publishing, 2006.

Cheatham, James T. *The Atlantic Turkey Shoot: U-Boats off the Outer Banks in World War II*. Greenville: Williams and Simpson Publishers, 1990.

Christensen, Rob. *The Paradox of North Carolina Politics*. Chapel Hill: University of North Carolina Press, 2008.

Collier, Peter. *Medal of Honor*. 3rd ed. New York: Artisan, 2011.

Cooper, Christopher A., and H. Gibbs Knott, eds. *The New Politics of North Carolina*. Chapel Hill: University of North Carolina Press, 2008.

Covington, Howard E., Jr. *Belk: A Century of Retail Leadership*. Chapel Hill: University of North Carolina Press, 1988.

———. *The Good Government Man: Albert Coates and the Early Years of the Institute of Government*. Chapel Hill: University Library, University of North Carolina, 2010.

Covington, Howard E., Jr., and Marion Ellis, eds. *Tar Heels Who Made a Difference*. Charlotte: Levine Museum of the South, 2002.

Crow, Jeffrey D., Paul Escott, et al. *A History of African Americans in North Carolina*. Revised 2nd ed. Raleigh: North Carolina Department of Cultural Resources, 2011.

Dallek, Robert. *Franklin Roosevelt and American Foreign Policy, 1932–1945*. New York: Oxford University Press, 1981.

Daniels, Jonathan. *Frontier on the Potomac*. New York: Macmillan, 1946.

———. *White House Witness, 1942–1945*. New York: Doubleday, 1975.

Davis, Anita Price. *North Carolina during World War II*. Jefferson: McFarland, 2014.

Davis, Anita Price, and James M. Walker. *Rutherford County in World War II*. 2 vols. Charleston, S.C.: Arcadia Publishing, 2003 and 2004.

Davis, Kenneth S. *Experience of War: The United States in World War II*. Garden City, N.Y.: Doubleday and Co., 1965.

———. *FDR: Into the Storm: 1937–1940*. New York: Random House, 1993.

Dew, Stephen H. *The Queen City at War: Charlotte, North Carolina during World War II, 1939–1945*. New York: University Press of America, 2001.

Dick, Bernard F. *The Star Spangled Screen: The American World War II Film*. Lexington: University Press of Kentucky, 1985.

Dolan, Edward F., Jr. *Hollywood Goes to War*. New York: Gallery Books, 1985.

Duffus, Kevin P. *War Zone: World War II Off the North Carolina Coast*. Raleigh: Looking Glass Productions, 2012.

Duvall, John S. *North Carolina during World War II: On Home Front and Battle Front*. Fort Bragg: Airborne and Special Operations Museum Foundation, 1996.

Eagles, Charles W. *Jonathan Daniels and Race Relations: The Evolution of a Southern Liberal*. Knoxville: University of Tennessee Press, 1983.

Eamon, Tom. *The Making of a Southern Democracy: North Carolina Politics from Kerr Scott to Pat McCrory*. Chapel Hill: University of North Carolina Press, 2014.

Egerton, John. *Speak Now against the Day: The Generation before the Civil Rights Movement in the South*. Chapel Hill: University of North Carolina Press, 1995.

Ehle, John. *Dr. Frank*. Chapel Hill: Franklin Street Books, 1993.

Ford, Gerald R. *A Time to Heal*. New York: Harper and Row, 1979.

Freeze, Gary. *North Carolina: Land of Contrasts*. Atlanta: Clairmont Press, 2009.

Fussell, Paul. *Wartime: Understanding and Behavior in the Second World War*. New York: Oxford University Press, 1989.

Gannon, Michael. *Operation Drumbeat: The Dramatic True Story of Germany's First U-Boat Attacks along the American Coast during World War II*. Annapolis: Naval Institute Press, 1990.

Gansberg, Judith M. *Stalag USA: The Remarkable Story of German POWs in America*. New York: Crowell, 1977.

Glass, Brent D. *The Textile Industry—North Carolina: A History*. Raleigh: Division of Archives and History, 1992.

Gorell, Dick, and Bruce Roberts. *USS North Carolina: The Showboat*. Charlotte: Heritage Publishers, 1961.

Greene, John Robert. *The Presidency of Gerald R. Ford*. Lawrence: University Press of Kansas, 1995.

Griffin, Clarence W. *History of Rutherford County, 1937–1951*. N.p.: Inland Press, 1952.

Hargrove, Marion. *See Here, Private Hargrove*. New York: Paperback Library, 1968.

Hastings, Max. *Inferno: The World at War, 1939–1945*. New York: Alfred A. Knopf, 2011.

Hegarty, Marilyn E. *Victory Girls, Khaki-Wackies, and Patriotutes: The Regulation of Female Sexuality during World War II*. New York: New York University Press, 2008.

Henderson, Archibald. *The Campus of the First State University*. Chapel Hill: University of North Carolina Press, 1949.

Hersey, John. *Hiroshima*. New York: Bantam Books, 1946.

Hickam, Homer, Jr. *Torpedo Junction: U-Boat War off America's East Coast, 1942*. New York: Dell Publishing Company, 1989.

Honey, James E., and Ida C. Honey. *A History of Richmond County*. Rockingham: Edwards and Broughton, 1976.

Horowitz, James. *They Went Thataway*. New York: Ballantine Books, 1976.

Hyman, Mac. *No Time for Sergeants*. New York: Random House, 1954.

Jackson, Ray D., and Susan Jackson. *America's Youngest Warriors*. 2 vols. Conroe, Tex.: Veterans of Underage Military Service, 1996.

James, Rawn, Jr. *The Double V: How Wars, Protests and Harry Truman Desegregated America's Military*. New York: Bloomsbury Press, 2013.

Jeffries, John W. *Wartime America: The World War II Homefront.* Chicago: Ivan R. Dee, 1996.

Jones, Edwin L. *J. A. Jones Construction Company: 75 Years Growth in Construction.* New York: Newcomen Society in North America, 1965.

Jones, Wilbur D. *The Journey Continues.* Shippensburg, Pa.: White Mane Books, 2005.

———. *A Sentimental Journey: Memories of a Wartime Boomtown.* Shippensburg, Pa.: White Mane Books, 2002.

Jordan, Joye E. *The Wildcat Division.* Raleigh: State Department of Archives and History, 1945.

Kandel, I. L. *The Impact of the War on American Education.* Chapel Hill: University of North Carolina Press, 1948.

Keegan, John. *The Second World War.* New York: Penguin Books USA, 1989.

Kiernan, Denise. *The Girls of Atomic City: The Untold Story of the Women Who Helped Win World War II.* New York: Touchstone, 2013.

Kilpatrick, Carroll. *Roosevelt and Daniels: A Friendship in Politics.* Chapel Hill: University of North Carolina Press, 1952.

King, Spencer Bidwell, Jr. *Selective Service in North Carolina in World War II.* Chapel Hill: University of North Carolina Press, 1949.

Koppes, Clayton R., and Gregory D. Black. *Hollywood Goes to War: How Politics, Profits and Propaganda Shaped World War II Movies.* Berkeley: University of California Press, 1990.

Lane, Tony. *The Merchant Seaman's War.* Manchester, UK: Manchester University Press, 1990.

Larrabee, Eric. *Commander in Chief.* New York: Simon and Schuster, 1987.

Lawson, Steve. *Black Ballots: Voting Rights in the South, 1944–1969.* New York: Columbia University Press, 1976.

Lemmon, Sarah M. *North Carolina's Role in World War II.* Raleigh: State Department of Archives and History, 1964.

Lemmon, Sarah M., and Nancy S. Midgette. *North Carolina and the Two World Wars.* Raleigh: Office of Archives and History, 2013.

Leuchtenburg, William E. *Franklin D. Roosevelt and the New Deal, 1932–1940.* New York: Harper and Row, 1963.

Lingeman, Richard. *Don't You Know There's a War On?: The American Home Front, 1941–1945.* New York: Thunder's Mouth Press, 2003.

Link, William A. *North Carolina: Tradition and Change in a Southern State.* Wheeling, Ill.: Harlan Davidson, 2009.

———. *William Friday: Power, Purpose and American Higher Education.* Chapel Hill: University of North Carolina Press, 1995.

Lord, Walter. *Day of Infamy.* New York: Holt, Rinehart and Winston, 1958.

Lotchin, Roger. *The Bad City in the Good War.* Bloomington: Indiana University Press, 2003.

Lowden, John L. *Silent Wings at War: Combat Gliders in World War II.* Washington, D.C.: Smithsonian Institution Press, 1992.

Lucas, Jack H., and D. K. Drum. *Indestructible: The Unforgettable Story of a Marine Hero at Iwo Jima.* N.p.: Thorndike Press, 2007.

Maney, Patrick J. *The Roosevelt Presence: A Biography of Franklin Delano Roosevelt*. New York: Twayne Publishers, 1992.

Manning, Frances M., and W. H. Booker. *Martin County History*. Vol. 2. Williamston: Enterprise Publishing Company, 1979.

McLaurin, Melton A. *The Marines of Montford Point*. Chapel Hill: University of North Carolina Press, 2007.

Meacham, Jon. *Destiny and Power: The American Odyssey of George Herbert Walker Bush*. New York: Random House, 2015.

Merryman, Molly. *Clipped Wings: The Rise and Fall of the Women Air Force Service Pilots (WASPs) of World War II*. New York: New York University Press, 1998.

Meyer, Agnes E. *Journey through Chaos*. New York: Harcourt Brace and Company, 1944.

Mills, L. Barron, Jr. *Randolph County: A Brief History*. Raleigh: Office of Archives and History, 2008.

Mobley, Joe A. *Ship Ashore: The U.S. Lifesavers of Coastal North Carolina*. Raleigh: Division of Archives and History, 1994.

———. *USS North Carolina: Symbol of a Vanished Age*. Raleigh: Division of Archives and History, 2003.

———, ed. *The Way We Lived in North Carolina*. Chapel Hill: Office of Archives and History and UNC Press, 2003.

Morgan, Robert, and Ron Powers. *The Man Who Flew the Memphis Belle: Memoir of a World War II Bomber Pilot*. New York: New American Library, 2011.

Moss, George Donelson. *The Rise of Modern America: A History of the American People, 1890–1945*. Englewood Cliffs, N.J.: Prentice Hall, 1995.

Naisawald, L. VanLoan. *In Some Foreign Field: Four British Graves and Submarine Warfare on the North Carolina Outer Banks*. Raleigh: Division of Archives and History, 1997.

Olson, Lynn. *Citizens of London: The Americans Who Stood with Britain in Its Darkest, Finest Hour*. New York: Random House, 2011.

———. *Those Angry Days: Roosevelt, Lindbergh and America's Fight over World War II, 1939–1941*. New York: Random House, 2013.

O'Neill, William L. *A Democracy at War*. Cambridge, Mass.: Harvard University Press, 1993.

Parker, Roy, Jr. *The Best of Roy Parker*. Fayetteville: Pediment Publishing Company, 2007.

———. *Cumberland County: A Brief History*. Raleigh: Division of Archives and History, 1990.

Parmet, Herbert S. *George Bush: The Life of a Lone Star Yankee*. New York: Scribner, 1997.

Petty, Adrienne. *Standing Their Ground: Small Farmers in North Carolina*. New York: Oxford University Press, 2013.

Pleasants, Julian M. *Buncombe Bob: The Life and Times of Robert R. Reynolds*. Chapel Hill: University of North Carolina Press, 2000.

———, ed. *Dictionary of North Carolina Biography: Vol. 2, D–G*. Chapel Hill: University of North Carolina Press, 1986.

Powell, William S., ed. *Encyclopedia of North Carolina*. Chapel Hill: University of North Carolina Press, 2006.

Putney, William W. *Always Faithful: A Memoir of the Marine Dogs of World War II*. Detroit: Free Press, 2003.

Pyle, Ernie. *Brave Men*. New York: Popular Library, 1964.

Reynolds, C. Russell, ed. *We Remember: Stories by North Carolina Veterans of World War II*. Dallas: Taylor Specialty Books, 2011.

Rhodes, Richard. *The Making of the Atomic Bomb*. New York: Simon and Schuster, 1986.

Samuel, Lawrence R. *Pledging Allegiance: American Identity and the Bond Drive of World War II*. Washington, D.C.: Smithsonian University Press, 1997.

Schaller, Michael, et al. *Present Tense: The United States since 1945*. Boston: Houghton Mifflin Company, 2004.

Scott, Ralph Lee. *The Wilmington Shipyard: Welding a Fleet for Victory*. Charleston, S.C.: History Press, 2007.

Simon, Neil. *Biloxi Blues*. New York: Samuel French, 1986.

Sitkoff, Harvard. *Toward Freedom Land: The Long Struggle for Racial Equality in America*. Lexington: University Press of Kentucky, 2010.

Smith, Bell Laney, and Karen T. Kluever. *Jones Construction Centennial: Looking Back— Moving Forward, 1890–1990*. Charlotte: Laney-Smith, 1989.

Smith, Eddie L., and Ben Patrick. *Voices from the Field*. Butner: Camp Butner Fiftieth Anniversary Celebration Planning Committee, 1992.

Smith, Michael. *The Secrets of Station X: How the Bletchley Park Codebreakers Helped Win the War*. London: Biteback Publishing Company, 2011.

Snider, William D. *Light on the Hill: A History of the University of North Carolina at Chapel Hill*. Chapel Hill: University of North Carolina Press, 1992.

Soloman, Deborah. *American Mirror: The Life and Art of Norman Rockwell*. New York: Farrar, Straus, and Giroux, 2013.

Sperber, A. M. *Murrow: His Life and Times*. New York: Freundlich Books, 1986.

Stallman, David A. *Echoes of Topsail: Stories of the Island's Past*. Bethel, Conn.: Rutledge Books, 1996.

———. *Women in the Wild Blue: Target Towing WASPs at Camp Davis*. Wilmington: Echoes Press, 2006.

Steele, Richard W. *Free Speech in the Good War*. New York: St. Martin's Press, 1999.

Stevens, Lowell, and Tom MacCallum. *Camp Mackall, North Carolina: Its Origins and Times in the Sandhills*. Rockingham: Richmond County Historical Society, 2011.

Terkel, Studs. *The Good War: An Oral History of World War II*. New York: Ballantine Books, 1984.

Thomas, Gordon, and Max Morgan Witts. *Enola Gay*. New York: Pocket Books, 1977.

Tibbetts, Paul W. *Return of the Enola Gay*. Columbus, Ohio: Mid Coast Marketing, 1998.

Tilley, Nannie M. *The RJ Reynolds Tobacco Company*. Chapel Hill: University of North Carolina Press, 1985.

Time-Life Books, eds. *This Fabulous Century*. Vol. 5: *1940–1950*. New York: Time-Life Books, 1969.

Tindall, George Brown. *The Emergence of the New South, 1913–1945*. Baton Rouge: Louisiana State University Press, 1967.

Tomblin, Barbara Brooks. *GI Nightingales: The Army Nurse Corps in World War II*. Lexington: University Press of Kentucky, 1996.

Treadwell, Mattie. *The Women's Army Corps*. Washington, D.C.: Office of the Chief of Military History, 1954.

Tyson, Timothy B., and David S. Cecelski, eds. *Democracy Betrayed: The Wilmington Race Riot of 1899 and Its Legacy*. Chapel Hill: University of North Carolina Press, 1998.

Vandenburg, Timothy W. *Cannon Mills and Kannapolis: Persistent Paternalism in a Textile Town*. Knoxville: University of Tennessee Press, 2013.

Vickers, Thomas, et al. *Chapel Hill: An Illustrated History*. Chapel Hill: Barclay Publishers, 1985.

Watson, Alan D. *Onslow County: A Brief History*. Raleigh: Division of Archives and History, 1995.

Weatherford, Doris. *American Women and World War II*. Edison, N.J.: Castle Books, 2008.

Weigley, Russell. *The American Way of War: A History of the U.S. Military Strategy and Policy*. Bloomington: Indiana University Press, 1960.

Wellman, Manly Wade. *The Story of Moore County*. Carthage: Moore County Historical Association, 1974.

White, William Allen. *Defense for America*. New York: Macmillan, 1940.

Wilson, Louis Round. *University of North Carolina under Consolidation, 1931–1966*. Chapel Hill: University of North Carolina Press, 1964.

Winchell, Meghan K. *Good Girls, Good Food, Good Fun: The Story of USO Hostesses during World War II*. Chapel Hill: University of North Carolina Press, 2008.

Woodruff, David. *Tap Roots: Tales of Growing Up in Southern Pines*. Southern Pines: Sandspur Project, 2014.

Wyden, Peter. *Day One: Before Hiroshima and Afterwards*. New York: Warner Books, 1984.

Wynne, Nick, and Richard Moorhead. *Florida in World War II: Floating Fortress*. Charleston: History Press, 2010.

Zorgry, Kenneth Joel. *The University's Living Room: A History of the Carolina Inn*. Chapel Hill: University of North Carolina Press, 1999.

INDEX

Page numbers in *italics* refer to illustrations.

Julian M. Pleasants is professor emeritus of history at the University of Florida and the author of ten books, including *Buncombe Bob: The Life and Times of Robert R. Reynolds*; *Hanging Chads: The Inside Story of the 2000 Presidential Recount in Florida*; and *The Political Career of W. Kerr Scott*, winner of the Ragan Old North State Award for best nonfiction book on North Carolina in 2015.